China, Asia, and the New World Economy

China, Asia, and the New World Economy

Edited by

Barry Eichengreen, Charles Wyplosz,
and Yung Chul Park

OXFORD
UNIVERSITY PRESS

Great Clarendon Street, Oxford OX2 6DP

Oxford University Press is a department of the University of Oxford.
It furthers the University's objective of excellence in research, scholarship,
and education by publishing worldwide in

Oxford New York

Auckland Cape Town Dar es Salaam Hong Kong Karachi
Kuala Lumpur Madrid Melbourne Mexico City Nairobi
New Delhi Shanghai Taipei Toronto

With offices in

Argentina Austria Brazil Chile Czech Republic France Greece
Guatemala Hungary Italy Japan Poland Portugal Singapore
South Korea Switzerland Thailand Turkey Ukraine Vietnam

Published in the United States
by Oxford University Press Inc., New York

British Library Cataloguing in Publication Data

Data available

Library of Congress Cataloging in Publication Data

Data available

Typeset by SPI Publisher Services, Pondicherry, India
Printed in Great Britain
on acid-free paper by
Biddles Ltd., King's Lynn, Norfolk

ISBN 978–0–19–923588–9
ISBN 978–0–19–923589–6 (pbk.)

1 3 5 7 9 10 8 6 4 2

Contents

List of Figures   vii

List of Tables   xi

Introduction   xv
Barry Eichengreen, Yung Chul Park, and Charles Wyplosz

  1. China's Coming Demand for Energy   1
      Richard N. Cooper

  2. China and the Global Environment   18
      Warwick J. McKibbin

  3. The Spoke Trap: Hub-and-Spoke Bilateralism in East Asia   51
      Richard E. Baldwin

  4. The Proliferation of FTAs and Prospects for Trade Liberalization
      in East Asia   87
      Yung Chul Park and Inkyo Cheong

  5. Containing the PTA Wildfire   113
      Cédric Dupont and David Huang

  6. China and the Multilateral Trading System   145
      Robert Z. Lawrence

  7. Regional and Global Financial Integration in East Asia   168
      Soyoung Kim, Jong-Wha Lee, and Kwanho Shin

  8. Determinants of Liquidity in the Thai Bond Market   201
      Akkharaphol Chabchitrchaidol and Sakkapop Panyanukul

  9. Is East Asia Safe from Financial Crises?   233
      Charles Wyplosz

10. Chinese Macroeconomic Management: Issues and Prospects   254
      Yu Yongding

Contents

11. The Chinese Approach to Capital Inflows:
    Patterns and Possible Explanations   274
    Eswar Prasad and Shang-Jin Wei

12. Do China's Capital Controls Still Bind?   312
    Guonan Ma and Robert N. McCauley

13. Impact of Financial Services Trade Liberalization on
    Capital Flows: The Case of China's Banking Sector   341
    Li-Gang Liu and Elvira Kurmanalieva

14. Why Does China Save So Much?   371
    Charles Yuji Horioka and Junmin Wan

Index   393

List of Figures

2.1: China's total energy consumption and supply, 1980–2004   23

2.2: Energy production by fuel type, China, 1980–2004   24

2.3: Projections of energy consumption, China, 1990–2030   25

2.4: Projections of CO_2 emissions by fuel type, China, 1990–2030   25

2.5a: Labor-augmenting technical change for uniform productivity scenario   26

2.5b: Labor-augmenting technical change by sector in differential
     productivity scenario   27

2.6a: Projection of Chinese carbon dioxide emissions   28

2.6b: Projecton of Chinese real GDP growth   29

2.7: Sources of black carbon in China in 1995 and 2020   34

2.8a: Response of emissions to a carbon tax in each country   38

2.8b: Response of GDP to a carbon tax in each country   38

2.9: Stylized permit price for an allocation of double and triple China's
     2002 emissions   41

2.A1: Overview of the G-Cubed model (version 63E)   46

3.1: Hub-and-Spoke Bilateralism: A Numerical Example   55

3.2: Domino Effect in Hub-and-Spoke Bilateralism   60

3.3: HMs for the US, Canada, and Mexico   66

3.4: HMs for South Cone nations   67

3.5: HMs for Japan, China, and Korea   68

3.6: HMs for JKFTA, JKCFTA, and ASEAN   69

3.7: A possible FTA pattern: East Asian bicycle   71

3.8: Size distribution EU GDP shares   73

3.9: EFTA's near-hub status in 1993   76

5.1: Keywords percentage of fifteen keyword groups in leaders'
     declarations, 1993–2003   124

5.2: Keywords percentage of fifteen keyword groups in leaders' declarations   125

5.3: APEC-funded projects by years, 1993–2003   127

5.4: Keywords percentage of fifteen keyword groups in project
     descriptions, 1993–2003   128

List of Figures

5.5: Keywords percentage of fifteen keyword groups in project descriptions   129

5.6: Keywords in leaders' declarations and projects, 1993–2003   131

5.7: WTO keyword group in leaders' declarations and in project descriptions   132

5.8: Capacity-building keyword in leaders' declarations and project descriptions   133

5.9: Financial crisis keyword in leaders' declarations and project descriptions   134

5.10: Organizational principles in leaders' declarations and project descriptions   135

5.11: Security and terrorism keyword in leaders' declarations and project descriptions   136

8.1: Bond market capitalization relative to the stock market, bank loans, and GDP   203

8.2: Bond outstanding by instruments as of June 2004   204

8.3: Profile of government securities holders as of September 2004   205

8.4: Events affecting the bid–ask spread (September 1999–October 2004)   211

8.5: Refining the empirical model   218

8.6: The relationship between trading volume and issuance outstanding of the Government Bond in 2004   225

8.7a: Bid–ask spread for ten–year Treasury issued in 1998   226

8.7b: Bid–ask spread for ten–year Treasury issued in 1998   226

8.8a: Trading volume for ten–year Treasury issued in 1998   227

8.8b: Trading volume for all Thai Government Bonds with a residual maturity of at least one year   228

8.9a: Historical yield of ten–year Treasury issued in 1998   228

8.9b: Interpolated yield for Thai Government Bond with ten–year maturity   229

9.1: Exchange rate regimes (1985–2004)   239

9.2: Gross foreign exchange reserves (US$ billions)   241

9.3: Currency mismatch indicator   248

10.1: China's economic growth and inflation, 1990–2006   255

10.2: Fixed asset investment and GDP growth, 1990–2006   255

10.3: The trade-off between growth and inflation   256

10.4: China's twin surpluses, 1982–2006   260

10.5: China's accumulation of foreign exchange reserves   260

10.6: China's fiscal situation, 1990–2006   267

10.7: Exports, imports, and growth of net exports, 1990–2006   269

11.1: Level and composition of gross capital inflows, 1982–2005 (US$ billions)   277

11.2: Gross capital flows by component, 1982–2005 (US$ billions)   278

11.3: Asian economies and emerging markets: net capital flows, 1990–2005
(% of GDP)   280

11.4: China's share of foreign direct investment inflows to emerging
markets, 1994–2005   281

11.5: External debt: cross-country comparison, 1990–2004 (% of GDP)   287

11.6: External debt, 1985–2005 (% of GDP)   288

11.7: Errors and omissions and portfolio investment, net for 1982–2005
(US$ billions)   293

11.8: Reserve adequacy indicators, 1995–2005   297

12.1: China's gross cross-border flows   314

12.2: Average absolute onshore–offshore yield spreads   318

12.3: The onshore less offshore CNY yields, based on three-month Chibor   318

12.4: Onshore less offshore NDF-implied yields   320

12.5: Exchange rate, NDFs, and implied volatilities of the Renminbi   321

12.6: Domestic CNY yields less US dollar yields   322

12.7: Investment income and current transfers flows of China   326

12.8: Onshore foreign currency deposits and exchange rate expectations   328

12.9: Net errors and omissions on China's BoP   329

13.1: Financial services trade liberalization commitment by Mode of Supply   348

13.2: Foreign bank concentration in terms of assets by region   352

13.3: Foreign banks do follow their customers in China   352

13.4: Funding source of foreign bank loans in China   354

13.5: Interest rate differentials and short-term capital inflows   356

14.1: National gross investment rate and per capita GDP in China, 1952–2004   375

14.2: Population and life expectancy in China, 1949–2004   376

14.3: Age structure of the population in China, 1949–2004   376

14.4: The income sources of the aged in China in 2004   378

14.5: Household income and consumption in China, 1995–2004   378

14.6: Household saving rate in China, 1995–2004   379

List of Tables

1.1: GDP and population, 2000 and 2025   2

1.2: Demand for primary energy and for oil, 2001 and 2025   5

1.3: Chinese primary energy consumption   8

1.4a: China's imports of selected primary products quantities (metric tons)   15

1.4b: China's imports of selected primary products value ($ billion)   15

1.5: Commodity prices, 1990–2004   16

2.1: Shares in global energy consumption and CO_2 emissions (%),
1990–2030   19

2.2: Shares in global consumption of fossil fuel energy components (%)   20

2.3: Shares in global consumption of non-fossil fuel energy components (%) 23

2.4: Urban air quality   30

2.5: Emissions of main air pollutants from waste gases in recent years   31

2.6a: Acid rain situation in the monitored cities   32

2.6b: Acid rain situation in acid rain control zones   32

2.7: Ambient air quality in main cities (2004)   33

3.1: HMs for Japan, Korea, China, ASEAN, JKFTA, and JKCFTA   70

3.2: The world's top twenty FTAers   78

4.1: Progress of major FTAs in East Asia (2005)   90

4.2: Impacts of FTAs on GDP (%)   94

4.3: The impact of FTAs on regional GDP in East Asia   96

4.4: The impact of FTAs in East Asia on regional capital stock   97

4.5: Effects of tariff elimination and ROO on trade   101

4.6: Tariff elimination in FTAs   102

4.7: Summary of ROO in major FTAs   102

4.8: Overall assessment   103

5.1: PTAs signed and implemented between APEC members since 2000   115

5.2: PTAs under negotiation or discussion between APEC members   116

5.3: Other PTAs between APEC members and other countries in Asia   116

5.4: Other PTAs under negotiation or discussions in Asia   117

List of Tables

6.1: Trade policy profiles, 2004   150

6.2: Top ten WTO participants (written submissions, 2003)   152

6.A1: Distribution of submissions over areas and issues (2003)   165

7.1: Geographical distribution of total portfolio asset holdings in 2003   173

7.2: Geographical distribution of total equity assets in 2003   175

7.3: Geographical distribution of total long-term debt securities in 2003   176

7.4: Geographical distribution of total short-term debt securities in 2003   177

7.5: Geographical distribution of cross-border bank claims in 2003   178

7.6: Geographical distribution of asset holdings in Latin America in 2003   179

7.7: Summary statistics (1999–2003)   180

7.8: Portfolio estimation   182

7.9: Bank claims estimation   182

7.10: Portfolio estimation with regional dummies   183

7.11: Portfolio claims with regional and global dummies   185

7.12: Bank claims with regional dummies   186

7.13: Bank claims with regional and global dummies   186

7.14: Estimates of regional and global risk-sharing, 1961–2002   190

7.15: Estimates of regional and global risk-sharing (average), various
      subperiods   191

7.16: Cross-country output correlation   193

8.1a: Summary statistics (LB08DA) 1999–2004   213

8.1b: Summary statistics (aggregate level) 1999–2004   213

8.2a: Summary statistics (LB08DA) 1999   213

8.2b: Summary statistics (aggregate level) 1999   213

8.3a: Summary statistics (LB08DA) 2000   213

8.3b: Summary statistics (aggregate level) 2000   214

8.4a: Summary statistics (LB08DA) 2001   214

8.4b: Summary statistics (aggregate level) 2001   214

8.5a: Summary statistics (LB08DA) 2002   214

8.5b: Summary statistics (aggregate level) 2002   214

8.6a: Summary statistics (LB08DA) 2003   215

8.6b: Summary statistics (aggregate level) 2003   215

8.7a: Summary statistics (LB08DA) 2004   215

8.7b: Summary statistics (aggregate level) 2004   215

8.8: Regression results on BAS (individual, LB08DA issue)   217

8.9: EGARCH model for volatility (individual, LB08DA issue) (VOLEG08)   219

8.10: Regression results on average BAS (aggregate of all tradable government bonds)   221

8.11: EGARCH model for volatility (aggregate level)   222

8.12: Effect of outstanding issuance on trading volume (TRADE)   224

9.1: Average incidence of currency crisis   234

9.2: Crisis risk assessments (1996)   235

9.3: Macroeconomic indicators (1996)   236

9.4: Stock market capitalization (2004)   238

9.5: Gross foreign exchange reserves   242

9.6: Macroeconomic indicators (2005)   247

10.1: The PBOC's assets-liability sheet by the end of 2005 (Billion CNY)   259

10.2: Adjustment of reserve requirements   262

10.3: Changes in interest rates since 1995   263

11.1: FDI inflows by source country (% share)   282

11.2: Utilized FDI by sector (% share)   283

11.3: Foreign direct investment inflows into China by region (% of total FDI inflows)   284

11.4: Total outward foreign direct investment (top ten countries with the highest average % share between 2001 and 2004)   286

11.5: External debt   289

11.6: Balance of payments (US$ billions)   290

11.7: A decomposition of the recent reserve buildup (US$ billions)   291

11.8: Capital flows under the financial account (US$ billions)   294

11.9: Possible effects of valuation changes on reserves   295

12.1: Credit default swap rates for People's Republic of China and British Bankers Association's Libor panel banks   316

12.2: Interbank rate differentials: Renminbi–dollar and Euro–dollar (bps)   324

12.3: Ratio of foreign currency deposits to total deposits (2000–5)   334

13.1: Domestic versus international capital flows under GATS: Mode 1   344

13.2: Domestic versus international capital flows under GATS: Mode 3   345

13.3: Financial services trade (FST) and capital flows under different modes of supply (no capital account restrictions)   346

13.4: China's capital control and its effect on financial services trade liberalization   347

13.5: Chronology of foreign bank presence in China since 1979   349

13.6: Foreign bank presence in China (top ten banks by assets in millions of US$)   351

13.7: Foreign financial institutions in China   351

List of Tables

13.8: Comparison of subsidiaries and branches (billions of US$)   352

13.9: Foreign bank loans by sector (millions of RMB)   353

13.10: Chinese external debt data by borrowers   355

13.11: Determinants of China's short-term bank loans   356

13.12: Panel regression results (1999–2003)   360

14.1: Household saving rate by province (average for the 1995–2004 period)   380

14.2: Age structure of the population by province (average for the 1995–2004 period)   382

14.3: Descriptive statistics   385

Introduction

Barry Eichengreen, Yung Chul Park, and Charles Wyplosz

The rise of Asia, and China specifically, is the single most important force reshaping the world economy at the beginning of the twenty-first century. From a low of 20 percent in 1950, Asia's share of global GDP has now risen to 33 percent and will exceed 40 percent within a generation if current forecasts are realized. This is first and foremost a Chinese story, but the pattern is general. By the mid-1990s, what were formerly called the 'Newly Industrializing Economies' (Hong Kong, Singapore, South Korea, and Taiwan) had experienced more than a quarter of a century of rapid growth, and a number of China's neighbors, Vietnam for example, now appear to be joining the high-growth club. Even leaving aside China, Asia is the world's most rapidly growing region and is likely to remain so for an extended period.

Asia's growing weight in the world economy is elevating it to a central position in global economic and financial affairs. Asian demands figure increasingly prominently in discussions of global energy markets. Asian policies figure prominently in the debate over greenhouse gases and global warming. Asia's trade, especially trade among Asian countries themselves, is the most rapidly growing component of global merchandise transactions. Financial flows from China are the largest single source of external finance for the US current account deficit. China has joined the United States as one of the two leading national destinations for foreign direct investment. At the same time, China's investments in the energy- and raw-materials-producing sectors in Africa and Latin America are attracting growing attention and, in some circles, concern. Asia has developed a complex of regional supply chains and production networks, where China serves as an assembly platform for its higher-wage, more technologically sophisticated neighbors. The effects are strongly felt in the United States, where goods assembled and produced in Asia dominate the market in consumer electronics, and in Europe, where producers of speciality products from apparel to machinery feel the pinch. Asia is conscious of its influence, which it increasingly exerts in the negotiations of the World Trade Organization and the deliberations of the World Bank and International Monetary Fund. Other regions, for their part, are equally conscious of Asia's growing weight in the world economy. Thus, in the autumn of 2006 the United States announced that it would henceforth engage in regular bilateral economic consultations with China. It is not far-fetched to imagine that Europe will follow the American example.

With these new powers come new problems. The rapid growth of Asia's exports and its persistent current account surpluses, *vis-à-vis* the United States in particular, excite protectionist pressures and complicate efforts to successfully complete the Doha Round of multilateral trade negotiations. Asia's response has been to pursue trade liberalization agreements at the regional level and bilaterally, but whether these initiatives represent adequate substitutes for the multilateral process is an open question. Financially, Asia has sought to bulletproof its economies from global financial markets by accumulating foreign reserves and by strengthening its own financial markets and integrating them with one another. Increasingly, however, questions are being raised about whether reserve accumulation has now gone too far— whether Asia has made excessive sacrifices of consumption and investment in order to augment its war chest of reserves—and whether significant progress can be made in the development of regional financial markets, bond markets in particular, over the relevant time frame. Internally, the Asian economies continue to experience problems of economic management. China, in particular, faces growing problems of managing aggregate demand, especially investment demand, in an environment of limited exchange rate flexibility, an increasingly open capital account, and a dearth of conventional monetary instruments.

This volume is an attempt by leading social scientists to offer a more systematic and comprehensive analysis of these issues. It considers both Asia's new powers—that is, its increasingly powerful influence in the world economy—and its new problems at the national, regional, and global levels. Necessarily, topical coverage is selective. But the issues considered here are, in our view, the logical starting points for analysis: they include the energy and environmental implications of Asia's rise, and China's rise in particular; trade relations; financial development; and problems of economic management. Geographical coverage is also selective. We focus on China and, more generally, on emerging East Asia. Our rationale for excluding Japan is twofold: as a more advanced economy, an analysis of its problems requires a separate treatment; and the country's relatively slow growth since the mid-1990s and looming demographic problems imply that it is likely to exercise declining financial and commercial leverage, relative to China and emerging East Asia, going forward. We exclude the interesting but again rather different case of India and South Asia generally on the grounds that it deserves—indeed requires—separate treatment.

The book opens with Richard Cooper's analysis of the implications of China's growth for global energy markets. Cooper begins by imagining what China will look like two decades from now (answer: China will be the world's second largest economy but still only a third the size of the United States). Its demand for energy will grow three times as fast as that of the United States and more than eight times as fast as that of Japan if current projections are to be believed. At this point it will be consuming one of every eight barrels of oil available worldwide. It will account for nearly 40 percent of global coal consumption, which is more troubling given the association of coal-based power generation with greenhouse gas emissions. It will depend on foreign sources for much of this energy. Cooper suggests that this dependence on foreign sources, together with China's lack of a large navy and strong naval tradition, will incline it toward a cooperative rather than a confrontational approach to securing its energy supplies.

Warwick McKibbin analyzes the environmental impact in more detail. He emphasizes the tendency for countries to invest more in environmental quality as incomes rise. China is likely to be no exception: although it has privileged industrial growth for the last quarter century, its leadership has clearly begun placing greater weight on environmental issues. Illustrations include the experiments currently underway to facilitate trading in sulfur emissions permits. McKibbin suggests that a similar approach might be taken to pricing carbon dioxide emissions and that the trading of permits would be effective, notwithstanding the peculiarities of China's system of property rights.

The conclusion of these two chapters is thus that the implications of China's growth for global energy and environment may be less dramatic and less adverse than sometimes supposed. With higher incomes will come pressures to enhance environmental quality, together with the technological sophistication to adopt less energy-intensive modes of production. With the development of a more market-oriented economy, the use of price-based measures, which are the most effective modality for policy intervention, will become even more effective in addressing energy and environmental concerns.

The second section of the volume considers the impact of Asia's emergence on the global trading system. The difficulties of the Doha Round of WTO negotiations, together with the expansion of intra-Asian trade, have spawned a proliferation of bilateral agreements in the region. While creating additional trade among the contracting parties, bilateralism can also divert trade from more efficient suppliers; depending on the specifics of implementation it can either serve as a building block or a stumbling block to wider liberalization. Richard Baldwin argues that bilateral agreements between countries like Japan and Korea are likely to have domino effects—they will encourage additional bilateral agreements. The result will be less an efficient network of trade than a pair of inefficient hub-and-spoke arrangements, where China and Japan serve as hubs and the other Asian countries (the 'spokes') trade disproportionately with the two center countries. But the emergence of a two-hub or 'bicycle' system is not inevitable. Baldwin suggests strategies for resisting its development: creating a union of East Asian nations that extend duty-free treatment to one another's industrial exports; and agreement by Japan and Korea, the countries responsible for initiating this dynamic, to coordinate their subsequent trade negotiations with other Asian countries.

Yung Chul Park and Inkyo Cheung further analyze the implications of the nascent hub-and-spoke system. They argue that a proliferation of bilateral agreements will produce an outcome inferior to an East Asian free-trade agreement or even a China–Japan–Korea FTA because bilateral agreements will divert more trade from low- to high-cost producers within the region. If both China and Japan succeed in creating hub-and-spoke networks of bilateral FTAs, they argue, other countries could end up being marginalized economically and politically. In response, potential spoke countries may wish to negotiate as many FTAs as possible, leading to the further proliferation of bilateral arrangements. This spaghetti- or noodle-bowl pattern would also render East Asia less attractive to foreign direct investment.

Cédric Dupont is also pessimistic about the capacity of Asian countries to limit the trade distortions associated with the bilateral approach to negotiating trade agreements. If anything, he is even more pessimistic than Park and Cheung about the prospects for an East Asian free-trade agreement or a China–Japan–Korea FTA. But he suggests that APEC (Asia Pacific Economic Cooperation), while itself a victim of preferential trading arrangements, could in fact turn out to be the region's savior. Standards set by APEC could be used to encourage the negotiation of high-quality agreements that shun sectoral preferences and other forms of hidden protection. The preference of the United States for multilateral and regional trade initiatives could be used to tip the balance against a proliferation of bilaterals. This would be consistent with APEC's original mandate. It would also be a way of enlisting the United States and other extra-Asian economic powers in pursuit of broader interests.

In the final study addressing these topics, Robert Lawrence focuses on the implications of China's emergence for the global trading system. Lawrence asks whether China's bilateral and regional initiatives might undermine the multilateral trading order and whether China is seeking to establish an East Asian trading bloc that discriminates against nonparticipating countries. He concludes that concerns about a Fortress East Asia are misplaced. Both directly and through the induced reaction of other countries, China's bilateral agreements with regional partners could provide a powerful impetus to the process of competitive liberalization. Moreover, countries implementing agreements with China should find it relatively easy to open their markets to other developing countries. Lawrence acknowledges the risk that a proliferation of FTAs could lead to a web of overlapping agreements that renders the global trading system inefficiently complex, but he offers a solution: adoption by the WTO of a set of rules to ensure the uniformity of bilateral agreements.

Thus, the authors contributing to this section provide a clear preference ordering of approaches to trade liberalization, ranking the multilateral approach as best, followed by the regional approach, and finally the bilateral approach. They predict that, in practice, China specifically and Asia generally will continue to pursue all three strategies. While the regional and bilateral approaches may create domino effects and thereby encourage wider liberalization, there is also the possibility of inefficiencies. The authors therefore suggest additional mechanisms, such as the reinvigoration of trans-Pacific cooperation, to mitigate these dangers.

If Asia's impact on trade flows has been prominent, its impact on international financial flows has been more prominent still. Asian policy makers have identified regional financial integration as a priority, establishing an Asian Bond Fund and creating an Asian Bond Market Initiative to advance this goal. Soyong Kim, Jong-Wha Lee, and Kwanho Shin assess progress to date. They find that, by the standards of Europe, East Asian financial markets are well integrated with one other. They also find more evidence of regional financial integration in bank claims than financial securities, which they attribute to weak incentives for portfolio diversification, the instability of monetary and exchange rate regimes, and the underdevelopment of regional securities markets.

The limited integration of markets in debt securities of which the authors provide evidence can be seen as a specific instance of the general problem of bond market underdevelopment in the region. The problem of bond market underdevelopment is especially evident when one considers market liquidity, measures of which compare unfavorably even with other emerging regions, Latin America for example. Akkharaphol Chabchitrchaidol and Sakkapop Panyanukul shed some light on this paradoxical behavior using detailed data on the Thai bond market. They identify inadequate policy transparency, underdeveloped derivatives markets, limits on short selling, the narrowness of the investor base, and small issue size as impediments to the development of bond market liquidity. Aside from the last, these are all problems that can be ameliorated through policy reform at the national level. In contrast, the negative impact of small issue size can only be solved over time (through economic growth that delivers larger economies and larger issuers) and by regional integration which encourages issuance by large borrowers from other countries (the strategy pursued by, *inter alia*, Singapore and Hong Kong).

The final chapter in this section, by Charles Wyplosz, asks whether progress in strengthening financial markets and institutions, together with changes in macroeconomic policies, have rendered East Asian countries less susceptible to financial crises. Wyplosz suggests that regional economies may have been rendered less vulnerable but by no means secure. The build-up of foreign reserves and modest moves in the direction of greater exchange rate flexibility enhance macroeconomic and financial resiliency but provide no guarantee against financial problems. Efforts to strengthen financial institutions and markets through the provision of better infrastructure and improved supervision and regulation have had positive effects, but the region—and not least countries like China—is even more exposed to capital flows than was the case a decade ago, a trend that works in the direction of heightening vulnerabilities.

Thus, the overall message from these chapters is that while policies have been strengthened, the development and integration of financial markets and institutions continues to disappoint. At the same time, there is no intrinsic reason why East Asia cannot overcome the obstacles to more rapid progress in the financial domain.

In the final section we return to China and its macroeconomic problems. China's macroeconomic performance is too important for the rest of Asia and, for that matter, other regions to ignore; that performance will hinge on how the authorities cope with challenges to growth and stability. Yongding Yu, a member of the Chinese Academy of Social Sciences and of the Monetary Policy Committee of the People's Bank, uses monetary policy as a window onto those policy challenges. As Yu explains, China is currently at a transitional stage between a government-led and market-led banking system, where neither official diktat nor market prices allow effective monetary control. Similarly, with the development of additional channels for capital flows into and out of the country, the authorities' limited tolerance for exchange rate flexibility increasingly poses a constraint on monetary control.

Solving these problems is straightforward in principle: the authorities should accelerate the commercialization of the banking system to enhance the effectiveness of market-based instruments and allow the exchange rate to fluctuate more freely so that policy can be tailored to domestic needs. But the problem is not so simple in practice. Commercializing the banking system is easier said than done when there is pressure for the continued extension of policy loans to state-owned enterprises that provide employment and social services to Chinese workers and their family members. Greater exchange rate flexibility is easier to advocate than implement when it continues to be resisted by an export sector accustomed to stable currency values and by leaders hesitant to tamper with success. This suggests that monetary management and macroeconomic management generally will continue to labor under significant handicaps for some time to come.

As noted, capital mobility is increasingly important in shaping the performance of the Chinese economy. Eswar Prasad and Shangjin Wei show that the authorities have adopted a coherent strategy toward capital account liberalization. They have privileged foreign direct investment over portfolio capital flows, building on the experience of other countries, although the authors also acknowledge the possibility that China's institutions and lack of market transparency may have contributed to the disproportionate importance of FDI. Prasad and Wei are skeptical that China's accumulation of foreign exchange reserves has functioned, as sometimes argued, as a kind of collateral that has rendered foreigners more confident of the security of their direct investments in the country.

Guonan Ma and Robert McCauley do not entirely agree with the emphasis placed by other authors on the opening of China's capital account. Chinese capital controls are still effective today, they observe, and there is no reason to think that market pressures will destroy their effectiveness tomorrow, assuming that the authorities continue to liberalize gradually. The magnitude of interest differentials also suggests that the Chinese authorities retain considerable room for running an autonomous monetary policy.

Be this as it may, over time Chinese depositors will become increasingly able to switch between domestic- and foreign-currency-denominated bank deposits. As this happens, the pressure for cross-border interbank capital flows to arbitrage differences with onshore dollar deposit and loan rates will intensify. The monetary autonomy consistent with a relatively rigid exchange rate will be reduced. It will then be imperative for the country to move in the direction of greater exchange rate flexibility in order to avoid ending up having to defend a fragile currency peg in the face of volatile capital flows.

Two other factors influencing capital flows in and out of China will be the liberalization of trade in financial services, considered by Li-Gang Liu and Elvira Kurmanalieva, and domestic savings behavior, which is the subject of Charles Horioka and Junmin Wan's chapter. China is a now a member of the WTO and as such is subject to the obligations of its General Agreement on Trade in Services (GATS). The experience of other countries suggests that liberalization measures adopted in response to GATS obligations have a significant impact on the volume of cross-border capital flows, especially in large middle-income countries like China. China's GATS obligations may thus end up exposing its economy to rapidly growing capital flows whether the authorities prefer gradualism or not.

Horioka and Wan's analysis of household data singles out demographic factors and habit formation as determinants of individual savings rates. From the perspective of Chinese macroeconomic management, their results suggest that the authorities will be dealing with a situation of high investment, financed out of abundant domestic savings, for some time to come, since the demographic situation will begin to change significantly only after 2015 and even then habit formation will limit the fall in savings rates. They thus suggest that China's current account surplus will not disappear anytime soon.

As a group, these studies highlight the existence of significant problems for Chinese macroeconomic management, from the difficulties of monetary control to the challenges of managing capital flows in an economy increasingly integrated internationally Whether the authorities are able to surmount these problems will be critical for determining whether the country sustains its rapid rate of growth in coming years. In turn this will have important implications for the development of the Asian and global economies. The papers collected here do not provide definitive answers to all these questions. But they at least provide a start.

* * * * *

The present book grows out of a trio of conferences in Berkeley, Geneva, and Seoul, reflecting our belief that a rounded perspective requires viewing the issues from different geographical and intellectual points of view. The Berkeley conference was supported by the National Science Foundation through its program to promote international scholarly collaboration, by the Korea Economic Institute, and by the University of California, Berkeley, through its Institute for East Asian Studies, Institute for European Studies, and Clausen Center for International Business and Policy. In Geneva support was provided by the Graduate Institute of International Studies. In Seoul we received both logistical and financial support from the Korean Institute for Economic Policy, Seoul National University, and the Bank for International Settlements. We are grateful to them all.

1

China's Coming Demand for Energy

Richard N. Cooper
Harvard University

We begin by sketching what China's economy will look like in 2025, two decades from now. It is desirable to do this quantitatively, both to indicate the practical possibilities open to China and to demythologize statements that suggest large magnitudes—'the next economic superpower'—without specifying what they are. Of course, no one really knows what China will look like in two decades, and indeed a range of outcomes is possible. In its 'Global Scenarios to 2025' the Royal Dutch/Shell (oil) Company allows China's growth to vary from 6.7 to 8.4 percent a year, depending on the nature of the external (world) economic and political environment. As we shall see, others would allow the possibility of even lower growth rates. For sake of concreteness, I will build here upon the 2025 projections of the US Department of Energy, yielding a growth in dollar terms of 7.2 percent a year. They will not necessarily be correct, but they represent an internally consistent projection that is reasonably optimistic about China's growth, and ties that growth to projections of energy demand, an important source of interaction between China and the rest of the world, both in economic and in environmental terms. We can then address the implications of this growth, and take excursions from the baseline projection.

Table 1.1 presents the projected GDP and population of China, India, Japan, and the USA in 2025, compared with 2000. GDP is reported in US dollars of 2005 (adjusted from 1997 dollars in the original source). We need to allow for some real appreciation of the Chinese currency (RMB) relative to the dollar over the next two decades. Similarly for India. I allow, somewhat arbitrarily, 1 percent a year. (The yen appreciated 0.8 percent a year against the dollar over the period 1950–75, although all this appreciation was concentrated in the period 1971–75.) This would bring China's GDP in 2025, measured in dollars, to $7.4 trillion, larger than Japan's projected GDP in that year if allowance is made for the upward revision of 16.8 percent in

Table 1.1: GDP and population, 2000 and 2025

	GDP (trillion 2005 dollars)		Population (millions)	
	2000	2025	2000	2025
China	1.30	7.40	1275	1445
India	0.57	2.75	1017	1369
Japan	5.09	7.61	127	120
USA	10.87	21.90	276	351

Source: Adapted from US Department of Energy, International Energy Outlook 2005.

China's GDP for 2004 made in December 2005, which is not included in these figures. (It would be larger still if the appreciation of the RMB is greater than 1 percent a year.) It would amount to about 10 percent of gross world product. It would be over one-third the projected size of the US economy in that year. India's GDP will reach $2.75 trillion, modestly larger than Germany today, but with an assumed growth rate (in dollars) of 6.5 percent remains much smaller than China. China's population will have grown to 1.4 billion, and India's to nearly 1.4 billion, while Japan's population will have *declined* to 120 million. The USA will have grown to 351 million, all figures drawn from medium projections by the US Census Bureau.

Several observations can be made about these projections. First, they assume that China will grow at 7.2 percent a year over the period, in dollar terms. This is only slightly lower than its 7.4 percent annual growth rate over the period 1980–98 as calculated by the economic historian Angus Maddison (1998), but considerably below the 9.9 percent official growth figures, and below actual growth in the past few years. The drop is partly due to a significant drop in the growth rate of the population, to 0.5 percent a year, and an even sharper drop in the growth of the potential labor force, as children born under the one-child policy reach adulthood. In other words, China is assumed to do well economically, meeting its official aspiration of quadrupling GDP when measured in dollars (although not quite when measured in RMB). Japan is assumed to grow at 1.7 percent a year, despite its drop in population and even sharper drop in labor force; the USA is assumed to grow at 3.1 percent—lower than in recent years—with population growing at 0.9 percent a year, also lower than in recent years when immigration is included, as it should be.

Second, however, China remains a relatively poor country, with GDP per capita only about one-twelfth that of Japan and the USA (the gap will be considerably lower in terms of purchasing power parity, on which more below). But Chinese will be five times richer than they were in 2000, and all Chinese under the age of 50 will have grown up in a period of rapid economic growth and increasing prosperity.

Third, the dynamics of population change are quite different in the four countries. America's population continues to grow, albeit at a somewhat slower rate. The number of 20 to 24 year-olds, the group that is just leaving its education and entering the labor force, will grow by 0.6 percent a year to 2025. The same age group in Japan, in sharp contrast, is expected to decline at 1.4 percent a year, so that by 2025 this age group will be only 70 percent as large as it was in 2000. China is in-between, with the 20 to 24 year-old group declining at 0.7 percent a year, down 16 percent from 2000. All three countries have aging populations due to increased longevity, but it is most rapid in Japan because of low natality. China will experience a significant drop in total population after 2035. India, in contrast, continues to grow albeit at declining rates.

A fourth observation is that China will be the world's second largest national economy, but little more than one-third the size of the USA in terms of economic output—roughly equal to the size of the USA in 1993. If it chooses, China will thus have considerable scope for internationally relevant policies, whether in military expenditure or in foreign aid, provided sufficient tax revenues can be raised. In 1993 Americans paid in taxes 29 percent of their GDP, compared with 17 percent in China in 2005.

One sometimes sees much larger numbers, even suggestions that China's economy could be larger than that of the United States by 2025 (see, e.g., *The Economist*, April 1–7, 2006, p. 84). These presentations compare GDPs using so-called purchasing-power parity conversion rates, rather than market exchange rates. Purchasing-power parity (PPP) is necessary when comparing standards of living between countries, since an important part of a family's expenditures is on locally produced goods and especially labor services, and these are much cheaper in poor countries, reflecting lower overall productivity. In terms of PPP, China's GDP in 2002 was 4.6 times what it was at market exchange rates, and already 70 percent larger than Japan's economy, whereas at market exchange rates Japan's GDP was 3.5 times that of China. There are, however, two serious problems with using PPP-based GDP for these comparisons.

The first is conceptual. China is tied to the world economy at market prices mediated by market exchange rates, not PPP. All trade in goods and services and foreign investment takes place at market exchange rates, and even local goods and services are linked to traded goods by the opportunity cost of land, labor, and capital factors that could earn more in the trade sector will move there, as circumstances permit. China is not a market economy in every respect, but prices and wages are largely determined freely, influenced by the prices of traded goods. These days some argue that the RMB is 'under-valued,' and suggest that it should be appreciated by as much as 25 percent. Such an adjustment, should it occur, would close only a small portion of the large difference between the existing exchange rate and the so-called PPP rate. As noted above, an allowance for appreciation by 1 percent a year, 28 percent over 25 years, has been assumed in the projection used here.

The second problem is practical. China's PPP exchange rate is based on fragile US–China price comparisons made in the mid-1980s for roughly 300 goods and services, some of which involved heroic assumptions to make them comparable. Many Chinese prices were still controlled, not market-determined, at that time. Moreover, the necessarily arbitrary choice of weights to add up these goods or services makes a large difference to the final result, by a factor of three between Chinese expenditure weights and US expenditure weights (see Maddison (1998)).

For geo-political or geo-economic purposes, market exchange rates, perhaps smoothed over several years, provide the relevant basis for comparing market economies. The choice makes a big difference: China's economy is already 70 percent larger than Japan's when calculated at PPP; but only slightly more than one-quarter of Japan at market exchange rates. China's ability to trade or invest abroad is determined by market exchange rates, not by PPP. China demonstrated the importance of market exchange rates even in the military arena when it purchased military aircraft and ships from Russia, at Russia's export prices, despite a known strong preference for producing military equipment at home. In effect, China indicated that it could not produce comparable weapons at competitive cost domestically.

A larger China of course has implications for the world economy. Demand for food, energy, and other resources will be much higher. By the same token, the supply of manufactures and other goods and services will be much higher. Of special interest will be China's demand for energy, especially coal (with its tendency to pollute) and oil (with its limited domestic supply). On the Department of Energy projection, China's total demand for energy will grow at 4.1 percent a year to 2025, as opposed to 1.3 percent in the United States and 0.5 percent in Japan. These growth rates allow for continued increases in energy efficiency, but no major breakthroughs during the next two decades. By 2025 China will be consuming 14.2 million barrels of oil a day, well over twice Japan's consumption, and over half that in the United States. By 2025, on these projections, China will account for 12 percent of world oil consumption, and for 22 percent of the increment in consumption between 2002 and 2025.

Coal consumption, mainly to generate electricity, will more than double to 3.2 billion tons, 39 percent of total world consumption, with important implications for air pollution, absent dramatic improvements in the way coal is consumed, and for emissions of carbon dioxide, an important greenhouse gas. These figures imply that energy efficiency in China remains much lower than in the USA and especially than in Japan, despite significant improvement. China will have great demand for infrastructure of all kinds—power, transport, housing, and urban services as the country becomes much more urbanized.

Table 1.2: Demand for primary energy and for oil, 2001 and 2025

	Primary Energy (quads)		Oil (million barrels per day)	
	2001	2025	2001	2025
China	40.9	109.2	4.9	14.2
India	13.8	29.3	2.2	4.9
USA	96.3	132.4	19.6	27.3
Japan	21.9	24.7	5.4	5.3
World	403.9	644.6	78	119.2

Normal units of measurement have been converted into quadrillion British Thermal Units (quads) at the following rates:
petroleum: 1 million barrels a day = 2.03 quads per year
coal: 1 million short tons = 0.0184 quads
gas: 1 trillion cubic feet = 1.034 quads
nuclear power: 1 billion kWh = 0.0105 quads

Source: US Department of Energy, International Energy Outlook 2005.

The DOE's reference case, reported in Table 1.2, is only a best guess, built on assumptions about world and national economic growth, changes in energy efficiency, and prices of energy. The DOE also provides 'high growth' and 'low growth' variants around its reference case. These raise and lower the assumed rates of economic growth, but do not change the relationship of energy consumption to growth, nor the assumed price trajectory for energy (especially oil). This latter point requires some explanation, since higher or lower world economic growth might be expected to influence energy prices. However, the projections are to 2025, two decades hence, so supply is assumed to respond to increased demand. The DOE's price trajectory assumes a gradual fall in the price of oil to $31 a barrel (2003 dollars) in 2010, whereupon oil prices rise at 0.8 percent a year through 2025, to just under $35. This price trajectory influences demand for energy, and also oil production by non-OPEC countries. OPEC is assumed to fill the gap between world oil demand and non-OPEC oil supply. Thus OPEC (in practice, Saudi Arabia and the neighboring Gulf oil producers, plus Venezuela) is assumed to be the residual supplier of oil under all the projections, adapting production as required. The assumption is that Saudi Arabia and others can produce the incremental oil profitably in this price range. Simmons (2005) has controversially questioned this assumption, arguing that Saudi Arabia is currently operating at or even beyond its optimal extraction rate. If Simmons is correct—his argument has been widely disputed—of course oil prices would have to rise further in the presence of steadily increasing world demand for oil, and that price increase would induce users to reduce their demand for energy, and to develop additional supplies of liquid fuels (especially oil sands and perhaps coal liquefaction).

Under the high growth projection, mature economies are assumed to grow 0.5 percent a year faster, and emerging markets 1.0 percent faster, than in the reference case. Under the low growth projection economic growth is assumed to be correspondingly lower. World demand for oil reaches 132.3 MBD under the high growth projection (versus 119.2 in the reference case), and China's demand for oil reaches 16.1 MBD, just over 12 percent of the world total. Under the low growth projection, world demand for oil reaches 107.7 MBD, and China's demand for oil is 12.5 MBD, just under 12 percent of the world total.

By 2025 China's total imports of goods and services will amount to perhaps $1.8 trillion, roughly three times Japan's imports and two-thirds of US imports but modestly more than imports by the European Union from non-member countries. Thus China will be a major market for the products of many countries, roughly on the scale of the United States at present (Cooper 2005).

China's transition period for full compliance with WTO rules and the terms of China's WTO accession expired at the end of 2006. Compliance was not complete by then, however, since many commitments run strongly contrary to well-established Chinese practices, and Beijing is unable to control the entire country except on a few issues of the highest priority. But compliance will gradually take hold in the coming decades, and by 2025 China is likely to be much more transparent and rule-bound, at least in the arena of commercial activity, than it is now. Foreign businessmen will play a significant role in that transformation, and not incidentally will provide an important source of information to the central government, independent of official channels, on what is happening around the country.

By 2025 completion of the Doha Round of trade negotiations will have been in the distant past and the ten-year transition period following completion of multilateral trade negotiations will have concluded, so the trading world of 2025 will be governed by the outcome of the Doha Round, even though a post-Doha round of trade negotiations may have been launched. If the aspirations of APEC of some years ago are realized (the target date was 2020), world merchandise trade will be completely free of tariffs and other restrictions on imports. The discriminatory features of the preferential trading arrangements which are currently proliferating rapidly will have been obliterated, or at least greatly attenuated, by such a development.

China has played a conservative, low-key role in international economic organizations, and that is likely to continue because the evolving status quo has served China's interests well. As noted, China will provide a huge domestic market for imports, giving the rest of the world a great interest in China's trade policy and practices.

All the above assumes China stays on its current growth path, which in turns assumes continued peace and prosperity in the world, so trade can continue to grow unimpeded. Even so, China's internal requirements remain formidable. It must grow the private and township sectors enough to compensate for declining employment in the state-enterprise sector. To close many loss-making enterprises it must create a social safety net (unemployment compensation, pensions, health care) for urban employees. It must deal with rapid growth in demand for water, waste disposal, and new housing in urban areas. It must greatly improve agricultural productivity, partly through large and more efficient irrigation projects, partly through improved seeds and techniques of farming. And it must address the widening regional inequalities of growth and income, in part through significant investments in infrastructure within and to the central and western parts of the country.

A team at the RAND Corporation, responding to a request by the US Defense Department, produced a study of various adverse scenarios, along with estimates of their negative impact on Chinese growth over the period 2005–15 (Wolf *et al.* 2003). The possible adversities cover a socially disruptive increase in unemployment, increased corruption, a major epidemic (focused on AIDS, written before SARS), failure to solve the emerging shortage of water in northern China, a major disruption in world oil supplies, a domestic financial crisis, a sharp decline in inward foreign direct investment, and a military conflict over Taiwan or elsewhere. Others are imaginable, for example a severe world recession or a significant reversion to protectionism in Europe and the USA, neither of which is likely but both of which are possible. Each scenario has an adverse impact on China's growth ranging from 0.3 to 2.2 percent a year on the assumptions made in the study, lowering China's GDP by 3 to 24 percent by 2015 from an unspecified base line. None of these adversities may materialize, but the Rand authors consider this implausible. If one occurs, others may be triggered, at least in part, because of interdependencies among them. Good luck as well as skillful management will be required for China to continue on a course of sustained growth.

Continued rapid growth in China requires peace and prosperity in the rest of the world. China thrives on a benign international environment, and China's current leaders understand that well. Legitimacy of the Chinese Communist Party (CCP) depends on delivering economic prosperity at home, as does the 'peaceful rise' of China in the society of nations. China will have at least two sets of new leaders by 2025. If the leaders of 2025 are around 60 years in age, they will have been born around 1965 and reached college age in the radically changed environment of 1985. Their parents will have been the victims, or in a few cases the perpetrators, of the Cultural Revolution.

As China grows, its dependence on imported materials will also grow. China has ample coal and is rich in some other minerals, but in general China is not a resource-rich country and it has already become dependent on imports of iron ore to feed its voracious demand for steel, copper, and especially oil, where domestic exploration has so far produced only disappointing results. China is also a large absorber of foreign technology, and so far has demonstrated only a limited capacity to generate new indigenous technology. That may change with the large increase in college graduates, including engineers, combined with greater incentives and fewer inhibitions to think creatively than has characterized China in the past—another major challenge.

1.1 China's Energy Consumption and Outlook

Table 1.3 provides basic information on China's primary energy consumption in 1990 and 2001, and the reference case projection of China's energy use to 2025 by the US Department of Energy. It can be seen there that China is heavily dependent (nearly two-thirds in 2001) on coal, the most carbon-intensive fossil fuel, mainly for electricity generation but also for industrial and household use. Oil accounted for just under one-quarter of primary energy use. Over the next twenty-five years the relative importance of coal is expected to decline, while that of oil rises (as more Chinese acquire automobiles, and truck traffic increases). But because of rapid growth, the use of coal is nonetheless expected to more than double by 2025, from an already large base. China is taking significant steps to increase the use of natural gas in households, industry, and especially for the generation of electricity, and to increase nuclear power, both of which are expected to grow rapidly, but by 2025 nuclear and hydro together still account for only 8 percent of China's primary energy consumption It is noteworthy that the DOE assumes that China over this period grows at 'only' 6.2 percent a year, over a percentage point less than China's 7.2 percent growth aspiration, and that energy growth, averaging 4.1 percent a year, is only two-thirds this expected growth in GDP, implying considerable improvements in efficiency in the use of energy as well as changes in the structure of the Chinese economy toward less energy-intensive activities. Despite lower growth, improvements in efficiency, and the relative decline of coal, China's CO_2 emissions are expected to grow by

Table 1.3: Chinese primary energy consumption

	(Quads)					
	1990	2001	2010	2020	2025	Growth (2002–25) percent
Coal	20.7	25	42.4	55.9	59.7	3.6
Oil	4.7	9.9	18.7	25	28.8	4.5
Gas	0.5	1.1	2.7	4.3	6.7	7.8
Nuclear	0	0.2	0.8	1.7	2.1	9.8
Hydro	1.3	2.6	5.2	6.2	6.7	3.4
Total:	27	40.9	73.1	97.7	109.2	4.1

Source: EIA (2005: app. A).

4.0 percent a year, the most rapid in the world, and will exceed those projected for the United States by 2025.

The demand for electricity grows with increases in income, for it is relatively clean and convenient at the point of use. In 1997 China had 263 GW in installed electricity-generating capacity, two-thirds coal-fired (74 percent of actual electricity generation), 23 percent hydroelectric, with the remaining 10 percent relying on oil, nuclear, gas, and renewables, in that order (IEA 2000: 204). The International Energy Agency expected China to add 500 GW of capacity by 2020, raising capacity by nearly a factor of three over existing capacity, two-thirds of which would be coal-fired, despite outsized increases in gas-fired, nuclear, and hydropower. This compares with a total of new generating capacity in the USA (Europe) of only 396 GW (477 GW), mostly gas, over the same period. China is expected to invest over 2001–30 a total of $795 billion in new power generation, compared with $654 billion in the USA and Canada, $525 billion in the European Union, and $274 billion in Japan (IEA 2003: 353). China faces a basic dilemma in framing its future energy policy. It has abundant coal resources, but has so far had difficulty finding abundant oil or gas. Coal accounts for much of the air pollution— 85 percent of sulfur dioxide (of which only 30 percent comes from power plants), for instance, and much particulate matter. In addition, coal mines are mainly located a considerable distance from the main sources of demand for energy, requiring extensive transportation. Switching to oil or gas, however, would involve extensive investments in infrastructure, and will prospectively increase China's dependence on the rest of the world for primary energy, to the discomfort of Chinese leaders. Their attempts to resolve this dilemma lead them to place heavy emphasis on hydro- and nuclear power; to explore intensively for oil and gas (but not to the point of inviting foreign equity participation, as distinguished from production-sharing, in Chinese production); to develop coal liquefaction; and to diversify their sources of imports, notably by considering (expensive) oil and gas pipelines from Kazakhstan and from Siberia, in order to reduce the inevitable growing dependence on seaborne oil (and, in the future, gas) from the Persian Gulf.

China has extensive hydroelectric potential, 290 GW estimated to be economically exploitable, of which only 60 GW was developed in 1997. The controversial Three Gorges Dam will bring on an additional 18 GW by 2009. IEA assumes the total will rise to 171 GW by 2020 (IEA 2000: 205). China's first nuclear power plant came online in 1991 and by 2000 China had 2.1 GW of capacity. By 2006 China had nine reactors in operation in two locations, two finished reactors in a third location, and four additional reactors approved for international bidding (*Wall Street Journal*, 3/22/06: A6). Official plans call optimistically for 40 GW by 2020 (CDF 2003: 71), but because of cost, long lead times, and other difficulties China is likely to reach only 21 GW.

(The capital costs of nuclear plants are about three times higher per kW than for new coal-fired plants in China.)

China has discovered the many attractions of gas-fired power plants, in cost, scale, and low pollution. China's problem is insufficient economical gas. It has approved two LNG terminals, both on the south coast, and has several more under consideration; it has contracted for Australian and Indonesian gas. Power plants will however have to compete with high-priority residential and industrial uses of gas. The IEA nonetheless projects a twentyfold increase in gas-fired power plants between 1997 and 2020, from a low base (IEA 2000: 205). The structure of the Chinese energy market is highly fragmented. While national policy is set in Beijing, actions by each province and municipality reflect local interests. As in many countries, end-use of energy, particularly gas and electricity, is subject to local price control. This is partly to prevent exploitation of local monopoly in delivery, but also reflects residual habits created during central-planning days in the energy sector, which is seen as critical to many industrial activities. Over 95 percent of China's population has access to electricity, but there are no national or even extensive regional electricity grids in China, so most power plants distribute only within the vicinity of the plants. Long-distance gas pipelines are few, although a West–East pipeline to bring gas from the Tarim Basin in Xinjiang province to Shanghai and other eastern destinations was completed in 2004 and is now in operation. Thousands of small coal mines also serve mainly local needs, although vast amounts of coal are also shipped east and south by rail and barge.

Furthermore, with few exceptions, energy is provided by state-owned enterprises (SOEs), many now owned by provinces or municipalities. Oil production and distribution have been concentrated in three large national SOEs, mostly non-competing. Electricity production is typically provided by provincial or municipal enterprises. China is having difficulty placing SOEs under tight budget constraints; they have historically had ready access to bank credit, and while banks (themselves SOEs) are under instruction to make loans only on a commercial basis, local politics continues to play an important role in credit allocation, especially to energy firms.

China is notably inefficient in its use of energy. China's energy efficiency is expected to improve over the projection period to 2025, at 1.9 percent a year, compared with 1.7 percent for the United States and 1.0 percent in Japan. This assumed rate of improvement seems too modest, given the scope for improvement and the concerns of Chinese leaders about growing dependence on imported energy. The 11th Five Year Program (2006–10) set as an objective a decline of 20 percent in the energy to GDP ratio, nearly 4 percent a year, although this target was not met during the first year of the plan.

According to the IEA, China's coal-fired generating plants operated at only 28 percent efficiency, 26 percent below the 38 percent average of the OECD countries in the late 1990s (IEA 2000: 204), despite more extensive pollution controls on the OECD plants. Generating plants in China were much smaller, coal consistency was uneven, and plants were down more often. New plants in China are typically much larger than average, over 300 MW, but generally remain behind world best practice.

China's authorities are well aware of their energy needs, problems, and constraints. They acknowledge that energy should not simply serve the requirements of growth, but should also take into account cost, environmental factors, and security. They also acknowledge the need to separate more sharply policy formulation from regulation and supervision (at all levels of government), and the need to move to price-incentives-based competitive markets subject to regulation to protect consumers from natural monopolies, particularly in final distribution, and taking into account environmental externalities (see statements by Qingtai Chen and Jiange Li of the Development Research Center at the China Development Forum on China's Energy Strategy and Reform, Beijing, November 2003). As is often the case in China, the difficult task is in translating coherent principles into actual practice.

One part of China's strategy seems to be to back out coal as rapidly as investment in gas, nuclear, and hydro permit, and to charge consumers of electricity whatever is necessary to finance the required investment.

Growing dependence on critical imported materials, including food and feed grains, creates new vulnerabilities for China. The clearest and most notable concerns oil. On the US Department of Energy's baseline projection, China will consume 14.2 MBD of oil in 2025, up 4.5 percent a year from the 4.9 MBD consumed in 2001. China was a small net exporter of oil in the early 1990s; by 2025 it will import nearly 11 MBD. China also desires to increase its consumption of natural gas, including liquefied natural gas (LNG), for environmental reasons—to replace coal in the home and workplace, and even to generate electricity in places close to the coast (or gas pipelines) and far from coal mines.

China's oil industry was reorganized in 1998 mainly into three large, vertically integrated oil firms, somewhat in emulation of the international oil majors: the China National Petroleum Corporation (CNPC), the China Petrochemical Corporation (Sinopec) and, for offshore development, the China National Offshore Oil Corporation (CNOOC). All are and are intended to remain state-owned firms, but each has floated minority shares in the international market and has as minority shareholders one or more of the major international oil companies, BP, Shell, and ExxonMobile. Regulatory oversight is by the State Energy Administration, created in 2003.

About a quarter of China's domestic oil production of 3.6 MBD is accounted for by a single field at Daqing in Manchuria, now in decline. About 15 percent of domestic production is offshore, mainly in the Bohai Sea east of Tianjin. Offshore exploration and development are occurring there and elsewhere, with the technical help and financing of a number of US firms such as

ChevronTexaco, ConocoPhillips, and Kerr-McGee, as well as Husky Oil of Canada.

New discoveries in China have been disappointing, imports have risen sharply, and Chinese firms have been not only buying in the market but also seeking oil development and production abroad. CNPC has acquired concessions in Azerbaijan, Canada, Indonesia, Iraq, Iran, Kazakhstan, Sudan, and Venezuela. Sinopec is directly involved in developing Iran's Yadavaran field, and has purchased 40 percent of Canada's Northern Lights oil sands project. Sinopec also has acquired offshore exploration rights in the Bight of Biafra, in territory jointly leased by Nigeria and Sao Tome. CNOOC has purchased a stake in an Indonesia field, and made an abortive effort in 2005 to purchase the US firm Unocal, whose oil reserves reside in South-East Asia. 'Street gossip' suggesting that China has been paying a significant 10–20 percent premia might have been warranted.

China's worldwide search for equity oil became politically sensitive in two areas: first, China's continued financial support of, and even sale of weapons to, the government of Sudan, despite that government's indirect involvement in mass displacement and deaths in Darfur, in western Sudan. Second, CNOOC's belated high bid for the US firm Unocal, which provoked a Congressional firestorm over implausible alleged national security concerns, but raised legitimate questions about the supposedly commercial nature of acquisitions by state-owned firms with privileged access to low-interest credit from state-owned banks, necessary for the purchase.

China's largest foreign project is CNPC's 60 percent stake in a Kazakh oil firm, with a promise to invest in development over the next twenty years. A pipeline has been constructed from Kazakhstan to western China which will initially supply three Chinese refineries with about 200,000 barrels a day. Chinese officials talk about eventually acquiring about half of imported oil 'through the market' and about half through China's overseas investments in equity oil. China's overseas ventures produced less than 10 percent of China's imported oil in 2005, however. This ratio may rise slightly with the opening of the Kazakh pipeline. About half of China's imported oil originates in the Middle East, with Saudi Arabia being the major supplier. China may discover, as the oil majors did in the 1970s, that 'owning' the oil provides no security of supply when oil supplies are tight; the oil-producing countries are capable of taxing away the higher earnings, or even nationalizing the foreign-owned reserves and operations.

China has been holding conversations with Russia about constructing an oil pipeline carrying as much as one million barrels a day from central Siberia to Daqing, where it would tie into China's pipeline system. An alternative eastbound pipeline route would skirt China and end up in the Russian port Nakhodka on the Sea of Japan, whence oil could be shipped to Japan, Korea, and China. Russia has so far been unable to decide which route to adopt, leaving China with growing reliance on seaborne oil. In March 2006 Russia's President Putin suggested that a branch could be built to China from a Nakhodka-bound pipeline, but specialists questioned whether there would be sufficient oil to serve both pipelines.

China's oil situation caught the world off guard when in 2004 China's imports of oil grew unexpectedly by 31 percent, 800,000 barrels a day, influenced in part by electric power shortages that were partially offset by use of diesel generators. World oil prices rose sharply, by $9 a barrel. But they rose even more sharply during 2005, when China's oil imports declined slightly, aided by supply disruptions in Nigeria, Venezuela, and the Gulf of Mexico, along with low inventories and little worldwide excess production capacity. Prices continued to rise into 2006, reaching $70 a barrel in early summer, before receding toward $50 a barrel by the end of the year. China has become a sufficiently large importer, at over three million barrels a day, to influence world prices; but prices continue to be influenced by many other factors as well.

China has discovered the advantages of natural gas, and has been working hard to develop its indigenous natural gas resources, mainly in Xinjiang in western China and in the Ordos basin in Inner Mongolia, and to build the infrastructure—pipelines and distribution systems—to make use of the gas. Hitherto China's modest gas use was mainly for feed stocks to the chemical industry, especially fertilizer, but it is increasingly being used as a fuel, including for electricity generation, where most of the significant incremental demand over the next two decades is expected to go.

China's potential demand for gas is much greater than prospective domestic supply, so China has been seeking foreign sources. One is the large gas resources of central Siberia, and letters of intent were signed with Russia (along with South Korea, another potential customer) in late 2003, to build a pipeline capable of transporting 2.9 billion cubic feet of gas per day, of which China would take 1.9 Bcf. Unresolved conflicts within Russia have so far prevented this $12 billion project from getting started. A summit meeting between President Putin and President Hu in March 2006 reaffirmed their joint commitment to this pipeline, but the price Russia wants to charge for gas (linked to oil prices, as in Russia's gas sales in Europe) is probably unacceptably high for China (*Wall Street Journal*, 3/23/06: A6). Another potential source is liquefied natural gas (LNG) imported by specialized ship. China is building two LNG terminals in south China (near Guangdong and Zhangzhou), is contemplating at least six additional LNG terminals along the east coast, and has begun to construct LNG carriers in China's shipyards. Guangdong province has contracted to build six gas-fired power plants, and to convert 1.8 GW of oil-fired generating capacity to gas.

As noted in Table 1.3, China's gas consumption is projected to rise at 7.8 percent annually over the next two decades. Even so, however, China's share of world gas consumption in 2025 will have risen to less than 3 percent of world consumption, so pressure on world gas supplies will be considerably less than in the case of oil. (According to some experts, by 2025 LNG will have become 'commoditized,' selling on the stock market as oil does today. That prognostication remains to be seen; it will require extensive investments in the total supply train—condensation, shipping, and re-gasification, all capital-intensive processes—without full commitment to long-term supply and demand contracts.)

1.2 Other Raw Materials

Chinese demand for imports has grown rapidly, if erratically, for a number of non-fuel primary products as well. Table 1.4 shows China's import quantities and values for 1985–2004. It is noteworthy that China is a physically large and highly diverse economy and it produces many primary products. Imports reflect the difference between demand and domestic supply. There has been an extraordinary growth in imports of inputs into China's steel industry, whose output is now the largest in the world and continues to grow rapidly: iron ore, steel scrap, and nickel. Imports of non-ferrous metals have also grown significantly, but much less dramatically (especially for aluminum) from 1985, since imports of both copper and aluminum fell between 1985 and 1990. China's inventories and stockpiling policy are not known, so it is possible that China from time to time has done some anticipatory buying, followed by inventory liquidation, making single-year comparisons problematic.

Table 1.4 also reports significant but by comparison with metals less dramatic increases in import demand for agricultural raw materials, and again there are intervening years in which imports for selected products fell. Imports of foodstuffs, both wheat and maize, while large in 2004 were both lower than they were in 1990.

Did growing demand from China strain world supply of non-fuel raw materials? If so, it would show up *inter alia* in unabated price pressures. Prices did indeed rise significantly (by more than 20 percent) in 2002–4 for iron ore, nickel, copper, aluminum, cotton, and rubber, among the items shown in Table 1.4, as well as for petroleum and other fuels. A number of other primary products, such as vegetable oils and lead, also experienced significant price increases. But for many products these price increases represented a recovery from the depressed prices of the late 1990s, and indeed the 2004 prices of aluminum, copper, cotton, and rubber were still below their levels of 1995 (Table 1.5).

China's share of world imports of primary products in 2004, a boom year in China, remained under 10 percent for most categories, the exceptions being agricultural raw materials (14 percent) and mineral ores (23 percent).

Table 1.4a: China's imports of selected primary products

	Quantities (metric tons)				
	1985	1990	1995	2000	2004
Iron ore (million)	10	14.2	41.1	70	208.1
Steel scrap (million)	—	0.1	1.3	5.1	10.2
Nickel ('000)	0.03	0.16	0.57	12	65.7
Aluminum ('000)	483	61	388	615	611
Copper ('000)	346	37	188	3316	5353
Rubber ('000)	228	333	631	1560	2379
Cotton ('000)	0.4	559	740	52	1907
Wool ('000)	105	44	284	301	245
Timber (m^3)	10.7	3.8	2.6	13.6	26.3
Wheat (mil.)	5.63	12.33	11.59	0.88	7.23
Maize (mil.)	6.17	13.56	20.27	3.15	9.75
Soybeans (mil.)	—	—	0.29	10.42	20.23
Petroleum *(mil.)	0.72	—	34.01	93.13	167.01

* including products
Source: China Statistical Yearbook, various issues.

For non-ferrous metals, iron and steel, industrial chemicals, and textiles, the share was between 5 and 10 percent (calculated from WTO 2005*b*: 212, 231). Of course these shares will grow over time if China's growth continues to exceed the world average and China's industrial structure does not change significantly.

Nonetheless, rapid growth from a low base can leave modest shares of world trade even after a few decades. Thanks to Boeing, we have forward projections of world demand for air freight to 2023. Intra-Chinese carriage is expected to grow by 8.1 percent a year from 2003, highest in the world except for within the Persian Gulf region and much higher than the 5.2 percent growth

Table 1.4b: China's imports of selected primary products

	Value ($billion)				
	1985	1990	1995	2000	2004
Iron ore	0.18	0.43	1.23	1.86	12.71
Steel scrap	—	—	0.02	0.51	2.23
Nickel	—	—	—	0.07	0.9
Aluminum	0.56	0.11	0.51	0.94	1.94
Copper	0.5	0.1	0.41	2.52	6.3
Rubber	0.22	0.38	0.75	1.35	2.94
Cotton	—	0.93	1.38	0.08	3.18
Wool	0.4	0.24	0.94	1.04	1.2
Timber	0.85	0.42	0.37	1.66	2.8
Wheat	0.76	1.82	2.03	0.15	1.64
Maize	0.86	2	3.58	0.59	2.23
Soybeans	—	—	0.08	2.27	6.98

Table 1.5: Commodity prices, 1990–2004 (1990 = 100)

	1995	2000	2004
Iron ore	87.7	88.9	117
Steel scrap			
Nickel	92.8	97.3	155.9
Aluminum	110.1	94.7	104.4
Copper	110.2	68.2	107.6
Rubber	182.8	79.9	156
Cotton	119.1	71.6	75.2
Wool (Aust. 48)	114.3	87.9	172.9
Timber (Malaysian Sawn)	143.1	115.8	112.6
Wheat	130.6	84.1	115.7
Maize	113	80.8	102.4
Soybeans	139.7	113.9	172.3
Petroleum (WTI)	74.9	123.2	168.4

Source: IMF, International Financial Statistics.

in worldwide air freight. By 2023, China's share will be 5 percent of world air freight, up from 2.9 percent in 2003 (WTO 2005*a*: 263–4).

1.3 Conclusion

Chinese leaders are of course aware of their growing dependence on imported oil and other raw materials and of the vulnerabilities it creates, both to physical and to market disruption. China has aggressively pursued oil exploration around the world, with a strong emphasis where possible on equity oil. In addition, China's leaders have launched a charm offensive throughout the developing world—in Southeast Asia, Latin America, Africa, even India—focused on cultivating trading partners, especially those that have resources necessary for China's development, including especially oil but not limited to oil. China also plans to create a strategic stockpile of oil. It would like to develop the hydrocarbons of the South China Sea cooperatively, without necessarily resolving the territorial disputes.

At the end of the day, practical considerations of high dependence on imports of critical materials, especially but not only oil, combined with a navy of limited capacity and no naval tradition since the fifteenth century, are likely to shape Chinese behavior in the international arena in a peaceful and even strongly cooperative spirit. Concretely, China has the same interest as Japan and the United States in a stable Persian Gulf region, from which most of the world's incremental oil must come over the next twenty years.

An alternative scenario is possible but implausible. Like Germany before 1914 and in 1941 (with the invasion of the Soviet Union), and Japan in the 1930s, China's sense of vulnerability regarding critical materials might lead to an aggressive policy of gaining control over such materials. In China's case, that points mainly to East Siberia, lightly populated and defended by Russia; or to acquisition through sponsored political coups in Southeast Asia, leading to governments that are in effect satellites of Beijing—although in the absence of significant new discoveries the latter course would not by itself assure sufficient oil for China's needs. In the long run, China might attempt to build a blue water navy (and collateral air support) capable of challenging the US Navy, not only in the western Pacific but also in the Indian Ocean, as Japan did with brief but transitory success in the 1930s. But that would require several decades of construction and naval training.

China is more likely to consider these alternatives, the more hostile is the political environment in which it must operate. Those who see China as a 'threat' and act accordingly may well be making a self-fulfilling prophecy.

References

China Development Forum (2003), *China's National Energy Strategy and Reform: Background Papers* (Beijing: Development Research Center of the State Council).

Cooper, Richard N. (2005), 'Global Public Goods: A Role for China and India,' background paper for UNIDO, *Public Goods for Economic Development* (Vienna, 2006).

International Energy Agency (2000), *World Energy Outlook 2000* (Paris: OECD).

——— (2003), *World Energy Investment Outlook* (Paris: OECD).

Maddison, Angus (1998), *Chinese Economic Performance in the Long Run* (Paris: OECD Development Centre).

Simmons, Mathew R. (2005), *Twilight in the Desert: The Coming Saudi Oil Shock and the World Economy* (Hoboken, NJ: John Wiley & Sons).

US Department of Energy, Energy Information Administration (2005) *International Energy Outlook 2005* (Washington, DC).

Wolf, Charles Jr., Yeh, K. C., Zycher Benjamin, Eberstadt, Nicholas, and Lee, Sung-Ho, *Fault Lines in China's Terrain* (Santa Monica, CA: RAND, 2003).

World Trade Organization (2005*a*), *World Trade Report 2005* (Geneva).

——— (2005*b*), *International Trade Statistics 2005* (Geneva).

2

China and the Global Environment[1]

Warwick J. McKibbin
Australian National University, The Lowy Institute for International
Policy, Sydney and The Brookings Institution

2.1 Introduction

China's remarkable rate of economic growth in recent decades is having
important impacts on the world economy. With roughly 20 percent of the
world's population being mobilized into the world economy, a critical input
into a growing Chinese economy is energy. China has large reserves of energy
and rising capacity, but rising demand for inputs into production in China
is already causing increases in global commodity prices. In addition to the
economic consequences of this rapid transformation, there are important
environmental consequences of increased industrialization in China, not only
within China but on its near neighbors and globally. By 2004 China was
the world's second largest energy producer and the second largest energy
consumer.[2] This massive use of energy has had important implications for
local environment problems such as air quality, public health problems and
local climate change. Energy generation and its related emissions of sulfur
dioxide from coal use, have caused local and regional problems with acid
rain. The large and growing emissions of greenhouse gases (particularly carbon
dioxide emissions from burning coal) are a critical input into the global issue
of climate change.

[1] This paper draws on early research funded by the China Economic Research and Advisory
Programme (CERAP). Many ideas in this paper have been developed jointly with Peter
Wilcoxen of Syracuse University. The author thanks Yan Yang for excellent research assistance
and Dr Tingsong Jiang for insights from an earlier collaboration. The views expressed in the
paper are those of the author and should not be interpreted as reflecting the views of the
institutions with which the authors are affiliated including the trustees, officers or other staff
of the ANU, Lowy Institute, or The Brookings Institution.
[2] All data, unless specifically indicated otherwise, are sourced from the Energy Information
Administration of the US Department of Energy and are for 2004 (revised in the Jan. 2007
online update).

Table 2.1: Shares in global energy consumption and CO_2 emissions (%), 1990–2030

	1990	2002	2003	2010	2015	2020	2025	2030
Energy Consumption								
China	7.8	10.3	10.8	15.1	16.3	17.4	18.3	19.3
India	2.3	3.4	3.3	3.8	4.0	4.2	4.4	4.5
Other Non-OECD	33.1	29.9	30.2	30.8	31.8	32.5	33.1	33.4
South Korea	1.1	2.0	2.0	2.1	2.2	2.2	2.2	2.1
Japan	5.3	5.4	5.3	4.5	4.2	3.8	3.6	3.4
United States	24.4	23.9	23.3	21.2	20.3	19.7	19.1	18.6
Other OECD	26.1	25.2	25.0	22.5	21.3	20.2	19.4	18.7
World Total	100.0	100.0	100.0	100.0	100.0	100.0	100.0	100.0
CO_2 Emissions								
China	10.6	13.5	14.1	19.3	20.8	22.2	23.3	24.5
India	2.7	4.2	4.1	4.5	4.7	4.9	5.0	5.0
Other Non-OECD	33.1	29.1	29.2	29.3	29.9	30.2	30.3	30.4
South Korea	1.1	1.9	1.9	2.0	2.0	2.0	2.0	1.9
Japan	4.8	4.9	4.8	4.0	3.6	3.3	3.0	2.8
United States	23.5	23.6	23.2	21.0	20.0	19.4	18.9	18.6
Other OECD	24.3	22.8	22.7	20.0	19.0	18.1	17.4	16.8
World Total	100.0	100.0	100.0	100.0	100.0	100.0	100.0	100.0

Source: Energy Information Administration/International Energy Outlook 2006.

As shown in Table 2.1, in 1990 China accounted for 7.8 percent of world energy use (roughly 1.5 times that of Japan and seven times that of Korea). By 2003 this share had risen to 10.8 percent. By 2030, China is projected to account for 19.3 percent of global energy use or more than six times the energy use of Japan and nine times that of Korea. Already China is the world's largest coal producer accounting for 37.9 percent of world coal production and as Table 2.2 shows 28.6 percent of world coal consumption by 2004. China's share of world coal consumption is projected to rise to a massive 44.0 percent by 2030 (Table 2.2). China's share of world oil consumption in 1990 was 3.5 percent but is projected to rise to 12.7 percent by 2030 (Table 2.2).

Until recently the focus of policy in China has been on economic growth and energy needs rather than the environmental consequences of rapid industrialization. This is beginning to change as rising income levels in China make the environment a more important issue and as environmental quality continues to deteriorate.

This study examines the environmental consequences of rapid growth in China with a focus on the environmental consequences of rising energy use. It explores the recent past as well as potential future developments and potential policy options.[3] Although economic growth is a priority, environmental

---

[3] There are many other environmental problems caused by a large population and rapid economic growth in China, such as water quality and air quality problems caused by

Table 2.2: Shares in global consumption of fossil fuel energy components (%)

	1990	2002	2003	2010	2015	2020	2025	2030
Coal Consumption								
China	21.3	26.9	28.1	36.4	39.1	40.8	42.3	44.0
India	4.9	8.2	7.9	8.4	8.8	9.0	8.8	8.4
Other Non-OECD	25.4	18.4	18.4	16.6	16.5	16.2	15.7	15.1
South Korea	0.9	1.5	1.5	1.7	1.7	1.6	1.7	1.7
Japan	2.4	3.3	3.2	2.5	2.3	2.0	1.8	1.6
United States	17.2	20.3	20.1	17.7	16.4	16.1	16.7	16.9
Other OECD	28.0	21.4	20.7	16.5	15.2	14.2	13.1	12.4
World Total	100.0	100.0	100.0	100.0	100.0	100.0	100.0	100.0
Oil Consumption								
China	3.5	6.6	7.0	9.5	10.2	11.2	11.9	12.7
India	1.8	2.9	2.9	3.2	3.4	3.6	3.7	3.8
Other Non-OECD	32.7	29.6	29.6	30.9	31.7	32.0	32.5	32.8
South Korea	1.5	2.7	2.7	2.8	3.0	2.9	2.9	3.0
Japan	7.8	7.0	7.0	5.9	5.6	5.2	5.0	4.6
United States	25.5	25.2	25.1	24.2	23.9	23.8	23.6	23.4
Other OECD	27.2	25.9	25.7	23.5	22.4	21.2	20.4	19.7
World Total	100.0	100.0	100.0	100.0	100.0	100.0	100.0	100.0
Natural Gas Consumption								
China	0.7	1.2	1.3	2.6	2.9	3.4	3.7	3.8
India	0.5	1.0	1.0	1.3	1.3	1.5	1.9	2.5
Other Non-OECD	48.5	44.2	45.1	48.0	49.3	50.6	51.7	52.9
South Korea	0.1	0.9	0.9	0.9	0.9	0.9	0.8	0.7
Japan	2.6	3.1	3.2	2.7	2.6	2.4	2.2	2.1
United States	26.2	24.9	23.4	20.1	19.3	17.9	16.3	14.8
Other OECD	21.3	24.8	25.0	24.5	23.8	23.3	23.3	23.2
World Total	100.0	100.0	100.0	100.0	100.0	100.0	100.0	100.0

Source: Energy Information Administration/International Energy Outlook 2006.

policy is already emerging as an important policy issue in China. This chapter summarizes the state of key aspects of environmental policy as related to energy use both in term of local issues as well as in the context of the current global debate on climate change.

A number of existing policies that China has already put in place to tackle local and regional environmental problems are also discussed.[4] Other issues relate to rising energy use, rising greenhouse gas emissions and the implications for China of a serious climate-change policy. This chapter outlines one way to address rising carbon dioxide emissions that could be implemented in

deforestation and desertification. China's demand for resources has made a significant impact on the environment, of other countries. These important problems are not the subject of this chapter but for an overview see Liu and Diamond (2005).

[4] China's Environmental Protection Law was promulgated in 1979—a nationwide levy system on pollution began in 1982. Fees for SO_2 pollution from coal began to be collected in 1992. See Jiang (2003) for an overview.

China in coming years. This approach[5] focuses on creating long-term property rights and both short-term and long-term pricing of carbon emissions in an effort to reduce greenhouse gas emissions at low cost over time. It is in many ways similar to experiments already underway in China with trading sulfur emission permits although with a few key differences related to time frames and the scale of carbon in the economy. Dealing with carbon emissions in China is critical for an effective global response. However it is particularly important for China as a large country that has ratified the Kyoto Protocol[6] and would be expected to take on binding targets for carbon emissions at some future stage, or at least a commitment to some realistic goal. China has shown a commitment to tackle local environmental problems with encouraging outcomes.[7] For example, Jiang and McKibbin (2002) find that Chinese policy has been effective in reducing environmental problems in a number of areas, relative to what otherwise would be the case, but other factors driven by strong economic growth have offset this underlying improvement. Despite some signs of progress, there is still much to be done.

This chapter is structured as follows. Section 2.2 presents a brief overview of energy use in China. It also provides projections from the US Energy Information Agency of energy use in China out to 2030 as well as projections from the G-Cubed model for carbon emissions under different assumptions about the sources of economic growth in China. As well as considering the environmental problems in China, policy responses and some quantitative evaluation of these for greenhouse emissions in China are considered in Section 2.3. The conclusion is in Section 2.4. An Appendix summarizes the G-Cubed multi-country model that forms the basis of some of the analysis in this chapter.

2.2 Energy Use and the Environment

2.2.1 *Energy*

The importance of China in world energy use and projected increases in this importance are summarized in Table 2.1. In 2004 China accounted for 13.3 percent of world energy use (compared to North America[8] at 27.0 percent) and 17.4 percent of global carbon dioxide emissions from fossil-fuel use (compared to the United States at 21.9 percent). Chinese GDP

---

[5] Developed jointly with the author and Peter Wilcoxen. See McKibbin and Wilcoxen (2002*a*, 2002*b*).

[6] Further details on the Kyoto Protocol can be found in Section 2.4.

[7] See Jiang (2003) and Panayatou (1998) for an overview of China's environmental problems.

[8] North America is the United States, Canada, and Mexico.

(in 2004) is estimated in PPP terms to be roughly 66 percent of the size of the United States.[9] This implies that although carbon emissions per unit of energy use are higher in China than in the United States, energy use per unit of GDP (in PPP terms) is slightly lower in China than in the United States. Many studies of energy intensity (i.e. energy use per unit of GDP) suggest that China is far more energy-intensive but these tend to use market exchange rates for this comparison rather than PPP. GDP measured at market exchange rates is inappropriate as a benchmark of energy intensity given the problems with comparing GDP across countries at different stages of development.[10] A better measure is what is physically produced and the quantity of energy required.

China has roughly 12.5 percent of the world's installed electricity generation capacity (second only to the United States) and over the next three decades is predicted to be responsible for up to 28.4 percent of the increase in global energy generation. China's size and composition of energy use are reflected in carbon dioxide emissions. China is estimated to have emitted 14.1 percent of global carbon emission from fossil fuels in 2003 (second only to the United States) and this share is projected to rise to 24.5 percent by 2030 (Table 2.1). In an attempt to move away from fossil fuel reliance, China currently has plans for another thirty nuclear power plants in the next two decades to supplement the nine nuclear reactors already existing.[11] It is estimated that China has the largest hydroelectric capacity in the world (largely in the south-west of the country) which is currently generating 19 percent of Chinese electricity. The Three Gorges hydroelectric dam on the Yangtze River will be the world's largest power plant when completed around 2009. In March 2005, the National Development and Reform Commission (NDRC) approved the largest wind farm in Asia to begin construction in 2006. Table 2.3 shows a quickly rising share of both nuclear energy and renewable energy (particularly hydro) in coming years. Although impressive in scale, the emergence of renewable energy will only slightly dent the overall dominance of coal in the foreseeable future in China under current relative prices of energy. This means that China will need to respond to a range of environmental problems resulting from burning fossil fuels, such as air quality (including black carbon emissions), acid rain (from sulfur dioxide and nitrogen oxide emissions), and climate change (from carbon dioxide emissions).

Figure 2.1 gives another perspective on the recent history of energy production and consumption in China. Energy demand and supply in China has been rising quickly—more than doubling between 1980 and 1997. In 1998, Chinese energy consumption began to outstrip Chinese energy production with China becoming a net energy importer.

[9] Source: 2005 UNDP Human Development Data.

[10] A large literature on using PPP for energy inter-country comparisons is summarized in Castles and Henderson (2003).

[11] Source: DOE (2004).

Table 2.3: Shares in global consumption of non-fossil fuel energy components (%)

	1990	2002	2003	2010	2015	2020	2025	2030
Nuclear Energy Consumption								
China	0.0	1.0	1.7	2.9	4.4	5.5	7.1	9.2
India	0.3	0.7	0.6	2.0	2.6	3.2	3.3	3.4
Other Non-OECD	14.0	12.8	13.1	13.5	15.0	17.0	18.3	17.5
South Korea	2.6	4.4	4.9	5.2	6.0	6.4	6.7	7.2
Japan	10.1	11.0	9.4	10.0	9.8	10.2	10.8	11.2
United States	30.2	30.6	30.3	29.5	28.2	27.9	26.9	26.4
Other OECD	42.7	39.5	40.1	36.8	34.0	29.8	26.8	25.0
World Total	100.0	100.0	100.0	100.0	100.0	100.0	100.0	100.0
Hydroelectricity and other Renewable Energy Consumption								
China	4.9	8.7	8.9	13.5	13.8	13.4	12.6	12.2
India	2.7	2.2	2.1	2.9	2.6	2.8	3.1	3.5
Other Non-OECD	31.6	34.5	35.5	35.8	38.1	39.5	41.5	43.1
South Korea	0.0	0.0	0.3	0.4	0.6	0.6	0.5	0.5
Japan	4.2	3.4	4.3	3.1	3.1	2.8	2.6	2.6
United States	23.2	18.3	17.4	15.9	15.3	15.3	15.1	14.6
Other OECD	33.1	32.9	31.2	28.5	26.5	25.6	24.6	23.6
World Total	100.0	100.0	100.0	100.0	100.0	100.0	100.0	100.0

Source: Energy Information Administration/International Energy Outlook 2006.

Figure 2.2 shows that an abundance of low-cost coal has been the predominant source of Chinese energy supply (mainly located in the northern part of the country). Crude oil is the next largest source of energy supply followed by hydroelectricity, natural gas, and nuclear energy. The major source of demand for energy in China is industry which accounts for 70 percent of the total in 2003. This is followed by the residential sector at 11.3 percent and transportation at only 7.5 percent.

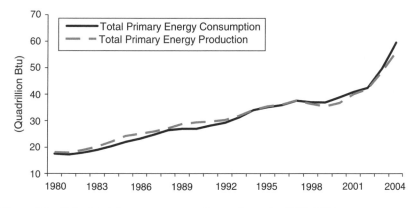

Figure 2.1: China's total energy consumption and supply, 1980–2004
Source: Energy Information Administration, 2006.

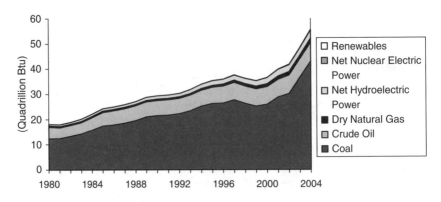

Figure 2.2: Energy production by fuel type, China, 1980–2004
Source: Energy Information Administration, 2006.

Projecting future energy use in China is difficult. It is tempting to base future projections on recent trends. However as shown by Bagnoli, McKibbin, and Wilcoxen (1996) and McKibbin *et al.* (2004), overall economic growth is not the key determinant of energy use—the sources of economic growth are critical. A number of projections are available. The Energy Information Administration in its Annual International Energy Outlook provides one source of projections. These are shown in Figure 2.3 for scenarios of high and low economic growth and a reference case. Figure 2.4 shows the composition of energy use for the mid scenario.

Next we generate emissions projections from the G-Cubed multi-country model[12] under two sets of assumptions (or scenarios) about the nature of economic growth. A summary of the approach is provided here but further details on the technique used in the G-Cubed model can be found in McKibbin *et al.* (2004). In the following discussion the actual source of growth is labor-augmenting technical change and population growth. The population growth assumptions are the same across both scenarios and are based on the 2004 UN population projections (mid scenario). In order to simplify the discussion, labor-augmenting technical change is referred to as 'productivity growth' throughout this chapter.

In the G-Cubed model, productivity growth by sector and by country is assumed to be driven by productivity catch-up. The United States is assumed to be the technological leader in each sector. Other countries are allocated an initial productivity gap by sector and a rate at which this gap is closed. For industrial countries and China this is assumed to be closed at the rate of 2 percent per year. For other developing countries it is assumed to close at 1 percent per year reflecting the empirical literature. In this chapter

---

[12] See McKibbin and Wilcoxen (1998) and documentation at <http://www.gcubed.com>.

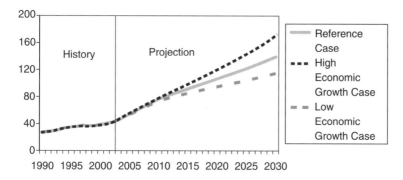

Figure 2.3: Projections of energy consumption, China, 1990–2030 (Quadrillion (10^{15}) Btu)

Source: Energy Information Administration, International Energy Outlook 2006.

Chinese productivity is assumed to be 20 percent of productivity in the equivalent sector in the United States. In the first scenario, the United States is assumed to have the same productivity growth across all sectors. This is the typical assumption in models where aggregate GDP drives energy use and therefore emissions. This scenario is labeled 'uniform productivity growth'. The implications for growth are shown in Figure 2.5*a*. Productivity growth in all Chinese sectors is the same given the same initial gaps to the US and the same catch-up rate across sectors.

In the second scenario it is assumed that the differential productivity growth across sectors in the United States is similar to that experienced over the past thirty years. The growth rates are adjusted so that the aggregate

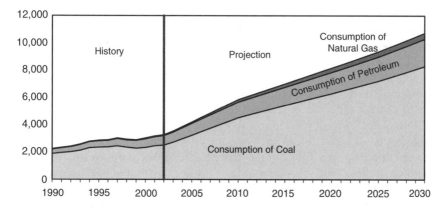

Figure 2.4: Projections of CO_2 emissions by fuel type, China, 1990–2030 (Million Metric Tons Carbon Dioxide)

Source: Energy Information Administration, International Energy Outlook 2006.

25

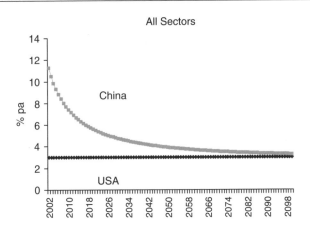

Figure 2.5a: Labor-augmenting technical change for uniform productivity scenario

GDP growth rate for the US is similar to GDP growth generated in the first scenario so that the main difference between the scenarios is the composition of growth. It is not possible to target GDP growth exactly.

Figure 2.5b shows the productivity growth assumptions for each sector in the United States and the implications for the equivalent sector in China under the assumptions of the same initial gaps and rates of convergence. Although the initial productivity gaps are the same, note that different sectors in China experience different rates of productivity growth. This is important because capital accumulation is endogenous in the G-Cubed model, responding to changes in actual and expected rates of return to capital.

The results from the G-Cubed model for Chinese carbon dioxide emissions and GDP growth under two scenarios are shown in Figures 2.6a and 2.6b. By 2020 emissions under the 'uniform productivity' scenario are 20 percent higher than under the 'differential productivity' growth scenario even though GDP growth is slightly higher under the 'differential productivity growth' scenario. This suggests that future projections of carbon emissions and energy use in China need to be interpreted carefully.

Despite this warning on the importance of structural change in energy projections—it is difficult to see a major shift in trends away from coal under current energy prices. Interestingly there is also little change in the real price of oil or any fossil fuels throughout the projection period in the International Energy Outlook results presented earlier, yet there are significant changes in the projections from the G-Cubed model, depending on assumptions about the sources of growth.

Under most scenarios, the emergence of China as a key supplier of energy and producer of energy is one of the most important issues in the debate over

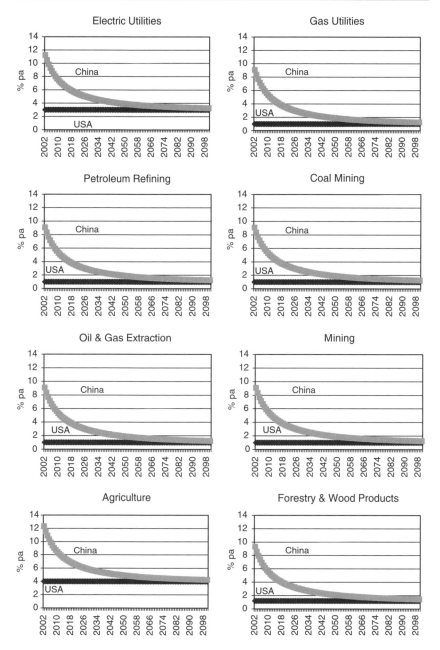

Figure 2.5*b*: Labor-augmenting technical change by sector in differential productivity scenario

Source: G-cubed Model version 63E.

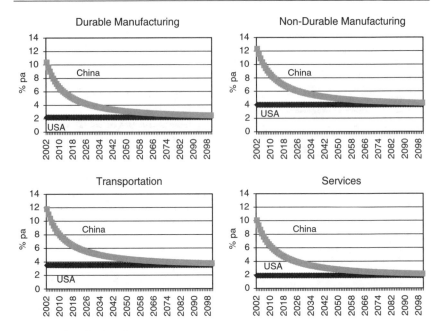

Figure 2.5b: (*Continued*)

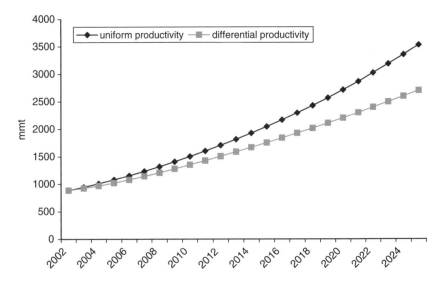

Figure 2.6a: Projection of Chinese carbon dioxide emissions

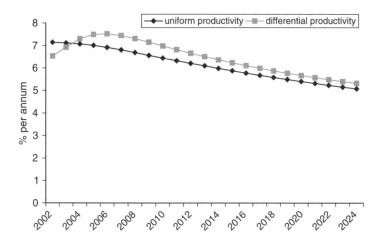

Figure 2.6b: Projection of Chinese real GDP growth
Source: G-cubed Model version 63E.

global energy use for the foreseeable future. As shown below, this is also a critical issue for environmental issues in China, Asia, and globally.

2.2.2 Environment

The impact of energy use on the environment (and public health) involves a range of problems from local particulate emissions to acid rain and carbon dioxide emissions. These have corresponding consequences for local, regional, and global environmental outcomes.

At the local level, a number of studies have explored air pollution caused by energy use in China. The term 'air pollution' covers a wide range of problems including emissions of particulates, sulfur dioxide, nitrous oxides, and carbon dioxide. The estimated costs of air pollution, largely due to the burning of fossil fuels, vary in size. A study by the World Bank (1997) valued health damages from air pollution at 5 percent of GDP in 1995[13] although other studies such as Yang and Schreifels (2003) suggest this is closer to 2 percent of GDP. Garbaccio, Ho, and Jorgenson (1999) found that local health costs could be reduced by 0.2 percent of GDP annually for a reduction in carbon emissions of 5 percent every year. A recent report by the State Environmental Protection Agency (SEPA)[14] on the environment notes that air quality in cities across China has generally improved but this is from a base of significant problems in most major Chinese cities. This can be seen in Table 2.4 which

---

[13] Panayotou and Zheng (2000) estimate that the cost to China from air and water pollution is 14.6% of GDP in the late 1990s. See also Wang and Smith (1999).

[14] See SEPA (2005).

Table 2.4: Urban air quality

Year	1998	1999	2000	2001	2002	2003	2004	2005
Numbers of monitored cities	322	338	332	341	343	340	342	522
Air quality reaching or better than National Air Quality Standard for Grade II (%)	27.6	33.1	34.9	33.4	34.1	41.7	39.3	51.9
Air quality reaching Grade III standard (%)	28.9	26.3	30.1	33.4	34.7	31.5	40.2	37.5
Air quality worse than Grade	43.5	40.6	34.9	33.1	31.2	26.8	20.5	10.6
Cities with TSP exceeding the standard (TSP$\leq$0.20 mg/m3)	63.8	60.0	61.6	64.1	63.2	54.4	52.5	40.5
Cities with SO_2 exceeding the standard ($SO_2 \leq$0.06 mg/m3)	36.2	28.4	21.7	19.4	22.4	25.6	25.7	22.6
Cities with NOx exceeding the standard (%)	0.0	0.0	0.0	0.0	0.0	0.0	0.0	0.0

Source: SEPA, Report on the State of the Environment in China 1998–2005.

contains results for Urban Air Quality for a number of Chinese-monitored cities from 1998 to 2005. Also see Table 2.7 for a snapshot of major cities and the main problems in air quality in 2004. The picture is mixed with an improvement in air quality for the worst-affected cities but deterioration for others. A large part of these air quality problems are directly related to energy use.

Whether the projections of rising energy use over the coming decade directly lead to projections of increased environmental problems is a critical issue facing policymakers in China. This is well understood in China. Premier Wen Jiabao in his March 5, 2005 report to the National People's Congress argued that improved energy conservation was necessary to reconcile rapid economic growth with limited energy resources—he also called for stronger pollution controls. The State Environmental Protection Administration (SEPA),[15] originally established in 1988 as the National Environmental Protection Agency, has also been implementing more stringent monitoring and enforcement of environmental legislation.

Particulate emissions cause serious health problems with identifiable economic costs as well as human costs. A recent study by Ho and Jorgenson (2003) finds the largest sources of Total Suspended Particulates (TSP) are the largest users of coal—electricity, nonmetal mineral products, and metals smelting, as well as transportation.

---

[15] The formerly named National Environmental Protection Agency was set up in 1988 and renamed SEPA in 1998 when it was upgraded to a Ministry.

Table 2.5: Emissions of main air pollutants from waste gases in recent years (in 10,000 tons)

	1998	1999	2000	2001	2002	2003	2004	2005
SO_2 Emission	2091.4	1857.5	1995.1	1947.8	1926.6	2158.7	2254.8	2549.3
Industrial	1594.4	1460.1	1612.5	1566.6	1562	1791.4	1891.4	2168.4
Household	497	397.4	382.6	381.2	364.6	367.3	363.5	380.9
Soot Emission	1455.1	1159	1165.4	1069.8	1012.7	1048.7	1095	1182.5
Industrial	1178.5	953.4	953.3	851.9	804.2	846.2	886.5	948.9
Household	276.6	205.6	212.1	217.9	208.5	202.5	208.5	233.6
Emission	1321.2	1175.3	1092	990.6	941	1021	904.8	911.2

Source: SEPA, Report on the State of the Environment in China 1998–2005.

One of the worst pollutants from burning fossil fuels is sulfur dioxide (SO_2) emissions. Table 2.5 shows SO_2 emissions and soot from 1998 to 2005. Surprisingly, SO_2 emissions remained reasonably steady from 1999 until 2002 but in recent years have been rising again. SO_2 emissions have local (health and acid rain) as well as regional (acid rain) implications. SO_2 mixing with nitrogen oxides (NOX) causes acid rain. The WHO (2004)[16] estimates that acid rain seriously affects 30 percent of China. Tables 2.6*a* and 2.6b give a mixed picture on acid rain in China although it appears that acid rain occurrences and intensity have stabilized over the past five years.

However, acid rain is not just a problem for China. Streets (1997) estimates that China accounted for 81 percent of SO_2 emissions in North-East Asia in 1990. China is the major source of acid rain across Northeast Asia. Without any control policies, Streets estimated in 1997 that this share would change little by 2010 except that the quantity of emissions is expected to grow by 213 percent from 1990 to 2010 by 273 percent by 2020. Assuming installation of state-of-the-art flue-gas desulfurization systems, Streets estimated that this scenario could be transformed so that SO_2 emissions fall to 31 percent of 1990 emissions by 2020. China has begun to address this problem with pilot sulfur dioxide emission trading systems in a number of control zones and closing of high sulfur coal mines as well as other direct controls. In fact sulfur dioxide emissions have fallen gradually from 1995 to 2002 but rose again in 2003 (see Table 2.5). The decline was a result of direct controls and other policies, although acid rain problems have not fallen because of a substitution of emission towards high stack sources which spread SO_2 over greater areas.[17] Direct policy to deal with sulfur dioxide emissions would seem to have a significant benefit for China and across the region and the Chinese authorities

---

[16] WHO (2004: 6) and SEPA (2004).   [17] See Yang and Schreifels (2003: 7–8).

Table 2.6a: Acid rain situation in the monitored cities

	2000	2001	2002	2003	2004	2005
Frequencies of Acid Rain Occurrence (Percentage of Cities)						
0%	38.2	41.2	49.7	45.6	43.5	51.3
> 0%	61.8	58.8	50.3	54.4	56.5	48.7
Annual Average PH Value of Precipitation (Percentage of Cities)						
PH$\leq$5.6	36.2	36.9	32.6	37.3	41.4	38.4
PH$>$5.6	53.8	63.1	67.4	62.7	58.6	61.6
Numbers of monitored cities	254	274	555	487	527	696

Source: SEPA, Report on the State of the Environment in China 2000–5.

Table 2.6b: Acid rain situation in acid rain control zones

	1998	2000	2001	2002	2003	2004	2005
Percentage of Cities with Different Frequencies of Acid Rain Occurrence							
0%	0	6.86	8.41	8.65	10.4	9.8	7.2
0–20%	17.9	19.6	21.5	20.19	20.8	17	21.6
20–40%	16.1	21.57	18.69	23.08	15.1	13.4	7.3
40–60%	33	26.47	16.82	15.38	16	19.6	20.7
60–80%	21.4	13.72	20.56	17.31	24.5	21.4	20.7
80–100%	11.6	11.76	14.02	15.38	13.2	18.8	22.5
Annual average PH Value of Pecipitation (Percentage of Cities)							
PH$\leq$4.5	9.8	3.9	7.5	15.38	15.1	21.5	24.3
4.5$<$PH$\leq$5	45.5	31.4	38.3	28.85	33	33	34.2
5$<$PH$\leq$5.6	27.7	35.3	27.1	25.96	22.6	19.6	14.5
5.6$<$PH$\leq$7	16.1	29.4	23.4	27.88	28.3	25.9	27
PH $>$7	0.9		3.7	1.92	0.9		
Numbers of monitored cities	112	102	107	104	106	112	111

Source: SEPA, Report on the State of the Environment in China 1998–2005.

are acting on this.[18] The encouraging results from experimentation with price-based charging and emissions trading systems suggest that these approaches should be used more extensively to reduce the emission of sulfur. This is particularly important given the projected rising use of coal for generating energy in the coming decade.

A more recent and potentially more important problem identified by Streets (1997, 2004) and others is the emission of black carbon. Black carbon is made up of fine particulates that are released from imperfect combustion of carbonaceous materials. Current research suggests that direct action to reduce the emissions of black carbon from household energy use and burning of forests and agricultural waste is an important issue that needs urgent attention in China. Understanding of black carbon emissions is only fairly recent due to

---

[18] Nakada and Ueta (2004) estimate that the current sulfur price is well below the socially optimal price.

Table 2.7: Ambient air quality in main cities (2004) (milligram/cu.m)

City	Paticulate Matters (PM_{10})	Sulphur Dioxide (SO_2)	Nitrogen Dioxide (NO_2)	Days of Air Quality Equal to or Above Grade II (days)
Bejing	0.149	0.055	0.071	229
Tianjin	0.111	0.073	0.052	299
Shijiazhuang	0.123	0.087	0.042	279
Taiyuan	0.175	0.087	0.022	224
Hohhot	0.080	0.045	0.038	311
Shenyang	0.137	0.052	0.035	301
Changchun	0.085	0.013	0.032	345
Haerbin	0.113	0.042	0.060	298
Shanghai	0.099	0.055	0.062	311
Nanjing	0.121	0.045	0.055	295
Hangzhou	0.110	0.049	0.055	292
Hefei	0.110	0.013	0.017	313
Fuzhou	0.074	0.010	0.041	358
Nanchang	0.099	0.057	0.029	330
Jinan	0.149	0.045	0.038	210
Zhengzhou	0.111	0.057	0.037	298
Wuhan	0.130	0.048	0.054	247
Changsha	0.140	0.084	0.033	219
Guangzhou	0.099	0.077	0.073	304
Nanning	0.078	0.061	0.034	348
Haokou	0.033	0.007	0.013	366
Chongqing	0.142	0.113	0.067	243
Chengdu	0.115	0.067	0.048	309
Guiyang	0.083	0.094	0.024	337
Kunming	0.085	0.069	0.040	351
Lasa	0.052	0.003	0.020	358
Xi'an	0.142	0.049	0.033	260
Lanzhou	0.172	0.071	0.045	204
Xining	0.127	0.024	0.027	280
Yinchuan	0.122	0.054	0.040	323
Urumuqi	0.114	0.102	0.058	258

Source: National Bureau of Statistics of China, China Statistical Yearbook 2005.

the work of Hamilton and Mansfield (1991), Hansen *et al.* (1998) and Streets (2004). Black carbon is classified as an aerosol and is therefore not included in the Kyoto Protocol. However, studies by Streets and others suggest it is a critical issue for China, particularly because the impacts of black carbon are wide–ranging, including reduced visibility, serious health problems, reduced agricultural productivity,[19] and damage to buildings. Streets (2004: 3) argues that black carbon is the second most important warming agent behind carbon dioxide. Using circulation models, Menon *et al.* (2002) estimate that black carbon is responsible for local climate problems in China such as summer floods in southern China and increased drought in northern China. The time

[19] Studies contained in Streets (2004) estimate that agriculture crop productivity might be reduced significantly (by up to 30% for rise and wheat) due to the impact of black carbon on photosynthesis by plants.

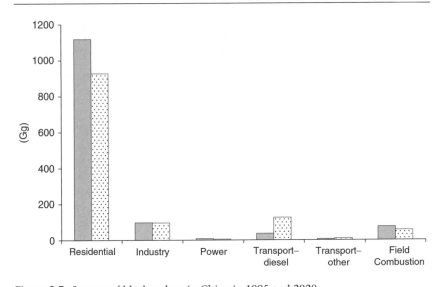

Figure 2.7: Sources of black carbon in China in 1995 and 2020

Source: D. Streets (2004), 'Black Smoke in China and Its Climate Effects.' Paper presented to the Asian Economic Panel, Columbia University, October.

lag between reducing black carbon emissions and significant local climate effects is estimated to be around five years—a much faster effect on climate than the many decades involved in affecting global climate from changing carbon dioxide emissions.

Figure 2.7 contains the main estimated sources of black carbon. Surprisingly a vast majority of emissions are from residential energy use rather than electricity generation or transportation. Residential burning of coal accounted for 83 percent of emissions in 1995. This is due to the fact that 80 percent of Chinese households use solid/biomass fuels for cooking and heating (WHO 2004). Black carbon is likely to be an important issue that authorities are yet to tackle, partly because it is a relatively recently understood problem and partly because the solution doesn't lie in the energy generation sectors but in the use of energy by households.

The significant environmental problems associated with energy use in China appear to have had large economic costs. With the expected large rise in energy use in China over coming decades outlined in Section 2.2, the environmental problems associated with rising Chinese energy use are likely to be accentuated. Policy responses to these problems will need to broaden in scale and scope. While existing problems are beginning to be tackled, new problems such as global climate change are emerging and China due to its size and speed of economic growth is a major player at the global level.

2.3 Responding to Energy-related Environmental Challenges

As outlined above, China has begun to respond to the local environmental problems. In terms of the problems emanating from energy use, there has been an attempt to substitute non-fossil-fuel energy sources such as wind, hydro, and thermonuclear energy for fossil fuels in energy generation. China has also attempted to reduce the emissions of sulfur dioxide from burning fossil fuels by implementing a range of policies. A greater focus in required to address the emissions of black carbon. From a global perspective the one area where China will need to take greater action is in the emissions of carbon dioxide. This is the focus of this section.

The most important cause of human-induced climate change is the accumulation of greenhouse gases in the atmosphere over many decades. The most important greenhouse gas is carbon dioxide. The global community has been struggling with how to effectively respond to the threat of climate change for several decades. The United Nations Earth Summit in Rio de Janeiro in 1992 produced a landmark treaty on climate change that undertook to stabilize greenhouse gas concentrations in the atmosphere. The agreement, signed and ratified by more than 186 countries, including the United States and China (the world's largest CO_2 emitters), spawned numerous subsequent rounds of climate negotiations aimed at rolling back emissions from industrialized countries to the levels that prevailed in 1990. Unfortunately the negotiations have had little effect on greenhouse gas emissions and have not produced a detectable slowing in the rate of emissions growth.[20] The treaty's implementing protocol, the 1997 Kyoto Agreement, was heavily diluted at subsequent negotiations in Bonn and Marrakech.[21] The Kyoto Protocol entered into force on February 16, 2005 after ratification by Russia yet there are still many problems to be faced before it will be evident that Kyoto is actually reducing emissions. More than a decade of negotiations has produced a policy that is likely to be ineffective in practice.

The difficulty at the international level is actually worse than it appears from the troubled process of Kyoto ratification. The Kyoto Protocol only places restrictions on the industrial economies, excluding the world's largest greenhouse emitter, the United States. Developing countries, including China, have ratified the agreement but have not taken on any responsibilities for reducing emissions except those that emerge from mechanisms such as the Clean Development Mechanism (CDM) and joint implementation (JI). That

---

[20] See McKibbin and Wilcoxen (2002a) for a summary of the negotiations and critique of the approach.

[21] Earlier estimates of the cost of Kyoto can be found in Weyant (1999). Direct comparisons of the COP3 and COP7 versions of the Protocol can be found in Bohringer (2001), Buchner Carraro, and Cersosimo (2001), Kemfert (2001), Löschel and Zhang (2002), and McKibbin and Wilcoxen (2004).

developing countries are not taking on targets as commitments is one of the reasons claimed by both the United States and Australia for not ratifying the Kyoto Protocol. Because there are no binding commitments by the key developing countries of China, India, Brazil, and Indonesia (amongst others), effective action against possible climate change is still largely a hypothetical debate.

Developing countries have legitimately argued that while they are prepared to be part of a regime to tackle climate change, they should not be required to bear a disproportionate part of the costs of taking action. Current concentrations of greenhouse gases in the atmosphere are primarily the result of economic activities in the industrial economies since the Industrial Revolution. Because it is the stock of carbon in the atmosphere that matters for temperature changes, any climate change in the near future will be largely the result of the historical activities of industrial economies. One of the main dilemmas for developing countries is not just the reality that at some stage they need to make some form of commitment to curbing greenhouse gas emissions but the fact that most estimates of the damages from climate change are borne by developing countries.[22]

It is worth clarifying several important facts about the costs and benefits of climate policy and exploring whether there are approaches possible in China and other developing countries that are available but are delayed by countries clinging to the Kyoto Protocol. Given the uncertainties of climate change and the decisions on energy systems being made in the regions of the developing world that are growing rapidly, this delay in providing clear incentives for moving away from fossil-fuel-based systems may prove to be extremely costly.

Fossil-fuel combustion is one of the largest sources of anthropogenic greenhouse gas emissions. Given the cost of changing existing energy systems substantially in the short run, one of the cheapest means of making the global energy system less reliant on fossil fuels is to remove these carbon emissions from future energy systems. As was shown in Section 2.2, China is heavily reliant on coal for energy production and is likely to be for many decades to come. Technology will ultimately be the source of reductions in emissions whether through the development of alternative sources of energy or through ways of sequestering carbon released from burning fossil fuels. Developing countries have huge potential to avoid the pitfalls in terms of carbon intensities, experienced by industrialized economies in their development process. The key issue is how to encourage the emergence of energy systems in developing countries that are less carbon-intensive over time. Ultimately if climate change does emerge as a serious problem, developing countries will have to move towards a less carbon-intensive future. It is likely to be

[22] See IPCC (2001).

significantly cheaper to do this over time than to face a massive restructuring at some future period—the sort of problems being faced within industrialized economies today.

The current state of global policy on climate is that the United States (the largest emitter of greenhouse gases) has rejected Kyoto and is arguing in favor of policies that directly or indirectly reduce emissions through technological change; the European Union is committed to emission targets (assuming Russia provides a great deal of those reductions required through selling emission permits) and implemented a Europe-wide emissions trading scheme (that exempts key sectors such as aluminium, motor vehicles, and chemicals) on January 1, 2005, but with actual caps that appear only to bind by the end of 2008; Japan is considering what it can do given that current emissions are 16 percent above target in an economy recovering from a decade of recession; and developing countries have refused to officially discuss taking on commitments.

Against this background, there are a number of ways a country like China could begin to address carbon emissions and make a major contribution to a global response. One policy would be to move energy prices closer to world levels by the removal of energy subsidies. The second would be to further raise the price of energy to further reflect the true economic and environmental cost of burning fossil fuels. A further approach could be direct importation of less carbon-intensive technologies provided by the CDM. This latter outcome is possible but not likely as already outlined above. Thus the focus in this study will be on the other alternatives.

Economic theory provides guidance about the structure of a possible climate change policy for China.[23] Since greenhouse gases are emitted by a vast number of highly heterogeneous sources, minimizing the cost of abating a given amount of emissions requires that all sources clean up amounts that cause their marginal cost of abatement to be equated. To achieve this, the standard economic policy prescription would be a market-based instrument, such as a tax on emissions or a tradable permit system for emission rights. This type of market-based incentive for environmental pollution is already being undertaken in China through pollution charges and permit trading in sulfur dioxide. Richard Cooper (2005) has advocated a carbon tax for China. Garbaccio, Ho, and Jorgenson (1999) and McKibbin and Wilcoxen (2004) find that a price signal would be effective in changing China's future emissions profiles. Figures 2.8a and 2.8b show results from the G-Cubed model for a tax of $US10 per ton of carbon for both the United States and China from 2005 to 2055. The short-run response of emissions in China is much larger than in the United States because the tax is a much larger proportional rise

---

[23] See McKibbin and Wilcoxen (2002a) for a survey and Pezzey (2003) for a comparison of taxes and permits.

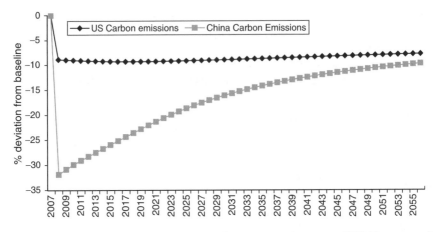

Figure 2.8a: Response of emissions to a carbon tax in each country ($US 10 per ton of carbon)

Source: G-cubed Model version 63E.

in the price of carbon-intensive energy in China (because initial prices are much lower than in the United States). The response in the short run reflects substitution and conservation by households as well as larger contraction in economic activity relative to base. Over time, substitution in production and use of energy allows a larger carbon reduction with less impact on GDP. GDP initially falls in both countries and in the longer run is higher in China due to efficiency gains from better use of energy. These results suggest the importance of prices in changing energy use in China.

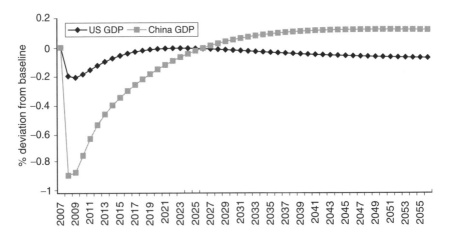

Figure 2.8b: Response of GDP to a carbon tax in each country ($US 10 per ton of carbon)

In the absence of uncertainty, the efficient level of abatement could be achieved under either a tax or a permit trading system, although the distributional effects of tax and emissions trading policies would be very different. Under uncertainty, however, the situation becomes more complicated. Weitzman (1974) showed that taxes and permits are *not* equivalent when marginal benefits and costs are uncertain, and that the relative slopes of the two curves determine which policy will be better.[24] Emission permits are better than taxes when marginal benefit schedules are steep and marginal costs are flat: in that situation, it is important to get the quantity of emissions down to the threshold. A permit policy does exactly that. In the opposite situation, when marginal costs are rising sharply and marginal benefits are flat, a tax would be a better policy. The potential inefficiency of a permit system under uncertainty is not just a theoretical curiosity: it is intuitively understood by many participants in the climate change debate by the expression of the concern about a policy that 'caps emissions regardless of cost'.

Applying this analysis to climate change McKibbin and Wilcoxen (2002a) show that a tax is likely to be far more efficient than a permit system under the uncertainties surrounding climate change. All evidence to date suggests that the marginal cost curve for reducing greenhouse gas emissions is very steep, at least for developed countries. Although there is considerable disagreement between models on how expensive it would be to achieve a given reduction in emissions, all models show that costs rise rapidly as emissions targets become tighter. At the same time, the nature of climate change indicates that the marginal benefit curve for reducing emissions will be very flat.

Given the advantages and disadvantages of the standard economic instruments, McKibbin and Wilcoxen (2002a, 2002b) show that it is possible to combine the attractive features of both systems into a single approach. They also show that it is possible to develop a system which is common in philosophy across developed and developing economies but in which developing economies do not incur the short-run costs to the economy in the form of higher energy prices until they have reached a capacity to pay. This approach is summarized below.

There are a number of goals that should be at the core of any climate change regime. These involve recognizing the trade-off between economic efficiency and equity within and between countries. The policy should also be based around clear property rights over emissions and clear long-run emission targets but near certainty in the short-run costs to the economy. A sensible climate policy should also create domestic institutions that allow people to self-insure against the uncertainties created by climate change. There should be market mechanisms that give clear signals about the current and expected future costs of carbon. There should be coalitions created within countries

---

[24] See also Pizer (1997) for a more recent discussion of the issue.

with the self-interest of keeping climate change policy from collapsing rather than creating a system of international sanctions in order to sustain the system.

The McKibbin Wilcoxen Blueprint (see McKibbin and Wilcoxen 2002*a*, 2002*b*) was created as an attempt to explicitly deal with these issues. It is a hybrid system that blends the best features of taxes and emission permit trading.[25] It is a system that can be applied across developed and developing countries but which recognizes that developing countries should not bear the same economic costs as industrial countries in the short run.

The basic idea is to impose a requirement that energy producers have an annual emission permit to produce energy each year, based on the carbon content of that energy. A fixed quantity of long-term permits would be created that allow a unit of emission every year for 100 years. These long-term permits are traded in a market with a flexible price. The government would also be able to create additional annual permits in any year at a guaranteed price. Permits which satisfy the annual constraint for energy production can be either a long-term permit or an annual permit that is provided by the government at a fixed price. The price of emissions in any year would never be higher than the fixed price set by the government and the amount of emissions in any year would be whatever the market delivers. Thus we have a long-term target in terms of emissions but an annual target in terms of the maximum cost of carbon to industry. In a developing country like China, the annual price would initially be zero if we allow an allocation of long-term permits well in excess of current emissions. However, the price of long-term permits would reflect the expectation that China would eventually reach the emission levels that caused the carbon emission constraint to be binding. Thus the market for long-term permits with positive prices would provide a financial incentive to begin to change Chinese carbon emissions over time even though the annual cost to industry of a carbon permit would initially be zero.

McKibbin and Wilcoxen (2002*a*) argue that the allocation of long-term permits would be determined by each country. The long-term permits could be auctioned, in which case the permits are actually a tax. The long-term permits could be given away to existing carbon emitters in which case the permits are a way of grandfathering or compensating existing emitters. The allocation mechanism of long-term permits is a wealth transfer that has little impact on the subsequent economic incentives facing emitters of greenhouse gases.

The implication of differential allocations of long-term permits is illustrated in Figure 2.9. The numbers for the annual permit price are hypothetical and

---

[25] The intellectual idea actually dates back to Roberts and Spence (1976) for general environmental policy and McKibbin and Wilcoxen (1997) for climate change policy.

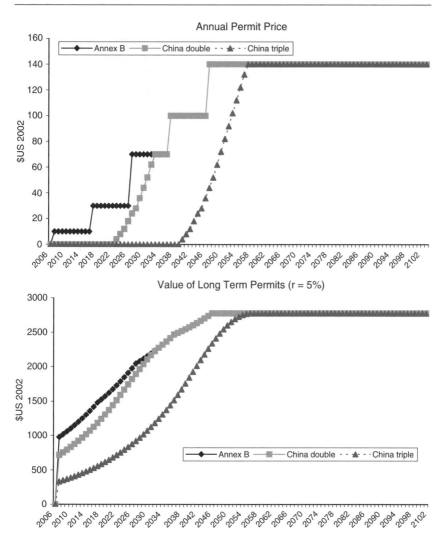

Figure 2.9: Stylized permit price for an allocation of double and triple China's 2002 emissions

Source: Hypothetical response based on author's calculations.

intended to show the relationship between the annual permit price trajectories and the long-term permit price under different assumptions. The top chart shows the annual permit price for industrial economies and for China when allocated a doubling of emissions from 2002 levels ('China Double') and a tripling of emissions from 2002 levels ('China Triple'). The bottom chart shows the value of long-term permits in each case where a discount rate of 3 percent real is used in the calculation. In the upper panel it is assumed that permit prices in industrial countries begin at US$10 per ton for a decade beginning in 2007. It then rises each decade by agreement, reaching $140 per ton by 2047. In China, because there are more long-term permits than annual emissions in the earlier years of the agreement, the price of annual permits is zero. In the case where double emissions are allocated, the annual permit price will be zero until the emission reaches the number of long-term permits. At that time (assumed to be 2023 in this example), the annual price begins to rise towards the price on annual permits in the industrial economies. In the example, the price is equalized by 2033. In the second example for China it is assumed that three times 2002 emissions are allocated and that the constraint begins to bind by 2040. In both cases the price of annual carbon emissions is equalized in China and the industrial economies eventually but allowance is built in for China's level of economic development. There is a differential cost to economies in the short run which is intended in the policy design.

Now consider the value of long-term permits in both regions. Even though China is given significant time to adjust, the price of long-term permits is positive from the beginning of the policy. These prices reflect the expected future price of annual permits which in the example is assumed to be known by the market. This long-term permit price is used for making energy investment decisions in China whereas the short-term prices are the cost to Chinese industry. In the industrial economies (under the assumed profile) the long-term permit value is $977 per ton of carbon emissions. In China in the double allocation case, the price of long-term permits is US$716 per ton and in the triple allocation US$333 per ton. These prices give a powerful incentive for carbon-saving technological investment in China even though initially the annual permit price is zero.

The attractiveness of the Blueprint for creating institutions to aid in economic development in a developing country like China should not be underestimated. The ability of investors in energy systems to effectively hedge their investment over a long period of time should be very attractive for the development of energy systems in developing countries. The time frame of the assets we propose to be created (by committing to a global climate regime) is currently unparalleled. China could use this new asset as a way of attracting foreign investment and enhance the development process by creating what is effectively a futures market in energy (for example by not allocating all long-term permits to current emitters by holding a reserve for foreign investors). This is far more likely to induce foreign investment than the CDM or other similar mechanisms that face very high administrative costs. Critics might argue that the problem with China is the inability to create the sorts of institutions the above scheme would require. This is a problem in the near term but it is easier for China to create property rights and institutions within China according to the philosophy and characteristics of China, than it would be to impose within China the sorts of institutions and property rights based on Western approaches that would be required under the Kyoto Protocol for China to be able to sell carbon rights into a global markets. The required synchronization of property rights globally in a form reflecting developed countries' practices is exactly why it is difficult to see how the Kyoto Protocol could be implemented outside the small group of industrialized countries with similar institutional structures that are already involved.

2.4 Policy Implications and Conclusion

China currently faces serious environmental issues and these are likely to become more important over coming years, particularly given the likely rise in energy use in China that will be required to sustain the momentum of economic growth generated through economic reforms. It is likely, given current global energy price structures, that future energy will be largely generated by use of coal which under current technologies in China is likely to have serious environmental consequences. Current plans to increase the use of nuclear energy and renewable energy such as hydroelectric power and wind power are impressive but will likely have little impact in a rapidly expanding energy sector unless there is a significant change in the expected relative price of carbon.

China is already taking action on local environmental issues. This has been particularly true in dealing with air and water quality as well as sulfur dioxide emissions. Action is already under way to reduce emissions of sulfur dioxide by substituting away from high-sulfur coal, by closing small, high-sulfur coal mines, with direct controls on SO_2 emissions, implementation of pilot schemes for SO_2 emission charges, and pilot schemes for SO_2 emissions trading. These are having an impact on emissions of sulfur although the impact on acid rain has been less clear. As Nakada and Ueta (2004) point out, there are likely to be gains for other economies in the region, such as Japan and Korea, to cooperate with China in controlling sulfur emissions since these economies are also directly affected by acid rain emanating from China.

Black carbon and its direct health, economic, and environmental consequences are a promising area for close attention and direct policy intervention within China. This is not an issue of technological change at the power utilities as might usually be the focus of energy policy. A reduction in emissions of black carbon will require a technology shift in the way households generate heating and cooking and in the way farmers clear their land after harvest. It appears that it would be feasible to implement a phase-in of alternative technologies at the household level over coming years with the potential to generate a range of environmental, health, and economic benefits. Addressing black carbon is a good candidate for consideration under the 'Asia Pacific Partnership for Clean Development and Climate' (APPCDC) announced on July 28, 2005 which consists of the United States, Japan, Australia, South Korea, China, and India. Black carbon is an aerosol and therefore is not covered by the Kyoto Protocol and the pay-offs for taking action in both development terms and climate outcomes are likely to be large and achieved within a decade.

The largest issue facing the global environment from Chinese energy use is likely to be the emissions of carbon dioxide. China has yet to take effective action on greenhouse gas emissions. However this is not surprising since there has been insufficient action in most industrial economies. Even if rapid action is possible, the pay-off in terms of potential climate change won't be realized for many decades into the future. Although some researchers believe that global responses such as through the clean development mechanism (CDM) of the Kyoto Protocol are one way to proceed,[26] it is doubtful that much can be achieved through this approach alone. This may change in coming years if Japan takes its Kyoto target seriously but it is unlikely given the current state of international negotiations. A strong case can be made for responses to be developed in China, Korea, Japan, and other economies in the Asia Pacific region for dealing with carbon dioxide emissions. This has already begun to emerge within the APPCDC. The idea within this group of countries of technology transfer without a carbon price signal, which currently underlies that approach, is unlikely to be an effective way forward. However, within the APPCDC framework, potential exists for experimenting with hybrid market/government control schemes such as the McKibbin-Wilcoxen Blueprint in which important institutions are created to begin a long process of reduced carbonization of the Chinese economy. This would allow China to continue to grow but would put in place a pricing mechanism for future carbon emissions as an incentive to gradually shift Chinese energy systems to low-carbon-emitting technologies. Foreign investment in these technologies could be doubly rewarded directly through allocation of long-term permits within China to foreign technology investment and indirectly through the profits likely to be generated from trading these permits and from the technological innovation itself. The creation of institutions for environmental

---

[26] See Ueta *et al.* (2005).

management, particularly through market incentives between now and 2010 will be the most important steps to be taken in China. The demonstration effect of such an approach could have an even bigger impact on global emissions if it encouraged other developing countries and the United States to begin to price carbon more appropriately given the current state of knowledge about the potential of climate change.

China and other countries in the Asia Pacific region are at a critical juncture in determining the potential global environmental impact of a rapidly growing China. Many of the solutions to environmental problems open to China are also yet to be implemented in other Asia-Pacific economies. There are few areas in multilateral policy cooperation that could have a larger environmental and economic impact than working cooperatively within the region to address looming environmental problems from China's emergence into the world economy.

Appendix 2.1: The G-Cubed Model for Projecting Energy Use and Greenhouse Emissions in China

The G-Cubed model is an intertemporal general equilibrium model of the world economy. The theoretical structure is outlined in McKibbin and Wilcoxen (1998).[27] A number of studies—summarized in McKibbin and Vines (2000)—show that the G-Cubed modeling approach has been useful in assessing a range of issues across a number of countries since the mid-1980s.[28] Some of the principal features of the model are as follows:

- The model is based on explicit intertemporal optimization by the agents (consumers and firms) in each economy.[29] In contrast to static CGE models, time and dynamics are of fundamental importance in the G-Cubed model. The MSG-Cubed model is known as a DSGE (Dynamic Stochastic General Equilibrium) model in the macroeconomics literature and a Dynamic Intertemporal General Equilibrium (DIGE) model in the general equilibrium literature.

- In order to track the macro time series, the behavior of agents is modified to allow for short-run deviations from optimal behavior either due to myopia or to restrictions on the ability of households and firms to borrow at the risk-free bond rate on government debt. For both households and firms, deviations from intertemporal optimizing behavior take the form of rules of thumb, which are consistent with an optimizing agent that does not update predictions based on

---

[27] Full details of the model including a list of equations and parameters can be found online at <http://www.gcubed.com>.

[28] These issues include: Reaganomics in the 1980s; German unification in the early 1990s; fiscal consolidation in Europe in the mid-1990s; the formation of NAFTA; the Asian crisis; and the productivity boom in the US.

[29] See Blanchard and Fischer (1989) and Obstfeld and Rogoff (1996).

Regions
United States
Japan
Australia
Europe
Rest of the OECD
China
Oil Exporting Developing Countries
Eastern Europe and the former Soviet Union
Other Developing Countries

Sectors
Energy:
Electric Utilities
Gas Utilities
Petroleum Refining
Coal Mining
Crude Oil and Gas Extraction
Non-Energy:
Mining
Agriculture, Fishing and Hunting
Forestry/Wood Products
Durable Manufacturing
Non-Durable Manufacturing
Transportation
Services
Capital Producing Sector

Figure 2.A1: Overview of the G-Cubed model (version 63E)

new information about future events. These rules of thumb are chosen to generate the same steady-state behavior as optimizing agents so that in the long run there is only a single intertemporal optimizing equilibrium of the model. In the short run, actual behavior is assumed to be a weighted average of the optimizing and the rule-of-thumb assumptions. Thus aggregate consumption is a weighted average of consumption based on wealth (current asset valuation and expected future after tax labor income) and consumption based on current disposable income. Similarly, aggregate investment is a weighted average of investment based on Tobin's q (market valuation of the expected future change in the marginal product of capital relative to the cost) and investment based on a backward-looking version of Q.

- There is explicit treatment of the holding of financial assets, including money. Money is introduced into the model through a restriction that households require money to purchase goods.

- The model also allows for short-run nominal wage rigidity (to different degrees in different countries) and therefore allows for significant periods of unemployment depending on the labor market institutions in each country. This assumption, when taken together with the explicit role for money, is what gives the model its 'macroeconomic' characteristics. (Here again the model's assumptions differ from the standard market-clearing assumption in most CGE models.)

- The model distinguishes between the stickiness of physical capital within sectors and within countries and the flexibility of financial capital, which immediately flows to where expected returns are highest. This important distinction leads to a critical difference between the quantity of physical capital that is available at any time to produce goods and services, and the valuation of that capital as a result of decisions about the allocation of financial capital.

As a result of this structure, the G-Cubed model contains rich dynamic behavior, driven on the one hand by asset accumulation and on the other by wage adjustment to a neo-classical steady state. It embodies a wide range of assumptions about individual behavior and empirical regularities in a general equilibrium framework. The interdependencies are solved out using a computer algorithm that solves for the rational expectations equilibrium of the global economy. It is important to stress that the term 'general equilibrium' is used to signify that as many interactions as possible are captured, not that all economies are in a full market-clearing equilibrium at each point in time. Although it is assumed that market forces eventually drive the world economy to a neoclassical steady-state growth equilibrium, unemployment does emerge for long periods due to wage stickiness, to an extent that differs between countries due to differences in labor-market institutions.

References

Bagnoli, P., McKibbin, W., and Wilcoxen, P. (1996), 'Future Projections and Structural Change,' in N. Nakicenovic, W. Nordhaus, R. Richels, and F. Toth (eds.), *Climate Change: Integrating Economics and Policy*, CP 96-1 (Vienna: International Institute for Applied Systems Analysis), 181–206.

Blanchard, O. and Fischer, S. (1989), *Lectures on Macroeconomics* (Cambridge, MA: MIT Press).

Bohringer, C. (2001), 'Climate Policies from Kyoto to Bonn: from Little to Nothing?' ZEW Discussion Paper No. 01-49 (Mannheim).

Buchner, B., Carraro, C., and Cersosimo, I. (2001), 'On the Consequences of the US Withdrawal from the Kyoto/Bonn Protocol.' Paper presented at the 17th Annual Congress of the European Economic Association, Venice, August 2002.

Castles, I. and Henderson, D. (2003), 'The IPCC Emission Scenarios: An Economic-Statistical Critique,' *Energy & Environment*, 14 (2&3): 159–85.

China, Council for International Cooperation on Environment and Development (2001), Report of Environmental Working Group.

Cooper, R. (2005), 'A Carbon Tax in China?' Paper prepared for the Climate Policy Center, Washington, DC.

Department of Energy (2004), 'An Energy Overview of the People's Republic of China.' Available at online <http://www.fe.doe.gov/international/EastAsia_and_Oceania/chinover.html>.

Energy Information Agency (2006), 'International Energy Outlook', Department of Energy, Washington, DC.

Garbaccio, R. F., Ho, M. S., and Jorgenson, D. W. (1999), 'Controlling Carbon Emissions in China,' *Environment and Development Economics*, 4(4): 493–518.

Hamilton, R. S. and Mansfield, T. A. (1991), 'Airborne Particulate Elemental Carbon: Its Sources, Transport and Contribution to Dark Smoke and Soiling, *Atmos. Environ.*, 25: 715–23.

Hansen, J. E. *et al.* (1998), 'Climate Forcings in the Industrial Era,' *Proceedings of the National Academy of Sciences of the USA*, 95(22): 12753–8.

_____ and Sato, M. (2001), 'Trends of Measured Climate Forcing Agents,' *Proceedings of the National Academy of Sciences of the USA*, 98: 14778–83.

Ho, M. and Jorgenson, D. (2003), 'Air Pollution in China: Sector Allocation Emissions and Health Damage.' Paper prepared for the China Council for International Cooperation on Environment and Development.

Intergovernmental Panel on Climate Change (2001), *Climate Change 2001*, 3 vols. (Cambridge: Cambridge University Press).

International Energy Agency (2004), *Analysis of the Impact of High Oil Prices on the Global Economy*, May, Paris.

International Monetary Fund (2004), *World Economic Outlook*, September.

Jiang, T. (2003), *Economic Instruments of Pollution Control in an Imperfect World* (Cheltenham: Edward Elgar).

_____ and McKibbin, W. (2002), 'Assessment of China's Pollution Levy System: An Equilibrium Pollution Approach', *Environment and Development Economics*, 7: 75–105.

Kemfert, Claudia (2001), 'Economic Effects of Alternative Climate Policy Strategies,' *Environmental Science and Policy*, 5(5): 367–84.

Liu, J. and Diamond, J. (2005), 'China's Environment in a Globalizing World,' *Nature*, 435: 1179–86.

Löschel, A. and Zhang, Z. X. (2002), 'The Economic and Environmental Implications of the US Repudiation of the Kyoto Protocol and the Subsequent Deals in Bonn and Marrakech,' *Nota Di Lavoro* 23.2002, Venice: Fondazione Enie Enrico Mattei, April.

McKibbin, W., Pearce, D., and Stegman, A. (2004), 'Long Run Projections for Climate Change Scenarios,' Lowy Institute for International Policy Working Paper in International Economics, 1/04 (May).

_____ and Vines, D. (2000), 'Modeling Reality: The Need for Both Intertemporal Optimization and Stickiness in Models for Policymaking,' *Oxford Review of Economic Policy*, 16(4): 106–237.

_____ and Wilcoxen, P. (1998), 'The Theoretical and Empirical Structure of the G-Cubed Model,' *Economic Modelling*, 16(1): 123–48.

_____ _____ (2002*a*), *Climate Change Policy After Kyoto: A Blueprint for a Realistic Approach* (Washington, DC: The Brookings Institution).

_____ _____ (2002*b*), 'The Role of Economics in Climate Change Policy,' *Journal of Economic Perspectives*, 16(2): 107–30.

_____ _____ (2004), 'Estimates of the Costs of Kyoto-Marrakesh Versus The McKibbin-Wilcoxen Blueprint,' *Energy Policy*, 32(4): 467–79.

Menon, S., Hansen, J., Nazarenko, L., and Luo, Y. (2002), 'Effects of Black Carbon Aerosols in China and India,' *Science*, 297: 2250–3.

Nakada, M. and Ueta, K. (2004), Sulfur Emissions Control in China: Domestic or Regional Cooperative Strategies?' 21COE Discussion Paper 41, Kyoto University.

National Bureau of Statistics (2003), *China Statistical Yearbook 2003* (Beijing, China: Statistics Press).

Obstfeld, M. and Rogoff, K. (1996), *Foundations of International Macroeconomics* (Cambridge, MA: MIT Press.

Panayotou, T. (1998), 'The Effectiveness and Efficiency of Environmental Policy in China, in M. McElroy, C. Nielsen, and P. Lydon (eds.), *Energizing China, Reconciling Environmental Protection and Economic Growth* (Boston: Harvard University Press), 431–72.

—— and Zheng, Z. (2000), 'The Cost of Environmental Damage in China: Assessment and Valuation Framework,' China Council for International Cooperation on Environment and Development.

Pezzey, J. (2003), 'Emission Taxes and Tradable Permits: A Comparison of Views on Long Run Efficiency.' *Environmental and Resource Economics,* 26(2): 329–42.

Pizer, W. A. (1997), 'Prices vs. Quantities Revisited: The Case of Climate Change,' Resources for the Future Discussion Paper 98-02 (Washington: Resources for the Future).

Roberts, M. J. and Spence, A. M. (1976), 'Effluent Charges and Licenses under Uncertainty,' *Journal of Public Economics,* 5: 193–208.

SEPA (2005), 'Report on the State of the Environment in China: 2005,' State Environmental Protection Agency, Beijing.

Streets, D. G. (1997), 'Energy and Acid Rain Projections for North East Asia,' The Nautilus Institute, online at <http://www.nautilus.org/archives/papers/energy/streetsESENAY1.html>.

—— (2004), 'Black Smoke in China and Its Climate Effects.' Paper presented to the Asian Economic Panel, Columbia University, October.

—— Bond, T. C., Carmichael, G. R., Fernandes, S. D., Fu, Q., He, D., Klimont, Z., Nelson, S. M., Tsai, N. Y., Wang, M. Q., Woo, J.-H., and Yarber, K. F. (2003), 'An Inventory of Gaseous and Primary Aerosol Emissions in Asia in the Year 2000,' *Geophysical Research,* 108 (D21, November): 8809–31.

Ueta, K., Inada, Y., Fujikawa, K., Mori, A., Na, S., Hayashi, T., and Shimoda, M. (2005), 'Win-win Strategy for Japan and China in Climate Change Policy.' Report to the International Collaborative Project on Sustainable Societies.

Wang, X. and Smith, K. (1999), 'Secondary Benefits of Greenhouse Gas Control: Health Impacts in China', *Environmental Science and Technology,* 33(18), 3056–61.

Weitzman, M. L. (1974), 'Prices vs. Quantities,' *Review of Economic Studies,* 41: 477–91.

Weyant, John (ed.) (1999), 'The Costs of the Kyoto Protocol: A Multi-model Evaluation,' *The Energy Journal,* Special Issue.

World Bank (1997), *Clear Water, Blue Skies: China's Environment in the New Century.* (Washington, DC: World Bank).

World Health Organzation (2001), *Environment and People's Health* (Geneva: World Health Organization and UNDP).

—— (2004), *Environmental Health Country Profile—China,* August (Geneva: World Health Organization).

Wu, Libo, Kaneko, S. and Matsuoka, S. (2005), 'Driving Forces behind the Stagnancy of China's Energy Related CO2 Emissions from 1996 to 1999: The Relative Importance of Structural Change, Intensity Change and Scale Change.' *Energy Policy*, 33(3): 319–35.

Yang, J. and Schreifels, J. (2003), 'Implementing SO_2 Emissions in China,' *OECD Global Forum on Sustainable Development: Emissions Trading* (Paris: OECD), 1–22.

Zhang, Z. (1998), *The Economics of Energy Policy in China: Implications for Global Climate Change* (Cheltenham: Edward Elgar).

3

The Spoke Trap: Hub-and-Spoke Bilateralism in East Asia

Richard E. Baldwin
Graduate Institute of International Studies, Geneva February 2007[1]

3.1 Introduction

The first draft of this chapter (written as a paper in 2003) opened with: 'East Asia finds itself on the eve of rampant regionalism.' In early 2007, we can say that regionalism is plainly rampant. ASEAN, which has signed agreements with China and Korea, is negotiating with Japan. Japan has signed bilateral agreements with some of the big ASEANs (Malaysia, Singapore, Indonesia, Thailand, the Philippines, and Vietnam) and is likely to conclude a deal with ASEAN as a group this year. ASEAN is also exploring the possibilities with Australia, New Zealand, India, and a raft of other Asian nations; Japan, Korea, and China are following suit. The Asian Development Bank counts 192 FTAs in the Asian Pacific region as of January 2007. This is about half the FTAs in the world—quite remarkable for a region with almost no functioning FTAs just ten years ago.

The resulting liberalization is likely to be good for the region, but there is a danger. The political economy force that drives the domino effect tends to produce hub-and-spoke bilateralism. This would be problematic at two levels.

Economically, hub-and-spoke-ism produces an inferior outcome for the region as a whole. In particular, it may produce a profusion of Free Trade Agreements that can make the whole region less attractive to foreign direct

[1] This paper was written while I was visiting the Korea Institute for International Economic Policy (KIEP), where I first presented it at a seminar on December 8, 2003. I wish to thank KIEP President Choong Yong Ahn and the Director of the Center for Northeast Asian Economic Cooperation, Hyungdo Ahn, for providing excellent support during my visit. Inkyo Cheong offered many insightful comments and suggestions that I have incorporated into this paper; these made it a better and less naive paper than it would otherwise have been.

51

investment—an effect that might be called, in the Asian context, the 'noodle bowl problem.'

Politically, hub-and-spoke-ism could prove divisive. It tends to marginalize the spoke economies both economically and politically while at the same time granting leverage to the hub economy. Since there are two natural hubs in East Asia—Japan and China—there is a strong possibility that uncoordinated political economy forces could produce a two-hub system. This would be a worrying outcome in that it might foster regional divisiveness rather than regional cooperation. This sort of alignment between trade blocs and political/ military camps clearly heightened political tensions in the intra-Europe war.

EAST ASIA'S USUAL REGIONALISM

While the domino effect is clearly at work (once two nations sign an FTA, third nations want to sign FTAs to avoid the emergence of discrimination against their exporters) regionalism in East Asia is quite unlike that of other regions in the world. For starters, most of the trade within the region is in parts and components, with many of the final goods exported to the EU or US. Moreover, trade flows closely follow the extensive network of foreign direct investment in the region. Asia, in short, is like one big factory with intra-regional trade flows acting like conveyor belts moving partly processed goods to the next production bay. This system, which started to unfold in the mid-1980s, has been called market-driven regionalism (see Urata 2004 for details and the history of this phenomenon). Market-driven regionalism is unusual in two distinct ways. It was not driven by governments but rather by private companies establishing production sites in the various countries and pushing for unilateral liberalization of tariffs. Second, it involved little preferential tariff access—at least until a few years ago—since nations unilaterally set their applied MFN tariffs to zero, or close to zero on the 'Factory Asia' goods. Indeed, almost no traders take advantage of the oldest arrangement—the ASEAN FTAs (AFTA); less than 15 percent of intra-ASEAN trade benefited from AFTA's preferences in 2002 (JETRO 2003). By comparison, utilization rates below 50 percent are considered very low for European FTAs (Augier and Tong 2005).

ORGANIZATION OF THIS CHAPTER

This chapter begins with a summary of the negative effects of hub-and-spoke bilateralism, followed by a discussion of the political economy forces that tend to create hub-and-spoke arrangements. This theory is used in Section 3.4 to motivate an empirical measure of 'hub-ness.' My findings suggest that only Japan and China are likely to be hubs as individual nations, but that a

Japan–Korea FTA would create a clearly dominant hub in the region. With this analysis in hand, Section 3.5 considers the implications for the likely course of East Asian regionalism. I argue that unless explicit measures are taken, a 'bicycle system' is like to emerge, that is to say, a two-hub system with Japan and China as the hubs.

The paper then turns to possible solutions to the spoke trap. Section 3.6 reviews various anti-spoke strategies from around the world, and Section 3.7 puts forth two proposals for East Asia. The final section presents concluding remarks.

3.2 Why hub-and-spoke bilateralism is bad economically

As it is well known, a country that lowers tariffs on imports from only some of its trade partners provides an artificial incentive for domestic residents to switch their purchases away from the non-favoured trade partner. This may be harmful to the country since it may involve diverting trade from low-cost to high-cost producers (trade diversion). A hub-and-spoke trade arrangement, by favouring imports from the hub, may lead to this sort of trade diversion. By contrast, a regional free-trade area, which multilateralized the hub-and-spoke FTAs, reduces this possibility since it reduces the fraction of trade that is divertable.

Baldwin and Venables (1995) classify the economic effects of trade agreements into allocation effects (i.e. the impact on the allocation of resources within an economy), location effects (i.e. the impact on the spatial allocation of economic activity within and between nations), and accumulation effects (i.e. the impact on the main determinants of growth—the rate of accumulation of human, physical, and knowledge capital). We turn first to the allocation effects.

3.2.1 Allocation effects

NOODLE BOWL EFFECT

As I wrote in 1994, 'A web of trade deals can create a nightmarish tangle of administrative procedures that raise costs for enterprises and for governments. Most costly of all, are those dealing with rules of origin.'[2] This clearly is a danger for future East Asian regionalism. (This point has come to be known by Jagdish Bhagwati's catchy phrase the 'spaghetti bowl effect.')[3] On rules of

---

[2] See the chapter entitled 'Hub and spoke bilateralism' in Baldwin (1994). The final manuscript can be downloaded from <http://heiwww.unige.ch/~baldwin/>.

[3] It is difficult to track down the exact citation for this, since even Bhagwati does not provide a reference when he uses the term. The first reference I could find was a column by

origin, see Krishna and Krueger (1995) for detailed analysis and Krishna (2003) for survey.

RESTRICTED PRO-COMPETITIVE EFFECT

An additional allocation effect of a hub-and-spoke agreement is the way in which it restricts competition from spoke-based firms in each other's markets. For the most part, competition from hub-based firms would provide all the competition that is needed, but in certain industries and certain countries, spoke-based firms will be more competitive. See Baldwin and Wyplosz (2003: ch. 6) for an accessible presentation of the pro-competitive effect and its implications.

3.2.2 Accumulation and location effects

The next effect, which Krugman (1993) calls the 'hub effect', concerns the impact on investment in spoke economies. That is, just as an all-roads-lead-to-Rome transportation system favours industrial location in Rome, a hub-and-spoke arrangement favours industry in the hub nation at the expense of industry in the spoke nations. Baldwin, Forslid, Martin, Ottaviano, and Robert-Nicoud (2003) provide a formal analysis of this in the context of the new economic geography.

The marginalizing tendencies of hub-and-spoke FTAs can be illustrated with a numerical example that intentionally puts to the side several important issues. Imagine there are three locations being considered as the site for a new manufacturing facility, Japan and two other Asian sites, one in Korea and one in Malaysia. For simplicity, assume the division of sales among markets is fixed irrespectively of costs, with 75 percent sold in Japan and 12.5 percent sold in Korea and Malaysia. (This simplification lets us divorce cost considerations from demand considerations.) Imagine the unit production costs would be 10 if the plant is located in Japan, 8 if the plant is located in Korea or Malaysia and 15 if three separate plants must be built. Economies of scale explain the high cost of separating production; wages explain why the Japanese location means higher production costs.

To start the analysis, suppose initially there are no FTAs, and unit trade costs amount to 6 for all three trade flows (i.e. it costs 6 to ship a unit between any two nations). Internal trade costs are assumed to be zero. The simplified problem facing the potential manufacturer is to choose the location with the lowest costs. Without FTAs, the cost-minimizing location for the plant is Japan. The average cost in Korea or Malaysia is 13.25-8 for production plus an average trade cost of (3/4)*6 plus (1/8)*0 plus (1/8)*6. This surpasses the

New York journalist Peter Passel, where he quotes Bhagwati as saying: a 'spaghetti bowl of tangled, inconsistent trade standards that just can't be good for efficiency.' February 4, 1997.

cost of producing in Japan (this equals 11.5) since the high unit production cost in Japan is more than offset by the better market access (i.e. lower average trade cost).

Envision the impact of hub-and-spoke bilateralism on this outcome. Presume Japan–Korea and Japan–Malaysia FTAs take effect, cutting the unit cost for bilateral trade to 3. Korea–Malaysia trade costs remain at 6. Arithmetic shows that the average unit cost of locating the plant in the Japan is still lower (10.75) than locating in Korea or Malaysia (11). Although FTAs lower trade costs bilaterally, trade costs within Japan are lower yet, so there is still some market size effect favouring the Japanese location. In short, location in the hub, Japan in this case, confers preferential access to *all three* markets, not just two.

The moral of this simple arithmetic example is that a hub-and-spoke system tends to favour location of industrial firms in the hub.

Lastly, consider the impact of turning the hub-and-spoke FTAs into a free-trade zone by implementation of a Korea–Malaysia FTA. Here we see that the total unit costs of locating in Korea or Malaysia are now lower (10.625) than locating in Japan (10.75). Although location in Japan implies zero trade costs for 75 percent of the manufacturer's sales, the lower Korea–Malaysia production cost finally becomes the dominant issue.

Of course, this simple illustration is not general, and we do not mean to say that filling in the gaps between 'spokes' will lead to a tidal wave of foreign investment into Korea and Malaysia. Nevertheless, the basic message is clear. Hub-and-spoke FTAs tend to marginalize the 'spoke' economies, since factories in the 'spokes' have artificially lower market access than factories in the hub. Consequently, hub-and-spoke FTAs cause an artificial deterrent to investment in the outer economies. Filling in the gaps with spoke-spoke FTAs removes this policy-induced investment deterrent.

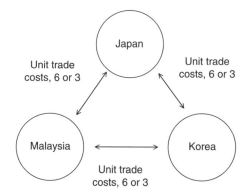

Figure 3.1: Hub-and-Spoke Bilateralism: A Numerical Example

Another way of saying this is that signing bilateral trade deals with the hub, without signing deals with the spokes, is self-inflicted peripherality. By making small economies smaller than they need be, hub-and-spoke bilateralism can be thought of as self-induced peripherality for spoke nations.

HYSTERESIS IN LOCATION

A key lesson of the 'new' economic geography (Fujita, Krugman, and Venables 1999) is that the location of economic activity is marked by multiple equilibria. That is to say, there is not a unique constellation of economic concentrations towards which Asia is inevitably heading. There is true uncertainty about what the economic geography of Asia will look like in fifty years. Moreover, once a particular location gets a head start, it may be extremely difficult for other regions to catch up. The import of all this is that the temporary investment-deterring effects of the current hub-and-spoke system may have consequences that last far beyond the termination of that system. In other words, bad policies–even when they are only temporary—may have very long-lived harmful consequences.

The importance of all this should be clear. Since hub-and-spoke bilateralism favours location in the 'hub', five or ten years of hub-and-spoke bilateralism will give Japanese locations a head-start on other Asian locations. Thus, more new industry may end up in Japan than would be the case with a free-trade area (i.e. FTAs among spokes as well). Given the logic of economic geography, circular causality will continue to favor regions that get a head start. The effect of a bad policy may be felt long after the policy is reversed. See Freund (1998) for a formal analysis of industrial hysteresis.

3.3 Why hub-and-spoke bilateralism? Some theory

The world is full of hub-and-spoke trade arrangements, and such an arrangement may well emerge in Asia. Before considering solutions to hub-and-spoke-ism, we discuss the political economy forces that so systematically yield hub-and-spoke bilateralism. One reward for this theorizing is an empirical methodology for measuring the 'hub-ness' of nations.

3.3.1 *The mercantilist view of trade negotiations*[4]

From a political perspective, exports are good and imports are bad. A more subtle expression of this idea is that trade is good because trade creates jobs. No matter how it is expressed, this idea is nonsense from the medium- or

[4] This section is taken almost verbatim from Baldwin (1994), which studied the then-emerging hub-and-spoke-ism in Europe. The main change has been to substitute 'EACs' (East Asian Countries) for 'CEECs' (Central and East European Countries).

long-run economic perspective. Be that as it may, the important fact is that this mistaken reasoning points governments in the right direction. It leads them to conduct trade negotiations based on an exchange of market access. Specifically, since exports are good and imports are bad, if country A wants better access to country's B's markets, then country A is expected to 'pay' for this market access by opening its own market to B's exports.

LAW OF THE JUNGLE, MFN RULES AND FTAs

Usually, the market opening that results from this mistaken reasoning is good for all nations involved. A drawback of this mechanism, however, is that it may create a sort of law of the jungle. That is, with market access as the currency of exchange, big countries are rich and small countries are poor. The rules of the GATT correct this imbalance with the principle of Most Favoured Nation (MFN) treatment. However, when it comes to negotiating regional trade arrangements, MFN does not apply, so the law of the jungle may prevail.

Political economy of hub-and-spoke bilateralism

Political economy forces created by an application of this law of the jungle support hub-and-spoke bilateralism. Take a country like the Czech Republic. On the pro-liberalization side, Czech exporters have a large interest in the EU market, but only a minor interest in the market of, say, Estonia. On the anti-liberalization side, Czech import-competing industries dislike imports whether they come from the EU, Estonia, or elsewhere. Now consider the line-up of political forces inside the Czech Republic. Czech exporters are willing to fight quite hard for market opening with the big EU market. They are willing to fight much less hard for market opening with Estonia. In other words, there are strong political forces backing market opening with the 'hub' but very little support for market opening with other 'spokes.' Since Czech protectionists simply want to reduce import competition from any source, the protectionists are likely to win when it comes to blocking spoke-spoke liberalization, though they lose when it comes to hub-spoke liberalization.

An interesting add-on effect may occur if foreign investment from the hub is important in the spoke economies. To attract foreign investors, the spoke governments may promise protection from imports. Moreover, given a credible trade agreement with the hub, it is much easier for the spoke government to promise long-term protection against imports from other spoke economies. If this sort of pandering-for-investment protectionism is common, the spoke economies may end up 'Balkanized.' That is, foreign multinationals may be enticed into locating inefficiently small production facilities in each spoke economy. Having done this, the multinationals may become a new anti-liberalization force. Companies from the hub that have invested in inefficiently small facilities in several spoke economies may resist efforts to liberalize spoke-spoke trade. This may make the hub governments more reluctant to take any initiative in redressing hub-and-spoke bilateralism.

WHY FTAs BETWEEN DEVELOPING NATIONS USUALLY FAIL

If some idiosyncratic event stirs a great wave of enthusiasm for brotherhood among the spoke economies, politicians in these countries may sign agreements promising to open spoke-spoke trade. Yet once the headlines fade and the enthusiasm wanes, the drab politics of protectionism usually reasserts itself. Promises are broken or never fulfilled and the expected liberalization never appears. Moreover, since protectionist forces reappear in both spoke economies, the broken promises are generally accepted without protest. Note how different the situation is for spoke-hub trade arrangements. Exporters in both the hub and the spoke (but especially those in the spoke economies) care a good deal about access to each other's market. Accordingly, exporters would raise their voices if promises were not kept. That is to say, the same sort of backsliding that is common in spoke-spoke agreements will not be tolerated in hub-spoke trade deals.

THE 'PASSING PARADE' PANDERING PROBLEM

Some competition among East Asian Countries' (EAC's) governments for foreign direct investment is probably a healthy thing for all parties. Inward investment is promoted by policies such as guaranteed profit remittances, property rights assurances (especially for intellectual property rights) and an absence of trade-related investment measures such as export requirements and local content rules. Although this is well understood, governments throughout the world often do not adopt such policies for domestic political reasons. Competition among EACs for foreign direct investment (FDI) is an effective way of ensuring that they stick to FDI policies that are in their best interest anyway.

However, too much competition among EAC policymakers could lead to an inferior, non-cooperative outcome. The basic problem can be exemplified with the so-called 'passing parade' parable. Imagine a crowd gathers to watch a parade. As the parade passes, people in the front stand on their toes to see better, thus forcing all those behind them also to stand on their toes. In the end, most see no better than before, but all have to stand on their toes.

In the EACs, potential investors, foreign and domestic alike, have an incentive to ask for import protection as a condition for making their investments. However if all EACs succumb to this pandering and erect trade barriers to attract investment or retain jobs, they could all end up 'standing on their toes' without results. This destructive competition could backfire. Each country's uncoordinated pandering to foreign investors could lead to trade barriers that lower the overall attractiveness of the region, thus resulting in less investment in each country. Of course, given the political power of EU exporters, it will be much more difficult for the EAC governments to promise protection against imports from the EU. But a hub-and-spoke system allows a free hand to put up barriers against imports from other EACs.

3.3.2 Domino effect applied to hub-and-spoke bilateralism

The domino theory asserts that the signing of one preferential trade arrangement triggers a chain reaction in that it tends to induce other such arrangements, with the force of this effect feeding on itself. The theory was originally conceived to account for NAFTA and the creation of pro-EU-enlargement pressures that emerged in the 1990s. Here we extend the domino theory to the specific case of hub-and-spoke bilateralism. Since the reasoning is fairly involved, it is best to organize it with the help of a simple analytic framework. In this case, import-supply and import-demand diagrams will be sufficient.

The above political economy reasoning suggests that exports to the hub are the key to the domino effect in this case, even though the full problem is radically more complex. To illustrate the basic logic as simply as possible, we make the extreme assumption that exports to the hub are the only thing that matters.

To be concrete, suppose we have three nations that are potential spokes, spokes 1, 2, and 3, and one potential hub. This situation is depicted in Figure 3.2. The right panel shows the hub's market, with MD reflecting its import demand curve. We assume that all of the spokes are symmetric to each other, so we can illustrate all effects with a single XS curve.

Presuming the hub initially imposes an MFN tariff of T on all three of its partners, the signing of the first hub-spoke FTA shifts the import supply curve down from MS_{MFN} to $MS_{1\text{-spoke}}$. As usual, this raises the price facing exporters based in the spoke nation that negotiated the FTA, with the size of the rise being from P'-T to P^1. Thus on the export side, the first FTA signer gains areas 3, 4, and 5 (before its border price as P'-T). The excluded spokes lose an area equal to area 2, because the FTA drives down the domestic price in the hub to P^1 and this drags down the excluded nations' border prices to P^1-T.

When the second hub-spoke FTA is signed, three things happen to spoke exports.

1. The second FTA signer sees its exports rise as the price it faces rises to P^2. This implies a gain to the second signer of areas 2, 3, and 4.
2. The first FTA signer sees its export volume to the hub fall as the price it faces in the hub market falls to P^2.
3. The remaining spoke sees its exports fall as the price it faces for exports to the hub falls to P^2-T.

Rising incentive for outsiders to get an FTA in a hub-and-spoke arrangement

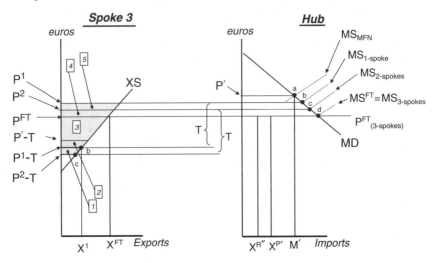

Figure 3.2: Domino Effect in Hub-and-Spoke Bilateralism

When the third and final hub-spoke FTA is signed, two things happen.

1. The first and second FTA signer see their exports fall as the price they face falls to the free-trade price, P^{FT} (at this point, the hub has eliminated all import duties). This implies an additional loss of area 4 for both.

2. The third FTA signer sees its export volume to the hub expand significantly, as all the discrimination is removed. And the price it earns on exports to the hub rises from P^2-T to P^{FT}. The gain to the third hub from this is the sum of areas 1, 2, and 3.

RACE TO BE FIRST

To summarize, when we focus only on spoke exports, the first FTA signer earns areas 3, 4, and 5. The second earns 2, 3, and 4. The third earns 1, 2, and 3. Because area 5 is bigger than area 2, and area 4 is bigger than area 1, we can say that the gain is greatest for the first, next biggest for the second, and smallest for the last. This ordering has important implications.

Let us suppose that for some reason or other, the hub cannot or at least might not be able to negotiate all three FTAs simultaneously. To keep things simple, make the artificial but useful assumption that the hub can do one FTA per year. It is obvious from the discussion above that any spoke that believes it will eventually sign an FTA with the hub would like to be the first one to do so. Or, to put it more colloquially, there will be a scramble for the head of the queue, once the spokes know that the hub is open to FTAs. Moreover, the same scramble would occur even if the hub can negotiate many FTAs at once but there is a possibility that some of these might be put off, or that at some point the hub would stop signing FTAs.

This is what happened when the US and Mexico announced their FTA in 1990. Within months, Chile, Brazil, Argentina, Uruguay, and Paraguay all formally or informally approached the US with requests for FTAs.[5] The Bush administration, fearing five separate battles with protectionists in Congress, discouraged these efforts and offered the Enterprise for the Americas Initiative (EAI) instead; this was launched in June 1990. According to CEA (1991: 255), the EAI created a process leading to free-trade agreements, the first step of which required nations to sign so-called Framework Agreements. These committed countries to reducing their investment restrictions, *inter alia*, in exchange for promises of closer US ties in the future. Although the Framework Agreements might be viewed as unilateral 'concessions' by mercantilists, twenty-six Latin American countries signed them in 1991.

The model discussed above leaves out two very important elements. First, it ignores the impact of FTAs on the spokes' economies. A full analysis would account for the political economy forces opposing an FTA with the hub. While these are surely important to the whole picture, post-war history shows that very few spoke economies can resist the appeal of an FTA with the hub once the hub starts signing such agreements. The second aspect has greater relevance to recent regionalism, namely, the attitude of the hub to further FTAs. In Europe, where the EU is clearly the hub, this is not an issue since the EU has committed itself to what might be called open FTA-ism. The EU will sign an FTA with almost any nation that is democratic and willing to accept the EU's insistence that agricultural trade be excluded. In the Americas, where the US is the dominant hub, things are quite different. The US has been extremely reluctant to accede to the many FTA offers it has received. Plainly, it would be nice to have a convincing analysis of why the EU and US approaches are so different, but I suspect that the real answer is non-economic.

3.4 An empirical measure of hub-ness

One unique feature of Asian regionalism is the extreme frequency with which the hub-and-spoke concept arises. Authors from virtually every nation in the region express a hope that their nation will become a hub for Asian regionalism. The harsh reality, however, is that very few Asian nations could attract the sort of mercantile interest necessary to attract a system of spokes. But how would one measure this attractiveness as a hub?

---

[5] At the time, I was working for the Bush Administration's Council of Economic Advisors following trade policy matters.

The above reasoning suggests that what really matters is the amount of extra exports that a nation would experience if it signed a bilateral FTA with the country in question. After all, a direct political benefit of an FTA is the extra exports it generates. While many other things will matter in every specific case, we can say that an FTA is quite unlikely to be politically viable unless it does generate sufficient mercantile interest. The basic idea is that we can measure a nation's hub-ness by looking at how interested other nations in the region would be in gaining preferential access. A hub will be the nation for whom preferential access is highly valued by most or all nations in the region.

Working out how an FTA changes a nation's exports is, in general, a complex matter. To make progress, it is useful to make some assumptions.

First, we assume that the exporters' interest will be proportional to the extra exports that such a bilateral opening would get them. Given this, the question is, 'How much would the nation's exports rise, if it got preferential access to another nation's market?'

To facilitate the reasoning, take an example. How much would Thailand's exports rise if it got better, preferential access to China's market? There are two parts to this. How much would a given opening raise bilateral exports? And how important are the affected bilateral exports in overall exports? We start with the second question.

MOTIVATING OUR HUB-NESS MEASURE

Here a simple calculation is useful. If Thailand's exports to China rose by 1 percent, how much would Thailand's overall exports rise? Defining Thailand's total exports as PT (a mnemonic for price times trade volume) and its exports to China as PT_C, Thailand's total exports can be written as $PT_C + \Sigma_i\, PT_i$, where PT_i represents Thai exports to all other nations. Simple log-differentiation shows that the percent increase in PT that comes from a one-percentage increase in PT_C is just China's initial share in Thai exports, PT_C/PT.[6]

Next, how much would preferential access raise Thai exports? To be concrete, we define 'preferential access' as a Chinese policy change that results in a 1 percent reduction in the price of Thai goods in the Chinese market relative to the price of other imports into China. The size of the resulting increase in Thai exports to China depends upon many things, but one important determinant is the share of Thai exports in the Chinese market. After all, if Thailand accounts for, say, 90 percent of all imported goods in China, 'preferential access' would not help that much. Thai firms would be gaining competitiveness only relative to the remaining 10 percent of imports. By

---

[6] For example, if China accounted for half Thailand's exports, total Thai exports would rise by $\frac{1}{2}$ percent if its exports to China rose by 1 per cent.

contrast, if Thai goods accounted for only, say, 1 percent of the Chinese imports, then the preference to Thai firms would have considerable effect.

Putting these together, we can very roughly estimate the increase in Thai exports to China that results from a marginal, preferential improvement in market access as:

$$HM_d = s_{od}^X(1 - s_{od}^M)$$

Where HM_d measures the 'hub-ness' of nation d (d stands for destination). The formula posits that this increases with the importance of d's market to nation o's exports (o stands for origin), and on the importance of o's sales in d's imports. In our example, s_{od}^X is the share of Thai exports that go to China, and s_{od}^M is the shared Chinese imports that come from Thailand.

For a more formal derivation of HM, see Box 3.1.

Box 3.1 DERIVING THE HUB-NESS MEASURE

The gravity model is by far the most empirically successful trade model. While it can be justified in many ways, the most natural is to view it as an application of the Helpman-Krugman trade model (Helpman and Krugman 1985). That model is based on Dixit-Stiglitz monopolistic competition, which entails CES demand functions. In particular, the exports of a typical variety made in the 'origin' nation is:

$$C_{od} = \frac{p_{od}^{-\sigma}\mu E}{\Delta}; \qquad \Delta \equiv \left(\int_i P_{id}^{1-\sigma}di\right) \qquad (1)$$

where p_{od} is the price of a typical origin-nation variety in the destination nation, E_d is expenditure in the 'destination' nations and and μ is the fraction of E_d that gets spent on all varieties in this sector. The integral is over all varieties sold in the destination nation (the subscript 'd' indicates a destination-nation variable).

If there are n_o varieties produced in the origin nation, the total value of exports from origin to destination, what we call PT, is:

$$PT \equiv n_o P_{od} C_{od} = \frac{P_{od}^{1-\sigma}}{\Delta} n_o \mu E; \qquad \Delta \equiv \left(\int_i P_{id}^{1-\sigma}di\right) \qquad (2)$$

Another handy aspect of Dixit–Stiglitz monopolistic competition is that each industrial firm is atomistic and thus rationally ignores the impact of its price on the denominator of the demand function. As a consequence, the typical firm acts as if it is a monopolist facing a demand curve with a constant elasticity equal to σ. Given the standard formula for marginal revenue, this implies that the profit-maximizing consumer price is a constant mark-up of marginal cost. More specifically, the first-order conditions for a typical industrial firm's sales to its local market and its export market are:

$$p = \frac{mc}{1 - 1/\sigma}, \qquad p^* = \tau p \qquad (3)$$

where p and p* are the local and export prices of an origin-nation based industrial firm, $\tau \geq 1$ reflects all bilateral trade costs (natural and man-made), and mc is the marginal cost of production in the origin nation (assumed to be flat in the Dixit–Stiglitz

---

Box 3.1 (*Continued*)

---

model). The second expression shows an important implication. Firms find it optimal to engage in so-called mill-pricing. That is to say, a firm charges the same producer price for sales to both markets. To see that this is true, note that the producer and consumer prices are identical for local market sales (there is no trade cost), but for export sales the consumer price is p*, while the producer price is p*/τ. This, together with inspection of (3), reveals that p = p*/τ, and this confirms the assertion that mill-pricing is optimal.

Using (3), we have:

$$P\,T_{od} = \frac{\phi_{od}\,p_o^{1-\sigma}}{\Delta}\,n_o\mu E; \quad \Delta \equiv \left(\int_i \phi_{pi}^{1-\sigma}di\right); \quad \phi_{id} \equiv \tau_{id}^{1-\sigma} \tag{4}$$

where ϕ_{od} measures the freeness of trade between nation o and nation d; in practice this will depend upon natural barriers, such as distance, and man-made barriers such as tariffs and non-tariff barriers.

Using this simple model we can easily calculate the export impact of a marginal opening of bilateral exports, i.e. a marginal increase in bilateral openness ϕ_{od}. Taking logs and differentiating, we have that:

$$\frac{dP\,T_{od}/P\,T_{od}}{d\phi_{od}/\phi_{od}} = 1 - \frac{n_o\phi_{od}\,p_o^{1-\sigma}}{\Delta} = 1 - s_{od}^M \tag{5}$$

where s_{od}^M is the share of nation-o's sales in nation-d's market.[1]

To see how important a change in PT_{od} is to nation-o's total exports, we simply log-differentiate the sum of o's exports to all destinations:

$$\frac{d\sum_i P\,T_{oi}/\sum_i P\,T_{oi}}{dP\,T_{od}/P\,T_{od}} = s_{od}^X \tag{6}$$

where s_{od}^X is the importance of d's market to o's exports, namely it is PT_{od} as a share of o's total exports.

Putting these together, we can see that the percent change in nation-o's total exports due to a 1 percent increase in bilateral openness with nation d is given by:

$$HM \equiv \frac{d\sum_i PT_{oi}/\sum_i PT_{oi}}{d\phi_{od}/\phi_{od}} = s_{od}^X(1 - s_{od}^M) \tag{7}$$

where HM stands for 'hub-ness.'

In our empirical implementation, we ignore domestic sales of the destination nation's firms; in essence this assumes that origin-nation varieties are only competing with other imported varieties in d's market.

Accounting for domestic varieties

The construction of HM rests on the simplifying assumption that imported goods compete only with other imported goods, ignoring domestic varieties. If one is willing to assume that all domestic GDP is in symmetric competition with all imported varieties, it is simple to account for this. In particular, the only thing that changes is the expression in (5); it becomes $1-(s_{od}^M)(s_Y^M)$, where s_Y^M is the destination nation's import to GDP ratio.

[1] To see this, note that from the expression for PT_{od}, $n_o\phi_{od}p_o^{1-\sigma}/\Delta = PT_{od}/\mu E$, i.e. it is the value of o's sales as a share of d's total spending on this sector.

With this theory in hand, we turn to the numbers.

3.4.1 *Application to Western Hemisphere*

In both the New World and the Old World, hub-and-spoke arrangements arose rather naturally. Unless Asian nations make a conscious effort to avoid this, the same is likely to occur in Asia. But who will be the hub? This is where our measure of 'hub-ness' comes in. By helping us to identify likely candidates for hub status, it will help us think about the course of Asian regionalism.

This, of course, presumes that our measure has relevance to the real world. Our first task is therefore to 'test' our hub-ness measure on existing data. In particular, we 'test' the validity of the measure by looking at what it says about an existing hub-and-spoke arrangement. While one may argue about who the hub will be in Asia, there is no question that the US is the hub in the Western Hemisphere. As we shall see, this is in line with what our hub-ness measure suggests. As such, it provides some very weak support for the relevance of our measure.

3.4.2 *Does the HM show the US to be a hub?*

Our proposed measure of hub-ness is simple to calculate since it requires nothing more than bilateral trade data. The results, which consider the hub-ness of the US, Canada, and Mexico, are shown in Figure 3.3.

The main fact that jumps out from the figure is the overwhelming importance of the US market to all the listed western hemisphere nations. This is not in any way new; an observer with even a passing knowledge of world trade flows would expect this. The importance of this result is that provides some weak support for the relevance of our HM index.

DOES THE HM SHOW BRAZIL TO BE A HUB FOR SOUTHERN CONE NATIONS?

US dominance is obvious, but given this dominance, one might argue that virtually any measure would show that the US, and not Canada or Mexico, were the hub. A slightly less obvious test comes by looking at the so-called Southern Cone of South America.

Trade in the Southern Cone is dominated by a regional arrangement called Mercosur—an agreement that started with a bilateral between Argentina and Brazil (Agreement on Argentina-Brazilian Integration, July 29, 1986). This bilateral gradually gathered depth as more sectors were added and bilateral tariffs were cut and triggered a domino effect. In August 1990, Paraguay and Uruguay asked to join, and on March 26, 1991, the Treaty of Asuncion created Mercosur (Portuguese abbreviation for Southern Common Market). The domino effect continued and in the mid-1990s, Chile and Bolivia asked

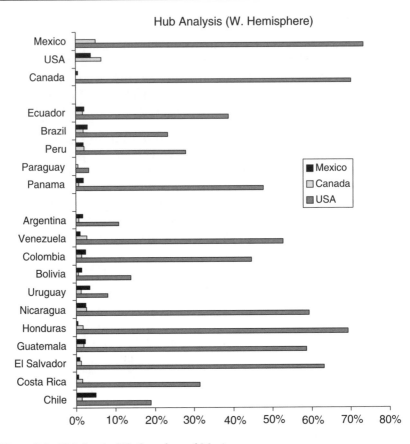

Figure 3.3: HMs for the US, Canada, and Mexico

for FTAs with Mercosur (which was by this time a customs union, at least in theory).

Brazil is widely viewed as the hub in this arrangement, although Brazil itself has made sure that the widening integration did not take a hub-and-spoke form. What does our HM say about Brazil's hub status?

As Figure 3.4 shows, Brazil is, even by itself, a hub to many South American nations, but not for Central American nations. When one takes Brazil and Venezuela together, the HM shows the pair's massive dominance of their neighbours, Bolivia, Uruguay, Paraguay and, less so, Chile.[7]

---

[7] Note that the HMs are based on trade figures from 2002. Since a severe crisis in Venezuela reduced its imports from all sources, the figures would be even more impressive for a more normal year.

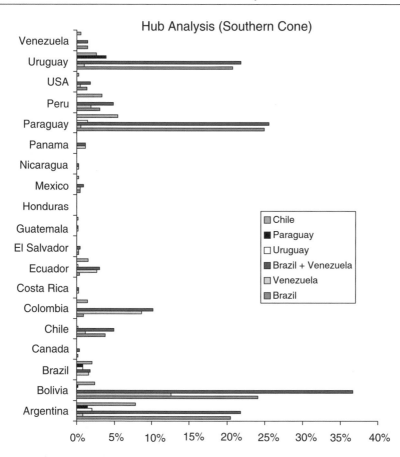

Figure 3.4: HMs for South Cone nations

3.4.3 *Application to East Asia*

What are the numbers for East Asia? The three most likely hubs in East Asia are plainly Japan, China, and Korea, so we start with these.

HUB-NESS OF JAPAN, CHINA AND KOREA

What our results show is the clear dominance of the Japanese market to East Asian nations. On average, Japan has twice the 'hub-ness' of China, and China has twice the hub-ness of Korea (see Figure 3.5). Indeed, for every East Asian nation listed, Japan has an HM that is at least twice that of China (Laos and Cambodia are the exceptions). Interestingly, the HM for China is higher than that for Japan from the Korean perspective.

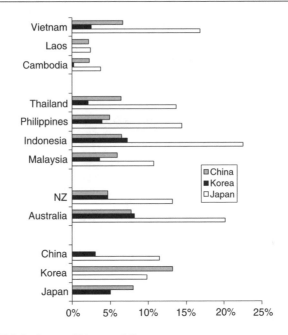

Figure 3.5: HMs for Japan, China, and Korea

It should be noted that the level of the HM in East Asia is nowhere close to that of the US in the Western Hemisphere. Indeed, it is below that of Brazil for many nations.

ASEAN, JKFTA, AND JKCFTA

While hubs are traditionally associated with individual nations, some regional integration agreements make groups of nations into a single hub. For example, the EU is a customs union, so it is not possible to sign an FTA with, for example, only Germany. As a consequence, the markets of the fifteen nations taken together are what matters.

In East Asia the only groupings that are likely, in the near future, are Japan and Korea (depending upon the exact nature of that FTA), or Japan, Korea, and China. ASEAN is a long way from implementing free trade among its members and it is unlikely to be able to negotiate with third nations as a body. For example, one of its main members, Singapore, has proceeded to negotiate a slew of bilateral FTAs on its own. Nevertheless, we present the figures for ASEAN for comparison.

The results show that a JKFTA could be a dominant hub in East Asia even without China. For example, the HM for a JKFTA is over 10 percent for all East Asian nations and over 20 percent for most. Adding China, and presuming

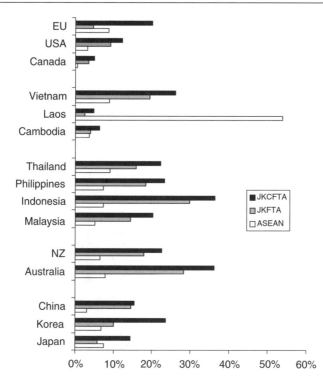

Figure 3.6: HMs for JKFTA, JKCFTA, and ASEAN

that the trio conducted third-party relations in lock step, would create a JKCFTA. The results show that although the HM for this combination is higher, it is not a great deal higher for East Asian nations. The big difference comes for the EU (see Table 3.1 for exact figures).

We turn now to looking at the implications of these numbers for the future of East Asian regionalism.

3.5 Implications for the likely evolution of East Asian regionalism

At the end of 2003, the first hints of the 'wildfire of regionalism' can clearly be seen. No one, however, is in charge. There is no overarching plan for managing it. Judging from the history of unplanned regionalism in other regions, the most likely outcome will be hub-and-spoke regionalism. As Section 3.3 argued, the mercantilist forces that drive nations' trade policies tend to free up major trade routes, leaving minor trade routes un-liberalized. Because bilateral

Richard E. Baldwin

Table 3.1: HMs for Japan, Korea, China, ASEAN, JKFTA, and JKCFTA

	Japan	Korea	China	ASEAN	JKFTA	JKCFTA
Australia	20%	8%	8%	8%	28%	36%
Brunei	44%	13%	4%	13%	56%	60%
Cambodia	4%	0%	2%	4%	4%	6%
Canada	3%	1%	1%	1%	4%	5%
China	11%	3%	0%	3%	15%	15%
EU	2%	2%	15%	9%	5%	20%
HK	2%	1%	1%	1%	2%	4%
Indonesia	22%	7%	7%	7%	30%	36%
Japan	0%	5%	8%	8%	6%	14%
Korea	10%	0%	13%	7%	10%	24%
Laos	2%	0%	2%	54%	3%	5%
Malaysia	11%	4%	6%	5%	14%	20%
NZ	13%	5%	5%	7%	18%	23%
Philippines	14%	4%	5%	7%	18%	23%
Singapore	5%	3%	6%	21%	9%	14%
Thailand	14%	2%	6%	9%	16%	22%
USA	7%	3%	3%	3%	9%	12%
Vietnam	17%	3%	7%	9%	19%	26%

Source: Author's calculations based on IMF DOT data (bilateral trade flows are an average of 2000–2).

trade flows in Asia form a hub-and-spoke pattern, the future pattern of FTAs is likely to follow the same pattern.

BUT WHO WILL BE THE HUB IN EAST ASIA?

The results of the calculations in the previous section suggest that both Japan and China will naturally emerge as hubs.

3.5.1 *East Asian bicycle: two hubs, many spokes*

Tying the hub-ness findings to our political economy reasoning, it seems likely that the pattern of FTAs that will be signed in the next ten years will have two hubs, Japan and China—something like a bicycle (Figure 3.7). Of course, our numerical results are not essential to this prediction; it would also be suggested by a careful examination of the regional trade pattern. The merit of the rough quantification of 'bilateral attractiveness' is that it imposes some discipline on what is usually an unruly analysis. One just cannot think of, say, Singapore or Vietnam, as a hub even if they signed an FTA with every East Asian nation.

Figure 3.7 is a schematic of this prediction for East Asian FTAs. While it does not show all the FTAs (e.g. Singapore has signed many bilateral FTAs), it stylizes the implications of rampant bilateralism. Since ASEAN is

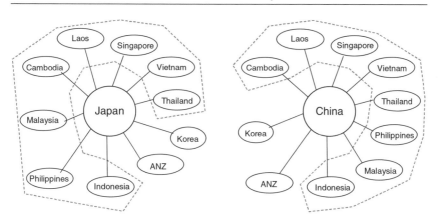

Figure 3.7: A possible FTA pattern: East Asian bicycle

not an effective free trade-area, it is shown as a dashed and irregular shaped line.

PROBLEMS WITH THE BICYCLE

Some readers may interpret Figure 3.7 differently. Indeed, I could have drawn it in a way that makes Japan and China the spokes with every other nation as a hub. This misses an important point. Hub status is about market access. For most industries, domestic market access is important, so it is worth noting the so-called 'border effect' (McCallum 1995). As it turns out, domestic firms have better access to the domestic market than foreign firms do, even when those foreign firms have duty-free access. Consequently, the market access provided to a firm in Korea may be much less than one in Japan or China, even if there are Korean FTAs with both China and Japan, but no Japan–China FTA.

Another problem is that 'law of the jungle' bilateral FTAs between big and small nations naturally tend to reflect the concerns of the big nation much more than those of small nations—after all, market access is the currency in an FTA negotiation, so negotiators from big-market nations can 'buy' more than those from small-market nations. Given this hard fact of bilateralism, a spoke's FTA with China and its separate FTA with Japan is likely to impose conditions that diminish the attractiveness of the spoke market.

While there many, many other possibilities, it seems to me that the two-hub scenario is the most likely for East Asia—unless something is done to prevent it.

That is the topic for the next section.

3.6 Anti-spoke strategies from around the world

The negative aspects of falling into the 'spoke trap' have long been recognized.[8] The natural question then is, 'How can East Asian nations avoid the spoke trap?' A first step towards answering this question is to review the strategies of small nations in other parts of the world.

Europe is the first place to look for effective anti-spoke strategies for the simple reason that Europe has more than a century of experience with discriminatory trade arrangements (German principalities and city-states were cajoled and coerced into joining Prussia's Zollverien between 1819 and 1867). Moreover, the other important precondition for the spoke trap—a very uneven distribution of economic size—is also met in Europe (see Figure 3.8).

CUSTOMS UNION SOLUTION: HOW TO JOIN THE HUB

Without a doubt, the most effective strategy for countering the spoke trap is a customs union. Not only does a customs union allow small nations to avoid the spoke trap, it automatically makes them part of the hub. This is the strategy adopted by the nineteen small, tiny, or miniscule European nations that will be members of the EU by mid-2004. For example, consider a small nation like Denmark, a nation that one might have expected to fall into the spoke trap—signing, for example, FTAs with its major trade partners Germany, France, the UK, and Sweden but not signing FTAs with, e.g., Germany's other partners.

Because Denmark joined the EU in 1975, it did not have the spoke option. All EU members are part of a 'full' customs union, and full customs union members must have, by definition, identical external trade policies. This means Denmark automatically has equal access to all the FTA partners of Germany and France. Or, to put it differently, since Denmark must have the same external trade policy as the natural hubs of Europe (Germany most of all, but also France, Britain, and Italy), Denmark cannot become a spoke in a hub-and-spoke system. Rather, it makes Denmark part of the hub.

CUSTOMS UNION DIFFICULTIES

Generally, customs unions require a level of political integration that very few nations can sustain politically. For example, Denmark has very little control over its own trade policy. For this reason, almost all successful customs unions are dominated by a hegemon (e.g. the South African Customs Union SACU), or involve deep political integration as in the case of the EU.

---

[8] For example, I devoted an entire chapter to them ten years ago in my book (Baldwin 1994).

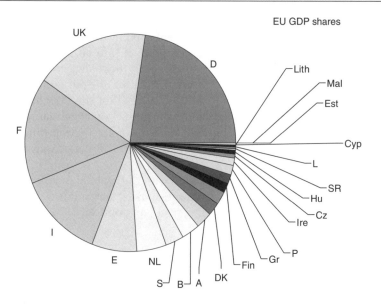

EU GDP shares

Figure 3.8: Size distribution EU GDP shares
Source: Author's calculations.

THE EXAMPLE OF TURKEY

In Europe, for instance, Turkey is in a 'partial' customs union with the EU, i.e. a customs union with respect to industrial goods. When the 1996 EU-Turkey customs union entered into force, Turkey dropped all duties on industrial goods from the EU and set its MFN tariffs to that of the EU's (the EU's MFN tariffs are called the Common External Tariff or CET). Turkey did not immediately adopt the EU's preferential tariffs (i.e. the EU's deviation from its MFN tariff structure), but phased this in progressively. Progress was especially slow for certain 'sensitive' products originating from third countries (e.g. ceramics, cars, and shoes). See Harrison, Rutherford, and Tarr (1996) for details and economic analysis.

This example illustrates an important nuance that is rarely stressed. Adopting a partner's MFN tariff structure is not the same as adopting the partner's external trade policy. One big difference is the partner's preferential tariff schedule; the other—contingent protection—does not concern us here.

A customs union's great advantage over FTAs is that a customs union makes rules of origin unnecessary. Any product that is physically inside the customs union must have paid the common external tariff (CET). Having paid the CET, the product should then be free to circulate among customs union members without having to worry about where it was made. However as far as the EU is concerned, the key is that Turkey's tariffs against third nations are never *lower* than the EU's because this ensures that third-nation exporters will never use Turkey as a tariff-avoiding entry point to the EU market. (The practice of avoiding duties by bringing a product into an FTA through the member with the lowest external tariffs is called 'trade deflection'.) For this reason, Turkey's adoption of the CET is sufficient to rule out tariff fraud and trade deflection. Turkey does not need to adopt all of the EU's preferential rates. However, if Turkey does not adopt all the EU's preferential rates, it is Turkey that runs the risk of tariff fraud, as, for example, cheap third-nation ceramics enter Turkey duty free after first having been imported duty free into Germany.

To summarize, forming a customs union with the regional economic power-house is a small nation's most effective anti-spoke strategy. It is not, however, a strategy that many nations are willing to accept politically. This brings us to the next best strategy.

EFTA's SOLUTION: AN 'FTA UNION' THAT 'SHADOWS' THE HUB

The distinction between a common external policy and a common MFN tariff structure provides another solution to the spoke trap, although one that does not allow the spokes to become hubs. I call this the 'FTA union' solution.

Phase 1: the FTA union

EFTA nations have lived with the spoke problem for three decades—ever since the dominant founding member of EFTA, the UK, left the organization to join the EU in 1975. Britain's joining the EU would have normally required the British to impose the CET against its former EFTA partners. To prevent this, the EU negotiated FTAs with all the non-joining EFTAns (Austria, Switzerland, Norway, Sweden, Finland, and Iceland). Importantly, however, the EFTAns in the 1970s did so in a coordinated manner—the FTAs were negotiated in parallel and the resulting EU–EFTA FTAs are almost identical. This helped them tame the usual law of the jungle where an FTA negotiation between a trade giant like the EU, and a tiny nation, like Norway, ends up as one-sided affair. Taken all together, the EFTAns were the EU's second-largest trading partner. Moreover, the EFTAns continued to maintain strong free-trade links among themselves to avoid economic marginalization.

Roughly speaking, the EFTAns became one big spoke, instead of a half dozen small spokes, due to the intra-EFTA free trade and the harmony across EU-EFTA FTAs.

It is critical to note that this was not the most natural outcome—it required a joint effort on the part of the EFTAns. As I wrote a decade ago, 'Although each EFTAn did most of their trade with the EEC, they managed to avoid the pitfalls of hub-and-spoke bilateralism. In this light, EFTA of the 1970s and early 1980s should not be thought of primarily as a club of countries that trade with each other. EFTA was a group of small countries that had free trade agreements with the EEC and wanted to band together to avoid hub-and-spoke bilateralism' (Baldwin 1994: 19 in the downloadable manuscript version). Plainly, this is a lesson from which many small East Asian nations might learn.

Phase 2: 'shadow' the hub

Throughout its history, the EU has almost continuously signed FTAs. For example, it signed an FTA with Greece in 1959 and one with Spain in 1970. The pace accelerated in the 1990s in part due to the emergence of a dozen new democracies in Central Europe and in part due to the domino effect of the EU's single market programme.

Be that as it may, the EU's predilection for FTAs posed a problem for EFTAn industry and governments. When the EU signed a free-trade agreement with, for example, Poland in the early 1990s, EFTA-based industry was threatened. The EU-Poland bilateral meant that German firms would have duty-free access to the Polish market.[9] Since Swiss, Swedish, and other EFTA-based manufacturers have to compete with German firms in Poland, the EU–Poland bilateral threatened the competitiveness of EFTA-based industry.

To redress this potential discrimination, EFTA followed an explicit policy of shadowing the EU's bilaterals. That is, every time the EU started on a new bilateral with a third nation, EFTA followed with its own bilateral with the same nation.

Near-hub status

Let's think about the implications of the 'shadowing' FTA policy combined with the free trade among EFTAns and between every EFTAn and the EU.

First, observe that the concatenation of the Stockholm Convention (EFTA's founding document that ensured free trade among EFTA members in industrial goods), the Treaty of Rome (EU's founding document that ensures free trade among EU members) and the EU–EFTA FTAs (which ensure free trade in industry goods between every EFTAn and every EU member) created a 'virtual Western European free-trade zone' for industrial goods. And note that this resulted from the efforts of EFTA leaders, not from the leadership of the EU (the EU would have been happy with the EU–EFTA bilaterals). This virtual free industrial trade zone is shown as the outer circle in Figure 3.9.

Second, note that by shadowing the EU's FTA policy as a team, the EFTAns made sure that EU-based manufacturers never had better access to any market. In effect, this allowed EFTAns to attain what might be called 'near hub' status.

---

[9] The deal was an 'Association Agreement', known as a 'Europe Agreement' that was an FTA plus some deeper integration measures. Signed in December 1991, it entered into force only in February 1994.

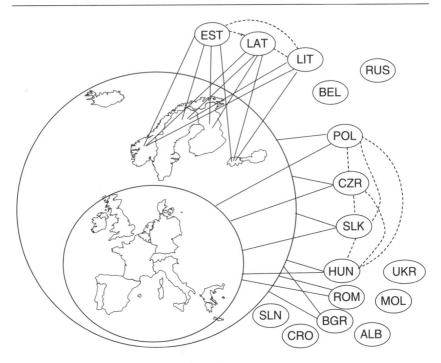

Figure 3.9: EFTA's near-hub status in 1993

Note: EFTA in 1993 consisted of Austria, Switzerland, Liechtenstein, Iceland, Norway, Sweden, and Finland. The dashed lines represent questionably effective FTAs among the Central European nations. Source: Baldwin (1994).

So why is this near-hub rather than hub status?

While near-hub status is good, it is not quite as good as hub status, at least as far as industrial competitiveness is concerned. The main differences require a more nuanced view of FTAs.

At the lowest level of analytical magnification, an FTA is simply bilateral free trade. But looking more closely, it is important to note that FTAs often exclude certain products—in Europe, for instance, the extremely protectionist agricultural policies of EU and EFTA nations mean that the above-mentioned FTAs excluded agriculture. Although the exclusion may in principle work in either direction (hub-based firms might face more or fewer exclusions), the economic size of the EU gives it a negotiating power that far exceeds that of the EFTAns. Consequently, one should not be surprised to see that EFTA firms face more exclusions than do EU firms.[10]

---

[10] Note that one advantage of EFTA lagging the EU FTAs is that the EFTA negotiators can take the EU FTA deal as a starting point for the negotiations.

Also, FTAs involve rules of origin that often have important protectionist content. This aspect tends to disfavour industrial location in the near-hub as opposed to the hub. This disadvantage comes in two ways. First, the relatively greater negotiating strength of the EU means that EU-spoke FTAs are likely to contain rules of origin that are more favourable to EU firms than EFTA-spoke FTAs rules are to EFTA firms. To put this point more colloquially, 'might' makes right in bilateral trade talks and the EU surely uses this 'might' to favour its firms. EFTA surely tries to do the same but with less effect.

Second, rules of origin do not usually cumulate over all the FTAs that a spoke has. For example, many Swiss-manufactured goods use German components, but the Swiss–Estonia FTA (negotiated together with other EFTAns) may not allow the German inputs to count towards Swiss origin even though Estonia also has an FTA with Germany. The general name for this class of distortions is 'cumulation'. Because relatively more EFTA firms rely heavily on EU inputs than EU firms rely on EFTA inputs, the cumulation problem is systematically more severe for firms located in the near-hub.

SINGAPORE: CASHING IN ON UNILATERAL FREE TRADE

Every international economist knows that the optimal trade policy for a small economy is unilateral free trade. This is correct, but it is an incomplete answer. Optimal policy for a small nation is to remove all of its own trade barriers and sign every free-trade agreement it can. After all, once the nation has dropped its own trade barriers, the trade-diverting features of FTAs disappear and all that remains is the possibility of improved access to foreign markets. This is what Singapore is doing.

Another way to think of Singapore's aggressive FTA strategy is as a means of 'cashing in' in terms of market access on the liberalization that it undertook unilaterally. It is less clear what Singapore's partners think they are getting out of the FTAs. On the whole, they have to view an FTA with Singapore as one of those low-costs-low-benefits-so-why-not-do-it type of policies.

Lessons?

One thing that is clear from this discussion is that Singapore's FTA policy is really quite unique. It is something that holds very few important lessons for normal-sized nations and nations with organized domestic resistance to liberalization.

MEXICO'S SOLUTION: AGGRESSIVE PURSUIT OF HUB STATUS

Leaving aside the EU (the perennial RTA champion) and its near-hub shadowers, Mexico is the biggest user of FTAs in the world (see Table 3.2). What

Table 3.2: The world's top twenty FTAers

		FTAs and CU, actual and under negotiation	FTAs and CU, actual
1	European Communities	36	33
2	Iceland	29	23
3	Norway	29	23
4	Liechtenstein	28	22
5	Switzerland	28	22
6	Turkey	21	16
7	Mexico	13	10
8	Bulgaria	13	10
9	Israel	12	12
10	Singapore	12	5
11	Estonia	11	11
12	Slovenia	11	11
13	Chile	11	4
14	Latvia	10	10
15	Lithuania	10	10
16	Croatia	10	8
17	United States	10	3
18	Czech Republic	9	9
19	Slovakia	9	9
20	Macedonia	9	8

Source: WTO (2003).

is Mexico up to? Mexico's first foray into real regionalism came in 1990. Until the 1980s, Mexico pursued protectionist and anti-foreign investment policies, especially *vis-à-vis* its giant neighbor. Its early 1980s debt crisis changed all that. Just like Asia's 1997 crisis, the macro shock precipitated a volte-face on many levels including a complete turn around on its inward-oriented development strategy. Mexico unilaterally cut its tariffs and non-tariff barriers on a non-discriminatory basis, joined the GATT, and signed several bilateral trade accords with the US and Canada. The process culminated with the Mexican President's proposal in June 1990 for an FTA with the US. According to Whalley (1993), Mexican objectives were to improve and lock in access to the US market and to underpin its domestic economic reforms with the aim of attracting foreign direct investment. US President Bush (Senior) rapidly agreed to bilateral talks. US motives had little to do with trade liberalization. The chief US aim was to foster stability in Mexico by boosting growth and locking in unilateral pro-market reforms. At Canada's insistence, the US–Mexico talks were trilateralized and NAFTA was born.

How to become a hub

Once NAFTA had been implemented, Mexico had zero tariffs on three-quarters of all of its imports. Moreover, because the US and Canada have very low MFN tariffs on their non-food, non-clothing imports, free trade with NAFTA is not much different than free trade with the world (with a few spectacular, but low-volume exceptions like steel). What all this means is that Mexico had little to gain from keeping its MFN tariffs on industrial goods. Like Singapore, it had already gutted the protectionist content of its MFN tariffs. Or, more to the point, NAFTA had already eliminated the domestic special interest groups that would normally be expected to resist further liberalization of industrial tariffs. Why not, then, go all the way for unilateral free trade? Or, better yet, why not get something in exchange and become a hub in a hub-and-spoke arrangement with the world's trade giants, the US, the EU, and Japan? This was Mexico's anti-spoke strategy.

While almost 90 percent of Mexico's exports go to NAFTA, Mexico sought FTAs with the EU and Japan. Having managed the EU-Mexico FTA, its exporters of industrial goods find themselves in the happy situation of being able to sell duty free to markets that accounted for 58 percent of world imports in 2002. If they get the Japanese FTA too, the figure will rise to 63 percent. In a nutshell, Mexico has become a hub (although obviously the above-mentioned importance of domestic market size still matters). It did this by aggressively pursuing FTAs with the world's largest importers, regardless of Mexico's rather meagre mercantilist interest in those markets.

Additionally, Mexico signed free-trade agreements with its poor and economically small neighbours, including Honduras, Costa Rica, Columbia, Venezuela, and many more. Since very little trade is covered by these bilaterals, one must assume that south–south politics rather than mercantile interest was the driving force. Indeed, Mexico has become the clear leader in Central America when it comes to trade relations. Like the EU, Mexico has adopted an all-FTAs-are-good attitude towards FTAs—what I call 'open FTAism'. And these Latin American FTAs do help the other nations avoid discrimination in the Mexican markets. Of course, open-FTAism is one key component in the forces that tend to foster hub-and-spoke bilateralism.

This FTA strategy has worked marvelously. Mexican exports have quadrupled since 1990 with all of the growth accounted for by its non-oil exports. It has also doubled its inflow of foreign direct investment, and, although it suffered a macro shock in 2001, its foreign debt has come down steadily and is now less than a third of what it was in 1990.

Korea as the Asian Mexico?

It is not hard to imagine Korea emulating the Mexican strategy—signing an FTA with Japan and then China and the EU in an attempt to become a hub. This could be followed by an open-FTAism that is likely to produce a slew of bilaterals with East Asia's many small nations. This may be more problematic for Korea than it was for Mexico. Mexico's strategy worked exactly because it was so dependent on the US for both its imports and exports. After the US–Mexico FTA, the rest was easy. Korea's trade pattern is much more diversified. Taken together, the Japan–Korea and China–Korea FTAs would cover only a quarter of Korean exports. Adding an EU–Korea FTA would boost the figure 38 percent, but it would need a US–Korea FTA to win duty-free status for over 60 percent of its exports, at least using 2002 trade shares.

3.7 Anti-spoke strategy for East Asian: A proposal

A Japan–Korea FTA (JKFTA) is likely to spark a wildfire of regionalism in East Asia. This is likely to create a web of hub-and-spoke bilateralism that will not be favorable for the region.

The best way to avoid this would be for the JKFTA to be a customs union with Japan and Korea agreeing in advance to allow any East Asian nation to join. While economically optimal, such a scheme is politically infeasible.

3.7.1 *Plan A: An East Asian Free-Trade Union*

The next best option would be for Japan and Korea to form a sort of 'Asian EFTA', an association or union of nations that provide duty-free treatment to each others' industrial exports. As pointed out above, this combination of two of the three largest economies in the region would create powerful forces for inclusion. Under this proposal, part of the JKFTA would be to establish procedures and an institutional framework that would allow other East Asian nations to join the Union, with China being at the head of the queue— indeed, Japan and Korea should probably consult with China to ensure that the new union was non-threatening to their north-east Asian neighbor. Under this scheme, each new member would automatically provide duty-free treatment to the industrial exports of all incumbent members in exchange for gaining duty-free access to all Union markets. Special rules to allow unilateral tariff concessions to least developed nations should also be considered (i.e. a Union-wide GSP policy that would operate like the US's Caribbean Basin Initiative).

The advantages of this Union of East Asian Free Trade are many. This plan would:

- prevent, or at least greatly reduce, the likelihood that hub-and-spoke bilateralism would emerge in Asia; this would be especially beneficial to small East Asian nations that might otherwise fall into the spoke trap.
- avoid the 'noodle bowl' problem (the Asian version of the spaghetti bowl) of a tangle of FTAs, thus making the region as a whole more FDI friendly.

- bring coherence to rules of origin (ROOs) in the region, since the Union would establish principles for the ROOs (e.g. limit them to involving either value-added rules, or change of tariff lines).

- create 'conditionally open regionalism' in East Asia, which would result in many of the efficiency aspects of Open Regionalism (Bergsten 1996) while still harnessing the critical political forces that are generated by reciprocal trade liberalization.

- Since Japan and Korea are developed nation WTO members, the Union would obey Article 24 disciplines. This would make the Union's market more attractive as a platform for production and as a market for third-nation exporters and foreign direct investment (since there would be one set of trade rules, not $n(n-1)$ bilateral FTAs for third-nation exporters to deal with). This discipline would also make the Union less threatening to third nations.

- Since Japanese MFN tariffs are very low, and Korean MFN tariffs are relatively low, membership in the Union would expose Union members to something close to world market prices. This has two merits:

- It greatly reduces the scope for inefficient switches from low-cost non-member suppliers to high-cost member suppliers (trade diversion)

- It means that joining the Union would almost surely foster further liberalization, as in the case of Mexico (see reasoning in Section 3.6).

3.7.2 Plan B: An FTA union

Japan and Korea may not be ready for the degree of institutionalization of regional trade implied by Plan A, so here is a less ambitious scheme that also avoids hub-and-spoke bilateralism.

As part of the JKFTA, the two nations would agree to tightly coordinate their FTA policies with other East Asian nations.

(1) All future FTAs between Japan and Korea on the one hand and other Asian nations on the other would be required to include accumulation in rules of origin. This would go a long way to reducing the noodle bowl problem.

(2) Japan and Korea would agree in advance that they would proceed on future FTAs in tandem.

(3) A stronger form of this would require that all future FTAs between Japan and Korea on the one hand and other Asia nations on the other would be 'multilateralized', i.e. if China and Indonesia want FTAs with Japan and Korea, then China and Indonesia should also sign an FTA between them.

While this might slow the pace of EA regionalism in the short term, it would result in a better long-run outcome.

3.8 Concluding Remarks

While the East Asian 'wildfire' of regionalism has not yet started, smoke is in the air and flames are likely to burst out very soon. The world should be concerned that there is no plan for managing regionalism in this critically important region. This chapter has presented an analysis that suggests that a two-hub arrangement of hub-and-spoke bilateralism is a likely outcome unless regional leaders take explicit action to prevent this divisive situation. It has also put forth two proposals to redress the problem, proposals that would allow East Asia to avoid the spoke trap.

References

Albertin, G. (2001), 'Will Regional Blocs Expand?' LSE (mimeo).

Artis, M. and Nixson, F. (2001), *The Economics of the European Union* (Oxford: Oxford University Press).

Augier, P., Gasiorek, Michael, and Lai Tong, Charles (2005), 'The Impact of Rules of Origin on Trade Flows' *Economic Policy*, 43 (July): 567–624.

Balassa, B. (1974), 'Trade Creation and Trade Diversion to the European Common Market', in B. Balassa (ed.), *European Economic Integration*, Amsterdam: North-Holland.

Baldwin, Forslid, Martin, Ottaviano, and Robert-Nicoud, Frederic (2003), *Economic Geography and Public Policy*, London: Princeton University Press.

Baldwin, Richard E. (1993), 'A Domino Theory of Regionalism', NBER WP 4465 (Cambridge). Published as: Richard E. Baldwin (1995), 'The Domino Theory of Regionalism,' in R. Baldwin, P. Haaparanta, and J. Kiander (eds.), *Expanding Membership of the European Union* (Cambridge: Cambridge University Press): 166–88.

____ (1994), *Towards an Integrated Europe*, CEPR, London. Manuscript freely downloadable from < http://heiwww.unige.ch/~baldwin/>.

____ (1997), 'The Causes of Regionalism,' *The World Economy*, 20(7): 865–88.

____ (2002), 'Asian Regionalism: Promises and Pitfalls.' Paper presented at KIEP Seminar on East Asia Free Trade Agreement, held in Seoul, Korea, September, 27 2002.

____ Forslid, Rikard, and Haaland, Jan (1996), 'Investment Creation and Diversion in Europe,' *The World Economy*, 19(6): 635–59.

____ and A. Venables (1995), 'Regional Economic Integration,' in *Handbook of International Economics*: Volume III, G. Grossman and K. Rogoff (eds.), North-Holland, Amsterdam: 1597–1644.

____ and Wyplosz, C. (2003), *The Economics of European Integration*, London: McGraw-Hill.

Bergsten, F. (1996a), *Competitive Liberalisation and Global Free Trade: A Vision for the Early 21st Century*, (Washington, DC: Institute for International Economics).

—— (1996*b*), 'Open Regionalism' (Washington, DC: Institute for International Economics).

Bhagwati, J. (1993), 'Regionalism and Multilateralism: An Overview,' in K. Anderson, and R. Blackhurst (eds.), Regional Integration and the Global Trading System (London: Harvester-Wheatsheaf): 22–57.

—— and A. Krueger (1995), *The Dangerous Drift to Preferential Trade Agreements* (Washington, DC: American Enterprise Institute).

Blomstrom, M. and Kokko, A. (1997), 'Regional Integration and Foreign Direct Investment', CEPR DP 1659 (London).

Brander, J. and Krugman, P. (1983), 'A Reciprocal Dumping Model of International Trade,' *Journal of International Economics*, 15: 313–21.

Cable, V. (1994), 'Overview', in V. Cable and Henderson, D. (1994), *Trade Blocs? The Future of Regional Integration* (London: Royal Institute of International Affairs).

Council of Economic Advisors (1991), *Economic Report of the President* (Washington, DC: Council of Economic Advisors).

CEPR (1992), *Is Bigger Better? The Economics of EC Enlargement* (London: CEPR).

Commonwealth Secretariat (1995), 'Impact of Uruguay Round and Nafta on Commonwealth Caribbean Countries' (London).

Cooper, C. and Massell, D. (1965), 'Towards a General Theory of Customs Unions in Developing Countries,' *Journal of Political Economy*, 73 (October): 461–76.

Davis, D. and Weinstein, D. (2002), 'Market Access, Economic Geography and Comparative Advantage: An Empirical Assessment,' *Journal of International Economics*, 59(1): 1–23.

De Melo, J. and Panagariya, A. (1993), 'Introduction,' in J. De Melo and A. Panagariya (eds.), *New Dimensions in Regional Integration* (Cambridge: Cambridge University Press for CEPR): 3–21.

De Torre, A. and Kelly, M. (1992), 'Regional Trade Arrangements,' IMF Occasional Papers, No. 93 (Washington).

Das, D. K. (2005), 'Market-Driven Regionalization in Asia,' *Global Economy Journal*, 5(3): Article 2.

Dixit, A., Grossman, G. and Helpman, E. (1997), 'Common Agency and Coordination: General theory and Application to Government Policy Making,' *Journal of Political Economy*, 105(4): 752–70.

Either, W. (1996), 'Multilateral Roads to Regionalism,' CIES DP (University of Adelaide).

Fernandez, R. (1997), 'Returns to Regionalism: An Evaluation of Non-Traditional Gains from RTAs,' CEPR DP 1634 (London).

Freund, C. (1998), 'Regionalism and Permanent Diversion', Board of Governors of the Federal Reserve System International Finance Discussion Paper Number 602.

Fujita, M., Krugman, P., and Venables, A. (1999), *The Spatial Economy: Cities, Regions and International Trade* (Cambridge, MA: MIT Press).

Galal, A. and Hoekman, B. (1997), *Regional Partners in Global Markets: Limits and Possibilities in the Euro-Med Agreements* (London: CEPR).

GATT (1993), GATT/1596, Press Communiqué, 16 September (Geneva).

Grossman, G. M. and Helpman, E. (1996), 'Rent Dissipation, Free Riding and Trade Policy,' *European Economic Review*, 40: 795–803.

Harrison, G., Rutherford, T., and Tarr, D. (1996), 'The Economic Implications for Turkey of a Customs Union with the EU,' Policy Research Paper, 1599, World Bank. <http://econ.worldbank.org/files/589_wps1599.pdf>.

Hillman, A. (1982), 'Declining Industries and Political-Support Protectionist Motives,' *American Economic Review*, 72(5): 1180–7.

____ (1989), *The Political Economy of Protection* (London: Harwood Academic Publishers).

Hufbauer, H. and Schott, J. (1992), *North American Free Trade: Issues and Recommendations* (Washington, DC: Institute for International Economics).

____ ____ (1993), *NAFTA: An Assessment* (Washington, DC: Institute for International Economics).

____ ____ and Clark, D. (1994), *Western Hemisphere Economic Integration* (Washington, DC: Institute for International Economics).

JETRO (2003), *Current Status of AFTA and Corporate Responses*. November. JETRO: Japan. <http://www.jetrobkk.or.th/japanese/pdf/3.10.3.pdf>.

Kemp, M. and Wan, H. (1976), 'An Elementary Proposition Concerning the Formation of Customs Unions,' *Journal of International Economics*, 6(1): 95–7.

Kowalcyz, C. and Wonnacott, R. (1992), 'Hubs and Spokes, and Free Trade in the Americas,' NBER WP 4198.

Krishna, K. (2003), 'Understanding Rules of Origin,' Pennsylvania State University mimeo.

____ and Krueger, A. (1995), 'Implementing Free Trade Areas: Rules of Origin and Hidden Protection,' NBER WP4983.

Krishna, P. (1998), 'Regionalism and Multilateralism: A Political Economy Approach,' *Quarterly Journal of Economics*, 113(1): 227–51.

Krueger, A. (1993), 'Free Trade Agreements as Protectionist Devices: Rules of Origin,' NBER WP 4352.

Krugman, Paul (1980), 'Scale Economies, Product Differentiation, and the Pattern of Trade,' *American Economic Review*, 70: 950–9.

Krugman, Paul (1993a), 'The Hub Effect: or Threeness in Interregional Trade,' in W. Ethier, E. Helpman, and J. Neary (eds.), Theory, Policy and Dynamics in International Trade (Cambridge: Cambridge University Press).

____ (1993b), 'Regionalism Versus Multilateralism: Analytic Notes,' in J. De Melo and A. Panagariya (eds.), *New Dimensions in Regional Integration* (Cambridge: Cambridge University Press for CEPR).

Lawrence, R. (1996), *Regionalism, Multilateralism and Deeper Integration* (Washington, DC: Brookings Institute).

Levy, P. (1997), 'A Political-Economic Analysis of Free-Trade Agreements,' *American Economic Review*, 87(4): 506–19.

Mankiw, G. (2000), *Principles of Economics* New York: Thomson Learning.

Martin, P. and Ottaviano, G. (1996), 'The Geography of Multi-Speed Europe,' *Economie Internationale*, 67:45–65. In English: CEPR discussion paper 1292.

McCallum, John (1995), 'National Borders Matter: Canada–U.S. Regional Trade Patterns,' *American Economic Review*, 85: 615–23.

Meade, James (1955), *The Theory of Customs Unions* (Oxford: Oxford University Press).

Panagariya, A. (1996), 'APEC and the United States,' CIES DP (University of Adelaide).

—— (1999), 'Preferential Trade Liberalisation: The Traditional Theory and New Developments,' University of Maryland mimeo. (Available online at <http://www.bsos. umd.edu/econ/panagariya/song/surveypt.pdf>.

Puga, Diego and Venables, A. (1997), 'Preferential Trading Arrangements and Industrial Location,' *Journal of International Economics*, 43: 347–68.

Robert-Nicoud, F. (2001), 'A Simple Model of Agglomeration with Vertical Linkages and Capital Mobility,' LSE (mimeo).

Sapir, A. (1992), 'Regional integration in Europe,' *Economic Journal*, 102: 1491–506.

—— (1997), 'Domino Effects in Western European Trade, 1960–1992,' CEPR DP.

Schott, J. (1988), 'The Free Trade Agreement: A US Assessment,' in J. Schott and M. Smith (eds.), *The Canada–US Free Trade Agreement: The Global Impact* (Washington, DC: Institute for International Economics): 1–35.

Schott, J. (1989), 'More free trade areas?' in J. Schott (ed.), *Free Trade Areas and US Trade Policy* (Washington, DC: Institute for International Economics): 1–58.

Schott, J. and Hufbauer, G. (1992), 'NAFTA: Questions of form and Substance,' in L. Waverman, (ed.), Negotiating and Implementing a North American Free Trade Agreement (Vancouver: The Fraser Institute): 66–72.

Serra, J. *et al.* (1997), *Reflections on Regionalism: Report of the Study Group on International Trade* (New York: Carnegie Endowment for International Peace).

Shujiro, Urata (2004), 'The Shift from 'Market-led' to 'Institution-led' Regional Economic Integration in East Asia in the late 1990s,' RIETI Discussion Paper 04-E-012.

Smith, M. (1988), 'The Free Trade Agreement in Context: A Canadian Perspective,' in *The Canada–United States Free Trade Agreement: The Global Impact* (Washington, DC: Institute for International Economics).

Summers, L. (1991), 'Regionalism and the World Trading System,' in L. Summers (ed.), *Policy Implications of Trade and Currency Zones*, Federal Reserve Bank of Kansas City.

Urata, S. (2004), 'The Shift from Market-led to Institution-led Regional Economic Integration,' RIETI Discussion papers 04-E-012.

USTR (1981), *North American Trade Agreements* (Washington, DC: Office of the US Trade Representative).

Viner, J. (1950), *The Customs Union Issue* (New York: Carnegie Endowment for International Peace).

Whalley, J. (1993), 'Regional Trade Arrangements in North America: CUSTA and NAFTA,' in J. De Melo and A. Panagariya (eds.), *New Dimensions in Regional Integration* (Cambridge: Cambridge University Press for CEPR): 352–87.

Whalley, J. (1996), 'Why do Countries Seek Regional Trade Agreements?,' NBER WP 5552 (Cambridge, MA).

Winters, A. (1996), 'Regionalism versus multilateralism,' World Bank Policy Research Working Paper 1687 (Washington, DC).

Wolf, M. (1994), *The Resistable Appeal of Fortress Europe* (Washington, DC: American Enterprise Institute).

Wonnacott, P. (1987), *The United States and Canada: The Quest for Free Trade* (Washington, DC: Institute for International Economics).

Wonnacott, R. (1990), 'U.S. Hub-and-Spoke Bilaterals and the Multilateral Trading System,' *C. D. Howe Institute Commentary* 23 (October): 1–22.

WTO (1995), Regionalism and the world trading system (Geneva: WTO Secretariat).

WTO (2003), 'The Changing Landscape of RTAs', Regional Trade Agreements Section of the Trade Policies Review Division, WTO Secretariat; paper prepared for November 14, 2003 seminar in Geneva.

Yeats, S. (1997), 'Does Mercosur's trade performance raise concerns about the effects of regional trade arrangements' World Bank Policy Research WP 1729 (Washington).

Yi, S. (1996), 'Endogenous Formation of Customs Unions Under Imperfect Competition: Open Regionalism is Good,' *Journal of International Economics*, 41: 151–75.

4

The Proliferation of FTAs and Prospects for Trade Liberalization in East Asia

Yung Chul Park
Seoul National University
Inkyo Cheong
Inha University, Korea

4.1 Introduction

There has been concerted movement toward freer trade in East Asia since the early 1990s. Individual countries have achieved a great deal in reducing tariffs and lowering non-tariff barriers (see, e.g., Berg and Krueger 2003). In parallel with domestic trade liberalization, East Asian countries have mounted collective efforts for region-wide free trade. In 1993, ASEAN states agreed to establish an ASEAN free-trade area (AFTA). Since then, they managed to reduce tariffs to a maximum of 5 percent among the original six members and brought four new members into AFTA in 2003. In 1995, APEC leaders proposed a plan for bringing about free trade in the Asia and Pacific region by 2020 in what is known as the Bogo Declaration.

Trade liberalization in individual countries as well as the regional movement for economic integration has contributed to a large increase in intraregional trade in East Asia. In terms of imports, intra-regional trade (ASEAN+3 and Taiwan) accounted for 46 percent of the region's total trade in 2001, when the entire region was still recovering from the crisis, up from 36 percent about a decade earlier. There is every indication that this trend will continue.

The most notable development in the process of trade integration has been the economic ascent of China: it has replaced the US as the most important destination of exports of all East Asian countries. Unlike other large countries, China exports a large share of its output. In recent years, its exports as a share of GDP have risen to almost 25 percent of GDP, twice the average share of other large countries. China has followed an export-led growth strategy but unlike other East Asian countries, its demand for imported raw materials and other intermediate and final goods is expected grow as fast as its exports. Assuming China is able to sustain its current rate of growth, it will be the growth engine for intra-regional trade in East Asia and reduce dependence on the US market.

In recent years, the APEC movement for region-wide free trade has lost its momentum and given way to a proliferation of bilateral free-trade agreements (FTAs). ASEAN has been negotiating or discussing a number of bilateral FTAs with other Asian countries including China, Japan, and Korea and also with the US and India from outside the region. Of the ASEAN states, Singapore has been the most aggressive, as it is prepared to talk to just about anyone willing to negotiate an FTA. The members of ASEAN+3 have concluded or have been negotiating or discussing altogether about forty FTAs with one another and with parties from outside of the region. When all the negotiations for these FTAs are completed, then East Asia will have constructed a thick web or a network of FTAs. What does this FTA development portend for trade liberalization in East Asia?

If China and Japan succeed in concluding their negotiations with neighboring East Asian countries for bilateral FTAs, they may emerge as hubs of FTAs (see the immediately preceding chapter by Richard Baldwin). Although China and Japan may be natural hubs, ASEAN has been at the center of the bilateral FTA movement. Indeed, ASEAN has been the most sought-after partner for bilateral FTAs to China Japan, Korea, the US, and India. ASEAN knows very well that it could easily be marginalized as a spoke in either China or Japan's network of bilateral FTAs. In order to avoid this marginalization and to gain access to other export markets, ASEAN has been seeking FTA partners from outside of the region including the US, India, Australia, and New Zealand.

The purpose of this chapter is to analyze the causes and possible consequences of proliferation of bilateral FTAs. In contrast to the preceding chapter by Richard Baldwin, whose compass is broader, we focus here specifically on the case of East Asia. We attempt to find clues to whether the bilateral FTAs in East Asia that are completed or under discussion could be building or stumbling blocks for regional as well as global trade integration. Section 4.2 discusses some of the factors behind the increase in bilateral FTAs. Section 4.3 is devoted to an analysis of economic effects of the proliferation of FTAs. Section 4.4 examines the quality of East Asia's FTAs in terms of the coverage of tariff elimination and rules of origin. This analysis is expected to help predict whether East Asian countries will end up creating a convoluted spaghetti bowl, hub-and-spoke system of bilateral FTAs or a single regional FTA in the end as they are entering into negotiations for a multiple of overlapping bilateral FTAs. Section 4.5 discusses consequences of the proliferation of FTAs in East Asia. This section concludes that for a number of institutional constraints, the proliferation is not likely to lead to the creation of a single East Asian FTA. Concluding remarks are in a final section.

4.2 FTAs in East Asia

4.2.1 *Recent Developments*

As shown in Table 4.1, the thirteen members of ASEAN+3 concluded twenty-two FTAs and have been under negotiation or discussion for another nineteen FTAs. Until recently, East Asia was not active in the formation of regional trade agreements (RTAs), which include FTAs and customs unions.[1] Indeed, the ASEAN Free Trade Area (AFTA) was the only major FTA until Japan and Singapore enacted the JSEPA in 2002. AFTA was established in 1992 with the six ASEAN member countries: Indonesia, Malaysia, the Philippines, Singapore, Thailand, and Brunei. The new ASEAN members—Cambodia, Laos, Myanmar, and Vietnam—joined AFTA in the latter half of the 1990s.

Among the East Asian economies, both ASEAN and its individual members have taken a great deal of interest in negotiating FTAs with countries within and from outside of the region since 2002. The FTA involving ASEAN that has received most attention is the one with China. ASEAN agreed to begin FTA negotiations with both Japan and Korea in 2005. Several ASEAN members have sought to establish bilateral FTAs independently of ASEAN's umbrella FTA negotiations. Singapore enacted or signed several FTAs with New Zealand, Japan, Australia, the US, the EFTA, and Korea. It has also been negotiating with India. Thailand, the Philippines and Malaysia concluded bilateral FTAs with Japan in 2005. Indonesia is expected to do the same with Japan in the near future.

Japan has so far concluded negotiations for five FTAs with ASEAN members and Mexico. Not to be outdone by Japan, China has been equally active in courting other Asian countries for bilateral FTAs. On November 4, 2002, China and ASEAN agreed on a framework to set up a large free-trade area that would have a total GDP of nearly $2 trillion. Since then they have been negotiating an FTA on trade in service and investment. At a

[1] In the GATT/WTO, regional trade agreements (RTAs), which violate one of its basic principles of non-discrimination, are permitted under GATT Article XXIV with several conditions, which include liberalization of substantially all the trade of the members, not increasing trade barriers on non-members, and completing the RTA process within ten years. For developing countries, more lenient conditions are applied under the enabling clause. An FTA is considered to be a shallow form of regional integration, because it only removes tariff and non-tariff barriers among the members, while a customs union is a deeper integration, as it adopts common external tariffs on non-members in addition to the removal of tariff and non-tariff barriers on trade among the members.

Table 4.1: Progress of major FTAs in East Asia (2005)

FTA	Stages of Evolution				
	Discussion	Joint study	Negotiation	Signed (year)	Implementation (year)
ASEAN					
ASEAN FTA					X (1993)
ASEAN–China (CEC)					X (2005)
ASEAN–Japan (CEP)			X		
ASEAN–India				X (2005)	
ASEAN + 3		X			
ASEAN–Korea				X (2005)	
ASEAN–CER		X			
Japan					
Japan–Singapore					X (2003)
Japan–Mexico					X (2004)
Japan–Malaysia				X (2005)	
Japan–Korea			X		
Japan–Philippines				X (2005)	
Japan–Thailand				X (2005)	
Japan–Chile		X			
Japan–India		X			
Korea					
Korea–Chile					X (2004)
Korea–Japan			X		
Korea–Mexico			X		
Korea–China	X				
Korea–Singapore				X (2005)	
Korea–Canada			X		
Korea–US	X				
Korea–EFTA				X (2005)	
Korea–MERCOSUR		X			
Korea–India		X			
China					
China–Hongkong					X (2004)
China–Macao					X (2004)
China–Australia			X		
China–Brazil		X			
China–Chile				X (2005)	
China–GCC		X			
China–Thailand			X		
Singapore					
Singapore–Australia					X (2003)
Singapore–New Zealand					X (2002)
Singapore–US		Signed TIFA with the US			X (2004)
Singapore–EFTA					X (2003)
Singapore–Canada					X (2004)
Thailand					
Thailand–China				X	
Thailand–Australia					X (2005)
Thailand–US	Signed TIFA with the US		X		
Thailand–Japan				X	
Thailand–India					X (2004)

Note: CER–FTA between Australia and New Zealand, GCC–Gulf Cooperation Council, MERCOSUR–South American Customs Union.

Source: Complied from various sources.

Northeast Asian summit meeting at the ASEAN+3 summit talks in November 2003, China proposed a study on a three-way free-trade agreement involving China, Japan, and Korea. It has also indicated its interest in a China-Korea FTA. China's eagerness for forging free-trade ties with ASEAN, where Japan has invested heavily for the past four decades, may turn the region into an economic battleground between the two countries.

At the Leaders Summit Meeting of ASEAN+3 in 1998, East Asian leaders agreed to create the East Asia Vision Group (EAVG), and East Asian Study Group (EASG) two years later. The mandate of the EAVG, which was composed of private sector experts, was to develop a long-term vision for economic cooperation in East Asia. The EAVG presented the leaders with its recommendations in 2001, which included establishment of an East Asia FTA (EAVG 2001). The EASG, consisting of government officials, concurred with the EAVG recommendation by acknowledging the potential role an East Asia FTA could play liberalizing trade and FDI in East Asia.

The recommendation for an East Asian FTA has not seen the light, however. East Asian leaders have been reluctant to initiate negotiations for an East Asian FTA, as they are faced with strong opposition from non-competitive sectors of their economies. More importantly, no country has been willing and able to provide the leadership needed for creating the FTA. However, the activities of the EAVG and EASG were followed up by establishing a 'Network of East Asian Think-Tanks (NEAT)' in 2003, which is supported by ASEAN+3. NEAT's meetings were held in 2003 and 2004 to discuss issues related to forming an East Asian Community, of which an East Asia FTA is an important component.

It should be noted that many of the FTAs discussed in this study cover not only trade liberalization but various types of economic cooperation. As such, some of the FTAs established in East Asia are termed as Economic Partnership Agreement (Japan–Singapore Economic Partnership Arrangement (EPA)), or Closer Economic Partnership Arrangement (China–Hong Kong CEPA). These new types of FTAs typically include the facilitation of foreign trade, liberalization and facilitation of foreign direct investment (FDI), and economic and technical cooperation, in addition to trade liberalization. It may be worth noting that the basic philosophy of these new types of FTAs is similar to that of the Asia Pacific Economic Cooperation (APEC) forum, whose three pillars are (1) liberalization, (2) facilitation of foreign trade and foreign investment, and (3) economic and technical cooperation.

4.2.2 Factors behind the Proliferation of FTAs in East Asia

There are a number of developments that have led to an upsurge in the number of FTAs in East Asia. Some of them are common to all East Asian economies whereas others are country-specific. One of the common developments has been the proliferation of FTAs in other parts of the world. By the mid-1990s the world's leading economies except those in East Asia had become members of FTAs. Indeed, both of the world's two largest economic regions—North America and Western Europe—formed FTAs. As a result of this FTA development, East Asian countries began to realize that they were being discriminated against in foreign markets. To overcome this disadvantage and secure markets for their exports, East Asian economies turned to forming their own FTAs beginning in 2002.

Another factor has been the slow progress in multilateral trade liberalization under the WTO. Despite years of multilateral efforts, trade liberalization under the WTO has become increasingly difficult and slow. With the increase in the number of WTO members, there has been a growing divergence of views on the pace and the extent of trade liberalization. The increasing difficulty of reaching consensus on trade issues delayed the start of a new round after the Uruguay Round. Although agreement was reached in Doha to launch a new round, it failed to initiate substantive negotiations. It was only in July 2004 that the modality for negotiations was more or less agreed. Faced with the difficulty in managing trade liberalization on a global scale, many countries opted to form FTAs with like-minded countries to open their trade regimes.

It should also be noted that the GATT/WTO rules could not adequately deal with newly emerging international economic activities such as FDI, trade in services, and labor mobility. Liberalization of border measures such as tariffs, which are the main focus of the GATT/WTO, is not adequate in providing a level playing field to both domestic and foreign firms. It is necessary to go deeper beyond border measures and establish rules governing domestic markets such as competition policy, which the GATT/WTO cannot provide.

A third development is that Japan and other East Asian economies have sought to rely on the external pressure FTAs can generate as a means of promoting deregulation and structural reform. Since the 1997–8 Asian financial crisis, domestic economic reforms in East Asian economies have slowed. In these economies, FTAs are viewed as providing an opportunity to break out of this stalemate. In the past Japan had made use of international frameworks such as GATT and OECD and external pressure (especially from the United States) to reform its industries, institutions, and policies through trade liberalization. Indeed, structural reform contributed significantly in improving the competitiveness of Japan's manufacturing sector. However, in the latter half of the 1990s, liberalization was getting more difficult under the WTO framework because of the slow progress in trade liberalization. Faced with a lack of external pressure, notably from the WTO's multilateral trade negotiations, Japan became interested in FTAs as a policy option to promote structural reform. Japan came to view FTAs in a positive light because it found that the EU and NAFTA were instrumental to structural reforms in the member countries.

Finally, there has been rivalry between China and Japan for economic and political leadership in East Asia. China and Japan use FTAs as a means of conducting regional policy, in particular for protecting their economic and security interests and influence in Southeast Asia. This strategy has made them choose to strengthen their relationships with other East Asian countries through FTAs. ASEAN and South Korea themselves have also come to use FTAs as a vehicle of maintaining their economic influences in East Asia.

4.3 Economic Effects of FTAs

In analyzing impacts of FTAs, two types of CGE models are used.[2] One is the GTAP model, and the other is the Michigan model. The GTAP model has been modified to incorporate a variety of features such as international capital mobility and investment dynamics. The Michigan model incorporates scale economies and imperfect competition.

According to Schiff and Winters (2003), for FTAs involving developing countries, trade creation is substantial while trade diversion is either non-existent or small. In contrast, for FTAs involving developed countries such as the EU and the EFTA, trade diversion is sizeable. They attribute this difference to the differences in their trade policies *vis-à-vis* non-FTA members: with regard to non-FTA members, developing countries substantially liberalize their trade regimes after joining FTAs, whereas developed countries do not as their protection levels are lower to begin with. Schiff and Winters (2003) interpret the results of developing countries as implying that it was non-discriminatory trade liberalization rather than the FTA itself that contributed to trade expansion.

Schiff and Winters (2003) also conduct simulation analyses using computable general equilibrium models to show that there are potential dynamic gains from FTAs. They caution, however, that gains cannot be expected automatically from tariff reduction alone and that it is important to lower

---

[2] It should be noted that CGE models, as other models, suffer from shortcomings, necessitating caution in interpreting the results. Specification of behavioral relationships is very simple, possibly missing intricate but important relationships. Parameters used in the model are generally not obtained from actual observations but based on educated guesses. Sectoral aggregation is rather broad, masking detailed variations. These problems in CGE models do not condemn such models, but they imply caveats.

barriers of entry to the market through measures such as FDI liberalization to increase the benefit from joining an FTA.

Scollay and Gibert (2001) obtain positive impacts on world trade for all FTAs they examine (twenty-nine combinations of different members) using a GTAP model, indicating that trade creation associated with FTAs is greater than trade diversion. They also find that the volume of trade of non-members declines as a result of FTAs, implying that there is bloc discrimination against non-members. For an ASEAN+3 FTA, they find that the export value of the members increases by 20.34 percent, while that of non-members declines by 0.65 percent, resulting in an increase in total world export value by 4.14 percent. According to the authors, the larger FTAs in terms of membership would lead to a larger increase in global trade: global trade liberalization would increase world export values by as much as 23.23 percent.

Table 4.2 shows the results of three CGE model simulations. Urata and Kiyota (2003) apply of a GTAP model with perfect competition and constant returns to scale, while Kawasaki (2003) incorporates 'dynamic' effects including capital accumulation and the increase in productivity resulting from trade liberalization. In addition, Kawasaki (2003) allows international capital movement. Kiyota (2004) uses the Michigan model. According to the three studies, emerging economies in Southeast Asia and China gain a great

Table 4.2: Impacts of FTAs on GDP (%)

FTA members	East Asia[1]	East Asia[2]	East Asia + Australia/New Zealand[3]
	Urata–Kiyota	Kawasaki	Kiyota
Australia/New Zealand	−0.23	—	0.1
China	1.27	3.68	2.9
Hong Kong	1.41	—	2.4
Japan	0.05	0.79	1.0
Korea	1.71	—	3.4
Taiwan	1.51	—	3.4
Indonesia	5.61	4.08	1.8
Malaysia	2.83	10.79	5.7
the Philippines	2.02	4.67	3.7
Singapore	2.26	5.66	8.1
Thailand	15.90	27.16	6.1
Vietnam	8.42	19.65	—
Other Asia	−0.31	—	0.0
United States	−0.06	—	0.0
EU	−0.01	—	0.0

Note: The figures indicate the percent change from the base.
[1] ASEAN+3, Hong Kong, and Taiwan
[2] ASEAN, China, and Japan
[3] ASEAN+3, Hong Kong, and Taiwan (excluding Vietnam)
Source: Urata and Kiyota (2003), Kawasaki (2003) and Kiyota (2004).

deal more in terms of the increase in GDP from joining an East Asian FTA than economies such as Korea and Taiwan in Northeast Asia. In particular, Thailand and Vietnam would be the largest beneficiaries of an East Asian FTA.[3]

An FTA will induce capital inflows from both within and outside the region. As trade, investment, and economic growth interact to produce dynamic synergies, concluding an FTA could bring about an outcome much more extensive than that of trade creation and diversion. Baldwin and Venables (1995) assert that trade liberalization produces investment incentives in addition to the static effects, which they call the 'capital accumulation effects.'[4] Capital accumulation is the result of increased domestic savings and investments and inflows of FDI. These investment incentives could constitute an important part of economic effects of an FTA.

This section estimates effects of FTAs on trade liberalization and capital accumulation using a modified GTAP model.[5] In this analysis, eight hypothetical FTAs are constructed. They are: FTAs between China–Japan, China–Korea, and Japan–Korea; and an FTA involving the three Northeast Asian economies (CJK); three FTAs between AFTA (ASEAN Free Trade Area) on the one hand and China, Japan, and Korea on the other; and an East Asia FTA including all East Asia economies. For each hypothetical FTA, effects of trade liberalization (TL) and capital accumulation (CA) are estimated. Trade liberalization refers to tariff elimination among the member countries in the GTAP database published in 2002, which is used to estimate the effective tariff rates of East Asian countries. Recent FTAs are comprehensive in that they include services, investments, trade rules on intellectual property rights, dispute settlement mechanisms, exclusion of anti-dumping rules. However, it is difficult to quantify the degree of improvement in trade rules for simulation. This paper chooses to focus on the effects of tariff elimination, which is the most important element of an FTA.

Table 4.3 presents effects of the eight hypothetical FTAs. It shows that, while the eight FTAs bring economic benefits to all member countries, non-members will suffer a loss. For example, if Japan and Korea conclude an FTA, the GDP of the two countries would increase, but those of non-member countries—ASEAN and Rest of World (ROW)—could decrease. Although the effects of TL alone are moderate, introducing those of capital accumulation (CA) increases substantially overall economic benefits. The effects of TL of a

---

[3] Urata and Kiyota (2003) find a disproportionate increase in intra-regional trade compared to extra-regional trade in their study of an East Asian FTA (ASEAN+3 + Hong Kong + Taiwan). Specifically, the share of intra-East Asia trade in world trade would increase from 11 percent to 14 percent, and the share of intra-East Asia exports (imports) in East Asia's total exports (imports) would increase from 44 (50) percent to 53 (59) percent. They also report that the trade intensity index would increase from 2.02 to 2.17 as a result of forming an East Asia FTA.

[4] Levin and Renelt (1992) and Grossman and Helpman (1995).

[5] This section draws on Cheong (2005).

Yung Chul Park and Inkyo Cheong

Table 4.3: The impact of FTAs on regional GDP in East Asia (unit: %)

FTAs in Northeast Asia

	China–Japan FTA		China–Korea FTA		Japan–Korea FTA		CJK FTA	
	TL	TL&CA	TL	TL&CA	TL	TL&CA	TL	TL&CA
China	0.27	1.11	0.12	0.45	−0.01	−0.03	0.34	1.29
Japan	0.05	0.12	−0.00	−0.04	0.01	0.04	0.06	0.13
Korea	−0.05	−0.26	0.76	1.76	0.22	0.92	0.94	2.45
ASEAN	−0.03	−0.36	−0.02	−0.19	−0.01	−0.08	−0.06	−0.59
ROW	−0.00	−0.06	−0.00	−0.06	−0.00	−0.02	−0.01	−0.12

FTAs in East Asia

	ASEAN–China FTA		ASEAN–Japan FTA		ASEAN–Korea FTA		East Asian FTA	
	TL	TL&CA	TL	TL&CA	TL	TL&CA	TL	TL&CA
China	0.076	0.441	−0.02	−0.12	−0.01	−0.07	0.36	1.39
Japan	−0.007	−0.076	0.04	0.09	−0.01	−0.05	0.10	0.17
Korea	−0.025	−0.177	−0.04	−0.20	0.13	0.65	1.01	2.84
ASEAN	0.229	2.077	0.43	3.19	0.41	2.17	0.73	4.00
ROW	−0.004	−0.075	−0.01	−0.05	−0.00	−0.04	−0.02	−0.22

Source: Cheong (2005).

China–Korea FTA would increase the GDP of the two partners by 0.12 percent and 0.76 percent respectively. When the effects of CA are added, the increases amount to 0.45 percent and 1.76 percent respectively.

Similarly, when ASEAN and China conclude an FTA, trade liberalization will increase ASEAN's GDP by 0.23 percent, and by 2.08 percent when the effect of capital accumulation is added. In the case of Northeast Asian FTAs, Korea is expected to gain relatively more from a CJK FTA than from a bilateral FTA with either China or Japan, as it can benefit from capital accumulation resulting from capital inflows from Japan. As far as Japan and Korea are concerned China is a more suitable FTA partner than they are to each other.

Economic effects of an FTA would in theory increase as its coverage area expands. As Table 4.3 shows, an East Asian FTA will bring more economic benefits to all members compared to a CJK FTA, but the difference between the two is relatively small. For example, China can expect a GDP increase of 0.34–1.29 percent in a CJK FTA compared to an increase of 0.36–1.39 percent in an East Asian FTA. This small difference is due to the fact that the economic size and volume of trade of ASEAN are relatively small. ASEAN's aggregate GDP is only about one-tenth of Northeast Asia's. For the same reason, Northeast Asian countries can expect smaller benefits from a bilateral FTA with ASEAN than from bilateral FTAs with each other. These results do not mean that a larger FTA like an East Asian one is not necessarily preferable to a smaller CJK FTA. The larger an FTA, the more economic benefits it will generate.

96

Table 4.4: The impact of FTAs in East Asia on regional capital stock (unit: %)

FTAs in Northeast Asia

	China–Japan FTA		China–Korea FTA		Japan–Korea FTA		CJK FTA	
	TL	TL&CA	TL	TL&CA	TL	TL&CA	TL	TL&CA
China	0.02	0.21	0.01	0.08	0.00	−0.01	0.02	0.24
Japan	0.00	0.02	0.00	−0.01	0.00	0.01	0.00	0.02
Korea	0.00	−0.05	0.02	0.23	0.01	0.16	0.03	0.36
ASEAN	0.00	−0.06	0.00	−0.03	0.00	−0.01	−0.01	−0.10
ROW	0.00	−0.01	0.00	−0.01	0.00	0.00	0.00	−0.03

FTAs in East Asia

	ASEAN–China FTA		ASEAN–Japan FTA		ASEAN–Korea FTA		East Asian FTA	
	TL	TL&CA	TL	TL&CA	TL	TL&CA	TL	TL&CA
China	0.01	0.09	0.00	−0.02	0.00	−0.01	0.02	0.26
Japan	0.00	−0.02	0.00	0.01	0.00	−0.01	0.00	0.02
Korea	0.00	−0.04	0.00	−0.04	0.01	0.12	0.03	0.43
ASEAN	0.02	0.33	0.03	0.49	0.02	0.31	0.03	0.58
ROW	0.00	−0.02	0.00	−0.01	0.00	−0.01	0.00	−0.05

Source: Cheong (2005).

Suppose that Korea establishes an FTA with ASEAN to avoid possible discrimination and negative effects from exclusion in response to the conclusion of the ASEAN–China FTA or an ASEAN–Japan FTA. Together with the CJK FTA, this addition will create a web of four FTAs in East Asia. Since the rules of origin differ in different FTAs, they would produce the spaghetti bowl effect and thus increase trade-related costs. A layer FTA would minimize the protective effects of FTA members' preferential rules of origin and also create a more competitive environment, which would generate dynamic synergy effects of economic integration. Since the simulation model of this study cannot capture these effects, the economic effects of an East Asian FTA reported in Table 4.3 are likely to be underestimated. East Asia will be better off with a region-wide FTA.

The CGE model used in this study cannot analyze the behavior of investors as it is a static one, but it can indirectly estimate the impact of an FTA on regional capital accumulation, using the method of François, McDonald, and Nordstrom (1997). As shown in Table 4.4, China gains more from a bilateral FTA with Japan than with Korea in terms of capital accumulation. China finds Korea a more desirable partner than ASEAN as far as the increase in GDP is concerned, but the other way around in terms of capital accumulation. For Korea, an FTA with China is preferable to one with Japan. Given those conflicting impacts of FTAs on different regions, a region-wide FTA such as an East Asian FTA would be preferable to a network of bilateral or subregional FTAs. An interesting result, though not unexpected, is that Japan is not affected by any of East Asia's FTAs regardless of its participation, though it suffers from a decrease in capital accumulation when excluded. This result follows from the fact that Japan is the second-largest open economy in the world.

The magnitude of the impacts of FTAs would vary from member to member. In general, impacts would be large for a country with high trade dependency and/or high import protection. For example, Thailand, which has relatively high trade dependency and high import tariff protection, gains more from joining an FTA, whereas Japan, which has a low trade dependency and low tariff protections except for a few agricultural products, cannot expect a large benefit.

4.4 Quality of FTAs: Market Access and Rules of Origin in FTAs in East Asia

4.4.1 *Rules of Origin in Major FTAs*

Most FTAs have several hundred pages of ROO protocol. The existing literature on the topic is limited.[6] For an analysis of different ROOs, several FTAs are chosen in this chapter. They are NAFTA and the EU–Mexico FTA, which represent the first generation of FTAs. Examples of FTAs signed or under negotiation by East Asian countries are the ASEAN Free-Trade Area (AFTA), China–ASEAN FTA, Japan–Singapore FTA (EPA), US–Singapore FTA, Korea–Singapore FTA, and Korea–Chile FTA. This section compares the stringency of ROOs of East Asian FTAs with that of the US and EU FTAs. Before presenting results, it is worth noting that the ROO of the AFTA and the ASEAN–China FTA, which specify a 40 percent regional value contents rule across all items are the simplest ROO in the world.[7] The 40 percent criterion of regional value contents was introduced by AFTA, when the Common External Preferential Tariff (CEPT) scheme was agreed upon in 1992. During the negotiations for an FTA between China and ASEAN, China accepted the AFTA ROO. But other East Asian FTAs have chosen to introduce more complicated ROOs.

ROOs of the US and EU FTAs

NAFTA is the first FTA with comprehensive coverage including trade, investment, services, and trade rules. In promoting FTAs, the US has imposed stringent ROOs based on change of heading, specific requirements for HS

---

[6] Comprehensive analysis of ROO in major RTAs can be found in Brenton (2003), Essevadeordal (2003), and the WTO (2002b).

[7] Similarly simple ROO can be found in ANZCER (Australia-New Zealand FTA), which has a 50 percent RVC rule. However, it specifies the additional requirement that the last manufacturing process should be performed in the exporting territory for some items. However, the 40 percent rule is applied in AFTA without extra requirements.

chapters, and complicated criteria for the regional value content. Essevade-ordal (2003: 348) concludes that the US specifies rules of origin of 'substantial transformation' in its FTAs. Changes in Tariff Classification (CTC) or 'tariff shift' in chapter, heading, and subheading are most widely used with additional requirements of a specific process and regional value contents. However, the de Minimis rule is 7 percent in NAFTA, lower than in other FTAs.

A number of FTAs have followed the structure of the NAFTA ROO with minor modifications for some items.[8] A rigid NAFTA ROO of 'wholly obtained or produced entirely' is applied to primary industries, and each of the non-originating materials used in the production of the good must undergo an applicable change in tariff classification set out in Annex 401 of the agreement. Technical processes are required for many items. Regional value content ratios are as high as 50–60 percent depending on calculation methods.[9] The agreement specifies a more stringent rule for automobiles (HS8702–8704) with 62.5 percent under the net cost method.

Other FTAs in which the US participates introduce a lower regional value contents ratio. For example, in the US–Chile FTA, 35 percent (Build-up) and 45 percent (Build-down) were adopted for some of HS34. A similar ROO is used for the US–Singapore FTA, although a little more rigid ROO was incorporated in the US–Australia FTA, especially for textile and footwear. In the case of footwear (HS64), the regional value contents ratio is set at 55 percent (Build-down) with an additional requirement of subheading change.

The EU's ROO heavily depends on PAN European Rules of Origin (PANEURO), which establishes a highly uniform ROO across the EU's FTAs such as the EU–EFTA FTA and the EU–Mexico FTA. The EU–Mexico FTA adopts a wide range of rules in defining the ROO. In general, the EU's ROOs are more restrictive than others in that it is dominated by changes in heading and imposes complicated rules for producers such as special requirements for sugar and cocoa for HS 18–22, although regional value contents ratios range from 20 percent to 50 percent with 20 percent for HS30.

ROOs in East Asian FTAs

Singapore adopted the US position on ROO in negotiating the US–Singapore FTA (concluded in 2003), which basically followed the framework of the NAFTA ROO. Chapter 3 of the US–Singapore FTA contains the rules of origin, and the requirements on specific items are given in Annex 3A. Heading changes are required for HS01-HS24, in addition to 'wholly obtained or produced entirely' for primary products.[10] These are also applied to HS49-HS60, although subheading changes are specified for HS27-HS48. For apparel and clothing (HS61), a stringent rule is adopted by specifying that, 'apparel and clothing must be both formed from yarn and finished in the territory of a Party.' For some HS chapters such as HS73, 78, 81, 84, 85, and 90, regional value contents ratios are at 35 percent in the Build-up method and 45 percent in the Build-down method respectively. De Minimis is set at 10 percent.

Given the strong domestic opposition to trade liberalization in their negotiation for FTAs Japan and Korea are predisposed to introduce a complex and stringent ROO.[11] Japan's first FTA—the Japan–Singapore EPA—specifies a 'wholly obtained or produced entirely' rule and products for preferential treatment in the FTA should have undergone sufficient transformation in a Party. Cumulation and de Minimis are accepted but the agreement specifies different shares of de Minimis with lower than or equal to 10 percent.

Heading changes are required for HS01-24, HS38 (chemical products), HS85 (machinery) with subheading changes or regional content requirements (liquor and cordials). A regional content requirement of 60 percent (with a combination of subheading changes) is required for other HS chapters. For textile fabrics and articles (HS59), fabric should be made with yarn from a Party.

The Japan–Mexico FTA has a less restrictive ROO than the Japan–Singapore EPA. De Minimis is introduced at 10 percent for all items. Changes in chapter, heading, and subheading are used for HS01-63. The rule for Mexico's major exports such as footwear (HS64) and natural resources like copper and zinc specifies heading or subheading changes with a 50–55 percent regional content requirement.

The ROO of the Korea–Chile FTA is a variant of NAFTA's rule with inflexible and complex specifications for sensitive items such as agricultural and fishery products, which require changes in heading (HS01-HS10). In order to prevent trans-shipment of agricultural products, de Minimis is specified at 8 percent. A combination of heading change and regional value contents is used for several chapters such as HS19, 29, 30, 31, 38, etc. In general, regional content ratios are relatively low: 45 percent for the Build-down and 35 percent for the Build-up method. For some of HS84, a 30 percent regional content ratio is specified for the Build-up method. However, HS200892-200899 (preparation of vegetables, fruits, nuts, or other parts of plants) are subject to an exceptionally high regional content ratio. This is designed to curb the export of illegal juices and similar products.

---

[10] This rule for primary products such as cattle, rice, etc. is widely accepted in RTAs.

[11] Essevadeordal (2003: 12) states that, 'the ROO of the Japan–Singapore EPA are complex, as evidenced by the more than 200-page ROO protocol.' Similar comments can be found in Essevadeordal (2003: p. 12) on the Korea–Chile FTA.

Table 4.5: Effects of tariff elimination and ROO on trade

	Stringency of ROO	
	Less	More
Coverage of tariff elimination		
Wide	High impact	Low impact
Narrow	Low impact	Limited impact

Although the conclusion of the Korea–Singapore FTA was announced, there are still several issues to be resolved between the two parties. According to reports in the media, the two countries agreed to a 10 percent de Minimis rule with the exception of textiles. Unlike the FTA with Chile, the Build-down method is extensively used with ratios of 45 percent, 50 percent and 55 percent.

4.4.2 Overall Assessment of Quality of East Asia's FTAs

Quality of FTAs can be evaluated in terms of several criteria, the most important being degree of market access. Market access is determined in general by the coverage of tariff reduction, elimination of non-tariff barriers (NTBs), simplicity of the ROO, and harmonization of trade rules. Some of these elements such as harmonization of trade rules cannot be easily quantified, but the coverage of tariff elimination and simplicity of the ROO can be measured. This section assesses quality of FTAs in terms of these two criteria as shown in Table 4.5, where FTAs are classified into four categories depending on their coverage of tariff elimination and complexity of their ROOs.

Table 4.6 summarizes the coverage of tariff elimination in major FTAs in the Western Hemisphere and East Asia. NAFTA, Australia–New Zealand Closer Economic Relations Trade Agreement (ANZCERTA), AFTA, and the ASEAN–China FTA have a broad range of tariff elimination. AFTA plans to impose low internal tariff rates of 0–5 percent on sensitive items instead of eliminating them completely. Other FTAs allow a large number of exceptions including agricultural products as in the FTAs concluded by Japan and Korea.

Different FTAs have quite different specifications for ROO, although all FTAs studied in this chapter employ the regional value content (RVC) ratio in defining the ROO. Many FTAs, including NAFTA, require substantial changes in tariff lines (CTC), making their ROOs highly complex. The ROOs become more complex and stringent when the CTC is combined with the RVC ratio. NAFTA, the EU–Mexico FTA, and bilateral FTAs Japan and Korea concluded introduce a ROO that stipulates both the CTC and RVC ratio for sensitive items.

Table 4.6: Tariff elimination in FTAs

	Coverage of Tariff Elimination	Remarks
ANZCERTA	Complete	Gradual liberalization (1983, 1988)
NAFTA	− 3% (HS8) of agriculture excluded	Quota for textiles is specified
EU–Mexico	− EU: 35.2% (HS8) of agriculture excluded	Mexico: 26.1% exception for agriculture
AFTA	− 98% of total tariff lines are included in liberalization package	− Intra-regional trade share: 20–25% −Utilization of CEPT is very low (3%)
China–ASEAN FTA	− Around 98% of tariff lines are liberalized	− Extremely sensitive items are excluded
JSEPA	− 58% of agricultural HS (6) excluded	Agriculture with positive tariffs are excluded
KCFTA	− 30% of agricultural HS (6) excluded	Additional liberalization will be discussed after the DDA

As shown in Table 4.7, the ROOs of East Asian FTAs are similar to those of Western FTAs in terms of the CTC, RVC ratio, cumulation, and de Minimis. However, AFTA and the ASEAN–China FTA have a very simple and uniform format for the ROO, which is simpler than the one the WTO recommends and which is not found in other RTAs. For example, AFTA and the ASEAN–China FTA do not specify a CTC criterion since they require a 40 percent RVC ratio. In negotiating FTAs with ASEAN for bilateral FTAs, both Japan and Korea are likely to yield to ASEAN's demand for a simple ROO.

Table 4.8 presents an overall assessment of market access in major FTAs. It shows that ANZCERTA and the ASEAN–China FTA receive high scores (Group I). AFTA can be placed in the same group but with some reservations, given its 0–5 percent tariff goal instead of complete tariff elimination. NAFTA is inferior to FTAs in Group I because of its complex and restrictive ROO. The Korea-Chile FTA, Japan-Singapore FTA and EU–Mexico FTA are included in Group IV with a relatively narrow coverage of tariff elimination and stringent ROOs. The three FTAs exclude a large number of agricultural items from tariff liberalization on top of introducing a ROO as stringent as that of NAFTA.

Table 4.7: Summary of ROO in major FTAs

	NAFTA	EU–Mexico FTA	AFTA	China–ASEAN FTA	Japan–Singapore FTA	Korea–Chile FTA
CTC	Yes	Yes	Not necessary	Not necessary	Yes	Yes
RVC Ratio	60–50%	50–30%	40%	40%	60–40%	45–30%
Cumulation	Yes	Yes	Yes	Yes	Yes	Yes
De Minimis	7%	10%	No mention	No mention	8–10%	8%

Table 4.8: Overall assessment

	Stringency of ROO	
	Less	More
Coverage of tariff elimination		
Wide	Group I: ANZCERTA CA FTA	Group II: NAFTA
Narrow	Group III: AFTA	Group IV: KCFTA EU-Mexico FTA JSEPA

4.5 Consequences of Proliferation of FTAs in East Asia

4.5.1 *Domino Effects: Emergence of an East Asian FTA?*

In reading an endless series of press releases by East Asian governments and ASEAN+3, journalistic accounts of bilateral FTAs under negotiation or discussion and the CMI and ABMI, many observers may be tempted to conclude that the region is at a historical turning point in economic integration. For the next several years, ASEAN+3 states will be preoccupied with negotiating bilateral FTAs with one another and with other countries from different regions. Will this enthusiasm for bilaterals usher in a new era of liberalization in East Asia?

R. E. Baldwin (1993) argues that once regional integration begins, it becomes difficult to resist and all trade arrangements within a region will eventually collapse into one. Could East Asia follow the pattern of development suggested by the domino theory? Are there any lessons East Asia could learn from the history of European economic integration? In the late 1950s and 1960s, Western Europe had two trade blocs: the European Economic Community (EEC) and the European Free Trade Association (EFTA). The member states of the EEC held a federalist view on economic integration whereas those of the EFTA were inter-governmentalists. As a large RTA, the EEC continued to enlarge and consolidate itself whereas the EFTA remained relatively inactive. This together with the fact that there were only two RTAs in Europe made it possible for the members of EFTA to decide to join the EEC on the basis of expected gains and losses. A bloc with the goal of deeper integration won over the inter-governmentalists and achieved deeper integration that eventually encompassed integration of the political system.

Many trade experts held the view until very recently that a similar development would take place in East Asia. Two large FTAs (the Japan–Korea FTA and the ASEAN–China FTA) would first come into existence competing for regional dominance. That is, it was argued that the two FTAs would initially divide East Asia into two trade blocs. But over time the Japan–Korea FTA, which is larger and more advanced in terms of institutions and markets, would develop into an East Asian FTA by absorbing the ASEAN–China FTA. This scenario was predicated on the assumption that China with its semi-market economic system would not be able to conclude a high-quality FTA with ASEAN or other countries. Against all expectations, the ASEAN–China FTA entered into force in July 2005, while the Japan and Korea have made little progress in their negotiation for an FTA. In the meantime, other East Asian economies have concluded or have been negotiating about forty FTAs among themselves and with outside partners. Instead of promoting region-wide economic integration, East Asian countries are showing competitive regionalism (Bergsten, 2000).

Since its inception, the ASEAN–China FTA has not engaged in any serious bloc discrimination against other East Asian economies. Japanese and Korean firms with large investments in both ASEAN and China see the ASEAN–China FTA as an opportunity for industrial agglomeration in an integrated market of the two partners. Loose rules of origin and the allowance of accumulation may also have moderated the discriminatory effect on non-member countries. ASEAN's ongoing negotiations for bilateral FTAs with Japan and Korea have also reduced the room for any bloc discrimination.

In addition to the absence of bloc discrimination and a dominant FTA, there are other impediments to trade integration in East Asia. One barrier is that there are simply too many FTAs with different rules of origin and different types of coverage of tariff elimination. Another, unlike in Europe, is the region's lack of historical experience and tradition in cooperation for economic and political integration. Whatever economic benefits trade and financial integration may bring, they are unlikely to be realized if each country is unwilling to cooperate in the political arena. Although ASEAN+3 members have so far shown considerable solidarity in working together for the development of the Chiang Mai Initiative (CMI) and Asian Bond Market Initiative (ABMI), it remains to be seen whether China, Japan, and other members of ASEAN+3 can overcome their differences in regional issues to sustain the integrationist movement and steer the proliferation of FTAs to regional trade integration.

A third constraint on regional trade integration is the failure of ASEAN+3 countries to coordinate their FTA negotiations. The two regional initiatives—the CMI and ABMI—were motivated and promoted to achieve financial stability and integration. As such, ASEAN+3 forums are organized around finance ministers and central bank governors and their deputies. Trade officials do not participate in any of the ASEAN+3 meetings, and as a result, trade issues are not included in the ASEAN+3 agenda: ASEAN+3 does not function as a regional arrangement for trade liberalization and there is no plan for expanding the ASEAN+3 framework for the coordination of trade policies. There is therefore an unfortunate dichotomy between trade and finance in the ASEAN+3 group.

A fourth institutional constraint is related to the need to coordinate the activities of ASEAN+3 with other regional forums such as APEC. At some point in the future, the leaders of ASEAN+3 may have to decide on the mode of cooperation and division of labor for trade liberalization in East Asia with APEC. Many of the thirteen ASEAN+3 countries have been engaged in policy reviews and dialogue through APEC sub-arrangements. They will have to decide on whether to work together with other members of APEC to achieve the APEC's goal of trade liberalization in Asia and Pacific or choose to concentrate on trade integration in East Asia.

The single most important obstacle to regional integration is the absence of leadership that could balance the different interests of different countries in East Asia. The European experience shows that regional integration cannot progress very far without the leadership that can keep participating countries as a coherent group dedicated to achieving a set of common objectives. China and Japan, which could and should provide the needed leadership, have not been able to agree on a number of regional issues.

China and Japan have different interests in and therefore different strategies for economic integration in East Asia. On regional economic issues, as far as China is concerned, its bilateral FTA with ASEAN may be more important than any other FTAs in consolidating its strategic interests in East Asia. Any economic gains its FTA with ASEAN offers are of secondary importance. From the perspective of Chinese policymakers, integration with ASEAN, South Asian, and central Asian countries may carry more significance both economically and geopolitically than, or take precedence over, free trade with either Japan or South Korea. Although China is a military superpower, it is still a developing economy with a huge gap in terms of technological and industrial sophistication *vis-à-vis* Japan. The country has been growing rapidly, but it has a long way to go before catching up with Japan.

In contrast, Japan has not been able to articulate its strategic interests in East Asia. For example, Japan suggested the formation of ASEAN+5, but did not specify which two countries were to be added to ASEAN+3. There is also the suspicion that Japan is not interested in free trade or financial integration *per se* in East Asia, but in countering China's penetration of ASEAN. In fact, Japan's economic influence in East Asia has declined following its decade long recession, allowing China to fill the gap. Many analysts believe that Japan's involvement in regional economic integration is therefore motivated by its desire to maintain its traditional pole position (Wall 2002). Given these differences in the economic and military status and strategies of the two countries, China and Japan may find it difficult to work together for a bilateral FTA and for regional integration in East Asia, even if they manage to reconcile their troubled past and to resolve territorial and other disputes.

Baldwin's domino theory is not likely to apply to East Asia in the short run, although it may in the long run, in that the members of ASEAN+3 are occupied with creating as many FTAs as they can without having a clear goal of and agenda for regional trade integration. Proliferation of FTAs would therefore make little headway in achieving region-wide free trade insofar as the East Asian bilateralism poses new trade barriers in terms of market access and the ROO.

What would then be the consequences of the proliferation of FTAs in East Asia? Would they bring about the formation of FTA hubs with China, Japan, or both serving as a center economy? Would they simply thicken the web of bilateral FTAs? These are the questions this study turns to in the next section.

4.5.2 *Emergence of China as an FTA hub in East Asia?*

In competition for creating or joining new FTAs, some of the economies in East Asia may develop into regional hubs of FTAs. There are three candidate economies for the hubs: ASEAN, China, and Japan. Which economy will succeed in forming a dominant hub in East Asia? The answer to this question will largely depend on future developments in China's trade relations with the rest of the region. China has become or will soon become the largest trading partner to all East Asian countries including Japan. This development will give China an edge in competing to become a hub country.

ASEAN has been active in forming FTAs with non-ASEAN countries in East Asia. As noted above, China was the first country to approach ASEAN for a bilateral FTA. In the beginning, many ASEAN countries regarded China as a threat rather than an opportunity and thus ASEAN's response was rather passive. However, their attitude toward China's proposal became more favorable as China not only offered a huge export market but various incentives such as an early harvest and economic assistance to new ASEAN members.

ASEAN has also been engaged in negotiating FTAs with Japan and Korea and has reached out to countries outside of East Asia such as Australia, New Zealand, and India. ASEAN's FTA with non-East Asian countries reflects its effort to enhance its bargaining power in East Asia, a region which is likely to be dominated by China and Japan. In allying with all these countries, ASEAN sees the opportunity to play a mediator role and to develop into a regional FTA hub.

However, it is unlikely that ASEAN will serve as an important regional hub of FTAs in East Asia. First of all, it is too small in economic size to provide a large export market to spoke countries. Although it has a history of more than ten years of integrating, AFTA remains a disparate group of economies. Despite the emerging consensus among the ASEAN members on the need to achieve a truly free-trade area, opposition from protected industries such as automobiles in Malaysia has delayed integration of ASEAN. In recent years, the rapid growth of China has provided added pressure on ASEAN to accelerate the AFTA process, but some of the large members with leadership potential have not been able to lead individually or collectively consolidation of AFTA into an efficient FTA. Non-member countries also find that access to the ASEAN market is very much limited. For these reasons, regardless of the number of FTAs ASEAN may establish, it is not likely to become an FTA hub in East Asia.

Japan had been rather passive in initiating FTA negotiations until it proposed ASEAN to establish an FTA in November 2002. It was Singapore, Mexico, and Korea that approached Japan for the possibilities of creating bilateral FTAs in the late 1990s. Until that time, Japan regarded trade negotiations under the multilateral GATT/WTO framework as desirable, and thus had a negative view on FTAs. In November 2002, it concluded a free-trade agreement with Singapore and also signed a joint declaration with ASEAN to negotiate a framework for a comprehensive economic partnership that includes a free-trade agreement. Since then, Japan has approached individual members of ASEAN such as the Philippines and Thailand for a bilateral FTA. Japan and Korea have also been exploring the possibility of forming a bilateral free trade area. Despite all these FTA gestures, it is well known that Japan initiated FTA negotiations with ASEAN largely in response to Chinese moves to establish closer links with other countries in the region. Partly for this reason, Japan has been perceived as a reluctant and difficult FTA partner to many East Asian countries.

Japan appears to be insensitive to and unwilling to resolve its wartime legacy and historical and territorial disputes, raising questions as to whether it is prepared to lead economic integration in East Asia. On trade in manufactures, Japan espouses the principle of market competition while protecting its agriculture. In negotiating FTAs, Japan has not been generous in making concessions as befits the second largest economy and has also shown the tendency of holding to the same position regardless of its partners for FTA negotiations. If there is a high probability that China will emerge as the dominant power in the region, then an economically integrated East Asia may not serve Japan's regional interests. From Japan's point of view, a better regional strategy may lie in forming as many FTAs with East Asian economies as it can and leave the region divided. Japan will manage to establish a network of FTAs, but it is not clear whether it will serve as a regional hub.

In view of the fact that China has already become Japan's largest trading partner in terms of exports, it is possible to speculate that despite the differences in their strategies, both China and Japan could come to realize that region-wide trade liberalization and integration would serve their interests in the long run. If Japan believes it inevitable that economic integration in East Asia will be centred on and led by China, and China realizes that Japan will continue to be the major source of capital and technology, then the two countries could cooperate in pushing for deeper trade integration in the region.

A more likely scenario is that of China assuming a central leadership role in regional integration and thereby forming an FTA hub. Knowing that ASEAN members will be more attracted to their FTA negotiations with China than with Japan, China may decide to use its market leverage to negotiate deeper financial and trade integration with ASEAN. As it was in negotiating with ASEAN, China is prepared to make concessions and to be flexible in dealing with agricultural issues in negotiating an FTA with South Korea. It is not clear whether South Korea will be receptive to China's proposal while it is negotiating with Japan. However, if South Korea decides to enter into discussion with China, trade experts believe that the two countries will be able to conclude an FTA within a relatively short period of time. A China–South Korea FTA will certainly elevate China's status as a regional hub in East Asia. However, it will take many years for the two countries to initiate and conclude negotiations for a bilateral FTA, even if South Korea gives priority to a China–Korea FTA over to a Japan–Korean FTA. This means that for the foreseeable future, East Asia will remain a thick web of bilateral FTAs.

As shown by Lee, Park, and Shin (2004), the benefits in terms of trade creation accruing from the proliferation and overlap of bilateral FTAs will decline. At the same time, the costs arising from different rules of origin and excluded sectors in different bilateral FTAs will increase. This development could discourage a further increase in bilateral FTAs or make East Asian countries realize the need for coordinating their trade policies, thereby producing incentives for laying the groundwork for regional trade integration in East Asia. Against this expectation, there has been an unmistakable shift in East Asia away from ASEAN+3 to a broader group of countries for trade integration. The movement may paradoxically defeat the very objective it has set out to achieve, which is regional economic integration centering on ASEAN+3. This development may or may not be bad depending on the outcome of the proliferation of FTAs. However, what is clear is that given the possibility on the basis of East Asia's experience that the proliferation will undermine multilateral trade liberalization efforts, the global community will have to come up with a new multilateral approach that could ensure smooth amalgamation of existing RTAs into a single global trading system.

4.6 Concluding Remarks

This chapter has examined details of the agreements of East Asia's bilateral FTAs that are completed or under negotiation for a better understanding of whether they will facilitate or stand in the way of regional trade integration. Many of East Asia's FTAs have been in existence for a relatively short period of time. As a result, they do not throw much light on how discriminatory the existing East Asian FTAs have been or will be, and whether they will collapse into a large single FTA or create a convoluted spaghetti or noodle bowl. Depending on how one interprets the objectives and performance of East Asia's FTAs, one can be either an optimist or pessimist on the prospects for multilateral trade liberalization.

There is indeed no shortage of arguments suggesting that bilateral FTAs could be complementary to and, to the extent that they can be concluded quickly, become building blocks for global trade liberalization under the WTO. Bilateral FTAs, it is often pointed out, have other advantages in that they could provide rules in various areas such as FDI and labor mobility that are not covered by the WTO.

While these advantages may be real, the spread of bilateralism in East Asia could have dangerous consequences. As simulation studies surveyed in Section 4.3 show, the bilateral movement is likely to produce an outcome inferior to a large FTA such as an East Asian FTA or a China–Japan–Korea FTA, because East Asian bilateral FTAs could, among other things, divert more trade from low-cost to high-cost producers. Indeed, if both China and Japan succeed in creating hub-and-spoke networks of bilateral FTAs, these networks pose a danger in that the spoke countries could be marginalized both economically and politically, as Baldwin notes in Chapter 3, Given this possibility, the potential spoke countries will attempt to join as many FTAs as they can, thereby leading to further proliferation of bilateral FTAs. This development would make East Asia less attractive to foreign direct investment, a problem Baldwin calls the 'noodle bowl' problem.

China and Japan may be motivated to negotiate bilateral FTAs with other East Asian countries in order to protect and strengthen their political and strategic interests in East Asia. If this were the case, then the proliferation of bilateral FTAs would not necessarily speed up trade liberalization in individual countries. This is because these politically motivated bilateral FTAs could turn into strategic alliances rather than economic unions. Furthermore, there is concern that some of the bilateral FTAs already concluded, negotiated, or under consideration in East Asia are examples of negotiated protectionism rather than negotiated liberalization, as they tend to leave out politically sensitive sectors, such as agriculture, by making a rather self-serving interpretation of GATT Article XXIV.8.

As countries engaged in negotiating bilateral FTAs in East Asia resort to many provisions for rules of origin to give selective protection to domestic industries as shown in the preceding section, they will strengthen domestic protectionist forces while weakening the domestic pro-liberalization coalition. At the same time, different rules of origin and coverage of imports for liberalization in different bilateral FTAs could create a bewildering spaghetti bowl effect of complex and incompatible agreements, thereby inhibiting a broadening of the geographic scope of integration (Ravenhill 2004). If this happens, then consolidating a large number of different bilateral FTAs for region-wide trade liberalization will be a Herculean task as it requires standardizing different FTAs into one agreement. It is therefore unlikely that an East Asian FTA will emerge by itself as a result of the amalgamation of bilateral FTAs (Cheong 2002). None of East Asia's FTA's makes any mention of a possible extension to other parties. The intensifying rivalry and the growing rift between China and Japan will also make it more difficult to create an East Asian FTA.

In the end, the pros and cons of bilateral FTAs will have to be judged on the basis of their performance. Many East Asian trade officials and experts argue that the pessimistic scenario is not firmly grounded in facts and the FTA strategies of ASEAN+3 members. All East Asian countries depend on trade for growth and industrialization, and in knowing that an economically integrated East Asia will offer new investment opportunities and help sustain rapid growth, East Asian policymakers cannot afford to have FTAs degenerate into a convoluted noodle bowl. That is, in light of the consensus among East Asian leaders that the establishment of an East Asian FTA is desirable as it would promote economic prosperity and social and political stability in the region, optimists argue that these separate FTA developments would in the end lead to the formation of an East Asia FTA. So far, however, there is little evidence that supports the optimistic view: the new wave of bilateral FTAs in East Asia is not likely to be supportive of region-wide free trade.

References

APEC (2004), 'Free Trade Agreements/Regional Trade Agreements (FTAs/RTAs) in the Asia-Pacific Region,' Part II in *APEC Economic Outlook*.

Baldwin, R. (1993), 'A Domino Theory of Regionalism.' *NBER* Working Paper No. W4465 (New York: National Bureau of Economic Research).

Berg, Andrew, and Krueger, Anne (2003), 'Trade, Growth, and Poverty: A Selective Survey,' IMF Working Paper No. 03/30, April.

Bergsten, F. (2000), 'East Asian Regionalism: Towards a Tripartite World,' *The Economist*, 356 (8179): 23–6.

Brenton, Paul (2003), 'Notes on Rules of Origin with Implications for Regional Integration on Southeast Asia.' Presented at PECC Trade Forum, Washington DC, April 22–3.

Cadot, Oliver, de Melo, Jaime, Essevadeordal, Antoni, Suwa-Eisenmann, Akiko, and Tumurchudur, Bolormaa (2002), 'Assessing the Effects of NAFTA's Rules of Origin,' *Mimeo*.

Cheong, Inkyo (2001), 'Analysis of Chile-MERCOSUR FTA,' unpublished manuscript, Seoul: Korea Institute for Economic Policy, July.

_____ (2002), 'The Economic Ellects of China's WTO Accession on Northeast Asian Economics,' *East Asian Review*, 14 (1): 61–88.

_____ (2003a), 'The Korea–Chile FTA: Contents and Assessment,' Seoul: Korea Institute for Economic Policy, March.

_____ (2003b), 'Korea's FTA Policy: Progress and Prospects,' in Yangseon Kim and Chang Jae Lee (eds.), *Northeast Asian Economic Integration: Prospects for a Northeast Asian FTA* (Seoul: Korea Institute for International Economic Policy).

_____ (2005), 'Estimation of Economic Ellects of FTAs in East Asia,' in Ahn Choong Yong, R. Chand, E. Baldwin, and Inkyo cheong (eds.), *East Asian Economic Regionalism'* (Amsterdam: Springer).

Committee on Regional Trade Agreements (CRTA) (2000), 'Draft Report on the Examination of the North American Free Trade Agreement,' Geneva: WTO CRTA, September.

Congressional Budget Office (CBO) (2003), *A Budgetary and Economic Analysis of the NAFTA*, Washington, DC, July.

Essevadeordal, Antoni (2003), 'Rules of Origin in FTAs: A World Map.' Presented at PECC Trade Forum, Washington DC, April 22–3.

Francois, J. F., McDonald, B. J., and Nordström, H. (1997), 'Capital Accumulation in Applied Trade Models,' in J. F. François and K. E. Reinert, *Applied Methods for Trade Policy Analysis: A Handbook* (Cambridge: Cambridge University Press), 364–82.

Grossman, G. M. and Helpman, E. (1995), 'The Politics of Free-Trade' Agreements,' *The American Economic Review*, 85 (4): 667–90.

Hai, Wen and Li, Hongxia, (2003), 'China's FTA Policy and Practice,' in Yangseon Kim and Chang Jae Lee (eds.), *Northeast Asian Economic Integration: Prospects for a Northeast Asian FTA* (Seoul: Korea Institute for International Economic Policy): 138–56.

Herin, Jan (1986), 'Rules of Origin and Differences between Tariff Levels in EFTA and in the EC,' EFTA Occasional Paper No. 13.

Kawasaki, Kenichi (2003), 'The Impact of Free Trade Agreements in Asia,' REITI Discussion Paper Series 03-E-018, Tokyo: Research Institute of Economy, Trade, and Industry.

Kiyota, Kozo (2004), 'The Role of Service Trade Liberalization in Japan's Trade Policies,' Faculty of Business Administration Working Paper #220, Yokohama National University, December.

Koskinen, Matti (1983), 'Excess Documentation Costs as a Non-Tariff Measure: An Empirical Analysis of the Effects of Documentation Costs,' Working Paper, Swedish School of Economics and Business Administration.

Lee, Jong-Wha, Park, Innwon, and Shin, Kwanho (2004), 'Proliferating Regional Arrangements: Why and Whither,' available online at <http://ssrn.com/abstract =604101>.

Levine, Ross and Renelt, David (1992), 'A Sensitivity Analysis of Cross-Country Growth Regressions,' *The American Economic Review*, 82 (4): 942–63.

OECD (2003), 'Analysis of Non-Tariff Measures: The Case of Export Duties,' Paris: OECD Trade Committee.

Palmeter, David (1997), 'Rules of Origin in Regional Trade Agreements,' in *Regionalism and Multilateralism after the Uruguay Round—Convergence, Divergence and Interaction*, published by European Interuniversity Press, Brussels.

Schiff, Maurice and Winters, L. Alan (2003), *Regional Integration and Development* (Oxford: Oxford University Press for the World Bank).

Scollay, Robert and Gibert, John P. (2001), *New Regional Trading Arrangements in the Asia Pacific?* (Washington, DC: Institute for International Economics).

Urata, Shujiro (2003), 'Japan's Policy toward Free Trade Agreements,' in Yangseon Kim and Chang Jae Lee (eds.), *Northeast Asian Economic Integration: Prospects for a Northeast Asian FTA* (Seoul: Korea Institute for International Economic Policy): 97–113.

—— and Kozo, Kiyota (2003), 'The Impacts of an East Asia FTA on Foreign Trade in East Asia,' NBER Working Paper 10173, December.

Wall, David (2002), 'North Korea and China—Nuclear Power,' *World Today*, 58 (12) (Dec.).

Winter, L. Alan (1991), *International Economics*, 4th edn. (London: HarperCollins Academic).

WTO (2002a), 'Compendium of issues related to regional trade agreements,' Geneva: WTO, May.

—— (2002b), 'Rules of Origin Regimes in Regional Trade Agreements,' Committee on Regional Trade Agreements, April 5.

5

Containing the PTA Wildfire

Cédric Dupont
Graduate Institute of International Studies, Geneva

David Huang
Academica Sinica, Taipeh

Pessimistic views about APEC which we hear occasionally today are overly affected by the fluctuation of expectation, ignoring the precise capability of APEC.

(Yamazawa 2001: 4)

5.1 Introduction

When created in 1989 under the leadership of Australia and Japan, Asia Pacific Economic Cooperation (APEC) was envisioned as a regional discussion forum for economic growth in the region. Its main objective was to softly foster trade liberalization through the promotion of transparency and coordination, thus becoming a kind of Asia OECD. As such, APEC was quickly considered to be the showcase of new regionalism (see Fawcett and Hurrell 1995; Mansfield and Milner 1999), characterized by voluntary commitments from members, openness with the rest of the world and the absence of a rigid institutional framework.

Early enthusiasm about the possible achievements of the forum led to a growth in scope to encompass more ambitious goals, in particular the objective of free and open trade and investment to be achieved no later than 2020, but also several measures of trade facilitation and economic cooperation to promote growth and reduce disparities and asymmetries in the region. Whereas most observers were initially optimistic about the ability of members to achieve APEC goals with minimal institutions, the dominant view now seems to be that APEC is 'adrift,' that it is going through a 'mid-life crisis,' currently experiencing a 'malaise,' that it is not more than a 'talk shop,' or a 'photo op.'

This change comes largely from disappointment with APEC's ability to promote fast trade liberalization on an open-access basis. For those observers, the rapid rise of PTAs, mainly bilateral, in the last five years is both the consequence of APEC's inability to deliver significant liberalization and the nail to its coffin. The result is an increasingly complex web of trading rules that makes transactions more costly. Accordingly, the PTA wildfire has raised significant concern among policymakers and the business community and prompted a search for remedies.[1]

APEC itself has reacted. The 2004 and 2005 annual meetings of ministers and heads of states in Santiago de Chile and Busan, Korea, underline the need to promote a practice for high-quality agreements. Transparency, coherence, liberalism and openness are important recommendations for ensuring the development of PTAs that help fulfill APEC's major goals. Whereas there can easily be a consensus on the relevance of these recommendations, the big question is whether APEC can be effective in fostering their implementation. To answer that question one should carefully evaluate APEC's past performance as a confidence-building forum based on 'open regionalism' and 'concerted unilateralism.' Such an analysis goes beyond an evaluation of an increase of trade and investment flows in the region. Indeed, empirical work should try to uncover consistencies or inconsistencies in APEC's efforts to build up voluntary commitment by members and common work on key issues, independent of substantive end results. Such work is clearly lacking and the objective of this study is to provide a first response to this gap. This will contribute to the ongoing debate on the role of international institutions on trade at the world level (Dupont 2003; Rose 2005a, 2005b, 2005c; Subramanian and Wei 2003; Tomz, Goldstein, and Rivers 2004, 2005) that has raised intriguing questions on the impact of GATT/WTO.

Analyzing the content of eleven APEC leaders' declarations, 845 APEC-funded projects, and 217 self-funded projects, we show that APEC leaders not only consistently emphasize certain topics relevant to APEC goals, but also that their emphases are largely met by APEC projects. While scholarly consensus is that the APEC is adrift, our analysis suggests consistency and coherence in the APEC agenda and institutional activities despite a minimal institutional set-up. This may constitute a significant convergence of expectations of members of the organization.

The chapter begins with a brief description of the recent evolution of preferential trading arrangements. In contrast to previous chapters, which

[1] Among early solution providers, see Baldwin (2003) and Dent (2003).

Table 5.1: PTAs signed and implemented between APEC members since 2000

Countries	Year of signing	Year of entry into force
New Zealand–Singapore	2000	2001
Japan–Singapore	2002	2002
Singapore–Australia	2003	2003
Chile–U.S.	2003	2004
Chile–Korea	2003	2004
China–Hong Kong SAR	2003	2004
China–Thailand	2004	2004
Singapore–U.S.	2003	2004
Australia–Thailand	2004	2005
Australia–US	2004	2005
Japan–Mexico	2004	2005
Thailand–New Zealand	2005	2005
Brunei–Chile–New Zealand–Singapore (TPSEPA)	2005	2006
Chile–China	2005	2006
Japan–Philippines	2005	2006?

Sources: APEC (2003); <http://www.bilaterals.org>; Feridhanusetyawan (2005); and <http://www.wto.org>

focus on Asia or East Asia alone, we consider trans-Pacific trade relations, not just those among countries on the Asian side of the Pacific but those on its American shores as well. Next we consider APEC, the only regional entity encompassing this entire region; its original aims; and its operation. We then provide new evidence on its activities since 1993, drawing inferences from the content of leaders' declarations and project submissions. We conclude with general lessons and by suggesting some avenues for future research.

5.2 PTAs in Asia and the Pacific

Whereas in the 1980s and 1990s trade liberalization in Asia and the Pacific took either the unilateral or regional routes, the new form in vogue is bilateralism. This development is particularly true for countries that are members of APEC (see Tables 5.1 and 5.2). Thirteen of APEC's twenty-one members have signed and implemented bilateral PTAs or FTAs, with notable countries like Singapore, Australia, and New Zealand participating in this rush for new agreements. The trend is unlikely to stop in the near future given the ongoing negotiations or discussions. On the basis of current developments, only four APEC member economies are unlikely to sign PTAs in 2006 or 2007: Russia, Papua New Guinea, Chinese Taipei, and Vietnam. Future PTAs will be less focused on pure bilateralism, though, with several attempts to connect ASEAN to selected neighbors, either individually or collectively.

It is also interesting to note that APEC members mostly look for preferential trade ties with other APEC members (see Table 5.3). There are currently only two PTAs in force between any APEC member and another Asian country, the

Table 5.2: PTAs under negotiation or discussion between APEC members

Negotiations	Negotiations	Discussions
ASEAN–China (ACCEC)	Japan–Malaysia	ASEAN–China–Korea–Japan
AFTA–CER	Japan–Philippines	ASEAN–US EAI
ASEAN–Japan (AJCEC)	Korea–Mexico	Chile–Australia
ASEAN–Korea (AKCCP)	Korea–Canada	Chile–Japan
Australia–China	New Zealand–China	Chile–Thailand
Australia–Japan	New Zealand–Hong Kong SAR	Korea–Malaysia
Australia–Malaysia	New Zealand–Malaysia	Korea–U.S.
Australia–Thailand	Singapore–Canada	US–New Zealand
Australia–U.S.	Singapore–Mexico	US–Philippines
Canada–Singapore	Singapore–Peru	
Japan–Indonesia	Singapore–Mexico	
Japan–Korea	Thailand–Peru	
	Thailand–US	

Sources: APEC (2003); <http://www.bilaterals.org>; Feridhanusetyawan (2005); <http://www.wto.org>

Table 5.3: Other PTAs between APEC members and other countries in Asia

Countries	Year of signing	Year of implementation
China–Macao SAR	2003	2004
India–Thailand	2004	2004
India–Singapore	2005	2006

Sources: APEC (2003); <http://www.bilaterals.org>; Feridhanusetyawan (2005); <http://www.wto.org>

two involving India. Interest in such deals is increasing, but compared to plans for deals between APEC members it remains quite restricted (see Table 5.4).

This rapid diffusion of PTAs in the region is raising concern within the business community.[2] Multiple trade rules increase the costs of transactions for traders. Give these costs, multiple PTAs are only useful if they meet some well-established criteria, including large and diverse membership, low external tariffs, comprehensive coverage, liberal rules of origin, trade facilitation measures as well as monitoring procedures (Feridhanusetyawan 2005). Current bilateral agreements between APEC members are problematic on almost all of these grounds. Particularly worrisome is the anarchic situation regarding rules of origin,[3] the long list of exceptions in terms of products, the systematic

[2] 'We're hearing from our business community that with all these different FTAs [free-trade agreements] in the region, it's getting hard for them to do business,' said a senior trade negotiator attending this week's annual meeting of the Asia-Pacific Economic Co-operation forum (APEC) (Financial Times, Nov. 18, 2005).

[3] As an illustration, note the differences between the Singapore–Australia and Singapore–Japan FTAs: for the former for most goods 50% or even for a limited number of electric or electronic goods 30% value-added rule; for the latter, product-specific rules of origin,

Table 5.4: Other PTAs under negotiation or discussions in Asia

Negotiations	Discussions
ASEAN–India (AICEP)	India-Australia
BIMSTEC (Bangladesh, India, Myanmar, Sri Lanka, Thailand, Bhutan, Nepal Economic cooperation)	India-Japan
SAFTA (South Asian Free Trade Area)	India-Malaysia
(Maldives, Pakistan, Sri Lanka, India, Nepal, Bhutan, Bangladesh)	
India–China	
India–Chile	
Pakistan–Malaysia	
Sri Lanka–Singapore	

Sources: APEC (2003); <http://www.bilaterals.org>; Feridhanusetyawan (2005); <http://www. wto.org>

exclusion of agriculture, the limited commitments in services as well as the underdevelopment of monitoring and dispute settlement mechanisms (APEC 2003).

Increasingly pressured by the business community, APEC members officially recognized the problem and have since 2003 made efforts to remedy the situation. Senior Officials' meetings launched work on how RTAs/FTAs can best support the achievement of the Bogor goals (free investment and free trade). Their conclusions materialized in a report *Best Practice for RTAs/FTAs in APEC* (APEC 2004) that was officially endorsed during the 2004 Annual Meetings of Ministers and Heads of States in Santiago de Chile and confirmed during the 2005 Annual Meetings in Busan, Korea. This reports aims on the one hand at promoting the design of high-standard agreements in a consistent and coherent fashion. The objective here is to develop model measures for as many commonly accepted FTA chapters as possible by 2008. On the other hand, the report seeks to promote transparency through an exchange of information and experiences. The basic idea is to help create a common understanding of RTAs/FTAs in the region.

More specifically, the report lists the following criteria to ensure high-quality agreements: (1) consistency with APEC principles and goals; (2) consistency with the WTO (art. XXIV GATT and V GATS); (3) going beyond WTO commitments; (4) comprehensiveness; (5) transparency; (6) trade facilitation measures; (7) mechanisms for consultation and dispute settlement; (8) simple rules of origin that facilitate trade; (9) accession of third parties; (10) provision for periodic review.

Against the benchmark mentioned above for 'good' FTAs, the APEC report includes all the right criteria. It even adds explicitly a notion of 'openness'

originating content must be no less than 60% of the total value of the materials (APEC 2003: 16).

with access by third parties, which would indirectly amount to multilateral-izing preferential treatment. As such it offers at least as interesting a solution to the problem as other proposals, such as an East Asian Free-Trade Area or a Free-Trade Union (Baldwin 2003). Furthermore, it would be more neutral in the signals that it would send to the rest of the world, either to the western hemisphere, or to the WTO. However, the key question is whether APEC can really have member states implement the recommendations of the *Best Practice Report*. We now turn to this issue in two stages. We first go back to the essence of APEC, and put the debate on its institutional weakness in theoretical perspective. We then turn to an empirical assessment of its evolution and performance.

5.3 APEC: original aim and possible role

When they formally created APEC in November 1989, Australia, Brunei, Canada, Indonesia, Japan, South Korea, Malaysia, New Zealand, Philippines, Singapore, Thailand, and the United States agreed on the broad objective to sustain growth and development in the region to contribute to improving living standards and, more generally, to enhance the growth of the world economy. In this perspective, they designed a very loose institutional frame-work. The mode of operation of this framework was defined during the Seoul ministerial meeting in 1991 and reproduced in Annex A of the joint statement that followed that meeting:

4. Cooperation will be based on:
   (a) the principle of mutual benefit...
   (b) a commitment to open dialogue and consensus-building, with equal respect for the views of all participants
5. APEC will operate through a process of consultation and exchange of views among high-level representatives of APEC economies, drawing upon research, analysis and policy ideas contributed by participating economies and other relevant organ-isations including the ASEAN and the South Pacific Forum (SPF) Secretariats and the PECC.

In sum, the basic idea of APEC is to foster cohesion and trust through regular meetings (Elek 1992), and to establish a regular dialogue to 'try and affect each other's policy making in a subtle way' (Yamazawa 1992: 1527). This basic idea has remained even with an expanding scope of activities since 1989.[4]

---

[4] See in particular the 1996 Osaka Action Agenda (OAA). In terms of scope, the OAA puts the focus on the promotion of convergence and harmonization of laws and regulations affecting trade and investment flows. More specifically, members should engage in: (*a*) trade liberalization (gradual liberalization through 'concerted unilateral actions,' that is unilateral non-binding commitments to undertake actions toward free trade and investment); (*b*) trade

Member states (member economies in the APEC wording) keep full control of the activities. Annual ministerial meetings prepare the direction and nature of APEC activities. Heads of states usually endorse ministerial recommendations during their subsequent annual summit. Decisions are then developed by senior officials' meetings (every four months) supported by a small secretariat and by a large set of working groups. Composed of representatives of the member states, these working groups each pursue one project on the work program.

The combination of open regionalism, voluntarism, and decentralized working structure was initially welcomed as the new regional road, in contrast to the supranational, closed, and compulsory approach pioneered by the EC. For some this was a pathbreaking development on the road to universal free trade (Bergsten 1994). But gradually skepticism has gained momentum. Less than one year after the Seattle summit, Manning and Stern (1994) and Linnan (1995) deplored the lack of concrete results and the absence of priorities. Still, at that time, most observers gave the benefit of the doubt to the capacity of the organization to carry out a useful role. Expectations were largely to let the structure be inhabited (Crone 1993), and several observers warned that APEC was not regionalism *à la* European Community, but something different meant to diffuse information (Kahler 1995) and generate consociational bonds (Foot 1995). As Ravenhill famously put it, APEC is 'regionalism by declaration rather than regionalism by treaty' (1995: 96). At the turn of the twenty-first century, pessimism had become dominant. In an authoritative book, Ravenhill (2001) led the charge. While he acknowledges some role for the summits in confidence-building (2001: 222), he argues that APEC has not developed into a collective dynamic pushing members toward more collaboration. In short, for him APEC as a regime can be considered as a failure, while acknowledging a risk of premature dismissal (2001: 154).

Can one therefore really think that APEC could help bring the wildfire of PTAs under control? Not if one believes that the way to address the problem is through some sort of coercion. Such a viewpoint is hardly realistic, though. Solutions clearly must be voluntary and self-convincing to countries in the region. From this second perspective, APEC may still have an interesting role to play as a 'support club of liberalizers in the region' (Yamazawa and Scollay 2003: 128), as a promoter of convergent trade practices and mutual understanding.

Putting the discussion into a larger theoretical context, institutions considered to be weak may not only turn out to have a significant impact on trade flows but also one that can be bigger than institutions with more teeth.

facilitation (cooperation on standards, customs procedures, competition policies, dispute mediation); (*c*) economic cooperation (regional development and assistance on projects in human resources, energy, transportation, telecommunications, and the environment).

In particular, work by Rose (2005c) suggests that the OECD may have had a bigger impact than the GATT/WTO. Such a finding (provided future research corroborates it) is hardly a mystery. The value of the OECD is to create an information-rich environment among members. Such an environment may lead to significant integration without further institutionalization (Kahler 1995). Given the parallels noticed between APEC and OECD (Ostry 1998), the relative success of the OECD is good news for APEC potential influence.[5]

Another interesting recent general empirical finding in the debate on the role of GATT/WTO pertains to the so-called embeddedness of trade agreements (Tomz, Goldstein, and Rivers 2004). Whereas membership in GATT/WTO in itself does not help achieve higher trade flows if members are members of PTAs, GATT/WTO is influential in that it provides the standards for liberalization and product coverage. A similar argument could be working for APEC. Ultimately, though, the question of APEC's capacity to carry through its new agenda of promoting best practice for FTA/RTA in the region should be based on empirical evidence of its past performance. This is the task of next section.

5.4 Where is APEC? A Twofold Empirical Assessment

Is APEC a hopeless case for harmonious trade liberalization in Asia and the Pacific? We provide in this section empirical evidence to answer this question. In contrast to most existing assessments, we do not focus on country-level indicators (such as investment inflows, growth in export and import) or intra-regional flows, but we restrict our analysis to the organizational dynamics located upstream and underneath.[6] APEC may be a worthwhile effort even though results on the above-mentioned indicators appear to be weak.[7] Indeed, APEC may be an underground force that gradually builds up, akin to an earthquake in the making. Uncovering such a force requires a novel empirical approach that carefully looks at apparently vain activities. Content analysis is such an approach for the case of APEC. We focus on two types of such activities, leaders' declarations and project submissions by members, and examine whether the build-up of activities may lead to an accumulation or on the contrary a dispersion of forces. Given that the annual APEC leaders'

[5] In particular, the OECD mode of operation involves: (a) regular meetings of senior officials; (b) annual meetings of ministers; (c) a myriad of lower level meetings that help promote the diffusion of knowledge (Ostry 1998: 329).

[6] To make an analogy with rivers, the mere fact that we do not see water at the surface does not mean that there is no water running underneath. That water may eventually come out some miles further down. As for APEC, the current absence of concrete results does not mean that such results are not in the making through a slow, hard-to-discern process.

[7] Dupont (1998) already argues that any expectation of a strong, direct impact of APEC was misplaced.

meeting introduces new ideas and sets up a working agenda for APEC in the following year, it is interesting to see whether APEC leaders' declarations provide a coherent agenda that commits APEC members consistently to its common goals, or an incoherent agenda that shifts APEC attention from year to year. This will give us a better indication of whether the focus on the promotion of high-quality PTAs in the 2004 and 2005 declarations are merely one additional fire in the span. It is also important to know whether the commitments made in APEC leaders' declarations are supported by its funded projects under the supervision of APEC working groups and committees.

LEADERS' DECLARATIONS: GETTING OUT OF HAND?

For the purpose of this study, we analyze all the declarations of heads of states' meetings between 1993, the first time such a declaration was issued, and 2003, leaving out the 2004 and 2005 declarations that contain a mention of high-quality PTAs. Textbox 1 lists the eleven summit locations since 1993 with a short summary of the key points of the respective declarations.

Textbox 1: ELEVEN APEC LEADERS' DECLARATIONS

1993—Blake Island, United States
APEC Economic Leaders meet for the first time and outline APEC's vision, 'stability, security and prosperity for our peoples.'

1994—Bogor, Indonesia
APEC sets the Bogor Goals of, 'free and open trade and investment in the Asia-Pacific by 2010 for developed economies and 2020 for developing economies.'

1995—Osaka, Japan
APEC adopts the Osaka Action Agenda (OAA) which provides a framework for meeting the Bogor Goals through trade and investment liberalization, business facilitation, and sectoral activities, underpinned by policy dialogues, economic and technical cooperation.

1996—Manila, The Philippines
The Manila Action Plan for APEC (MAPA) is adopted, outlining the trade and investment liberalization and facilitation measures to reach the Bogor Goals and the first Collective and Individual Action Plans are compiled, outlining how economies will achieve the free trade goals.

1997—Vancouver, Canada
APEC endorses a proposal for Early Voluntary Sectoral Liberalization (EVSL) in fifteen sectors and decides that Individual Action Plans should be updated annually.

1998—Kuala Lumpur, Malaysia
APEC agrees on the first nine sectors for EVSL and seeks an EVSL agreement with non-APEC members at the World Trade Organization.

Textbox 1: (*Continued*)

1999—Auckland, New Zealand

APEC commits to paperless trading by 2005 in developed economies and 2010 in developing economies. APEC Business Travel Card scheme is approved and a Mutual Recognition Arrangement on Electrical Equipment and a Framework for the Integration of Women in APEC is endorsed.

2000—Bandar Seri Begawan, Brunei Darussalam

APEC establishes an electronic Individual Action Plan (e-IAP) system, providing IAPs online and commits to the Action Plan for the New Economy, which, amongst other objectives, aims to triple Internet access throughout APEC region by 2005.

2001—Shanghai, People's Republic of China

APEC adopts the Shanghai Accord, which focuses on Broadening the APEC Vision, Clarifying the Roadmap to Bogor, and Strengthening the Implementation Mechanism. The e-APEC Strategy is adopted, which sets out an agenda to strengthen market structures and institutions, facilitate infrastructure investment and technology for online transactions and promote entrepreneurship and human capacity building. APEC's first Counter-Terrorism Statement is issued.

2002—Los Cabos, Mexico

APEC adopts a Trade Facilitation Action Plan, Policies on Trade and the Digital Economy, and Transparency Standards. APEC's second Counter-Terrorism Statement is delivered, along with the adoption of the Secure Trade in the APEC Region (STAR) Initiative.

2003—Bangkok, Thailand

APEC agrees to re-energize the WTO Doha Development Agenda negotiations and recognizes that Free-Trade Agreements, Regional Trade Agreements, the Bogor Goals and the multilateral trading system under the WTO can be complementary. Counter-terrorism is acknowledged as a complementary mission to APEC's Bogor Goals. The APEC Action Plan on SARS and the Health Security Initiative are agreed to further protect human security. Strengthening efforts to build Knowledge-Based Economies and to promote sound and efficient financial systems, and accelerating regional structural reform are also agreed.

To analyze whether members have kept consistency over these eleven declarations, we utilize content analysis. We first identified ninety-nine keywords or keyword strings informed by various theories in the existing APEC literature (see Appendix 5.1). Then, we performed a computerized search within the eleven declarations for these keywords. As a result, we found a total 2077 hits over a total of over 25,000 words. Next, we combined these keywords/strings into fifteen conceptual groups, such as WTO issues, APEC goals, APEC actions, trade and investment, economy and development, capacity-building, standard and harmonization, guiding principles, private/business and third sectors, biotechnology and disease, security and terrorism, technology and communication, global/regional dimensions, environmental protection, financial system/financial crises, and others. Obviously both our choice of the long list of keywords and of the combination of keywords into fifteen groups may have important implications for the results of our analysis. Our rationale for both these choices has been to set the odds against some concentration trend by allowing a large number of keywords to be used and then not reducing excessively the list. We also checked whether a further reduction of the 15 keyword groups alters the results below. It turns out that this reveals similar patterns.

As Figure 5.1 illustrates, during the period of 1993–2003 APEC leaders committed to different aspects of APEC agenda but clearly there was more emphasis on some keywords/strings in particular organizational principles, trade and investment, the global/regional dimension, APEC goals and actions, and economy and development issues. The frequency distribution of the keyword groups is more or less consistent with previous findings, in which APEC was regarded as talking more about principles than actions; APEC was said to mainly focus on trade/investment and economic/technology development; APEC was supposed to be WTO-consistent and private/business-friendly; APEC was believed to concern with global and regional dimensions.

Figure 5.2 shows changes in frequency distribution of keyword groups across three historical periods. The main keyword groups have remained similar across time, not without some varying trajectories though. Congruent with previous findings, APEC leaders place more emphasis on trade and investment and organizational principles in their earlier meetings, but pay a great attention to economic development in more recent meetings. Furthermore, APEC leaders seldom discuss the issue of capacity-building in their earlier meetings, but they have become more conscious of it in the 2001 and 2002 summit meetings. Figure 5.2 also helps to reveal short-term movements: APEC leaders emphasize the financial system and financial crisis during 1997 and 1998; while security and terrorism are seldom mentioned in the earlier summit meetings, they become major issues for leaders' discussions after the September 11 attack in 2001. Although APEC leaders' attention may be shifted to focus on some urgent events in each year, they nevertheless consistently stress APEC principles, trade/investment, economic development, and WTO-related issues.

Yet, relative differences in the use of keyword groups have declined across time. This can be seen from the category 'others' in Figure 5.2 that moves from 7.62 percent to 10.58 percent. It is confirmed by the share of the top three and top six keyword groups: in 1993, the top three and six keyword groups represent 54 percent and 76 percent of hits, respectively; in 2003, they represent 37 percent and 60 percent, respectively.

In sum, our data indicates that there has indeed been an expansion of the APEC agenda but this has not come at too big a price given the continuous focus on some core items.

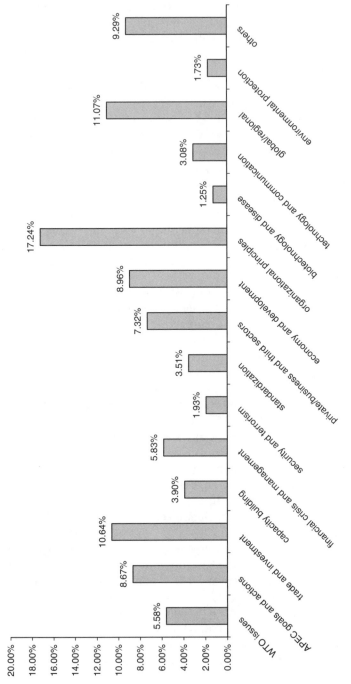

Figure 5.1: Keywords percentage of fifteen keyword groups in leaders' declarations, 1993–2003

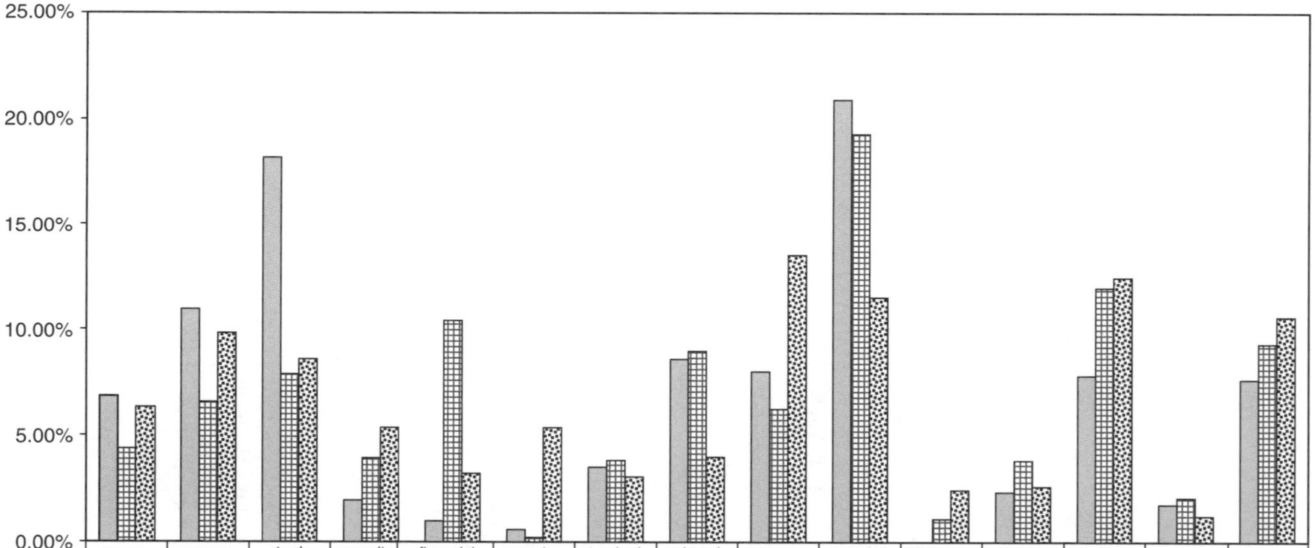

	WTO issues	APEC goals and actions	trade and investment	capacity building	financial crisis and management	security and terrorism	standard-ization	private/business and third sectors	economy and develop-ment	organiza-tional principles	biotechn-ology and disease	technology and commun-cation	global/regional	environ-mental protection	others
1993–1996	6.84%	10.94%	18.16%	1.95%	0.98%	0.59%	3.52%	8.59%	8.01%	20.90%	0.00%	2.34%	7.81%	1.76%	7.62%
1997–2000	4.38%	6.57%	7.89%	3.94%	10.41%	0.22%	3.83%	8.98%	6.24%	19.28%	1.10%	3.83%	11.94%	2.08%	9.31%
2001–2003	6.29%	9.82%	8.59%	5.37%	3.22%	5.37%	3.07%	3.99%	13.50%	11.50%	2.45%	2.61%	12.42%	1.23%	10.58%

Figure 5.2: Keywords percentage of fifteen keyword groups in leaders' declarations

CONTENT OF PROJECT DESCRIPTIONS AND LEADERS' DECLARATIONS IN COMPARATIVE PERSPECTIVE

Our discussion so far indicates that leaders' declarations have not gone out of control. Yet, even if one subscribes to Ravenhill's (1995) notion of regionalism by declaration, declarations alone would not lead APEC members very far. As we discussed in the previous section, APEC members as well as private actors are expected to take voluntary action to further the goals of the organization. A typical action is to submit a project that would be examined for funding (see Feinberg 2003*a* for a description of the process of project selection). Whereas the number of projects funded has significantly increased over time (see Figure 5.3), critiques have pointed to the lack of priorities among projects (in particular Linnan 1995; Ravenhill 2001) but have stopped short of providing careful evidence to support their claims.

Making use of APEC electronic data bank on all projects, we conducted a content analysis of all the projects funded by APEC funds as well as by self-contributions and by the Japanese-sponsored TILF fund, which amounts to a total of 1062 projects (see Figure 5.3 for the evolution of the number of yearly funded projects). Specifically, we scan several key paragraphs of projects' submission forms for our set of keywords presented above that we then aggregate in fifteen groups (see Appendix 1 and 2).[8] Given the number of projects, we end up with a total of almost 35,000 hits for our set of keywords.

Figures 5.4. and 5.5. show the distribution of keyword groups on the whole period as well as its evolution through time. Clearly there is some significant variation across groups of keywords although variation is more marked between sets of groups than across individual groups. As for evolution across time, we observe a pattern similar to the one for leaders' declarations. Relative differences in the use of keyword groups have declined across time. This can be seen in the category 'others' in Figure 5.5 that moves from 7.52 percent to 9.48 percent and is confirmed by the share of the top three and top six keyword groups: in 1993, the top three and six keyword groups represent 56 percent and 85 percent of hits, respectively; in 2003, they represent 32 percent and 58 percent, respectively.

On the basis of the evidence presented so far, one can see similar aggregate patterns in leaders' declarations and project descriptions regarding relative use of keyword groups. This does not constitute a big surprise, given that there is a clear necessity for project writers to 'respond to the priorities of the Leaders and Ministers, set out in their declarations, particularly by Bogor Declaration and its updates' (*Guidebook on APEC projects*, Annex B, paragraph A, section 1).

---

[8] We focus on part A of project proposals in particular on the description of project objectives and linkages (see Annex A of *Guidebook on APEC Projects* available on line at <http://www.apec.org>).

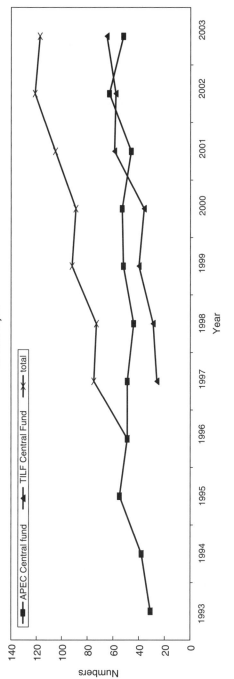

Figure 5.3: APEC-funded projects by years, 1993–2003

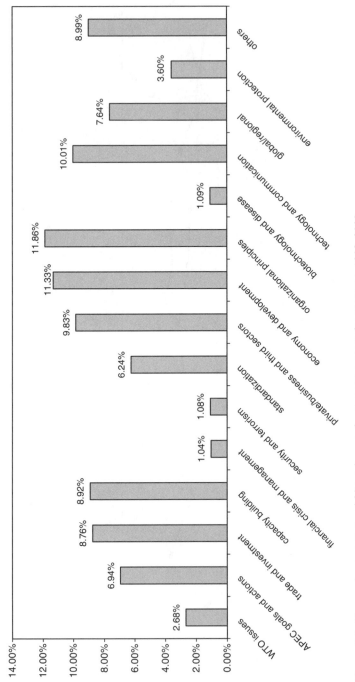

Figure 5.4: Keywords percentage of fifteen keyword groups in project descriptions, 1993–2003

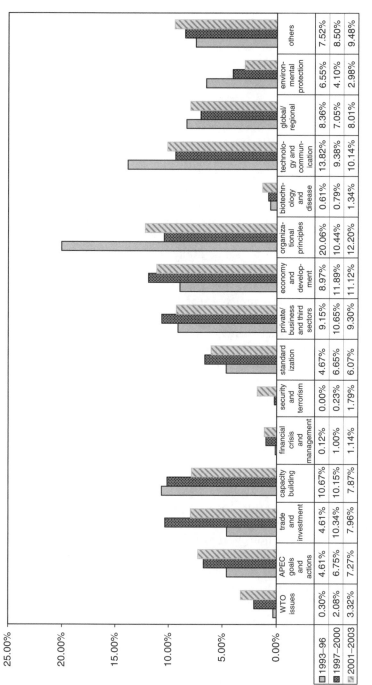

	WTO issues	APEC goals and actions	trade and investment	capacity building	financial crisis and management	security and terrorism	standard ization	private/ business and third sectors	economy and develop-ment	organiza-tional principles	biotechn-ology and disease	technolo-gy and commun-ication	global/ regional	environ-mental protection	others
1993–96	0.30%	4.61%	4.61%	10.67%	0.12%	0.00%	4.67%	9.15%	8.97%	20.06%	0.61%	13.82%	8.36%	6.55%	7.52%
1997–2000	2.08%	6.75%	10.34%	10.15%	1.00%	0.23%	6.65%	10.65%	11.89%	10.44%	0.79%	9.38%	7.05%	4.10%	8.50%
2001–2003	3.32%	7.27%	7.96%	7.87%	1.14%	1.79%	6.07%	9.30%	11.12%	12.20%	1.34%	10.14%	8.01%	2.98%	9.48%

Figure 5.5: Keywords percentage of fifteen keyword groups in project descriptions

On the other hand, the absence of a strong secretariat that could rigidly vet project descriptions makes it unlikely that one would find a strong correspondence between leaders' declarations and project descriptions. Furthermore, the decision-making process for project funding tends to put more focus on a leveling of projects through member economies rather than on the specific matching of priorities between leaders' declarations and project objectives and linkages.[9]

So, similar trends in the content of leaders' declarations and project descriptions do constitute an intriguing result for an institution like APEC, in contrast to one like the European Union. Yet, how similar are these trends? Figure 5.6 helps develop a more nuanced view. Priorities in project descriptions do not perfectly match those of the leaders' declarations.

Indeed, whereas the relative frequency of some groups is quite similar across the two groups of documents, including items such as APEC goals and actions, trade and investment (TILF)', or economy and development, differences are significant for some groups, including WTO issues, capacity-building, financial crisis, and organizational principles. There is a stronger emphasis on WTO issues and financial crises in Leaders' Declarations and a stronger emphasis on human capacity building, standard and harmonization and private/business sector. These differences are hardly surprising. Leaders tend to overreact to major systemic issues (WTO, financial crisis) while project submissions remain focused on more concrete actions. Figures 5.7, 5.8, 5.9, 5.10, and 5.11 provide a finer look for these keyword groups.

The Seattle and then Doha effects come out clearly from Figure 5.7. There has been an increasing gap between leaders' declarations and project descriptions for the keyword group WTO issues since 1999. APEC members have clearly been concerned with the evolution toward, and later within, a new round of negotiations at the world level and have repeatedly referred to it during the annual meetings. The large share of project activities connected to education and training explains the important gap between declarations and project description for the keyword group human capacity building. Yet, as Figure 5.8 reveals, this gap has been decreasing since 2000. Figure 5.9 confirms that APEC reactions to the financial crises of 1997–8 have remained at a rhetorical level. Despite a huge emphasis on this topic during the annual meetings, there has been no change of interest at the level of projects. A similar pattern may apply to security and terrorism. As can be seen from Figure 5.11, APEC members have greatly increased their focus on this item since 2001, whereas project activities have so far only moderately followed the trend. It is too soon to tell how behavior will evolve, but it is striking to see the resilience of project focus despite the pressure from heads of states.

[9] See Feinberg (2003a) for a discussion of the process of project funding.

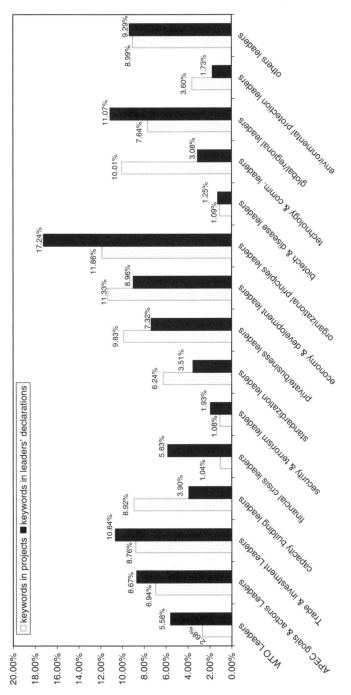

Figure 5.6: Keywords in leaders' declarations and projects, 1993–2003

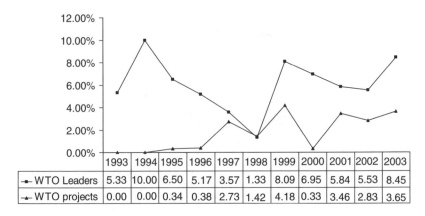

	1993	1994	1995	1996	1997	1998	1999	2000	2001	2002	2003
WTO Leaders	5.33	10.00	6.50	5.17	3.57	1.33	8.09	6.95	5.84	5.53	8.45
WTO projects	0.00	0.00	0.34	0.38	2.73	1.42	4.18	0.33	3.46	2.83	3.65

Figure 5.7: WTO keyword group in leaders' declarations and in project descriptions

Finally, Figure 5.10 reveals the responsiveness of project descriptions to key organizational principles laid out in leaders' declarations. The responsiveness of projects is quite striking for the initial period but has been diminishing in the recent years.

In sum, the contrast between leaders' declarations and project descriptions does not lead to the idea of that APEC has grown 'like Topsy without setting priorities' (Linnan 1995: n. 10). There has been consistency in emphasis both in leaders' declarations and in project descriptions. Furthermore, when emphasis has differed between declarations and project descriptions, this can be explained by the difference in purpose and audiences of the two vehicles.

5.5 Conclusion

PTAs are all the rage now in the Asia and the Pacific. They are a source of growing concern due to the anarchic multiplication of trade rules that could ultimately harm trade flows in the region. Significant success in the Doha round of talks at the WTO would probably slow down the rush to PTAs. But given the difficulties of talks at the world level, preserving multilateralism at the regional level should also be tried. This study brings evidence that APEC, the forum that many consider to be the first victim of PTAs, should not be dismissed too quickly. On the one hand, APEC did react to the wildfire of PTAs with a theoretically sound report on Best Practice for FTAs. On the other hand, the organization has since its creation demonstrated consistency, and some sense of priorities, two characteristics that could be crucial in the

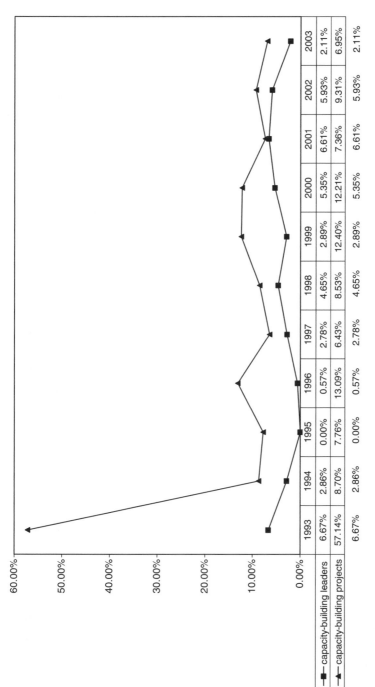

	1993	1994	1995	1996	1997	1998	1999	2000	2001	2002	2003
capacity-building leaders	6.67%	2.86%	0.00%	0.57%	2.78%	4.65%	2.89%	5.35%	6.61%	5.93%	2.11%
capacity-building projects	57.14%	8.70%	7.76%	13.09%	6.43%	8.53%	12.40%	12.21%	7.36%	9.31%	6.95%
	6.67%	2.86%	0.00%	0.57%	2.78%	4.65%	2.89%	5.35%	6.61%	5.93%	2.11%

Figure 5.8: Capacity-building keyword in leaders' declarations and project descriptions

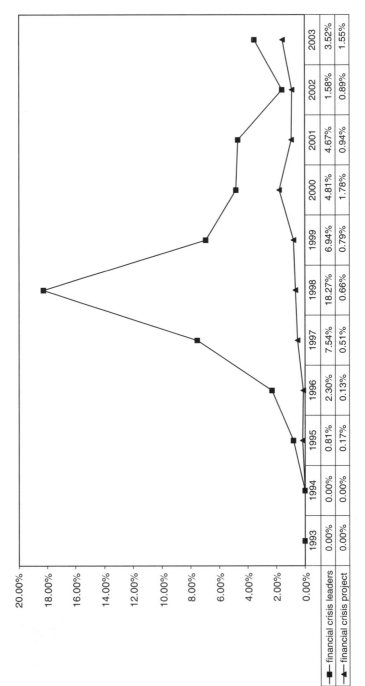

	1993	1994	1995	1996	1997	1998	1999	2000	2001	2002	2003
financial crisis leaders	0.00%	0.00%	0.81%	2.30%	7.54%	18.27%	6.94%	4.81%	4.67%	1.58%	3.52%
financial crisis project	0.00%	0.00%	0.17%	0.13%	0.51%	0.66%	0.79%	1.78%	0.94%	0.89%	1.55%

Figure 5.9: Financial crisis keyword in leaders' declarations and project descriptions

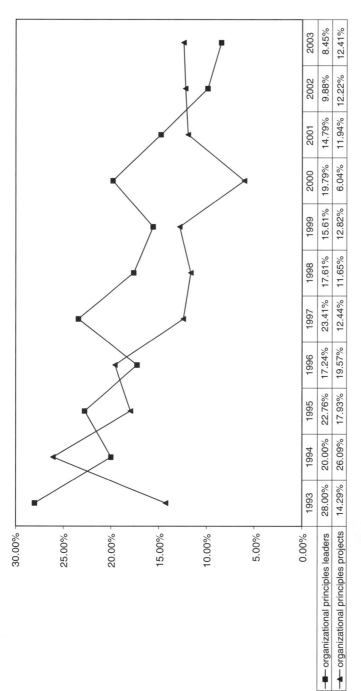

	1993	1994	1995	1996	1997	1998	1999	2000	2001	2002	2003
organizational principles leaders	28.00%	20.00%	22.76%	17.24%	23.41%	17.61%	15.61%	19.79%	14.79%	9.88%	8.45%
organizational principles projects	14.29%	26.09%	17.93%	19.57%	12.44%	11.65%	12.82%	6.04%	11.94%	12.22%	12.41%

Figure 5.10: Organizational principles in leaders' declarations and project descriptions

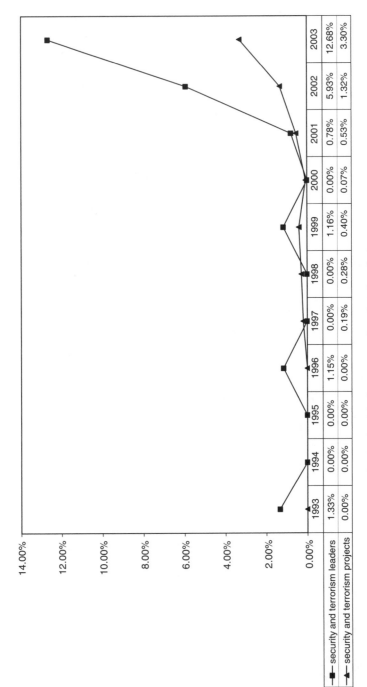

	1993	1994	1995	1996	1997	1998	1999	2000	2001	2002	2003
security and terrorism leaders	1.33%	0.00%	0.00%	1.15%	0.00%	0.00%	1.16%	0.00%	0.78%	5.93%	12.68%
security and terrorism projects	0.00%	0.00%	0.00%	0.00%	0.19%	0.28%	0.40%	0.07%	0.53%	1.32%	3.30%

Figure 5.11: Security and terrorism keyword in leaders' declarations and project descriptions

persuasion process aiming at bringing some order to the mushrooming of PTAs in the region. Specifically, this chapter highlights that, although APEC leaders' attention has been shifting and tended to focus on differing events in each year, they have nevertheless consistently stressed key APEC issues, trade/investment, economic development, and WTO-related issues. In other words, an expanding agenda has not come at the price of loss of priorities. Second, our analysis of project descriptions does not provide support for an anarchic development of activities within APEC. Most importantly, there has been consistency in emphasis both in leaders' declarations and in project descriptions. Furthermore, when emphasis has differed between declarations and project descriptions, it can easily be explained by the difference in purpose and audiences of the types of APEC products. In other words, it is not simply integration by 'declaration.' There has been a follow-up in terms of specific transactions among members.

Appendix 5.1: Codebook for Keywords

	Variable name	Label
1	cancun_d	Cancun (declaration)
2	gatt_d	GATT (declaration)
3	dda_d	Doha Development Agenda/DAA (declaration)
4	ur_d	Uruguay Round (declaration)
5	wto_d	World Trade Organization/WTO (declaration)
6	brunei_d	Brunei Goals (declaration)
7	imple_d	Implementation Plan (declaration)
8	borgor_d	Bogor goals/Bogor (declaration)
9	collec_d	Collective Action Plan(s) (declaration)
10	dialog_d	dialogue(s)/economic dialogue/policy dialogue(s) (declaration)
11	forum_d	forum/fora (declaration)
12	manila_d	Manila Framework (declaration)
13	iap_d	(Individual)Action Paln(s) (declaration)
14	oaa_d	Osaka/Osaka action agenda/OAA (declaration)
15	rule_d	rule-based (declaration)
16	shangh_d	Shanghai Accord (declaration)
17	span_d	SPAN (declaration)
18	three_d	three pillars (declaration)
19	a2010_d	APEC 2010 (declaration)
20	a2020_d	APEC 2020 (declaration)
21	free_d	free and open (declaration)
22	libera_d	liberalization/liberalisation (declaration)
23	multil_d	multilateral trading system/multilateral (declaration)
24	protec_d	protectionism (declaration)
25	facil_d	(trade)facilitation (declaration)
26	tilf_d	trade and investment/liberalization and facilitation/TILF (declaration)

(cont.)

(Continued)

	Variable name	Label
27	capaci _d	capacity building/capacities (declaration)
28	hcb_d	human capacity building/HCB (declaration)
29	hrd_d	human resource development (declaration)
30	financ_d	financial crisis/financial (declaration)
31	ifs_d	international financial system (declaration)
32	securi_d	security (declaration)
33	terror_d	terrorism/terrorist/counter-terrorism/ bio-terrorism (declaration)
34	transp_d	transparency/transparent (declaration)
35	harmon_d	harmonization/harmonize/harmonizing (declaration)
36	harnes_d	harness/harnessing/harnesses (declaration)
37	instit_d	institution/institutional (declaration)
38	stand_d	standard(s) (declaration)
39	adb_d	Asian Development Bank/ADB (declartaion)
40	g8_d	G-8 (declaration)
41	abac_d	ABAC (declaration)
42	bussi_d	business sector/business (declaration)
43	priva_d	private sector (declaration)
44	partne_d	partnership (declaration)
45	agricu_d	agricultural (declaration)
46	ecotec_d	economic and technical/ecotech (declaration)
47	ecogro_d	economic growth (declaration)
48	ecoinf_d	economic infrastructure (declaration)
49	energy_d	energy (declaration)
50	neweco_d	New Economy (declaration)
51	sustai_d	sustainable (economic) development (declaration)
52	struct_d	structural reform(s)/structural (declaration)
53	mirco_d	small and medium scale enterprises/micro-enterprises (declaration)
54	commun_d	community/international community (declaration)
55	cooper_d	cooperation/cooperative (declaration)
56	compre_d	comprehensiveness/comprehensive (declaration)
57	compar_d	comparability (declaration)
58	consen_d	consensus/consensus-building (declaration)
59	flexib_d	flexibility/flexible (declaration)
60	integr_d	integration (declaration)
61	member_d	membership (declaration)
62	nondis_d	non-discrimination (declaration)
63	openne_d	openness (declaration)
64	stasti_d	standstill (declaration)
65	stake_d	stakeholders (declaration)
66	region_d	(the)region (declaration)
67	unilat_d	unilateral (declaration)
68	volunt_d	voluntary/voluntarism (declaration)
69	biotec_d	biotechnology (declaration)
70	diseas_d	disease/SARS (declaration)
71	health_d	health (declaration)
72	hiv_d	HIV/AIDS (declaration)
73	eapec_d	digital/e-APEC/e-business/e-commerce/electronic commerce (declaration)

(*Continued*)

	Variable name	Label	
74	intnet_d	internet (declaration)	
75	techol_d	science and technology/technologies (declaration)	
76	telec_d	telecommunications/transportation (declaration)	
77	global_d	global/globally (declaration)	
78	globiz_d	globalization (declaration)	
79	gover_d	governance (declaration)	
80	intnat_d	international (declaration)	
81	intdep_d	interdependent/interdependence (declaration)	
82	regism_d	regional/regionalism/open regionalism (declaration)	
83	envir_d	environment/environmental (declaration)	
84	green_d	greenhouse (declaration)	
85	accoun_d	accountability (declaration)	
86	bilate_d	bilateral (declaration)	
87	compet_d	competitive/competitiveness (declaration)	
88	confid_d	confidence-building (declaration)	
89	educat_d	education/training (declaration)	
90	effici_d	efficiency/efficient (declaration)	
91	impion_d	implement/implementation (declaration)	
92	intact_d	interaction (declaration)	
93	politi_d	political will (declaration)	
94	prospe_d	prosperity/common prosperity (declaration)	
95	stabil_d	stability (declaration)	
96	tariff_d	tariff(s) (declaration)	
97	transa_d	tranction cost(s) (declaration)	
g1	i_w_d	Cancun + GATT + DDA + UR + WTO (declaration)	wto issues
g2	ii_a_d	Brunei + Bogor + Manila + OAA + Shangh + SPAN + three + 2010 + 2020 (declaration)	apec goals
g3	ii_a_d	Imple + Collec + dialog + forum + IAP + rule (declaration)	apec actions
g4	iii_t_d	free + libera + multi + prptec + facil + TILF (declaration)	trade and investment
g5	iv_c_d	Capaci + HCB + HRD (declaration)	capacity building
g6	v_f_d	finance + IFS (declaration)	financial system
g7	vi_ter_d	securi + treeor (declaration)	security and terrorism
g8	vii_s_d	transp + harmon + harnes + instit + stand (declaration)	standard and harmonization
g9	viii_p_d	ADB + G8 + ABAC + bussi + priva + partne (declaration)	private/business
g10	ix_e_d	agricu + ecotec + ecogro + ecoinf + energy + neweco + sustai + struct + mirco (declaration)	economy and development
g11	x_o_d	commun + cooper + compre + compar + consen + flexib + integr + member + nondis + openne + stasti + stake + region + unilat + volunt (declaration)	organizational principles
g12	xi_b_d	biotec + diseas + health + HIV (declaration)	biotechnology and communication
g13	xii_te_d	eapec + intnet + techol + telec (declaration)	technology and communication

(*cont.*)

(Continued)

	Variable name	Label	
g14	xiii_g_d	global + globiz + gover + intnat + intdep + regism (declaration)	global / regional
g15	xiv_en_d	envir + green (declaration)	environmental protection
g16	xv_oth_d	accoun + bilate + compet + confid + educat + effici + impion + intact + politi + prospe + stabil + tariff + transa (declaration)	others

Appendix 5.2: Fifteen Keyword Groups in APEC Leaders' Declarations and Project Descriptions

No.	Name of Keyword Groups	Keywords
1	WTO issues	Seattle Cancun GATT Doha Development Agenda/DDA Uruguay Round/Uruguay World Trade Organization/WTO
2	APEC goals and actions	Brunei Goals Implementation Plan (the) Bogor goals/Bogor Collective Action Plan(s) dialogue(s)/economic dialogue/policy dialogue(s) forum/fora Manila Framework Action Plan(s)/Individual Action Plan(s) Osaka/Osaka action agenda/ OAA rules-based Shanghai Accord SPAN three pillars 2010 2020
3	trade and investment	free and open liberalization/liberalisation multilateral/multilateral trading system protectionism facilitation/trade facilitation trade and investment/liberalization and facilitation/TILF
4	capacity building	education/training Capacity Building/capacities human capacity building human resource development
5	financial crises and management	financial crisis/financial international financial system
6	security and terrorism	security terrorism/terrorist/counter-terrorism/bio-terrorism

(Continued)

No.	Name of Keyword Groups	Keywords
7	standardization	transparency/transparent harmonization/harmonisation/harmonize/harmonizing harness/harnessing/harnesses institutional standard(s)
8	private/ business and third sectors	Asian Development Bank/ADB G-8 ABAC business/business sector private sector partnership
9	economy and development	agricultural economic and technical/ecotech economic growth economic infrastructure energy New Economy sustainable (economic) development structural reform(s)/structural small and medium scale enterprises/micro-enterprises
10	organizational principles	community/international community cooperation/cooperative comprehensiveness/comprehensive comparability consensus/consensus-building flexibility/flexible integration membership non-discrimination openness standstill stakeholders (the) region unilateral voluntary/voluntarism
11	biotechnology and disease	biotechnology disease/SARS health HIV/AIDS
12	technology and communication	digital/e-APEC/e-business/e-commerce/electronic commerce Internet science and technology/technologies telecommunications/transportation
13	global/ regional	global/globally globalization governance international interdependent/interdependence regional/regionalism/open regionalism
14	environmental protection	environment/environmental greenhouse
15	others	accountability bilateral competitive/competitiveness

(cont.)

(Continued)

No.	Name of Keyword Groups	Keywords
		confidence-building
		efficiency/efficient
		implement/implementation
		interaction
		political will
		prosperity/common prosperity
		stability
		tariff(s)
		transaction cost(s)

References

APEC (2003), 'Inventory of RTAs involving APEC Members,' APEC Market Access Group.
_____ (2004), 'Best Practice for RTAs/FTAs in APEC,' APEC 16th Ministerial Meeting.
Baldwin, Richard E. (2003), *The Spoke Trap: Hub and Spoke Bilateralism in East Asia* (Geneva: Graduate Institute of International Studies).
Bergsten, C. Fred (1994), 'APEC and World Trade. A Force for Worldwide Liberalization,' *Foreign Affairs*, 73(3): 20–6.
Büthe, Tim and Milner, Helen V. (2005), *The Politics of Foreign Direct Investment into Developing Countries: Increasing FDI through Policy Commitment via Trade Agreements and Investment Treaties* (Durham and Princeton: Duke University and Princeton University).
Crone, Donald (1993), 'The Politics of Emerging Pacific Cooperation,' *Pacific Affairs* 65 (1): 68–83.
Damond, Joseph M. (2003), 'The APEC Decision-Making Process for Trade Policy Issues. The Experience and Lessons of 1994–2001,' in Richard E. Feinberg (ed.), *APEC as an Institution* (Singapore: Institute of Southeast Asian Studies), 85–109.
Dent, Christopher M. (2003), 'Networking the region? The emergence and impact of Asia-Pacific bilateral free trade agreements projects,' *The Pacific Review* 16 (1): 1–28.
Dupont, Cédric (1998), 'European Integration and APEC: The Search for Institutional Blueprints,' in Vinod K. Aggarwal and Charles Morrison (eds.), *Institutionalizing the Asia-Pacific: Regime Creation and the Future of APEC* (New York: St. Martin's Press), 351–84.
_____ (2003), 'Trade Liberalization and Monetary Integration in the 19th Century: Parallel or Interdependent Contagions?' Paper presented at ISA Annual Meetings, Portland, Oregon, Feb. 25–March 1, 2003.
_____ and David Huang (2005), 'APEC on Track.' Paper presented at the International Studies Association Annual Meetings, Honolulu, Hawaii, Feb. 28–March 2, 2005.
Elek, Andrew (1992), 'Trade Policy Options for the Asia Pacific Region in the 1990's: The Potential of Open Regionalism,' *American Economic Review* 82 (2): 74–8.

Fawatt, L. and Hurrell, A. (eds.) (1995), *Regionalism in World Politics* (Oxford: Oxford University Press).

Feinberg, Richard E. (2003*a*), 'Project Selection and Evaluation. APEC's Budget and Management Committee and the Secretariat,' in Richard E. Feinberg (ed.), *APEC as an Institution* (Singapore: Institute of Southeast Asian Studies), 73–81.

Feinberg, Richard E. (ed.), (2003*b*), *APEC as an Institution*. Singapore: Institute of Southeast Asian Studies.

Feridhanusetyawan, Tubagus (2005), 'Preferential Trade Agreements in the Asia-Pacific Region.' *IMF Working Paper* 05/149.

Foot, Rosemary (1995), 'Pacific Asia: The Development of Regional Dialogue,' in Louise Fawcett and Andrew Hurrell (eds.), *Regionalism in World Politics* (Oxford: Oxford University Press), 228–49.

Funabashi, Yoichi (1995), *Asia-Pacific Fusion: Japan's Role in APEC* (Washington, DC: Institute for International Economics).

Hufbauer, Gary and Schott, Jeffrey J. (1995), 'Toward Free Trade and Investment in the Asia-Pacific,' *The Washington Quarterly*, 18 (3): 37–45.

Kahler, Miles (1995), *International Institutions and the Political Economy of Integration* (Washington, DC: Brookings Institution).

Linnan, David K. (1995), 'APEC Quo Vadis?' *American Journal of International Law*, 89 (4): 824–34.

Manning, Robert A. and Stern, Paula (1994), 'The Myth of the Pacific Community,' *Foreign Affairs*, 73 (6): 79–93.

Mansfield, Edward and Milner, Helen V. (1999), 'The New Wave of Regionalism,' *International Organization*, 53 (3): 589–627.

Ostry, Sylvia (1998), 'APEC and Regime Creation in the Asia Pacific: The OECD Model?' in Vinod K. Aggarwal and Charles Morrison (eds.) *Institutionalizing the Asia-Pacific: Regime Creation and the Future of APEC* (New York: St. Martin's Press), 317–50.

Ravenhill, John (1995), 'Competing Logics of Regionalism in the Asia-Pacific,' *Journal of European Integration*, 18 (2–3): 179–99.

—— (2000), 'APEC Adrift: Implications for Economic Regionalism in Asia and the Pacific,' *The Pacific Review*, 13 (2): 319–33.

—— (2001), *APEC and the Construction of Pacific Rim Regionalism* (Cambridge: Cambridge University Press).

Rose, Andrew K. (2005*a*), 'Do we Really Know that the WTO Increases Trade?' *American Economic Review*, 94 (1): 98–114.

—— (2005*b*). 'Does the WTO make trade more stable,' *Open Economies Review*, 16 (1): 7–22.

—— (2005*c*), 'Which International Institutions Promote International Trade,' *Review of International Economics*, 13 (4): 682–98.

Soesastro, Hadi (2003), 'APEC's Overall Goals and Objectives, Evolution, and Current Status,' in Richard E. Feinberg (ed.), *APEC as an Institution* (Singapore: Institute of Southeast Asian Studies), 29–45.

Subramanian, Arvind and Wei Shang-Jin (2003), 'The WTO Promotes Trade, Strongly but Unevenly,' *NBER Working Paper* 10024.

Tomz, Michael, Goldstein, Judith, and Rivers, Douglas (2004), 'How do Institutions Affect International Relations? Standing, Embeddedness, and the GATT/WTO' (Stanford: Stanford University).

Tomz, Michael, Goldstein, Judith, and Rivers, Douglas (2005), 'Membership has its Privileges: The Impact of GATT on International Trade' (Stanford: Stanford University).

Wesley, Michael (2001), 'APEC's Mid-Life Crisis? The Rise and Fall of Early Voluntary Sectoral Liberalization,' *Pacific Affairs*, 74 (2): 185–204.

Yamazawa, Ippei (1992), 'On Pacific Economic Integration,' *Economic Journal*, 102 (415): 1519–29.

—— and Scollay, Robert (2003), Towards an Assessment of APEC Trade Liberalization and Facilitation, in Richard E. Feinberg (ed.), *APEC as an Institution* (Singapore: Institute of Southeast Asian Studies), 110–29.

6

China and the Multilateral Trading System

Robert Z. Lawrence
Harvard University and Institute for International Economics

6.1 China and the Multilateral Trading System

For more than two decades, China's rapid growth has been driven by its global economic engagement. Since its accession to the WTO in 2001, foreign trade and foreign direct investment have made even more important contributions to Chinese growth. Between 2001 and 2005, for example, the dollar value of Chinese exports and imports increased at annual rates of 29.3 and 25.3 percent respectively, and in 2005 58 percent of Chinese exports originated from foreign-owned firms. As a result of this performance, China's share in world imports increased from 3.3 percent in 2001 to 5.9 percent in 2004 and its share in world exports from 3.9 percent in 2001 to 6.5 percent in 2004. This makes China a major participant in world trade and, having now surpassed Japan, the dominant trading power in East Asia.[1] China looms particularly large as an exporter of labor-intensive manufactured goods and components and as a major importer of capital goods, primary commodities, and semi-finished parts.[2] It is also the developing world's largest recipient of direct foreign investment.

Given its size, the pace of its expansion, and its outward orientation, China is likely to have a growing impact on global trading patterns and its policies

---

[1] In 2003 and 2004 China accounted for 10.6% and 8.9% of the growth in world imports and 10.5% and 9.7% of world exports.

[2] Having assumed the ranks of the world's third largest trader, Chinese trade policies will now be subject to the WTO trade review mechanism every two years—a treatment reserved for countries with large trade volumes.

are likely to have an important influence on the system's evolution. These policies have been as dynamic as its trade and investment performance. In 2001 after fourteen years of negotiations, China became a full member of the WTO, assuming obligations that are at the level of many developed economies. Since that time it has participated actively in the institution's activities and negotiations. In part to meet the conditions of its accession, China has also dramatically liberalized its domestic economy and introduced a large number of internal policies that consolidate its transition to a market economy. In addition, China has adopted a multi-track trade policy strategy, complementing its WTO and domestic liberalization policies with regional trading initiatives. By 2005, China had completed four FTA agreements (Thailand in 2003, Hong Kong and Macao in 2004 and Chile in 2005) and as estimated by Wong and Hufbauer had proposed and/or launched negotiations for at least another fifteen.[3]

What do these policies portend? When China proposed joining the WTO several concerns were raised. One was that the system as a whole could be weakened because China was not a fully market-driven economy and was therefore unlikely or unable to adhere to the WTO rules. China then acceded to the WTO under very demanding terms and there were fears that either deliberately or inadvertently it would not implement these commitments.[4] This would put other members in the difficult position of either (a) trying to compel compliance with trade retaliation and other sanctions that could increase frictions or (b) ignoring Chinese infractions, thereby undermining the WTO system in establishing an international rule of law to which all members adhered.

A second concern was that China would not participate constructively in the WTO. It would throw its weight around, try to obtain dispro-portionate influence, and use its influence to fundamentally change the WTO system. China was also seen as a potentially powerful addition to the ranks of developing countries, and many in the developed world wor-ried that it would seek to limit the obligations required of developing countries.

More recently a third set of questions is being raised with respect to China's trade policies in the East Asian region. Will Chinese regional initiatives under-mine the multilateral trading order? Is China seeking to establish an East Asian trading bloc under its leadership that discriminates against outsiders? Will it use its market to create a hub-and-spoke system in East Asia in which China

---

[3] Hufbauer and Wong (2005). Their list of proposed agreements includes APEC, East Asia, Southeast Asia, Brazil, GCC, India, Mexico, New Zealand, Peru, Singapore, South Africa, Mercosur, Australia, Chile, Iceland, Japan, Korea, and Pakistan.

[4] Mallon and Whalley (2004) for example express concern that Chinese policy instruments would generate many new trade disputes.

gains as the hub and the other countries serve as the spokes? Finally there is the fear that not only China but other countries in the region are creating a system of overlapping trade regimes—or a noodle bowl—that could impose unnecessary trading costs, induce harmful trade diversion, and actually fragment rather than integrate the regional economy.

This paper considers these questions. In contrast with previous chapters, which consider trade relations generally or trade relations within Asia or the Asia-Pacific region, the focus here is on China. Chinese policies are analyzed with a view to determining the direction they are taking and the effects they are likely to have on the multilateral system. The discussion first considers China's participation in the WTO. It reviews the terms of accession, China's current tariff and trade regime and its participation in the Doha Round negotiations, and the institution's regular activities. The analysis concludes that China's trade policies are broadly supportive of a rules-based multilateral trading order. China has accepted and implemented obligations that go far further than most developing countries. It has been interested in using the system to advance its interests rather than in changing it (Pearson 2003). Its behavior at the WTO is thus more akin to that of a status quo power than one seeking major systemic changes. The discussion then turns to China's FTA initiatives. These are still a work in progress, and their implications are uncertain. Concerns about an East Asian fortress appear misplaced. Directly, and through their impact in inducing others to respond, these FTAs could provide a powerful impetus to the process of competitive global liberalization. Countries that do implement agreements with China will find it relatively easy to open their markets to other developing countries. There is also a risk that the proliferation of FTAs will lead to web of overlapping agreements that could make the trading system unnecessarily complex.

China's policies both at home and abroad are still evolving. Thus major shifts in the direction and nature of those policies cannot be ruled out. Accordingly, the final section considers four factors that could play an important role in influencing outcomes in the future. These are the precise terms of the agreements that are concluded, China's domestic implementation of its commitments, the impact of currency appreciation on China's competitiveness, and protectionist responses to China by other countries.

6.2 China in the WTO

The WTO operates by consensus. Any country seeking to join must essentially satisfy all existing members before they will permit it to accede. To be sure, there is a requirement for decisions on accession to be approved by a vote of two thirds of the Members (Agreement Establishing the World

Trade Organization, Art. XII.1) and there are also provisions allowing existing and acceding members a one-time opportunity to opt out from extending MFN provisions when countries accede (Agreement Establishing the WTO Art. XIII) but in practice unanimity is sought and most countries receive full MFN treatment. The need to obtain such approval means that new members are often asked to assume obligations that are far more extensive than existing members at an equivalent stage of economic development.

ACCESSION COMMITMENTS

The terms of China's accession to the WTO exemplify these propositions. Although China is a developing country and thus in principle entitled by the WTO's 'enabling clause' to special and differential treatment, the United States and other WTO members were successful in insisting that China enter the WTO on 'commercial terms.' This meant that China assumed obligations that in many cases went far beyond those expected of existing members at its stage of development. These commitments involved not simply reducing border barriers but undertaking detailed changes in internal policies.

Upon accession China was required to make major tariff reductions and by 2007 to reduce average import-weighted tariffs to 6.8 percent (Sally 2004). This is a major additional decline in tariffs which had averaged 40.6 percent as recently as 1992 and is almost half the average level in place upon accession. Almost all of China's non-tariff trade barriers have to be removed. Nearly all import and export quotas and licenses had to be removed by 2005 and those that did remain to be administered in a transparent manner. By 2005, all firms were to be allowed to import and export goods. China also agreed to implement the WTO TRIMs agreement without exceptions and thus could no longer make the permission to invest or import contingent on performance requirements such as earning foreign exchange or using domestic content. Restrictions on foreign participation in the distribution sector were to be phased out within three years. China also agreed to the TRIPs and it adopted the WTO SPS and TBT Agreements immediately upon its accession.

There were also a host of commitments with respect to policy transparency including obligations to translate into English and publish new laws and regulations and to establish inquiry points for foreign firms and governments. Time is allowed for comment before laws are promulgated and new tribunals established to review administrative acts relating to WTO implementation with the right of appeal to higher judicial bodies.

Although the WTO is in principle based on non-discrimination, China was also compelled to agree, on a transitory basis, to permit members to subject it to discriminatory treatment. First, it agreed to a special selective safeguard that could be used against its exports for twelve years after its accession. It also agreed to an additional safeguard provision for textiles and apparel that would be in force until the end of 2008 and could be (and has been) used temporarily to deny it the full benefits of the expiration of the MFA in 2005.[5] Second, China agreed to accept non-market economy status for the purposes of anti-dumping rules until the end of 2015. This would allow countries to use specially constructed prices when evaluating claims of dumping brought against Chinese exporters; and third, China allowed the WTO to set up a transitional Review Mechanism that would monitor its implementation record annually for the first ten years of its membership.

These demanding terms were useful for Chinese reformers. Before its accession to the WTO, China's initial domestic reforms involved taking tentative steps towards introducing a market system to its economy. The enterprises that played a leading role in these reforms, however, were generally owned by foreign investors and local Chinese governments rather than private Chinese entrepreneurs. WTO membership strengthened the hand of reformers seeking to hasten China's movement towards a more developed market economy. The benefits from WTO accession became an added reason for undertaking the domestic reforms. WTO entry has allowed China's leadership to make a more credible commitment towards moving China towards a system that more fully recognizes private enterprise.

The requirements of WTO entry forced Chinese policymakers to confront politically difficult issues. These included reforming domestic banking institutions, subjecting state-owned enterprises to harder budget constraints, and allowing private firms to freely engage in international trade. WTO entry also mobilized domestic firms to become more competitive through restructuring, acquiring new technologies, and forming new alliances and mergers with both domestic and foreign firms.

The WTO accession process also served to promote better Chinese governance. The WTO requires policy transparency and the enforcement of domestic trade policies on the basis of rules rather than bureaucratic discretion. WTO membership also necessitates non-discrimination (i.e. national treatment) for imported goods and services. China remains a country with considerable domestic barriers and strong provincial governments. If provinces are forced to provide national treatment for imported goods and services, they will find it harder to discriminate against goods from other provinces.

Many of these reforms are changes that China might have chosen to implement anyway, but entry into the WTO served to advance their implementation.

In 2004, as reported in Table 6.1 below, these requirements were apparent in China's tariff regime and WTO commitments. China had bound 100 percent of its tariffs—a discipline which most other Asian and many developing countries and developed countries have not accepted. Unlike almost all developing countries that have average bound rates far in excess of their applied rates,

---

[5] Par. 242 of the 'Report of the Working Party on the Accession of China.'

Table 6.1: Trade policy profiles, 2004

Country	%						WTO Cases*	AD Cases
	bound	Final Bound	Applied Total	Agriculture Applied	Non-Agric. Applied	Services #sectors		
China	100	10	10.4	16.2	9.5	93	1/0	71
Other Asian:								
Indonesia	96.6	37.1	6.9	8.2	6.7	45	2/4	7
Korea	94.5	15.9	11.2	41.6	6.7	98	8,8	32
Malaysia	83.7	14.5	8.4	3.3	9.1	73	1,0	12
Philipines	66.8	25.6	6.3	9.5	5.8	51	0,0	0
Singapore	69.2	6.9	0	0	0	67	0,0	0
Taipei,Chinese	100	6.1	6.9	16.3	5.5	119	0,0	3
Thailand	74.7	25.7	15.4	29.6	13.3	75	5,1	22
Other developing								
Brazil	100	31.4	12.4	10.3	12.7	43	12,2	50
Costa Rica	100	42.8	5.9	12.2	4.9	44	0,1	0
Egypt	99.1	36.6	19.9	22.5	19.5	44	0,1	15
India	73.8	49.8	29.1	37.4	27.9	37	8,5	191
Mexico	100	34.9	18	24.3	17.1	77	5,3	63
South Africa	100	19.1	5.8	9.1	5.3	91	0,0	
Developed								
Australia	97	9.9	4.2	1.2	4.6	103	5,2	52
Canada	99.7	5.1	3.9	3	4	105	12,10	59
EU	100	4.1	4.2	5.9	4	116	26,21	167
Iceland	95	13.4	2.9	6.5	2.4	113	0,0	0
Israel	76.4	20.8	5.6	15.9	4	58	0,0	6
Japan	99.6	2.9	3.1	7.3	2.5	112	8,6	2
Norway	100	3	1.2	na	0.6	111	1,0	0

* Defendant/claimant

Source: http://stat.wto.org/CountryProfiles/SG_e.htm

there is almost no water in China's tariffs. Its average applied rates in 2004 of 10.4 were converging closely to its final bound rate average of 10 percent. China's average applied rates on non-agricultural products of 9.5 percent in 2004 were similar to those of Malaysia (9.1) and converging to the levels of Korea and other East Asian economies of around 6 percent. They were already far below the average non-agricultural rates applied by other major developing countries such as Brazil (12.7), Egypt (19.5), India (27.9), and Mexico (17.1). China's average applied tariffs on agricultural products of 16.2 percent are similar to those of the Philippines and Chinese Taipei and far below those of Korea, Thailand, Egypt, India, and Mexico.

China's services liberalization is also very impressive. Commitments have been made for 93 sectors, a number way above the typical developing country or ASEAN member and in line with the commitments of Korea (98 sectors) and South Africa (91 sectors.) Among noteworthy commitments: the banking sector is to be completely open to foreign competition by the end of 2006. In telecommunications up to 49 percent ownership is to be allowed by 2006. The insurance sector was also extensively liberalized. Foreign securities houses were allowed minority equity and several professional services, most notably legal, were liberalized as well.

WTO PARTICIPATION

Appraisals of China's performance at the WTO are generally positive.[6] Its delegation is regarded as being of high quality. It has participated actively in regular WTO activities. Remarkably, it has only been involved in one dispute as a complainant (US steel safeguards) and two as a defendant. There was a case initiated by the United States in March 2004 relating to preferential value-added tax for domestically designed integrated circuits[7] and currently there is a case regarding auto parts in which both the US and the EU allege China has violated its commitments. In several other cases where China has been challenged they have quickly come into compliance.[8] China has also participated in forty-seven cases as a third party, something which both the EU and US routinely do to ensure that they have the right to defend their interests should the need arise. This participation is a clear demonstration that China views its interests as systemic and that these go beyond only those disputes in which it is directly involved.

China has also been active in the Doha Round negotiations. Non-Agricultural Market Access (NAMA) is the area of greatest importance as an offensive objective. China would like to see as much liberalization as possible by other countries while at the same time insisting on special treatment for countries that have recently acceded. China has engaged actively in NAMA discussions of formulas that should be employed for tariff reduction. In agriculture its positions are more mixed. It is very interested in reducing subsidies and protection in developed countries. It chose to participate in the G20 in order to press these claims although it has not been particularly active in joining other groups. It would also like to see lower barriers to its agricultural exports to developing countries. On the other hand, China also seeks some flexibility in commitments assumed by developing countries to assist poor farmers and promote rural development. In the services area, China also has a particular interest in mode-four liberalization: the movement of natural persons. This would increase opportunities for Chinese workers to work abroad. China is particularly concerned about rules. It seeks more disciplines on anti-dumping practices such as zeroing for example. China has also voiced its support for trade facilitation although it is not particularly interested in such assistance for itself. It has also not been a vociferous advocate of S&D treatment because it clearly has an important interest in seeing developing

---

[6] According to Pearson, 'on a personal level, China's interlocutors at the WTO, as at APEC, are uniformly complimentary about the quality of China's delegation'.

[7] The case resulted in a mutually agreed solution in October 2005 China agreed to amend or revoke the measures at issue.

[8] Author's private communication with a US trade lawyer based in China.

Table **6.2**: Top ten WTO participants (written submissions, 2003)

Rank	Member	Category	Overall	Individual	Joint
1	EC	D	120	105	15
2	USA	D	116	109	7
3	China	DC	65	48	17
4	Japan	D	61	44	17
5	Australia	D	50	44	6
6	India	DC	48	16	32
7	Switzerland	D	46	23	23
8	Chile	DC	45	16	29
9	Thailand	DC	44	16	28
10	Canada	D	43	36	7

Source: Nordström (2005)

countries with large markets such as India and Brazil making meaningful liberalization commitments.[9]

Overall, therefore, in the Round, China has not tried to take as a strong a leadership role as Brazil, but it has by no means been passive. This is also true of its activity at the WTO more generally. Håkan Nordström has undertaken a very interesting analysis of country participation in WTO activities. He has collected data on all written submissions members have undertaken both individually and with others in 2003. These reflect activities undertaken both in the ruling bodies of the WTO as well as in the Doha Round negotiations. *China emerges in these data as the most active developing country and the third most active WTO member.* Its total of 65 written submissions was considerably below those for the EU (120 submissions) and the USA (116), but greater than India, the second most active developing country participant. The detailed data reported in Table 6.2 indicate that China was especially active in the Rules Committee with eighteen submissions, ten of which related to subsidies and countervailing duties.

In most respects, therefore, China appears as a constructive member working to pursue its interests which for the most part correspond to the organization's goals of greater multilateral liberalization. There are however two matters in which China has been more aggressive and even recalcitrant. Both reflect powerful domestic political concerns. The first relates to Taiwan. Members of the WTO are officially customs territories rather than sovereign nations. As such China could tolerate the accession of Taiwan which also occurred at Doha. At the same time, however, the government of China has fiercely fought any gesture by WTO members that could imply that Taiwan enjoyed sovereign status. This has led to testy interactions when Taiwan

---

[9] Pearson makes the interesting point that China has not been a participant in coalitions of developing countries that have resisted liberalization such as the 'Like-minded Group' that focused on the difficulties of developing country implementation (2003: 23).

attempted to exercise its right to formal consultations. In 2003, there was also considerable friction in response to Chinese efforts to downgrade Taiwan status from 'permanent mission' which could imply an independent country to office of permanent representative' (Pearson 2003: 16).

China has also been visibly unenthusiastic about the annual Transitional Review Mechanism. China is required by the terms of accession agreement each year to provide an extensive amount of data regarding its policies and performance and then to submit to questioning by other members. These reviews are a nagging reminder about the terms of its accession that some in China viewed as having been a sell-out. They also appear to question China's integrity and its willingness to honor its legally binding commitments. China grudgingly sticks to the letter of law in meeting this commitment, giving only oral answers to questions that are often less than forthcoming. It is clearly an unwilling participant and does not take kindly to the treatment.

All told, therefore, China is seeking normalcy, not special treatment, and this is something it will gain once the transitory arrangements associated with its accession expire. Within a decade, special safeguards, non-market status, and transitional review mechanisms will expire and China will gladly assume its role as a more normal but very important WTO member.

What accounts for the way in which China has participated in the WTO? Why has it chosen to be constructive and yet not highly assertive? China is constructive because the WTO is a very attractive institution for China that clearly serves its interests. To be sure, China was important enough to receive MFN treatment from almost all countries even prior to joining, and some suggested that by joining under such demanding terms, it was opening itself up to challenges that could have actually reduced its market access (Mallon and Whalley 2004). But, for the most part such challenges have been conspicuous by their absence, and China now enjoys unconditional MFN treatment and the ability to enforce its rights through the dispute settlement system.

China's political relations with other countries are often problematic because of the undemocratic nature of its system of government and its poor record on human rights. This gives China a great interest in a strong, rules-based WTO because it allows its trade and investment issues to be placed on a less political, more technical track. In addition, since China does not have FTAs or benefit from preferences in its major developed-country markets—the US, EU, and Japan (so far)—the MFN terms on which access to these markets is granted is especially important for China.

Bargaining at the WTO is done on the basis of reciprocal concessions. This means that those with the largest markets exercise the greatest power. China's large and growing market and its willingness and ability to liberalize position it to exercise influence. But, so far, it has been prudent in the way it has exercised this power. This is because China also seeks to be a leader of the developing countries and its economic interest in liberalization and competitiveness in exporting come into conflict with the desire of many developing countries to seek special and differential treatment and benefit from preferential access. This leads it to be less outspoken about its interests than it might be otherwise and allows China to leave the demands for developing-country liberalization to the developed countries.

Historically, times during which new powers are arising on the global stage have been filled with tension. The real challenge for the rest of the world lies in ensuring that an emergent China has incentives to engage the rest of the world in a cooperative and peaceful fashion. China's performance at the WTO suggests that at least so far, by allowing China to join, the rest of the world has helped meet this challenge.

6.3 Regional Arrangements

Like almost every other WTO member, China has not confined its trade policy to the WTO.[10] Instead, it has both embraced and stimulated the current global trend towards Free Trade Agreements (Antkiewicz and Whalley 2004). China has concluded several agreements and is in the process of negotiating many more. In 2001, it began talks with ASEAN that resulted in an agreement to eliminate tariffs and continue with a view to obtaining agreements with respect to investment and services. In 2003, an agreement in agriculture was concluded with Thailand. In 2004, Hong Kong and Macau signed agreements with the Mainland. In 2005, an agreement with Chile was concluded and there are currently ongoing FTA negotiations with Australia, New Zealand, Pakistan, the Southern Africa Customs Union, and the Gulf Cooperation Council. Other discussions that are ongoing include Brazil, Iceland, India, Japan, and South Korea. In what follows, I first describe some of these agreements and then appraise their significance.

ASEAN

In 2002 a framework agreement on Comprehensive Economic Cooperation was signed with ASEAN to serve as guide for achieving an FTA that covers goods, services and investment. The goal is to have an FTA in place by 2010 among the more advanced of these countries. The newer ASEAN members (Vietnam, Laos, Myanmar, and Cambodia) will have until 2015 to comply.

[10] Some countries, embarrassed by the need to explain why they are departing from a pure multilateral strategy use the excuse of slow movement in the Doha Round as the reason why they are suddenly launching into a large number of FTAs, but this is not generally very persuasive since some of the countries making this excuse are among the least forthcoming. This is not, however, an argument made by the Chinese government.

An early harvest program reduced or eliminated tariffs in about 10 percent of lines by 2006. Most other tariffs are to be eliminated on between 2005 and 2010, by which time 90 percent of tariff lines should be covered. The remaining 10 percent are deemed sensitive and will be removed at a slower pace.[11] According to a Singapore government website, there are also ongoing negotiations with respect to services and investment and expectations that ASEAN could obtain benefits from acceleration in China's WTO service liberalization commitments.[12]

China has heralded this agreement. Its press observes:

The China-ASEAN FTA will form a huge market, with 1.85 billion consumers and a combined gross domestic product of almost US$2.5 trillion. The value of imports and exports of this zone will hopefully exceed that of the NAFTA (North America Free Trade Agreement) by 2010 and its GDP will likely be higher than that in the European Union market. These three, China-ASEAN free trade zone, NAFTA and the EU, will become the three pillars of the world economy.[13]

China has also had talks on bilateral FTAs with some of the ASEAN countries. In particular it concluded the agreement with Thailand that focused on fruits and vegetables in 2003. It also started talks with Singapore but these were suspended over a fallout on Taiwan.

HONG KONG AND MACAO

The Closer Economic Partnership Arrangement (CEPA) Agreement signed by China and Hong Kong was the first completed FTA agreement signed by both parties. Its stated purpose is 'to strengthen trade and investment cooperation by liberalizing tariff and non-tariff barriers on substantially all trade, liberalizing services and promoting trade and investment facilitation' (CEPA Preamble).

The CEPA Agreement specifically makes clear that the parties will not apply the provisions of China's WTO accession that allow countries to (a) subject China to non-market economy status in the application of antidumping; and (b) impose special safeguards on all trade until 2012 and on

---

[11] The sensitive groups of products would have their tariffs slashed starting in 2012 to reach a level between zero and 5 percent by 2020, while highly sensitive goods may maintain their import duties but only to a maximum 50 percent in 2020.

[12] It has been agreed that the ASEAN Investment Agreement (AIA) would be used as a template for investment negotiations. ASEAN and China have also agreed to cooperation focusing on five priority sectors namely: agriculture, ICT, HRD, investment, and the Mekong River Basin development, and eleven other activities including the acceleration of the Singapore–Kunming Railway Project.

[13] Remarks made by Wang Jinzhen, spokesman of China Council of Promotion of International Trade (CCPIT), in Xiamen, Sept. 7, 2002.

textiles through 2008.[14] The schedules of the Agreement provide for the Mainland to eliminate duties on all products of Hong Kong origin (except prohibited articles) provided that CEPA rules of origin are met. Both sides also eliminate the application of anti-dumping measures or countervailing measures although they can apply safeguards. Services are liberalized using a positive list approach which in accordance with WTO practice extends the preferential treatment to 'service suppliers of other WTO members that are engaged in substantive business operations.' Financial cooperation is given a lot of attention. The Mainland supports state-owned banks in relocating their treasury and foreign exchange trading centers to Hong Kong, in making acquisitions, using Hong Kong financial intermediaries, cooperative financial regulation, and the listing of insurance companies in Hong Kong. 'The liberalization permits earlier access for Hong Kong service suppliers to the Mainland market, ahead of China's World Trade Organization (WTO) timetable. In some sectors, like audiovisual services, transport services and distribution services, the concessions go beyond China's WTO commitments.'[15] There are specific provisions for cooperation in financial services (banking, securities, and insurance) tourism, and trade and investment facilitation, and for encouraging the mutual recognition of professional qualifications and exchange of 'professional talents.' 'The two sides shall resolve any problem arising from the interpretation or implement of the "CEPA" through "consultation in the spirit of friendship and cooperation."' A Joint Steering Committee with officials designated by both sides will make decisions by consensus (Art 19: 5). The Agreement signed with Macao follows a very similar template.

Since Hong Kong did not apply tariffs on Chinese goods, for China this agreement clearly was not about eliminating tariffs on its exports. It was given greater security from anti-dumping and countervailing actions. However there are additional advantages. First, it signaled the special status of Hong Kong. Second, it gained relief from the discriminatory treatment in the WTO agreement. Third, it clearly used the agreement to signal government support for Mainland financial institutions in Hong Kong. In addition it provided services firms in Hong Kong first foreign mover advantages. Indirectly, it also provided advantages for Hong Kong over Taiwan.

CHILE

In 2005 China and Chile concluded an FTA. The two countries took less than a year to negotiate the accord, which immediately eliminates tariffs on

[14] These are contained in Articles 15 and 16 of the 'Protocol on the Accession of the People's Republic of China to the WTO' and par. 242 of the 'Report of the Working Party on the Accession of China.'

[15] See Trade and Industry Department of Hong Kong website, <http://www.tid.gov.hk/english/cepa/details/note.html#goods>.

92 percent of Chile's exports to China and 50 percent of the products that China sends to Chile. The pact does not cover services.[16] In ten years after the start of the tariff concession process, the import tariffs on 97 percent of the tariff lines of both sides will be zero. Furthermore, the Agreement provides that the two Parties may accelerate the tariff concession upon consensus through consultation.

NEW ZEALAND

New Zealand hopes to become the first developed country to sign an FTA with China. It has already become the first developed economy to grant it market economy status. The FTA talks have gone on for several years. The New Zealand government, which was criticized for signing an agreement with Thailand that failed to include services, is insistent that the deal should be comprehensive and in addition covers goods, services, and investment, include provisions for rules of origin, trade remedies, intellectual property, and government procurement.

AUSTRALIA

China is also involved in FTA talks with Australia. Again the memorandum of understanding that launched the talks granted China market economy status. The Australian government has also made clear that it is seeking a comprehensive agreement that applies to 'substantially' all goods, trade in services 'as well as other non-tariff issues such as the recognition of standards, customs cooperation, protection of intellectual property rights and regulation of foreign investment.'[17] Australia is a highly competitive producer of agricultural and mineral products. In 2005, it accounted for 98 percent of all Chinese beef imports, 12 percent of dairy imports, and significant amounts of cotton and wool. There are significant exports of barely, wheat, hides and skins, and wine and very substantial quantities of iron ore, uranium, and non-ferrous metals. Given Chinese tariffs on agricultural products of 15.3 percent and on Australian manufactured goods of up to 45 percent, the amount of liberalization for China could be substantial.[18] On Australia's

[16] China–Chile FTA will start the comprehensive tariff concession in the latter half of 2006. On the Chilean side, the import tariff rates of 74% of the tariff lines will be lowered to zero immediately after the Agreement takes effect, while on the Chinese side, 63% of the import tariff lines will have zero rate within 2 years; The remaining import tariff lines of both Parties, will be zero rated 5 to 10 years after the Agreement becomes effective. Each party may keep only 3% of the tariff lines as exceptions with tariff rates unchanged.

[17] Australia–China Free Trade Agreement, Australian Government, Department of Foreign Affairs and Trade, March 2006. The Government also stresses 'we will not be rushed. The Australian Government has stressed that any FTA with China must deliver real gains for Australian businesses across the board. That is, it must be comprehensive—covering goods, services and investment—and be completed as a single undertaking.' Ibid.

[18] In a model done for the Australian government the authors assume Chinese barriers in agriculture have the following tariff equivalents: Wool 15 percent, Sugar 25 percent, Oi-lseeds

part, the quid pro quo would be liberalization of tariffs on labor intensive manufactured goods. In the textiles and clothing sector, Australian average tariffs are 9.1 percent. There are 234 tariff lines with rates of between 16 and 20 percent, and 387 between 6 and 10 percent; in footwear there are 4 lines between 16 and 20 percent and average rate of protection of 5.6 percent.[19]

The fact that China is willing to conclude FTAs with these two developed countries that are highly competitive agricultural producers is very significant, since it indicates a willingness to contemplate major adjustments in agriculture while also indicating these countries willingness to contemplate free trade in labor-intensive manufacturing.

OTHERS

China has also launched talks with India and Pakistan. New Delhi does not quite share the enthusiasm for a conventional FTA although it is willing to talk about cooperation. But Pakistan and China have signed a framework agreement, implemented an early harvest, and Pakistan has provided China with the requisite market economy status. China is also discussing FTAs with many other potential partners in Latin America (Brazil, Peru), South Africa, the Gulf (GCC), Iceland, Asia (Korea), and with regional groupings such as APEC and East Asia (ASEAN plus three).

6.3.1 IMPLICATIONS

China has numerous goals in signing these agreements. One immediate concern is to use them to obtain market status recognition and relief from being subject to special safeguards. Ironically China is using these discriminatory agreements as a way to *remove* the discrimination to which it has been subjected at the WTO. A second motive is to secure access to important raw materials—many of the countries are major suppliers of minerals (Chile—copper, Australia—iron-ore and uranium, and GCC—oil). A third is to solidify its relations and influence both inside and beyond the East Asian region. A fourth, the most basic, is to gain improved market access for its exports which as labor-intensive manufactured and agricultural goods are often subject to high tariff protection. Individual agreements are also used to achieve specific goals. For example, the Hong Kong and Macao agreements help underscore the privileged relationship between the Mainland and these economies and ensure that despite their differences measures such as anti-dumping and

13 percent, Cereals 3 percent, Wheat 30 percent, Processed rice 10.6 percent. Source: Adams, Fan, Li, and Zheng (2005).

[19] Source: <http://www.dfat.gov.au/geo/china/fta/feasibility_3.pdf>.

countervailing duties could not be used to segment them. In addition these agreements were used to implement specific joint initiatives and signal clearly that Beijing would permit state-owned banks to move some of their operations to Hong Kong.

China is well aware of concerns that it is trying to dominate East Asia and/or close it to outsiders. It has gone to great pains to allay such fears. It is particularly reluctant to appear domineering in its interactions with ASEAN and it prefers that ASEAN take the leading role in the bilateral relationship. China also does not want to be seen as building a fortress Asia. Consider this official statement:

We should continue to support ASEAN in playing the leading role in East Asia cooperation. On the other hand, we should give due consideration to the legitimate interests of the non-East Asian countries in this region, so as to gain their understanding of and support for East Asia cooperation.[20]

In general, China's approach to FTAs has been pragmatic. It has shown a willingness to negotiate with countries individually and in groups (e.g. ASEAN and ASEAN+Korea+Japan), with developed (New Zealand and Australia) and developing countries, and with those that are heavily specialized in agriculture (New Zealand and Australia), manufactured goods (ASEAN, South Korea), and services (Hong Kong). It has been focused on East Asia but also quite willing to deal with countries in Latin America, South Asia, and Africa. It has sought to signal that its interests are global.

The agreements have not followed a single template. Some have included goods, services, investment and cooperation (e.g. Hong Kong, Macao), others cover only goods (e.g. Chile), while some have started with goods liberalization with the intention to add services and investment later (e.g. ASEAN). Several have been launched with an early harvest in which some liberalization has come into effect as soon as talks have commenced. The deepest agreements thus far are with Hong Kong and Macao, although even these do not cover issues that are part and parcel of agreements that are typically signed by the US (e.g. intellectual property, labor and environment, government procurement, dispute settlement by panels) or the EU (e.g. competition policy).

STUMBLING BLOCS?

These Chinese initiatives raise several concerns that are traditionally mentioned in debates about regional trade arrangements. The first is the concern that these regional arrangements are likely to undermine the multilateral trading system. This fear is misplaced. If (and this is an important qualification)

---

[20] 'Be Open and Inclusive And Achieve Mutual Benefit and Common Progress.' Statement by Premier Wen Jiabao at The First East Asia Summit, Kuala Lumpur, Malaysia, December 14, 2005:<http://www.fmprc.gov.cn/eng/topics/wjbfw/t228275.htm>.

they do achieve liberalization in 'substantially all trade', FTA agreements that involve China are likely to *hasten* global liberalization. China has not insisted on covering services and investment in its agreements, but its agreements do include liberalization in most merchandise products. Since China is such a competitive supplier of labor-intensive manufactures, for most countries, an FTA signed with China is very likely to be trade-creating on the import side. Indeed, any country that adjusts domestically to Chinese competition is most likely to require little additional adjustment before it opens up to developing countries as a whole. (The same would be true of countries opening up in services mode four—the movement of natural persons—if this is included in agreements.) If China is able to sign FTAs with the Asian Pacific region, this region will be readily positioned to extend this liberalization to the rest of world.

A similar argument holds for those signing FTAs with the US with respect to services and investment. The US has insisted on deep agreements that cover services with a negative list and investment in addition to trade in goods including agriculture. Any country that signs with both China and the US could surely extend these benefits to the rest of the world without major additional dislocation.

The dominoes appear to falling. Each time China concludes an FTA with another significant trading partner, it puts pressure on others to preserve their access to the world's most rapidly growing market. In numerous sectors, China's MFN tariffs remain significant and thus FTAs could give producers of those products a significant competitive advantage. Likewise, each time China succeeds in obtaining preferential access to another market it adds to the pressure for others who sell in *that* market to obtain similar access. Korea and Japan for example, reacted to the agreement between China and ASEAN by proposing FTAs of their own with ASEAN—something they probably would not have done before.[21]

The FTA between Korea and ASEAN is still being finalized. It is expected to remove duties on 80 percent of goods traded by 2009. Korea and ASEAN have also pledged to conclude negotiations on liberalization in services and investment by the end of this year. Korea also has FTAs with Chile and Singapore and is seeking similar deals with several Latin American and other countries.

---

[21] The Korea International Trade Association (KITA) said the China–ASEAN FTA, which will come into force soon, is expected to create the world's largest economic bloc, with bilateral trade amounting to US$1.2 trillion. The pact will cause disadvantages such as high tariffs for South Korean industries such as petrochemicals, textiles, shoes and electrical and electronic products. More than 21 percent of South Korean exports to China will be subject to tariffs over 10 percentage points higher than those for China-bound ASEAN shipments in 2010, when the FTA is fully implemented. The FTA will impose no duties on more than 90 per cent of the trade between China and ASEAN members by that time.

Currently, Japan is reported to be in the process of developing a concerted response to the pressures it is feeling from the Chinese and US initiatives. It is developing new policies with respect to agriculture and the movement of labor and planning a host of additional agreements to preserve its competitive position.[22] It appears that powerful forces of competitive liberalization are operating effectively.

FORTRESS ASIA?

A second, related concern is that East Asia could become a 'fortress' in which barriers are raised or at least not lowered with respect to the rest of the world. China is, however, clearly willing to negotiate with countries outside the region. Indeed this is true of the rest of Asia as well. The countries in the Asia Pacific are global traders and there is no evidence that they are confining their FTAs to the region. Instead, they are actively scouring the globe to find FTA partners. Singapore has FTAs with the US and a host of countries outside the region.[23] Likewise Thailand, Malaysia and South Korea are all negotiating with the United States[24] and Japan has an FTA with Mexico.

HUB AND SPOKE?

A third concern is that China is going to erect a hub-and-spoke system in which it has access to the regional economy duty-free, but the other countries do not have similar access to one another. But in fact, almost all countries in the region are now negotiating with each other. For example, ASEAN is negotiating with both South Korea and Japan and Australia with many countries in the region. So this fear is also misplaced.

NOODLE BOWL

The one concern that is legitimate is that these FTAs are creating a system of overlapping agreements with respect to rules of origin and other provisions that are unnecessarily cumbersome. By proceeding piecemeal in these negotiations, there is the danger for China and its other trading partners that trade could be enveloped in the proverbial noodle bowl of agreements. Producers could have to meet different standards and rules of origin when selling to different partners. This is an area in which the WTO and APEC have both seriously failed. In particular Article XXIV 5(b) of the GATT only states that the 'duties and other regulations of commerce' once the FTA is concluded

---

[22] Japan has reached Agreements for Economic Partnership Arrangements with Philippines, Malaysia, and Thailand. It is negotiating with Korea, Asean, Indonesia, and engaged in collaborative research with Chile, India, Australia, Switzerland, and in talks in ASEAN, plus 3.

[23] Singapore's government webpage lists eleven FTAs that are in place and fifteen more under negotiation < http://app.fta.gov.sg/asp/index.asp>.

[24] Thailand's negotiations with the US have confronted problems with respect to light trucks as well as agriculture and have become a domestic political issue.

shall not be higher or more restrictive than they were before. But it does little to discipline the crafting of these to meet specific circumstances in a manner that is protectionist and inefficient. The simplest solution would be a single system of rules that would be applied by all WTO members in all preferential agreements.

6.4 Qualifications

I have argued that thus far, China has promoted trade liberalization in both the WTO and through its FTAs. However, it should be stressed that many of the FTAs have yet to be completed and thus China's trade and domestic policies remain very much a work in progress. In this final section, therefore I offer four qualifications to this conclusion.

AGREEMENT DETAILS

First, the history of free-trade agreements is a mixed one. In thinking about their implications it is important to pay attention both to their content and their prospects for implementation. Countries enter into FTAs with different motives. Some are genuinely interested in promoting trade liberalization and deep economic integration and view the agreements as a complement to multilateral liberalization. For the most part, for example, the United States is using FTAs as part of such an offensive strategy.[25] A second group of typically smaller countries is driven by the desire to improve their competitiveness as a location for production. It is often said that preferential trade arrangements are 'second best' and that multilateral liberalization is first best. But for individual countries even better than free trade could be the combination of no barriers at home and preferential access to all foreign markets. This competitiveness motive seems to explain why Chile and Singapore have pursued these agreements so avidly. A third group of countries, however, are as yet unwilling to liberalize fully and are basically driven by defensive considerations to undertake these agreements. For these countries, there is often a temptation to conclude agreements that go by the name of FTAs but (*a*) take a long time to implement; (*b*) exclude significant amounts of potential trade in goods and services; (*c*) have highly restrictive rules of origin that limit their impacts; and (*d*) fail to include adequate provisions for enforcement.

China basically seeks to use FTAs to secure market access, i.e. for offensive purposes, and it is prepared to open its market at home to do this. But its initiatives are also being driven by political considerations and the

---

[25] To be sure there is resistance in the US particularly from sugar and clothing producers.

desire to reassure other countries. Unlike the US or the EU, China does not seem to have developed a demanding comprehensive FTA template that is used with minor changes with all its FTA partners. Instead China has proceeded opportunistically, signing agreements with quite different degrees of depth and coverage. In part this is because China is using FTAs as much as an instrument of foreign policy as an instrument of trade policy.[26] This means that where a partner is willing to contemplate full liberalization in the context of a deep integration agreement, the result could be trade creation on a large scale. Indeed that would appear to be the implication of the types of agreements being aimed at by the Australian and New Zealand governments. In negotiations with countries that fall into the defensive category, however, some of the agreements that are actually concluded could be quite limited and there may be less there than meets the eye.

CHINESE IMPLEMENTATION

A second key issue relates to the institutional capacity to ensure that the agreements China signs are implemented at home. This holds with respect both to China's WTO and FTA commitments. The United States Trade Representative for example publishes an annual report on Chinese WTO compliance filled with complaints of compliance failures. The most recent report for example is 101 pages long.[27] It is particularly concerned with the still incomplete transition from a state-planned economy. Other concerns include: the lack of enforcement of intellectual property laws, the continued use of industrial policies in sectors such as auto-parts, steel, and high-tech, regulatory intervention to support domestic enterprises, export restrictions on coke, the use of standards to favor domestic high-tech producers, and sanitary and phytosanitary standards to favor domestic farmers. Nonetheless, the USTR report does acknowledge that China has made great strides towards coming into compliance and it is surely the case that trade agreements make it more likely that these issues can be resolved.

LOSS OF COMPETITIVENESS

A third key qualification relates to the continuation of China's competitiveness and its impact on Chinese domestic politics. The competitiveness of its traded goods sector has facilitated China's adjustment to its WTO accession and contributed significantly to the character of the trade policy that I have described in this chapter. China is basically eager to

---

[26] The greater flexibility in these agreements may reflect domestic decision-making differences. In the case of the US, agreements must get through Congress.
[27] United States Trade Representative (2005).

erect a legal and political superstructure to ensure its access to key inputs and markets and it is prepared to expose its domestic firms and farmers to increased foreign competition in order to do so. Nonetheless, even with the success it has enjoyed in recent years, domestic tensions have arisen with respect to the dislocation caused by the spread of the market economy.

There is a widespread view that the Chinese currency is seriously undervalued and there are strong external political pressures for a substantial appreciation.[28] The verdict of undervaluation is supported by China's very large current account surplus and its significant accumulation of foreign exchange reserves over the past few years. In March 2006, these amounted to $853.7 billion, surpassing the reserves held by Japan and making Chinese holdings the world's largest. There is considerable debate over the appropriate course of action to deal with this issue. For our purposes it should be recognized that if a significant appreciation of the reminbi was to undermine Chinese competitiveness, the broad thrust of the policies described here could be adversely affected. Domestic protectionist pressures would surely increase and China would be considerably less eager to pursue reciprocal free-trade agreements if it was less confident in its ability to compete. Whatever the costs of China's exchange rate policies might have been, therefore, the liberal nature of its recent trade policies should be counted among its benefits.

HYPER-COMPETITIVENESS

On the other hand, there could be problems abroad, if China becomes too competitive. Protectionism abroad could then offset Chinese liberalization at home. It could also undermine the application of MFN treatment. In both the United States and the European Union, for example, the very large bilateral trade deficits with China have heightened trade frictions. The surge in Chinese clothing exports in 2005 when the Multi-Fiber Agreement expired led to the use of special safeguards in both economies. While these were legal, they are certainly discriminatory.

In many developing countries, the highest non-agricultural tariffs are placed on precisely the labor-intensive products in which China specializes. So while China's trade policies are a force for a more liberal trading order, China's trade performance exerts countervailing pressures in other countries. Some may rise to the challenge, but others could become even more reticent to embrace global engagement.

[28] See Bergsten (2006), Goldstein (2005) and Goldstein and Lardy (2004).

Table 6.A1: Distribution of submissions over areas and issues (2003)

Series	WTO body	China				WTO		
		DDA	Ind.	Joint	Total	Individual	Joint	Total
			48	17	65	838	1387	2225
	Ruling Bodies							
WT/MIN (03)/	Ministerial Conference, Doha	X	1	4	5	20	195	215
WT/GC/	General Council		1	5	6	24	268	292
TN/C/	Trade Negotiations Committee	X	1	1	2	1	92	93
	Agriculture							
G/AG/	Committee on Agriculture			2	2	13	52	65
TN/AG/	Committee on Agriculture—Special Session	X	1		1	24	92	116
G/SPS/	Committee on Sanitary and Phytosanitary Measures		3		3	76	11	87
	Non-Agriculture Market Access (NAMA)							
G/C/	Council for Trade in Goods (except trade facilitation)		1		1	23	4	27
TN/MA/	Negotiating Group on Market Access	X	1		1	33	56	89
G/MA/	Committee on Market Access		1		1	8		8
G/RO/	Committee on Rules of Origin					3	2	5
G/VAL/	Committee on Customs Valuation		1		1	9		9
G/LIC/	Committee on Import Licensing		1		1	10		10
G/IT/	Committee of Participation on the Expansion of Trade in IT prod.				4			4
G/TBT/	Committee on Technical Barriers to Trade		3		3	60	2	62
G/TRIMS/	Committee on Trade-Related Investment Measures		1		1	3		3
G/STR/	Working Party on State Trading Enterprises					1		1
	Rules							
TN/RL/	Negotiating Group on Rules	X	4	2	6	84	185	269
G/ADP/	Committee on Anti-Dumping Practices					10		10
G/ADP/AHG/	Committee on anti-Dumping Practices—WG on Implementation					9		9
G/SCM/	Committee on Subsidies and Countervailing Measures		10		10	136	8	144
G/SG/	Committee on Safeguards		2		2	11		11
WT/REG/	Committee on Regional Trade Agreements					5	49	54
	Gats							
S/C/	Council for Trade in Services		2		2	14	2	16
TN/S/	Council for Trade in Services—Special Session	X	1	3	4	46	103	149
S/CSC/	Committee on Specific Commitments					5		5
S/FIN/	Committee on Trade in Financial Services					10	16	26
S/WPDR/	Working Party on Domestic Regulation					10		10
S/WPGR/	Working Party on GATS Rules					4		4
	TRIPS							
IP/	Council for TRIPS		3		3	66	105	171
TN/IP/	Council for TRIPS—Special Session	X				4		4
	Singapore Issues							
WT/WGTI/	WG on Relationship between Trade and Investment	X	2		2	8	3	11

(cont.)

Table 6.A1: (*Continued*)

Series	WTO body	China				WTO		
		DDA	Ind.	Joint	Total	Individual	Joint	Total
WT/WGTGP/	WG on Transparency in Government Procurement	X				4		4
WT/WGTCP/	WG on Interaction between Trade and Competition Policy	X	2		2	18		18
G/C/	Trade facilitation (dedicated meetings of the General Council)	X				5		5
	Development							
WT/COMTD/	Committee on Trade and Development						13	13
TN/CTD/	Committee on Trade and Development—Special Session	X				1	41	42
WT/BOP/	Committee on Balance-of-Payments Restrictions					1		1
WT/WGTTT/	Working Group on Trade and Transfer of Technology					2	7	9
WT/TDF/	Working Group on Trade, Debt and Finance						1	1
	Trade and environment							
WT/CTE/	Committee on Trade and Environment					18		18
TN/TE/	Committee on Trade and Environment—Special Sessions	X	2		2	22		22
TN/DS/	**DSU Review**		4		4	32	81	113

Source: Nordström (2005).

References

Adams, Philip, Fan, Mingtai, Li, Ronglin, and Zheng, Zhaoyang (2005), An Independent Report Prepared for The Australia–China FTA Feasibility Study the Centre of Policy Studies, Monash University, March 2.

Antkiewicz, Agata and Whalley, John (2004), 'China's New Regional Trade Arrangements,' NBER Working Paper 10992, December.

Australia–China Free Trade Agreement (2006), Australian Government, Department of Foreign Affairs and Trade, March. Available online at <http://www.dfat.gov.au/geo/china/fta/feasibility_3.pdf>.

Bergsten, C. Fred (2006), 'Clash of Titans,' *Newsweek*, International Edition, April 2.

Goldstein, Morris (2005), 'Reminbi Controversies,' Paper prepared for the Conference on Monetary Institutions and Economic Development Cato Institute, November 3.

——— and Lardy, Nicholas R. (2004), 'What kind of Landing for the Chinese Economy?', Policy Briefs in International Economics No. PB04.7 November 2004 (Washington, DC: Institute for International Economics).

Hufbauer, Clyde and Wong, Yee (2005), 'Prospects for Regional Free Trade in Asia,' Working Paper Number WP-o5-12, October, [Washington, DC: Institute for International Economics.]

Mallon, Glenda and Whalley, John (2004),'China's Post Accession WTO Stance,' NBER Working Paper No. 10649, August.

Nordström, Håkan (2005), 'Participation of Developing Countries in the WTO—New Evidence Based on the 2003 Official Records,' National Board of Trade, Sweden (mimeo).

Pearson, Margaret M. (2003), 'China's Multiple Personalities in Geneva: Constructing a Template for Future Research on Chinese Behavior in WTO,' University of Maryland (mimeo).

Sally, Razeen (2004), 'China's Trade Policies and its Integration into the World Economy.' Paper prepared for IGD/SAIIA SACU-China FTA Workshop, Johannesburg, September 28–9.

Singapore's government webpage <http://app.fta.gov.sg/asp/index.asp>.

Trade and Industry Department of Hong Kong website <http://www.tid.gov.hk/english/cepa/details/note.html#goods>.

United States Trade Representative (2005), 'Report to Congress on China's WTO Compliance' (Washington, DC: GPO).

Wang, Jinzhen, Spokesman of China Council of Promotion of International Trade (CCPIT), in Xiamen, September 7.

Wen, Jiabao (2005), 'Be Open and Inclusive and Achieve Mutual Benefit and Common Progress', Statement by at The First East Asia Summit Kuala Lumpur, Malaysia, December 14; <http://www.fmprc.gov.cn/eng/topics/wjbfw/t228275.htm>.

7

Regional and Global Financial Integration in East Asia[1]

Soyoung Kim, Jong-Wha Lee, and Kwanho Shin
Korea University

7.1 Introduction

In East Asia, there has been a rapid increase in international capital mobility, as East Asian countries have been deregulating their financial markets since the early 1990s. This continuous financial opening process has enabled the economies of the region to become integrated into global financial markets. The available empirical evidence suggests that the East Asian financial markets have become increasingly integrated with the markets of developed countries over the last decades. (Bekaert and Harvey 1995, World Bank 1997; and Eichengreen and Park 2005a).

However, it is not clear that the global financial liberalization and integration process has contributed to the integration of financial markets within the region. In general, trade liberalization tends to bring about trade integration on both global and regional levels, though possibly more on the regional level. In a similar vein, we might expect that capital market liberalization will also make these economies more closely linked with one another through cross-border financial transactions. On the contrary, several studies have claimed that the degree of financial market linkage in East Asia still remains low and that, unlike trade integration, the integration of financial markets in this region has been occurring more on a global level rather than on a regional level.

The majority of empirical studies provide evidence that the level of financial market integration in East Asia is relatively lower compared to Europe and that

[1] We are grateful to Galina Hale, Gyutaeg Oh, and Andrew Rose for helpful comments and Chi-soo Chung and Ju-Hyun Pyun for data assistance.

East Asia is integrated through global financial markets rather than through regional ones. Park and Bae (2002) and Eichengreen and Park (2005*b*) analyzed the distribution of the nationality of the lead managers, Japanese overseas portfolio investment, and co-movement of interest rates and stock prices. They concluded that East Asian countries have developed stronger financial ties with the US and Western Europe than with one another. Based on various tests utilizing cross-country interest rate and stock price data, Jeon, Oh, and Yang (2005) and Keil, Phalapleewan, Rajan and Willett (2004) also support this finding. Kim, Kim, and Wang (2004, 2006) estimated the degree of risk-sharing for East Asia by using a cross-country consumption correlation and formal regression analysis. They found that the degree of regional risk-sharing within East Asia is quite low.

Despite this research that indicates a low degree of financial integration in East Asia, some studies provide opposing evidence. For instance, McCauley, Fung, and Gadanecz (2002) assert that the financial markets of East Asia are more integrated than is often suggested. They show that in the international bond market and the international syndicated loan market, East Asian investors and banks have on average committed half of the funds in bonds underwritten and loans syndicated for borrowers in East Asia.

The progress and prospects of regional financial integration in East Asia have been an important area to study among economists, as well as public officials in the region. Greater financial integration in East Asia can be beneficial in several ways. With mobile international capital flows, each country can smooth its consumption and finance investment, regardless of its temporary income level. With full international financial integration, each country can be insured against country-specific income risks. These are general benefits which can be enjoyed at various levels of international financial integration. For example, when global financial integration is not complete, an increase in financial integration within East Asia can enhance the welfare of East Asia.[2]

However, there has been surprisingly little attempt to justify making regional financial integration even deeper than its global equivalent. Rather, there is an argument that supports the opposite. In order to diversify portfolios, investors may prefer to buy equities from a distant country rather than a neighboring one, since business cycle co-movements tend to be lower for the pair of countries that are more distant.

One compelling argument for regional financial integration is that it can contribute to monetary integration. Monetary integration entails

---

[2] Kim, Kim, and Wang (2004, 2005) reported that East Asia would have substantial benefits from regional financial integration if the financial integration within East Asia is strengthened substantially.

virtually no role for individual monetary policy and a very limited scope for individual fiscal stabilization. As such, monetary integration may imply substantial costs for individual member countries, especially when the business cycles of the member countries are not synchronized. Regional risk-sharing through regional financial market integration can insure against country-specific income/consumption risks. Therefore, the costs of monetary integration may decrease substantially through regional financial market integration even when business cycles are not synchronized.

Further, regional financial integration can strengthen financial cooperation. Since the financial crisis of 1997–8, various financial arrangements have been started to promote financial and monetary cooperation in East Asia. Although regional cooperation has already produced some concrete results, such as a network of bilateral swap agreements under the Chiang Mai Initiative, its future remains uncertain. Further financial integration among East Asian economies will go hand in hand with financial and monetary cooperation in the region. For instance, in recent years, there have been discussions on how to pool accumulated international reserves and use them to develop an East Asian regional bond market.

In addition, regional financial integration can help to develop local financial service industries by enhancing the role of financial intermediaries. Many western banks and nonblank financial institutions have established an extensive network of branches and intermediaries throughout East Asia. Because these western financial institutions have superior financial technology and expertise, East Asian corporations and banks are likely to rely more on them for financial services. However, global financial institutions may not always serve local needs best. For example, small and medium enterprises in the region, even the most efficient ones, may not easily get access to international bond markets. Countries in East Asia have been working together to develop regional financial markets as a part of their strategy to deepen regional financial cooperation.

Given that the extent to which East Asian economies are financially integrated is still unclear, this chapter aims to reassess the degree of regional financial integration with new data and new methodologies. First, we compile data on cross-border holdings of international financial assets including equity portfolios, debt securities, and bank claims for 1997 through 2004. By analyzing the geographical composition of the portfolio investment and bank asset holdings, we will assess the degree of regional and global financial market integration in East Asia and compare it to that in Europe and Latin America. We adopt a gravity model of bilateral financial asset holdings to test whether East Asian financial markets are relatively less integrated with each other than global markets, particularly European ones. To our knowledge, no empirical study to date has systematically assessed the degree of regional and global financial integration in East Asia utilizing this data set.[3]

We also implement an alternative analysis to provide insights into the extent of regional and global financial market integration. By extending the standard empirical analysis on consumption risk-sharing, we estimate the degree of regional and global consumption risk-sharing. In contrast to previous studies, such as Kim, Kim, and Wang (2004, 2006), we assess both regional and global consumption risk-sharing models in one empirical framework.

The remainder of the paper is organized as follows. In Section 7.2, we analyze the data on geographical distribution of international portfolio assets and bank claims for East Asia compared to that for Europe, in order to judge the degree of regional and global asset diversification of East Asia. A gravity model of bilateral financial asset holdings is adopted to formally test if East Asian financial markets are relatively less integrated within the region than in global markets, particularly compared with ones in Europe. Section 7.3 introduces the empirical framework on consumption risk-sharing, and estimates the degree of regional and global consumption risk-sharing for East Asia and Europe. Section 7.4 discusses several hypotheses for the low degree of regional financial integration in East Asia. Concluding remarks follow in Section 7.5.

7.2 Regional and Global Diversification of Financial Assets

We look at the stylized pattern of the regional composition of the portfolio investment and bank asset holdings. The degree of financial market integration can be judged by the share of East Asia in international asset holdings for East Asia, compared to the comparable figures for European or Latin American countries. In addition, the intra-regional investment of East Asia can be compared to their investment in the US and global financial markets. Thus, we can judge the degree of regional and global asset diversification of East Asia. We have compiled data on cross-border holdings of financial assets including portfolio assets and bank claims.

7.2.1 Data

We are interested in comparing cross-border financial transactions within East Asia and other regions. Therefore, we require data on international

---

[3] An exception is Eichengreen and Park (2005a), which has adopted the gravity model to assess the extent and causes of the East Asia's intra-region at integration. But this study looks at evidence in the international bank-loan market for 2000 only.

asset holdings on a bilateral basis that distinguish the country of origin and destination.

Data on international portfolio asset holdings have recently been published by the International Monetary Fund (IMF). The IMF conducted the Coordinated Portfolio Investment Survey (CPIS) for the first time in 1997, and annually since 2001.

The first CPIS involved twenty economies, and the 2001 CPIS was expanded to sixty-seven source economies, including several offshore and financial centers. In each case, the bilateral positions of the source countries in 223 destination countries/territories are reported.[4] The CPIS provides a breakdown of a country's stock of portfolio investment assets by country of residency of the nonresident issuer. Problems of survey methods and under-reporting of assets by participating countries are pointed out as shortcomings of the CPIS data (Lane and Milesi-Ferretti 2003). Nevertheless, the CPIS survey presents a unique opportunity for the examination of foreign equity and debt holdings of many participating countries.

Data on international bank claims are from the Bank for International Settlements (BIS). We use the consolidated international bank claims of BIS reporting banks by nationality of lenders and borrowers. We gathered these data for twenty-five reporting countries including two reporting banks from East Asia (Japan and Taiwan) and fifteen European countries from the BIS Quarterly Review.[5] The data are available from 1983 on a biannual basis, but most countries report more complete bilateral data from 1999. We have also obtained compatible data for South Korea from its supervisory authority. Note that although the data set includes only three countries in East Asia reporting consolidated foreign bank claims, the other countries, such as Hong Kong, Indonesia, Malaysia, the Philippines, Singapore, and Thailand, are included as the country of destination for the bank loans.

7.2.2 Regional and Global Structure of International Financial Assets: Stylized Facts

PORTFOLIO INVESTMENT

Table 7.1. provides the geographical distribution of total portfolio investment asset holdings for East Asian and European countries in 2003. The table highlights that the degree of cross-country asset holdings within East Asia is lower than that of Europe. The share of intra-East Asia holdings is about 14 percent on average for eight East Asian economies.[6] It is only 1.3 percent in Japan and 7.9 percent in South Korea. Malaysia has the largest intra-East Asia share,

---

[4] See the IMF website at <http://www.imf.org/external/np/sta/pi/cpis.htm> for details.

[5] See the BIS website at <http://www.bis.org/statistics/histstats10.htm> for details.

[6] The weighted average is much smaller. The eight East Asian economies hold only 4.9% of their total portfolio asset holdings, amounting to $2.2 trillion US dollars, in East Asia.

Table 7.1: Geographical distribution of total portfolio asset holdings in 2003

Source Country	% of Portfolio Assets Held in Each Region				Total	
	East Asia*	Europe	(UK)	USA	(bln US $)	(percent in GDP)
Hong Kong	16.3	27.0	14.5	13.9	334.9	213.8
Indonesia	11.3	15.2	2.1	24.8	1.8	0.9
Japan	1.3	35.3	5.8	36.0	1721.3	40.0
Korea	7.9	16.6	6.4	45.9	17.3	2.9
Malaysia	45.9	23.4	5.2	18.1	1.7	1.6
Philippines	7.0	19.5	10.6	68.9	3.7	4.6
Singapore	20.2	38.9	18.2	15.7	143.9	157.5
Thailand	2.9	20.5	4.6	64.2	2.7	1.9
Average	*14.1*	*24.6*	*8.4*	*35.9*	*278.4*	*52.9*
Austria	1.3	70.6	5.0	9.9	206.8	81.7
Belgium	0.8	68.3	4.2	7.8	417.8	138.4
Denmark	4.4	56.5	7.5	22.9	127.0	59.9
Finland	1.5	82.3	8.7	8.1	107.4	66.4
France	2.8	72.7	9.2	11.1	1367.0	77.8
Germany	2.7	63.5	6.4	11.1	1205.1	50.1
Greece	0.2	47.1	14.7	14.2	34.0	19.7
Iceland	4.6	36.9	15.0	23.9	3.7	35.1
Ireland	3.3	56.3	19.2	27.4	811.6	528.0
Italy	2.0	48.2	5.3	12.5	791.1	53.9
Netherlands	3.8	58.8	9.5	27.8	782.6	153.0
Norway	7.7	60.1	10.4	22.9	184.4	83.5
Portugal	0.1	66.4	6.4	6.0	97.3	65.8
Spain	0.6	69.0	8.9	8.5	432.7	51.6
Sweden	5.1	46.0	12.4	30.7	213.7	70.9
Switzerland	2.5	43.4	5.0	14.6	654.4	204.4
United Kingdom	10.9	41.7	0.0	25.0	1729.5	96.4
Average	*3.2*	*58.1*	*8.7*	*16.7*	*539.2*	*108.0*
United States	14.3	52.8	21.2	0.0	3134.2	28.6

* 9 economies including China
Source: International Monetary Fund, the Coordinated Portfolio Investment Survey, 1997, 2001, and updated data from the IMF website at http://www.imf.org/external/np/sta/pi/cpis.htm

amounting to 46 percent of its international portfolio assets. Respectively, the intra-region share is about 16 percent and 20 percent for Hong Kong and Singapore.

In comparison, most of Europe holds more than one half of their portfolio assets within Europe. On average, the share of intra-Europe asset holdings is 58 percent for seventeen European countries.[7] It reaches 82 percent in Finland and 73 percent in France. Iceland (37 percent) and the UK (42 percent) have relatively lower intra-Europe share percentages. For the UK, the below-average Europe share in holdings of international assets reflects the fact that London is a global financial center. In fact, UK residents hold relatively larger share positions in East Asia (11 percent) than other residents of European countries do.

[7] The weighted average is also similar to this simple average figure. The intra-Europe share of total portfolio asset holdings for 17 European economies is 57%.

Table 7.1 also reports information for the US. At the end of 2003, the share of East Asia in the international investment portfolio of the US (14.3 percent) is far above the average of Europe (3.2 percent).

Table 7.1 also presents data on the size of total international portfolio asset holdings. The total recorded level of portfolio investment in the 2003 CPIS is US $16.5 trillion (tln). The G-5 countries are the major investors in international securities markets. The largest foreign investor is the US. It holds cross-border assets amounting to about US $3.1 trillion or 19.1 percent of the total international portfolio assets. In East Asia, Japan, Hong Kong, and Singapore are the major investors. Japan holds international portfolio assets of about US $1.7 trillion or 10.5 percent of the total international portfolio asset. Hong Kong and Singapore hold US $335 and US $144 billion, respectively. Their investment in East Asian financial assets amounts to US $54.6 billion in Hong Kong, $29.1 billion in Singapore, and $22.4 billion in Japan. In comparison, the other East Asian countries such as South Korea, Thailand, and Indonesia hold a very small amount of East Asian financial assets. In total, the eight East Asian countries hold about US $2.2 trillion of the total international portfolio assets and about US $108.7 billion of East Asian financial assets. They are smaller than the comparable figures for Europe, which hold US $9.2 trillion of the total international portfolio assets and about US $389.3 billion of European assets.

When scaling portfolio holdings by GDP, small economies with financial and offshore centers dominate the picture. For instance, Hong Kong, Singapore, Ireland, and Switzerland have assets amounting to several times their own domestic output. For a typical East Asian economy, on the other hand, bilateral financial linkages are a relatively small fraction of its GDP.

Tables 7.2, 7.3, and 7.4 provide the geographical distribution of portfolio investment holdings separately for each asset—equity, long-term debt, and short-term debt securities.

The distribution of equity and debt securities asset holdings shows a stylized pattern similar to that of total portfolio assets. Table 7.2 shows that the share of intra-East Asia equity asset holdings for most East Asian economies is, in general, far lower than that of intra-Europe equity asset holdings for Europe. The share of intra-East Asia equity holdings is about 20 percent on average for eight East Asian economies. This is lower than the average intra-Europe share of 44 percent in Europe. Japan, Hong Kong, and Singapore—the three largest investors in East Asia—hold international portfolio assets of about US $274.5 billion, US $152.8 billion, and US $42.7 billion respectively, and their intra-East Asian shares are 3.9 percent, 17 percent and 28 percent, respectively. The intra-East Asian share is exceptionally high in Malaysia, which invests 75 percent of its cross-border equity assets in East Asia. But Malaysia is a very small investor, of which total international portfolio assets amount to only US $3.4 billion.

Table 7.2: Geographical distribution of total equity Assets in 2003

Host Country	% of Equity Assets Held in Each Region				Total	
	East Asia*	Europe	(UK)	USA	(bln US $)	(percent in GDP)
Hong Kong	17.4	22.7	20.1	5.2	152.8	97.5
Indonesia	12.5	56.3	0.0	6.3	0.02	0.0
Japan	3.9	30.9	12.0	52.0	274.5	6.4
Korea	8.4	5.7	3.0	28.1	3.4	0.6
Malaysia	75.0	5.5	1.8	10.9	0.9	0.8
Philippines	1.2	—	—	86.1	0.2	0.2
Singapore	27.9	21.0	8.9	16.3	42.7	46.8
Thailand	12.5	13.3	1.2	16.9	0.2	0.2
Average	*19.9*	*22.2*	*6.7*	*27.7*	*59.3*	*19.1*
Austria	4.0	50.2	7.2	19.2	44.0	17.4
Belgium	1.7	42.0	4.9	8.6	140.3	46.5
Denmark	9.8	48.8	12.6	27.0	52.1	24.6
Finland	4.3	67.0	15.8	13.5	36.5	22.5
France	6.2	60.3	10.0	15.8	337.7	19.2
Germany	4.2	45.1	7.6	14.5	440.8	18.3
Greece	1.1	36.6	18.6	35.7	3.9	2.3
Iceland	5.1	33.0	15.7	24.9	3.4	32.0
Ireland	9.3	44.8	20.4	31.3	211.4	137.5
Italy	4.1	31.0	4.7	11.6	331.0	22.5
Netherlands	7.4	39.4	15.5	42.8	327.1	64.0
Norway	8.7	49.1	15.9	30.2	76.4	34.6
Portugal	0.9	45.7	9.6	9.5	11.5	7.7
Spain	2.5	60.2	16.3	10.5	83.4	9.9
Sweden	6.3	36.9	13.9	32.9	141.7	47.0
Switzerland	4.0	28.2	5.0	17.7	293.7	91.7
United Kingdom	18.4	34.9	0.0	26.8	749.8	41.8
Average	*5.8*	*44.3*	*11.4*	*21.9*	*193.2*	*37.6*
United States	18.9	52.9	20.2	0.0	2080.3	19.0

* 10 economies including China

Source: International Monetary Fund, the Coordinated Portfolio Investment Survey, 1997, 2001, and updated data from the IMF website at http://www.imf.org/external/np/sta/pi/cpis.htm

In comparison to equity investment, the intra-East Asia share is relatively low in international debt securities markets. Table 7.3 shows the geographical distribution of long-term debt securities. On average, the share of intra-East Asian long-term debt securities is about 10 percent for eight East Asian economies and ranges from 0.8 percent in Japan to 15.3 percent in Malaysia. For the short-term debt securities market, the intra-East Asia share is only 5.7 percent. In contrast, the average intra-Europe share for seventeen European countries is about 68 percent and 66 percent of long- and short-term debt securities, respectively.

BANK LENDING

Table 7.5 reports level and geographical distribution of cross-border bank claims for East Asia, Europe, and the US at end-2003. We have data for three East Asian reporting countries (Japan, South Korea, and Taiwan). The share

S. Kim, J-W. Lee, and K. Shin

Table 7.3: Geographical distribution of total long-term debt securities in 2003

Source Country	% of Debt Securities Held in Each Region				Total	
	East Asia*	Europe	(UK)	USA	(bln US $)	(percent in GDP)
Hong Kong	14.4	31.7	10.0	21.8	154.1	98.4
Indonesia	11.8	15.6	2.2	21.4	1.7	0.8
Japan	0.8	36.4	4.4	32.9	1407.2	32.7
Korea	7.8	19.0	6.8	50.3	13.8	2.3
Malaysia	15.3	41.3	8.9	26.0	0.8	0.8
Philippines	11.0	6.8	1.4	72.7	2.2	2.7
Singapore	17.2	35.0	5.7	24.9	57.6	63.0
Thailand	2.2	23.1	5.6	68.6	2.2	1.6
Average	*10.1*	*26.1*	*5.6*	*39.8*	*205.0*	*25.3*
Austria	0.5	76.1	4.4	7.2	159.5	63.0
Belgium	0.3	81.9	3.5	7.1	264.3	87.5
Denmark	0.6	61.9	4.0	19.9	73.6	34.7
Finland	0.0	89.7	5.0	5.6	66.3	40.9
France	1.7	76.7	7.4	9.2	909.7	51.8
Germany	1.8	74.5	5.7	8.6	750.0	31.2
Greece	0.1	47.8	12.8	11.4	29.4	17.1
Iceland	0.0	77.7	7.2	13.5	0.3	3.0
Ireland	1.8	67.9	14.3	18.0	385.7	250.9
Italy	0.5	60.2	5.6	13.3	453.7	30.9
Netherlands	1.2	73.1	5.1	16.9	449.0	87.8
Norway	7.1	67.9	6.6	17.3	105.2	47.6
Portugal	0.0	67.0	7.2	6.4	71.1	48.1
Spain	0.1	72.4	7.4	8.3	327.5	39.0
Sweden	2.9	64.0	9.4	26.5	66.0	21.9
Switzerland	1.3	56.9	4.8	12.5	335.4	104.8
United Kingdom	0.9	44.8	0.0	24.1	875.7	48.8
Average	*1.2*	*68.3*	*6.5*	*13.3*	*313.1*	*59.4*
United States	6.2	46.3	16.5	0.0	868.9	7.9

* 10 economies including China
Source: International Monetary Fund, the Coordinated Portfolio Investment Survey, 1997, 2001, and updated data from the IMF website at <http://www.imf.org/external/np/sta/pi/cpis.htm>

of intra-East Asia bank claims is 7.3 percent in Japan, 36 percent in South Korea, and 26 percent in Taiwan. The intra-region shares of bank claims for Japan and South Korea are larger than the comparable figures of equity or debt securities asset holdings for these countries. This may indicate that bank-loan market integration is greater than portfolio market integration. Nevertheless, East Asia is a small investor in the international bank lending markets. While Europe holds about US $10.7 trillion of international bank claims in total and about US $5.5 trillion claims within Europe, East Asia holds only about US $1.4 trillion total claims in international bank lending markets and US $130 billion within East Asia.

East Asian banks tended to have large bank claims within East Asia. But, lending to East Asian banks dropped after the Asian financial crisis in 1997. This occurred not only due to a reduced willingness to lend, but also because

Table 7.4: Geographical distribution of total short-term debt securities in 2003

Source Country	% of Debt Securities Held in Each Region				Total	
	East Asia*	Europe	(UK)	USA	(bln US $)	(percent in GDP)
Hong Kong	21.8	24.0	8.7	17.9	28.0	17.9
Indonesia	0.0	0.0	0.0	100.0	0.1	0.0
Japan	1.3	28.2	13.7	35.4	39.7	0.9
Korea	0.0	59.6	59.6	40.4	0.09	0.0
Malaysia	0.0	100.0	0.0	0.0	0.01	0.0
Philippines	—	—	—	60.1	1.3	1.6
Singapore	16.9	61.7	43.9	3.0	43.6	47.7
Thailand	0.0	6.2	0.0	71.1	0.3	0.2
Average	*5.7*	*40.0*	*18.0*	*41.0*	*14.1*	*8.5*
Austria	0.5	73.0	5.8	12.6	3.2	1.3
Belgium	0.1	74.9	8.8	12.9	13.2	4.4
Denmark	0.0	60.9	2.6	31.9	1.4	0.6
Finland	0.0	97.0	6.3	2.2	4.6	2.9
France	1.5	78.1	21.1	12.4	119.6	6.8
Germany	0.0	54.2	7.2	34.4	14.3	0.6
Greece	0.0	83.1	82.4	7.5	0.6	0.3
Iceland	0.0	50.0	0.0	16.7	0.01	0.1
Ireland	0.0	46.5	26.8	40.4	214.5	139.5
Italy	0.5	87.3	18.4	2.8	6.4	0.4
Netherlands	2.0	49.6	13.3	16.0	6.5	1.3
Norway	0.0	64.8	1.5	34.5	2.8	1.3
Portugal	0.0	80.0	0.0	1.3	14.8	10.0
Spain	0.0	51.5	3.0	3.5	21.8	2.6
Sweden	0.0	62.4	10.5	24.7	6.0	2.0
Switzerland	0.0	41.0	9.6	6.7	25.4	7.9
United Kingdom	0.3	60.8	0.0	19.3	104.1	5.8
Average	*0.3*	*65.6*	*12.8*	*16.5*	*32.9*	*11.0*
United States	0.5	82.2	53.6	0.0	185.0	1.7

* 10 economies including China

Source: International Monetary Fund, the Coordinated Portfolio Investment Survey, 1997, 2001, and updated data from the IMF website at <http://www.imf.org/external/np/sta/pi/cpis.htm>

of a weaker demand for loans in the region. In this region, the shift to current account surpluses, corporate deleveraging, and an increase in equity investment inflows made external bank financing less needed (Jeanneau and Micu 2002). BIS data show that the share of intra-East Asian bank claims for Japanese banks continued to decline from 14.4 percent in 2001 to 7.3 percent in 2004.

While East Asian economies tend to be more integrated in the commercial bank-loan market, the degree of cross-border bank claim within East Asia is still lower than that of Europe. The intra-Europe share in holdings of international bank claims is 60.4 percent on average for sixteen European countries. A notable exception is the UK, which holds only 30 percent of international bank claims within Europe. Again, this reflects London's status as a global financial center.

Table 7.5: Geographical distribution of cross-border bank claims in 2003

Source Country	% of Bank Claims Held in Each Region				Total	
	East Asia*	Europe	(UK)	USA	(bln US $)	(percent in GDP)
Japan	7.3	35.6	8.3	39.5	1238.2	28.8
South Korea	35.7	21.2	9.8	21.2	50.8	8.4
Taiwan China	26.2	22.9	6.2	37.1	83.2	29.1
Average	*23.1*	*26.6*	*8.1*	*32.6*	*457.4*	*22.1*
Austria	4.1	53.1	10.0	3.8	97.8	38.6
Belgium	3.7	73.6	16.5	12.3	658.0	218.0
Denmark	0.1	86.4	23.2	5.0	82.2	38.8
Finland	1.5	75.8	6.2	13.5	57.8	35.7
France	13.2	49.5	13.6	23.1	1353.4	77.0
Germany	6.3	61.1	20.2	18.1	2576.4	107.2
Greece	0.9	49.3	12.4	14.9	49.9	29.0
Ireland	4.8	82.4	27.9	4.1	341.7	222.3
Italy	2.8	58.1	15.3	7.7	328.8	22.4
Netherlands	6.4	54.5	12.9	26.9	1190.8	232.8
Norway	0.8	60.8	8.6	12.0	17.2	7.8
Portugal	0.2	72.0	16.3	10.0	68.9	46.6
Spain	0.4	49.9	7.7	6.6	409.4	48.8
Sweden	0.9	75.4	11.9	11.5	216.9	71.9
Switzerland	6.9	34.3	17.6	48.2	1565.0	488.9
United Kingdom	16.8	29.9	0.0	33.0	1637.4	91.2
Average	*4.1*	*60.4*	*13.8*	*15.7*	*665.7*	*111.1*
United States	19.8	48.9	16.9	0.0	838.3	7.7

* 10 economies including China
Source: The Bank for International Settlements, available from the BIS website at <http://www.bis.org/statistics/histstats10.htm.>

Comparing the intra-East Asian share of cross-border financial assets for East Asia to that of Europe may not be appropriate, because the two regions are quite dissimilar in terms of economic development and financial infrastructure. For comparison, the geographical distribution of international financial asset holdings for the Latin American countries is presented in Table 7.6.

The share of intra-Latin America total portfolio asset holdings is low. For instance, it is 3 percent in Argentina, 4 percent in Chile, and 6 percent in Mexico. Panama has an exceptionally high intra-regional share of 42 percent, reflecting its hosting of offshore financial centers. Similar patterns are also visible in the separate categories of equity, long- and short-debt securities. The intra-Latin America share in bank claims is relatively higher than that in portfolio assets, ranging from 6 percent in Brazil to 48 percent in Panama. The intra-regional shares of international financial assets for most of Latin America are similar in magnitude to those of East Asian economies.

Table 7.6: Geographical distribution of asset holdings in Latin America in 2003

Source country	% of Assets held in each Region				Total	
	Latin America	Europe	(UK)	USA	bln US $	% in GDP
TOTAL PORTFOLIO						
Argentina	3.0	6.3	0.8	86.7	13.1	10.1
Brazil	15.3	18.0	7.1	35.3	4.5	0.9
Chile	3.6	23.5	4.8	25.4	13.0	17.9
Colombia	1.4	7.4	2.1	62.6	1.9	2.4
Mexico	6.0	6.0	2.0	76.4	5.1	—
Panama	42.3	6.0	2.9	45.1	3.6	27.8
EQUITY						
Argentina	1.8	8.1	1.0	83.2	7.5	5.8
Brazil	14.2	18.2	3.3	29.2	2.5	0.5
Chile	0.3	22.4	4.9	23.0	10.7	14.8
Colombia	0.0	5.4	2.7	37.8	0.7	0.9
Mexico	—	—	—	23.8	0.4	0.1
Panama	71.3	1.2	0.2	8.3	0.8	6.5
LONG-TERM DEBT						
Argentina	4.6	3.9	0.5	91.2	5.5	4.2
Brazil	23.2	8.5	1.4	51.9	0.6	0.1
Chile	19.5	28.5	4.0	36.7	2.2	3.1
Colombia	2.6	7.7	1.7	77.2	0.9	1.2
Mexico	7.8	2.8	2.5	85.1	4.0	0.6
Panama	31.9	7.2	4.1	57.8	2.4	19.0
SHORT-TERM DEBT						
Argentina	0.0	0.0	0.0	100.0	0.2	0.1
Brazil	13.7	21.7	16.5	39.3	1.4	0.3
Chile	0.0	0.0	0.0	0.0	0.0	0.0
Colombia	0.7	10.9	1.5	77.0	0.3	0.3
Mexico	—	26.1	—	59.1	0.8	0.1
Panama	45.4	9.2	0.3	44.0	0.3	2.3
BANK CLAIMS						
Brazil	5.9	49.3	19.4	28.6	23.8	4.8
Chile	24.4	27.0	2.8	39.0	2.2	3.0
Mexico	14.3	2.8	0.0	37.1	2.1	0.3
Panama	48.1	10.7	3.0	27.6	7.9	61.2

Source: The International Monetary Fund and the Bank for International Settlements.

7.2.3 A Gravity-Model Test of Regional Financial Integration in East Asia

To the data set on international portfolio asset holdings and bank claims, we added a number of other variables that are necessary to estimate the gravity model. We collected population and real GDP data from the IMF, *International Financial Statistics* (IFS). The bilateral trade data are from the *Direction of Trade* (DoT) data set.[8] The nominal values were converted to real

---

[8] *Direction of Trade* reports bilateral trade on FOB exports and CIF imports recorded in American dollars. We deflate trade by the American GDP deflator. Then we calculate an average value of bilateral trade between a pair of countries by averaging all of the four possible measures potentially available.

Table 7.7: Summary statistics (1999–2003)

	Portfolio (N=13,971)		Bank claims (N=11,974)	
	Mean	Std. Dev	Mean	Std. Dev
Year	2001.975	0.823	2001.203	1.409
Log of trade	3.797	2.634	4.560	2.617
Log of distance	8.129	0.834	8.075	0.837
Log of GDP in pairs	40.794	2.814	41.649	2.640
Log of per capita GDP in pairs	8.004	1.869	8.552	1.699
Log of area in pairs	24.431	3.076	24.298	2.866
Common land border dummy	0.028	0.166	0.024	0.153
Common language dummy	0.150	0.358	0.130	0.336
Real Portfolio	22.343	170.739	—	—
Bank Claims	—	—	1.245	1.688
East Asia	0.012	0.111	0.010	0.102
Europe	0.059	0.233	0.104	0.305

Note: The summary statistics are based on the bilateral variables for the portfolio holdings and bank claims data sets. See the text for an explanation of variables and sources of them.

values using the common US GDP deflator for every country.[9] A number of country-specific variables such as distance, land area, language, and land border were obtained from Rose (2000).[10] Finally for Taiwan, we acquired the data on GDP and population from the website of the Asian Development Bank and bilateral trade data from the Bureau of Foreign Trade in Taiwan.

The data set has features of a panel structure consisting of 13,971 annual observations from 1999 to 2003 clustered by 4,475 country pair groups for the portfolio data and 11,974 annual observations clustered by 4,364 country pair groups for the bank claims data.[11] The number of observations varies by year. Summary statistics are presented in Table 7.7. East Asian country pairs constitute about 1 percent of each data set, while the proportion of European country pairs is much larger, amounting to about 6 percent for the portfolio data set and about 10 percent for the bank claims. The average size of portfolio asset holdings (22.343) in the logarithm value is much larger than that of bank claims (1.245).

We set up a gravity model of the bilateral financial asset holdings. Initially, the model was adopted by economists to study foreign trade without firm theoretical grounds. In its basic form, trade between two countries depends positively on their total income and negatively on the distance between

---

[9] It would be preferable to use a separate deflator for each country, but such deflators in a unified framework are not available.

[10] The data set is available on the web page <http://faculty.haas.berkeley.edu/arose/>, maintained by Andrew Rose.

[11] Since most asset holdings data start from 1999, we have ignored the observations before then. Due to the lack of bilateral trade data, we end the sample period at 2003.

them. The model can be extended to include other variables, depending on the study's purpose. The empirical success of the gravity model to explain the bilateral trade flows has motivated a number of theoretical models that can justify it.[12]

While using the gravity model to explain bilateral trade flows has a long history, there have been relatively few attempts made to use it in explaining exchanges of financial assets. The main reason is that unlike goods, financial assets are weightless, hence distance cannot represent for transaction costs. Recently, however, Portes and Rey (2005) find that a gravity model performs at least as well in asset trade as goods trade.[13] Portes and Rey suggest that information friction is positively correlated with distance, justifying that financial asset trade is also negatively related to distance. Following their model, this paper also used a gravity model as a basic framework that takes the following form:

$$\ln(Assets_{ijt}) = \beta_0 + \beta_1 \ln(GDP_i * GDP_j) + \beta_2 \ln(GDP_iGDP_j/Pop_iPop_j)_t \qquad (1)$$
$$+ \beta_3 \ln Dist_{ijt} + \beta_4 \ln(Area_iArea_j) + \beta_5 Border_{ij} + \beta_6 Language_{ij} + \varepsilon_{ijt}$$

where i and j denote countries, t denotes time, $Assets_{ijt}$ denotes the financial assets of country j held by country i at time t, GDP is real GDP, Pop is Population, $Dist$ is the distance between i and j, $Area$ is the size of land area of the country, $Border$ is a binary variable which is unity if i and j share a land border, and $Language$ is a binary variable which is unity if i and j have a common language.

Tables 7.8 and 7.9 present the estimation results of specification (1) for total portfolio assets and for bank claims respectively. Column (1) reports random-effect estimation and column (2) between-effects estimation results.[14] In columns (3) and (4) we also added bilateral trade flows to the explanatory variables, reporting the estimation results.[15]

Consistent with Portes and Rey, we find that the gravity model fits the data very well and that most estimated coefficients were statistically significant

---

[12] See Anderson (1979), Bergstrand (1985), and Evenett and Keller (2002).

[13] See Buch (2002, 2003), Yildrim (2003), and Lane and Milesi-Ferritti (2003).

[14] We omit the fixed-effect 'within' estimation results. This method can provide more consistent estimates by controlling for the influences from omitted country-specific factors. One drawback is, however, that since the fixed-effect estimator exploits variation over time, we cannot obtain the estimates for time-invariant factors such as distance, area, land border, and common language as well as a regional dummy. We believe that the fixed-effect estimation is not appropriate for our analyses since the time span of our sample is too short. A more serious problem is that the regional dummy variables that will be investigated later are time-invariant and hence cannot be estimated by the fixed-effect regression.

[15] Adding bilateral trade flows as an explanatory variable may be subject to an endogeneity problem. However, as will be confirmed later in this section, the existence of bilateral trade flows does little to change major regression results.

Table 7.8: Portfolio Estimation

	(1) Random effects	(2) Between effects	(3) Random effects	(4) Between effects
Log distance	−0.203** [0.017]	−0.193** [0.017]	−0.118** [0.019]	−0.082** [0.019]
GDP in pair	0.150** [0.008]	0.145** [0.008]	0.063** [0.011]	0.031* [0.012]
Per capita GDP in pair	0.136** [0.011]	0.131** [0.011]	0.141** [0.010]	0.134** [0.010]
Common language	0.120** [0.035]	0.111** [0.035]	0.065 [0.035]	0.038 [0.035]
Border	0.641** [0.094]	0.635** [0.095]	0.488** [0.093]	0.428** [0.096]
Area in pair	−0.001 [0.006]	−0.002 [0.006]	0.008 [0.006]	0.009 [0.006]
Log trade			0.106** [0.010]	0.139** [0.012]
Observation	13,971	13,971	13,971	13,971
R-squared	0.38	0.37	0.39	0.39

Note: All the variables are bilateral between country i and country j. The dependent variable, real portfolio investment asset holdings, refers to the case where country i is a source country and country j is a destination country. It is in log form after adding 1 to include all the observations with value zero. All other explanatory variables except the dummy variables are also in logs. Robust standard errors are reported in parentheses. Intercept and year dummy variables are included (not reported). ** and * indicate that the estimated coefficients are statistically significant at 1% and 5% levels respectively.

Table 7.9: Bank claims estimation

	(1) Random effects	(2) Between effects	(3) Random effects	(4) Between effects
Log distance	−0.280** [0.023]	−0.289** [0.024]	−0.194** [0.024]	−0.110** [0.026]
GDP in pair	0.339** [0.011]	0.335** [0.012]	0.230** [0.015]	0.123** [0.018]
Per capita GDP in pair	0.146** [0.015]	0.154** [0.015]	0.148** [0.014]	0.146** [0.014]
Common language	0.415** [0.049]	0.416** [0.049]	0.347** [0.048]	0.273** [0.048]
Border	1.100** [0.137]	1.063** [0.138]	0.988** [0.133]	0.841** [0.134]
Area in pair	−0.059** [0.009]	−0.058** [0.009]	−0.045** [0.008]	−0.037** [0.009]
Log trade			0.121** [0.011]	0.242** [0.016]
Observation	11,974	11,974	11,974	11,974
R-squared	0.63	0.62	0.64	0.63

Note: All the variables are bilateral ones between country i and country j. The dependent variable, real bank claims of country i on country j, is in logs after adding 1 to include all the observations with value zero.

with the expected sign. The estimated coefficients for the bilateral distance were significantly negative and the estimated coefficients for the log of GDP in pair, log of per capita GDP in pair, common land border dummy, and common language dummy were significantly positive. When we add bilateral trade flows, most coefficients preserve the same sign and statistical significance. The coefficient of bilateral trade flows is also positive and significant, indicating that even after taking consideration of the conventional explanatory variables of the gravity equation, trade may independently foster financial integration.

Table 7.10: Portfolio estimation with regional dummies

	(1)		(2)		(3)		(4)	
Log distance	−0.201**	[0.018]	−0.106**	[0.020]	−0.028	[0.017]	0.059**	[0.018]
GDP in pair	0.151**	[0.009]	0.068**	[0.012]	0.158**	[0.008]	0.081**	[0.011]
Per capita GDP in pair	0.135**	[0.011]	0.133**	[0.011]	0.067**	[0.010]	0.065**	[0.010]
Common language	0.120**	[0.035]	0.066	[0.035]	0.155**	[0.031]	0.105**	[0.031]
Border	0.642**	[0.094]	0.493**	[0.093]	0.496**	[0.083]	0.361**	[0.082]
Area in pair	−0.002	[0.007]	0.003	[0.007]	−0.020**	[0.006]	−0.016*	[0.006]
EA_single	−0.01	[0.040]	−0.074	[0.040]	−0.066	[0.037]	−0.124**	[0.037]
EA_pair	0.022	[0.157]	−0.118	[0.154]	0.191	[0.137]	0.058	[0.135]
Europe_single					−0.109**	[0.027]	−0.107**	[0.026]
Europe_pair					2.461**	[0.068]	2.423**	[0.067]
Log trade			0.110**	[0.010]			0.102**	[0.009]
Observations	13,971		13,971		13,971		13,971	
R-Squares	0.38		0.47		0.39		0.48	

Note: The dependent variable is real portfolio investment asset holdings.

Next, we investigate how deeply financial integration is entrenched in East Asia by introducing two dummy variables, *EA_single* and *EA_pair*, as additional regressors. *EA_single* is a dummy variable that takes one if either a host or destination country belongs to East Asia, and *EA_pair* a dummy variable that takes one if both countries do. The estimated coefficient of *EA_single* captures the additional asset exchanges involved with an East Asian country in general. The estimated coefficient of *EA_pair* represents the additional asset exchanges when both countries are East Asia. Hence, the depth of financial integration among East Asian countries, relative to their integration with the rest of the world, can be measured by subtracting the estimated coefficient of *EA_single* from that of *EA_pair*.

Table 7.10 reports estimation results for portfolio asset holdings when the new dummy variables are added. Since the between-effects estimation results are very similar, only random-effects estimation results are presented.[16] In column (1), we find that the coefficient of *EA_single* is negative while the coefficient of *EA_pair* is positive, indicating some evidence of regional financial integration. However, neither coefficient is statistically significant. Furthermore, when we added bilateral trade to explanatory variables in column (2), while the coefficient of bilateral trade is positive and statistically very significant, the coefficient of *EA_pair* turned negative. Hence, the evidence of regional financial integration is very weak, if any, and most of it might be explained by trade integration in the region.

In order to compare the degree of financial integration in East Asia with that for Europe, we have also added the same two dummy variables for Europe,

---

[16] The between-effects estimation results are available upon request.

that is, *Europe_single* and *Europe_pair*, and reported the estimation results in columns (3) and (4) without and with trade as an additional regressor, respectively. Even after the European dummies were added, the estimated coefficients of East Asian dummies were hardly changed, except that the coefficient of *East_single* became statistically significant. In contrast, the coefficients of Europe dummies were very significant with the opposite sign to each other. The coefficient of *Europe_pair* was particularly large and positive, which implies that European countries tend to make portfolio investments among themselves. Since the coefficient of *Europe single* is negative, its subtraction from the coefficient of *Europe_pair* is even larger, implying that European countries invest more heavily in each other than they do in the rest of the world. The estimated coefficients indicate that European countries invest thirteen times more among themselves.[17]

So far, we have confirmed that regional financial integration is deeper in Europe than in East Asia. Is this because East Asia is more closely linked to the global financial markets? To answer the question, we added three more dummies: *Global*, *EA_global*, and *Europe_global*; the first dummy takes a value of one if either a host or destination country represents a global financial market and zero otherwise; the second dummy takes a value of one if the pair of countries represent an East Asian country and a global financial market; and the third dummy takes a value of one if they were a European country and a global financial market. A global financial market is defined in two ways. The first case includes only the US market and the second case, both the US and the UK markets.

In Table 7.11, we find that the coefficient of *Global* is positive and statistically significant in both column (1) when the US represents the global market, and in column (2) when the US and the UK do. This indicates that the global financial markets do indeed play an important role in world financial integration. However, the global link is more important for East Asian and European countries: the coefficients of *EA_global* and *Europe_global* were positive, much larger, and statistically very significant. Surprisingly the coefficient of *Europe_global* was even larger, indicating that European countries are more deeply linked to the global markets as well.

Only when we compared the importance of the global market *vis-à-vis* the regional market for East Asia (*EA_global* vs *EA_pair*) with that for Europe (*Europe_global* vs *Europe_pair*), we realize that East Asia places relatively more importance on global financial integration rather than regional financial integration. The estimated coefficients of East Asia were 2.571 or 2.313 for the global integration vs 0.272 or 0.323 for the regional integration, depending on the definition of *global*, while the corresponding figures for Europe were 3.957

---

[17] This figure is calculated as $e^{2.462-(-0.109)} = 13.1$.

Table 7.11: Portfolio claims with regional and global dummies

	(1) US		(2) US and UK		(3) US		(4) US and UK	
Log distance	−0.048**	[0.016]	−0.041**	[0.015]	0.028	[0.017]	0.035*	[0.017]
GDP in pair	0.128**	[0.008]	0.117**	[0.008]	0.061**	[0.010]	0.050**	[0.010]
Per capita GDP in pair	0.049**	[0.009]	0.070**	[0.009]	0.048**	[0.009]	0.068**	[0.009]
Common language	0.123**	[0.029]	0.093**	[0.029]	0.081**	[0.029]	0.051	[0.029]
Border	0.524**	[0.075]	0.588**	[0.075]	0.406**	[0.075]	0.468**	[0.074]
Area in pair	−0.022**	[0.006]	−0.013*	[0.006]	−0.018**	[0.006]	−0.009	[0.006]
Global	0.493**	[0.068]	0.371**	[0.047]	0.477**	[0.067]	0.362**	[0.047]
EA_global	2.571**	[0.227]	2.313**	[0.162]	2.437**	[0.224]	2.215**	[0.160]
EA_single	0.022	[0.035]	−0.004	[0.035]	−0.029	[0.035]	−0.054	[0.035]
EA_pair	0.272*	[0.123]	0.323**	[0.123]	0.153	[0.122]	0.203	[0.121]
Europe_global	3.957**	[0.163]	2.793**	[0.119]	3.898**	[0.161]	2.755**	[0.117]
Europe_single	−0.042	[0.025]	−0.082**	[0.025]	−0.042	[0.025]	−0.080**	[0.024]
Europe_pair	2.604**	[0.062]	2.228**	[0.062]	2.569**	[0.061]	2.199**	[0.061]
Log trade			0.090**	[0.009]	0.090**	[0.009]		
Observations	13,971		13,971		13,971		13,971	
R-squares	0.42		0.43		0.56		0.56	

Note: The dependent variable is real portfolio investment asset holdings. For other information see the note for Table 7.7.

or 2.793 for the global integration vs 2.604 or 2.228 for the regional integration. The estimated coefficient of the global integration is dominatingly larger than that of the regional integration in magnitude only for East Asia.

When we added bilateral trade as an additional regressor in columns (3) and (4), the above findings were still preserved. Further the coefficient of trade is positive and statistically significant, indicating a possibility that trade additionally plays an independent role in fostering financial integration. The coefficient of *EA_pair* is no longer statistically significant if trade is used as an additional regressor. This again supports the view that the regional financial integration in East Asia, while low, is mainly due to the trade integration taking place in the region.

Now we turn to the same regression results based on the bank claims data set. In Table 7.12, we present evidence of how deep financial integration is in both regions by relying on the same set of equations as in Table 7.10. Unlike the case of portfolio asset holdings, we now find much stronger evidence of regional integration in East Asia. The coefficient of *EA_pair* in column (1) is positive and statistically very significant. Even after bilateral trade is added as a regressor, the coefficient of *EA_pair* in column (2) becomes even larger and still statistically very significant. When we compared the degree of regional financial integration in East Asia with that of Europe, in columns (3) and (4), the degree of regional financial integration in East Asia (0.819 or 1.099) is quite comparable to that of Europe (1.116 or 1.103). Subtracting the estimated coefficients of *EA_single* (−0.231 or −0.075) and *Europe_single* (0.295 or 0.276)

Table 7.12: Bank claims with regional dummies

	(1)		(2)		(3)		(4)	
Log distance	−0.244**	[0.025]	−0.090**	[0.027]	−0.142**	[0.026]	0.01	[0.027]
GDP in pair	0.346**	[0.013]	0.330**	[0.012]	0.243**	[0.015]	0.229**	[0.015]
Per capita GDP in pair	0.143**	[0.015]	0.099**	[0.015]	0.136**	[0.015]	0.092**	[0.015]
Common language	0.400**	[0.049]	0.478**	[0.048]	0.332**	[0.048]	0.405**	[0.047]
Border	1.159**	[0.137]	1.115**	[0.133]	1.050**	[0.132]	1.003**	[0.129]
Area in pair	−0.066**	[0.009]	−0.051**	[0.010]	−0.058**	[0.009]	−0.045**	[0.009]
EA_single	−0.152**	[0.049]	0.014	[0.055]	−0.231**	[0.048]	−0.075	[0.053]
EA_pair	0.994**	[0.192]	1.284**	[0.188]	0.819**	[0.186]	1.099**	[0.181]
Europe_single					0.295**	[0.045]	0.276**	[0.044]
Europe_pair					1.116**	[0.085]	1.103**	[0.082]
Log trade			0.125**	[0.011]			0.125**	[0.011]
Observations	11,974		11,974		11,974		11,974	
R-Squares	0.63		0.65		0.64		0.66	

Note: The dependent variable is real bank claims of country *i* on country *j*. For other information see the notes for Tables 7.8. and 7.9.

from these figures, yields even higher estimates of regional integration in East Asia.

Table 7.13 reports the same set of estimation results as Table 7.11 to verify the relative degree of regional integration compared with that of global integration based on the bank claims data. Generally, we found that the importance of global integration is higher in East Asia. The estimated coefficients of global vs regional integration were 2.208 (or 2.280) vs 1.351 (or 1.412) in East Asia, while the corresponding figures for Europe were 1.190 (or 1.790) vs 1.190

Table 7.13: Bank claims with regional and global dummies

	(1) US		(2) US and UK		(3) US		(4) US and UK	
Log distance	−0.103**	[0.026]	−0.101**	[0.025]	−0.005	[0.026]	−0.002	[0.026]
GDP in pair	0.315**	[0.013]	0.304**	[0.013]	0.217**	[0.015]	0.205**	[0.015]
Per capita GDP in pair	0.086**	[0.015]	0.096**	[0.015]	0.078**	[0.014]	0.088**	[0.014]
Common language	0.451**	[0.047]	0.414**	[0.047]	0.381**	[0.046]	0.345**	[0.046]
Border	1.131**	[0.129]	1.206**	[0.127]	1.020**	[0.125]	1.095**	[0.123]
Area in pair	−0.054**	[0.009]	−0.050**	[0.009]	−0.048**	[0.009]	−0.044**	[0.009]
Global	0.003	[0.091]	0	[0.059]	−0.027	[0.088]	−0.005	[0.057]
EA_global	2.208**	[0.285]	2.280**	[0.200]	2.069**	[0.274]	2.180**	[0.192]
EA_single	0.018	[0.056]	−0.03	[0.055]	−0.073	[0.055]	−0.115*	[0.054]
EA_pair	1.351**	[0.183]	1.412**	[0.179]	1.162**	[0.177]	1.225**	[0.173]
Europe_global	1.190**	[0.210]	1.790**	[0.148]	1.175**	[0.202]	1.774**	[0.142]
Europe_single	0.288**	[0.048]	0.256**	[0.044]	0.264**	[0.047]	0.239**	[0.043]
Europe_pair	1.190**	[0.083]	0.983**	[0.082]	1.175**	[0.080]	0.973**	[0.079]
Log trade					0.123**	[0.011]	0.124**	[0.011]
Observations	11,974		11,974		11,974		11,974	
R-squares	0.64		0.67		0.66		0.69	

Note: The dependent variable is real bank claims of country *i* on country *j*. For other information see the note for Table 7.7.

(or 0.983). Since the values in parentheses were estimated when the UK was included among global markets, it tended to overstate the global integration and underestimate the regional integration in Europe. In both cases, however, global integration is deeper in East Asia.

Why did we reach a different conclusion when we used the bank claims data instead of the portfolio investment data? At the first glance, one may argue that this is solely due to the different definition of the regional dummy, *EA_pair*. Since we have bank claims data available only for three host countries, Japan, South Korea, and Taiwan, no observation was included if bank loans were made between any pair of the remaining seven countries. Since relatively fewer bank loans were expected to occur between them, the estimated measure of the regional integration derived from the bank claims data may be overstated. We tested this possibility by redefining the regional dummy, *EA_pair*, for portfolio investment in the same way as bank claims—that is, by assigning a value of one only when any of the three countries is a host country. We reestimated the same set of equations in Tables 7.10 and 7.11 and found that the estimated coefficients hardly change (not reported), implying that the distinction is not due to the difference in the definition of the regional dummy.

Another possibility is that, since bank loans were more likely to reflect with trade than portfolio investments, the evidence of regional financial integration in the bank claims data may only reflect heavy trade integration in the region. The extent of intra-regional trade did indeed increase substantially in East Asian economies between the 1980s and the 1990s. In 2000, the share of intra-region trade in total trade was above 50 percent in most East Asian economies, except for Japan and the Philippines. However, we believe that this argument is not supported by the data either, since the importance of the regional financial integration in East Asia does not disappear even after trade flows are added.

We conjecture that the difference is due to the special role played by the banks in East Asia. Traditionally, financial systems in East Asia are largely bank-oriented. While most banks in East Asia are small and have a limited access to international capital markets, some must have been active in providing funds to East Asia.

7.3 Regional versus Global Consumption Risk-Sharing

7.3.1 *Regional versus Global Risk-Sharing*

Empirical studies of risk-sharing have grown rapidly in recent years. The formal literature started by testing the hypothesis of full risk-sharing at various aggregation levels, such as among individuals in a village (Townsend, 1994), households (Altug and Miller 1990; Cochrane 1991; Mace 1991), and countries (Canova and Ravn 1996; Lewis 1996). These papers were based on the consumption Euler equation under complete (asset) markets as the implication of the perfect risk-sharing. For example, in a simple theoretical model, the consumption growth rate of an individual country is equal to (the world) aggregate consumption growth rate under perfect risk-sharing.

Most of these studies rejected the null of perfect risk-sharing. Subsequently, the literature investigate how incomplete the risk-sharing arrangement is. Crucini (1999), Crucini and Hess (2000), Obstfeld (1994, 1995), Hess and Shin (2000), and Asdrubali and Kim (2003) addressed such issues. A simple version of such empirical framework can be described as follows:

$$\Delta \log(c_{it}) = \alpha + \lambda \Delta \log(c_{wt}) + (1 - \lambda) \Delta \log(y_{it}) + e_{it}, i = 1, 2, \ldots, R \tag{2}$$

where c_{it} is the consumption of the country i, y_{it} is the income of the country i, c_{wt} is the consumption of the world, the constant term, α, may reflect the difference in the discount factor across countries, the error term, e_{it}, may reflect the preference shocks, and λ represents the degree of risk-sharing. To the extent that risk-sharing arrangements are established (λ), the consumption growth rate follows the aggregate consumption growth rate since country-specific risks are shared. However, the rest (fraction $1-\lambda$) of the consumption growth rate follows its own income growth rate since that is what is domestically available.[18, 19] Equation (2) can be estimated by non-linear least squares. The restrictions, $0 \leq \lambda \leq 1$, can be imposed to exclude unrealistic cases.

The above framework is simple and intuitive, but it only considers risk-sharing with the world economy as a whole. However, there is a possibility that the risk-sharing arrangements of a country are more intensive with countries in a specific region than with the remaining countries. For example, the countries in the European Union may have more intensive sharing arrangements with EU member countries than with the remaining countries. By extending the framework of the past studies, we have developed a framework

---

[18] Crucini (1999) uses permanent income instead of current income by assuming that international intertemporal trade is perfect. On the other hand, Obstfeld (1995) uses current income by assuming financial autarky. Asdrubali and Kim (2003) discuss intermediate cases. If an income process follows a random walk, changes in current income and permanent income would be equal. For more details, see Asdrubali and Kim (2003).

[19] The presence of common shocks does not strongly bias the estimate. The above regression equation can be reorganized as:

$$\Delta \log(c_{it}) - \Delta \log(c_{wt}) = \alpha + (1 - \lambda)[\Delta \log(y_{it}) - \Delta \log(c_{wt})] + e_{it}, i = 1, 2, \ldots, R$$

When aggregate income changes are similar to aggregate consumption changes, the regression is similar to using country-specific variables.

to analyze the risk-sharing arrangements of a country not only with the world but also within a region.

By extending the logic of the empirical framework of the previous section, we argue the following. To the extent that a country established risk-sharing arrangements within the region (λ_r), its consumption growth rate its follows the consumption growth rate of the aggregate consumption of the region. Similarly, to the extent that a country established risk-sharing arrangements with the world (λ_w), its consumption growth rate follows the consumption growth rate of the aggregate consumption of the world. The rest of the consumption growth rate of the country follows its income growth rate $(1 - \lambda_r - \lambda_w)$. This idea can be expressed as the following equation:

$$\Delta \log(c_{it}) = a + \lambda_w \Delta \log(c_{wt}) + \lambda_r \Delta \log(c_{rt})$$

$$+ (1 - \lambda_w - \lambda_r) \Delta \log(y_{it}) + e_{it}, \quad i = 1, 2, \ldots, R \qquad (3)$$

By rearranging equation (3), the following equation can be obtained:

$$\Delta \log(c_{it}) - \Delta \log(c_{wt}) = a + \lambda_r (\Delta \log(c_{rt}) - \Delta \log(c_{wt}))$$

$$+ (1 - \lambda_w - \lambda_r)(\Delta \log(y_{it}) - \Delta \log(c_{wt})) + e_{it},$$

$$i = 1, 2, \ldots, R \qquad (4)$$

In the above equations, λ_r, λ_w, and $1 - \lambda_r - \lambda_w$ can be interpreted as the degree of regional risk-sharing, the degree of global risk-sharing, and the extent that neither of risk-sharing arrangements is arranged. Equation (4) can be estimated using non-linear least squares. The restrictions, $0 \leq \lambda_r \leq 1$, $0 \leq \lambda_w \leq 1$, and $0 \leq \lambda_w + \lambda_r \leq 1$ can be imposed to exclude unrealistic cases.

We applied this empirical framework to infer the degree of regional risk-sharing (risk-sharing with the region) and the degree of global risk-sharing (risk-sharing with the world). Asian countries under consideration were: China, Hong Kong, Indonesia, Japan, South Korea, Malaysia, the Philippines, Singapore, Taiwan, Thailand. European countries under consideration were: Austria, Belgium, Denmark, Finland, France, Germany, Greece, Ireland, Italy, Luxemburg, the Netherlands, Norway, Portugal, Spain, Sweden, Switzerland, and the UK. The world in our model is assumed to consist of these ten Asian countries, seventeen European countries, other G-7 countries (the US and Canada), Australia, and New Zealand.

For consumption and income growth rates, the real per capita consumption growth rate (in domestic currency) and real per capita GDP growth rate (in domestic currency) are used. The aggregate consumption growth rates of the two regions and the world were constructed as the weighted average of the real per capita consumption growth rates of the individual countries. Here, the weight was determined by the relative size of the country's total consumption

Table 7.14: Estimates of regional and global risk-sharing, 1961–2002

	Regional (λ_r)	Global (λ_W)	None ($1\text{-}\lambda_W\text{-}\lambda_r$)	Adjusted R^2
(1) Asia				
China	0.570* (0.038)	0.000 (0.000)	0.430* (0.038)	0.727
Hong Kong	0.238* (0.091)	0.000 (0.000)	0.762* (0.091)	0.396
Indonesia	0.224 (0.176)	0.000 (0.000)	0.776* (0.176)	0.248
Japan	0.045 (0.090)	0.218* (0.052)	0.738* (0.060)	0.845
South Korea	0.212* (0.080)	0.000 (0.000)	0.788* (0.080)	0.619
Malaysia	0.000 (0.000)	0.000 (0.000)	1.000* (0.000)	0.568
Philippines	0.000 (0.000)	0.464* (0.042)	0.536* (0.042)	0.412
Singapore	0.000 (0.000)	0.335* (0.056)	0.665* (0.055)	0.598
Taiwan	0.198* (0.057)	0.000 (0.000)	0.802* (0.059)	0.292
Thailand	0.000 (0.000)	0.210* (0.059)	0.790* (0.059)	0.678
Average 1	0.149 (0.053)	0.123 (0.021)	0.729 (0.066)	0.538
Average 2	0.122	0.123	0.729	—
(2) Europe				
Austria	0.158 (0.161)	0.189 (0.239)	0.653* (0.260)	0.519
Belgium	0.757* (0.234)	0.075 (0.178)	0.167 (0.137)	0.365
Denmark	0.000 (0.000)	0.000 (0.000)	1.000* (0.000)	0.512
Finland	0.170* (0.050)	0.000 (0.000)	0.830* (0.050)	0.820
France	0.597* (0.092)	0.000 (0.000)	0.402* (0.094)	0.702
Germany	0.467* (0.217)	0.063 (0.144)	0.470* (0.136)	0.486
Greece	0.347 (0.290)	0.191 (0.269)	0.462* (0.091)	0.456
Ireland	0.377 (0.334)	0.129 (0.356)	0.494* (0.113)	0.319
Italy	0.258* (0.094)	0.000 (0.000)	0.742* (0.094)	0.668
Luxemburg	0.887* (0.062)	0.000 (0.000)	0.113 (0.059)	0.280
Netherlands	0.124 (0.106)	0.000 (0.000)	0.876* (0.106)	0.526
Norway	0.170 (0.431)	0.021 (0.278)	0.808* (0.173)	0.409
Portugal	0.157 (0.141)	0.000 (0.000)	0.843* (0.141)	0.362
Spain	0.000 (0.000)	0.000 (0.000)	0.876* (0.051)	0.863
Sweden	0.378* (0.099)	0.000 (0.000)	0.621* (0.101)	0.455
Switzerland	0.501* (0.044)	0.000 (0.000)	0.499* (0.044)	0.636
UK	0.056 (0.222)	0.152 (0.162)	0.792* (0.156)	0.398
Average 1	0.318 (0.152)	0.048 (0.096)	0.626 (0.106)	0.516
Average 2	0.236	0.000	0.610	—

(in PPP) to the aggregate total consumption (in PPP). Individual countries' real per capita variables were obtained from the WDI, and consumption (in PPP units) was obtained from Penn World Tables 6.1.

7.3.2 Empirical Results

Table 7.14 reports estimation results for individual countries for 1961–2002.[20] The numbers in parentheses are standard errors. '*' indicates that the coefficients are significant at 5 percent level. The restrictions of $0 \le \lambda_r \le 1$, $0 \le \lambda_w \le 1$, and $0 \le \lambda_w + \lambda_r \le 1$ are imposed in the estimation. So that Asian and European countries can be easily compared, the table reports the average numbers in the two regions. In addition, another average number, which

---

[20] The constant term was dropped since it was insignificant in most estimates.

Table 7.15: Estimates of regional and global risk-sharing (average), various subperiods

		1961–96	1961–80	1981–2002	1973–2002
Regional (λ_r)	Asia	0.197 (0.056)	0.184 (0.146)	0.166 (0.025)	0.204 (0.042)
	Europe	0.340 (0.146)	0.372 (0.190)	0.329 (0.107)	0.402 (0.134)
Global (λ_w)	Asia	0.140 (0.021)	0.164 (0.153)	0.119 (0.029)	0.121 (0.025)
	Europe	0.060 (0.086)	0.127 (0.118)	0.019 (0.031)	0.037 (0.080)
None ($1-\lambda_w-\lambda_r$)	Asia	0.668 (0.047)	0.652 (0.131)	0.724 (0.049)	0.676 (0.102)
	Europe	0.628 (0.109)	0.501 (0.123)	0.645 (0.089)	0.550 (0.099)

treats the insignificant estimate as zero, is calculated and reported, in order to exclude the influence of large insignificant estimates.

The pattern of regional and global risk-sharing for Asian and European countries is quite different. Compared to European countries, Asian countries have a lower degree of risk-sharing within the region but a higher degree of global risk-sharing. The simple average for the estimates for the degree of regional risk-sharing for Asian countries is 0.149, which is lower than that for European countries, 0.318. The number for the degree of global risk-sharing for Asian countries is 0.123, which is larger than that for European countries, 0.048.

When we only consider the estimates which are statistically significant, we reach the same conclusion. Out of the ten Asian countries, there are four countries where regional risk-sharing is statistically significant and four countries where global risk-sharing is statistically significant. In contrast, out of the seventeen European countries, there are nine countries where regional risk-sharing is statistically significant and no countries where global risk-sharing is statistically significant. The conclusion is similar when we use the average that treats the insignificant estimate as zero. The estimates for the degrees of regional and global risk-sharing for Asian countries are 0.122 and 0.123, respectively, while those for Europe are 0.236 and 0.[21] When we do not impose the restrictions on λ_r and λ_w, the conclusion is similar.

On the other hand, the overall extent of risk-sharing is larger in Europe; the average of the estimates for the extent of no risk-sharing arrangement ($1-\lambda_r-\lambda_w$) is 0.729 for Asia and 0.626 for Europe. Except for two European countries, the estimates are significantly different from zero. This implies that risk-sharing arrangements are not perfect in most countries, which is consistent with the results of the past studies.

Table 7.15 reports the simple averages for Asian and European countries for various subperiods. First, we cut the sample up to 1996, in order to exclude the effects of the Asian crisis. Second, we divide our sample into two

[21] The average is zero since none of the estimates is significantly different from zero.

subperiods, 1961–80 and 1981–2002. Third, we estimated for the period of 1973–2002, in order to account for exchange rate regime changes in early 1970s. For all these subperiods, we reached similar conclusions. Asian countries tend to have weak regional risk-sharing arrangements but strong global risk-sharing arrangements, compared to Europe. In addition, the degree of overall risk-sharing tends to be higher in Europe than in East Asia.

7.4 Why is Regional Financial Integration Low in East Asia?

Empirical results in previous sections from the gravity model of international asset holdings and the consumption risk-sharing model indicated that East Asia tends to be more integrated with regional financial markets than global financial markets, compared to Europe. In this section we discuss three hypotheses that may help explain the low financial integration within East Asia: incentives for portfolio diversification/risk-sharing, the development and deregulation of financial markets, and the monetary and exchange rate regime.

7.4.1 Incentives for Portfolio Diversification/Risk Sharing among East Asia

Theoretical models such as International Capital Asset Pricing Model (I-CAPM), imply that investors should diversify their portfolios to the greatest possible extent by investing more in securities that show a low degree of correlation with the home portfolio. This implies that countries with different structures, subject to different economic shocks, and with low business cycle correlations, will find it more advantageous to develop financial links with one another. In this regard, extensive portfolio diversification within East Asia may not be necessarily an optimal strategy, considering the homogeneity of East Asian economies.

Eichengreen and Park (2005a) refute this hypothesis. They claim that Europe is more homogenous in income and structure, and more synchronized in business cycles, but more integrated than East Asia. In this regard, we report the cross-country output correlation for East Asian and European countries for various subperiods in Table 7.16. The number under 'Reg' shows the correlations of the growth rate for each country's output and the growth rate of regional aggregate output.[22] The number under 'Glob', on the other hand, shows the correlations of the growth rate for each country's output and the growth rate of world aggregate output. The table also indicates the average correlation for East Asia and Europe. The average of regional correlation for East

[22] The regional and global aggregates are constructed by a similar method to that used in Section 7.3.

Table 7.16: Cross-country output correlation

	1961–2002		1961–96		1961–80		1981–2002		1973–2002	
	Reg	Glob	Reg	Glob	Reg	Glob	Reg	Glob	Reg	Glob
Asia										
China	0.81	0.34	0.86	0.36	0.90	0.45	0.50	0.39	0.60	0.27
Hong Kong	0.24	0.47	0.11	0.42	0.17	0.51	0.57	0.39	0.40	0.48
Indonesia	0.23	0.11	0.03	−0.02	−0.02	−0.07	0.76	0.29	0.54	0.22
Japan	0.20	0.48	0.12	0.46	0.21	0.53	0.57	0.39	0.67	0.59
Korea	0.50	0.44	0.45	0.44	0.45	0.53	0.77	0.39	0.59	0.49
Malaysia	0.21	0.27	0.01	0.15	−0.03	0.33	0.68	0.24	0.43	0.32
Philippines	−0.03	0.05	−0.09	0.01	−0.11	0.13	0.04	−0.07	0.02	0.05
Singapore	0.21	0.29	0.09	0.18	0.11	0.10	0.64	0.47	0.50	0.43
Thailand	0.42	0.64	0.41	0.66	0.48	0.69	0.50	0.57	0.53	0.69
Taiwan	0.44	0.32	0.38	0.34	0.42	0.51	0.81	0.31	0.69	0.38
Average	*0.32*	*0.34*	*0.24*	*0.30*	*0.26*	*0.37*	*0.58*	*0.34*	*0.50*	*0.39*
Europe										
Austria	0.10	0.34	0.10	0.32	0.22	0.38	−0.14	0.17	−0.18	0.22
Belgium	0.12	0.49	0.09	0.46	0.14	0.40	0.27	0.65	0.06	0.50
Denmark	0.06	0.52	0.05	0.52	0.06	0.57	0.08	0.36	0.23	0.58
Finland	0.09	0.34	0.12	0.34	0.24	0.23	−0.11	0.42	0.00	0.31
France	0.11	0.52	0.12	0.52	0.27	0.68	−0.12	0.31	0.00	0.50
Germany	0.26	0.62	0.25	0.61	0.36	0.73	0.18	0.43	0.23	0.59
Greece	0.18	0.47	0.18	0.49	0.31	0.53	−0.07	0.32	0.30	0.48
Ireland	−0.08	0.10	−0.01	0.13	−0.13	−0.02	−0.09	0.30	0.09	0.23
Italy	−0.14	0.35	−0.20	0.33	−0.24	0.19	0.30	0.65	0.06	0.52
Luxemburg	0.22	0.49	0.28	0.51	0.30	0.65	0.05	0.41	0.20	0.54
Netherlands	0.31	0.60	0.37	0.61	0.47	0.57	0.02	0.61	−0.02	0.56
Norway	−0.19	0.01	−0.27	−0.05	−0.49	−0.52	0.24	0.41	−0.10	0.06
Portugal	0.13	0.45	0.13	0.45	0.18	0.53	0.08	0.21	0.27	0.52
Spain	−0.17	0.31	−0.17	0.31	−0.21	0.22	0.04	0.44	0.00	0.36
Sweden	0.02	0.33	0.05	0.33	0.09	0.14	−0.08	0.53	−0.06	0.31
Switzerland	−0.05	0.36	−0.05	0.36	−0.04	0.23	−0.05	0.56	0.06	0.43
UK	0.32	0.69	0.36	0.71	0.38	0.77	0.23	0.61	0.47	0.78
Average	*0.08*	*0.41*	*0.08*	*0.41*	*0.11*	*0.37*	*0.05*	*0.43*	*0.10*	*0.44*

Asia ranges between 0.24–0.50 while that for Europe ranges between 0.05–0.11. The average global correlation for East Asia ranges between 0.30–0.39, while that for Europe ranges between 0.37–0.44. In contrast to Eichengreen and Park (2005a)'s claim, the regional correlation of East Asia is higher than that of Europe, while the global correlation of East Asia is not higher than that of Europe.[23] This result may imply that the welfare gains for regional financial integration are lower in East Asia than in Europe. This might alternately

---

[23] The simple output correlation does not suggest the sources of shocks. Therefore, the substantial synchronization of business cycles among the countries within a region can be caused by a common global shock rather than a regional shock. But Lee, Park, and Shin (2004) show that, based on dynamic factor models that isolate independent regional and global components, the regional component explains more than half of output variance for individual East Asian economies in 1990s.

explain why East Asia has a lower degree of regional financial integration than Europe.

In general, investors tend to invest the bulk of their financial wealth in domestic assets. An interesting question is whether this 'home bias' in portfolio investment is weaker at the country level than the regional level. If a country is strongly integrated with regional financial markets but weakly integrated with global financial markets, 'home bias' at the country level can be weaker than 'home bias' at the regional level. However, for East Asian countries, 'home bias' at the country level does not seem to be weaker than 'home bias' at the regional level, based on our results that regional financial integration within East Asian countries is very weak.

As surveyed by Lewis (1999), there are a number of reasons in the literature explaining home bias at the country level. First, domestic equities can provide a better hedge for risks that are specific to the home country. For example, hedges against domestic inflation and hedges against wealth (not traded in capital markets) such as human capital, are better provided through domestic assets. Second, the gains from global diversification may not be large, compared to the costs involved. If the costs of acquiring and holding foreign equities are sufficiently large, then investors may find it preferable to keep their savings at home. Third, information is more easily communicated at the country level. This information superiority enables portfolios solely based on domestic assets to perform better than global portfolios.

These arguments do not seem to generalize well for East Asia. First, business cycle synchronization within East Asian countries is not much weaker than business cycle synchronization of East Asian countries with the rest of the world. Therefore, East Asian countries may not find hedges through regional markets to be far superior to those through global markets. Second, investing in East Asia may involve even larger costs since most East Asian countries have underdeveloped financial markets. Third, information sharing may not be easier among East Asian countries than among European countries, and East Asian countries may have better information on the financial markets of developed countries like the US than on the financial markets of mostly underdeveloped East Asian countries. On the other hand, these factors seem to be more applicable to European countries. Therefore, East Asia would be less inclined than European countries to intensify their financial linkages with one another.

7.4.2 Development and Deregulation of Financial Markets[24]

Several institutional and structural characteristics of East Asian financial systems may constrain regional financial integration. In East Asia, where

---

[24] See Lee, Park, and Shin (2004) and Eichengreen and Park (2005a, 2005b).

financial systems have been largely bank-oriented, securities markets have been relatively underdeveloped. Inadequate financial and legal structure, low auditing and accounting standards, and weak corporate governance must have hampered the development of regional capital markets. After a long period of bank-oriented systems and financial repression, East Asian capital market institutions are not well equipped for the management of external financial transactions. Brokerage services for investing in foreign securities have mostly been provided by Western financial institutions. It is therefore natural that financial market liberalization and opening have contributed to integrating East Asia's financial markets into global financial markets more than to creating integrated regional financial markets.

Except for the Japanese banks, most other East Asian banks—which are small in size—have relatively limited experience in international corporate banking, and small branch networks. There are not that many domestic investment banks, securities firms, and mutual funds able to compete against their counterparts from developed countries. In the absence of these institutions, securities underwriting in East Asia has been mostly dominated by American and European investment banks.

Although Hong Kong and Singapore have been important regional financial centers, East Asia still lacks a center that can mediate financial transactions within the region, helping to attract regional investors into the regional securities markets. These two centers were serving East Asian borrowers and lenders well before financial market opening got underway in the region. However, they were essentially outposts of major international capital markets in advanced countries. Thus, they may have gravitated more toward linking the East Asian economies with the advanced economies than integrating them with one another.

It is also true that a number of countries in East Asia still rely on capital controls. Restrictions on capital account transactions and on entering foreign financial institutions must be an impediment to the process of financial integration involving these economies.

Consistent with this, Eichengreen and Park (2005b) provide evidence that a lower level of capital market liberalization and an underdevelopment of financial markets and institutions particularly in potential lending countries are the main factors contributing to the difference between the intra-Europe and intra-East Asia integration in the cross-border bank lending market.

7.4.3 Monetary and Exchange Rate Regime

A number of studies focus on how the choice of exchange rate regime affects the volume of cross-border financial transactions. Most of these show that higher exchange rate volatility leads to less trade in assets, as well as trade in goods. Blanchard and Giavazzi (2002) show that correlations between current account positions and per capita incomes increased more for future European Monetary Union (EMU) countries in 1990s, suggesting that monetary integration enhanced financial integration. Danthine, Giavazzi and von Thadden (2000) and Fratzscher (2001) provide evidence that the introduction of the Euro has increased the degree of financial integration in Euro countries. Spiegel (2004) also argues that overall international borrowing is facilitated by the creation of monetary unions, particularly based on the evidence from Portugal's accession to the EMU. Evidence supports the idea that the degree of financial integration has increased significantly after the introduction of euro. In addition, based on a broad set of more than 150 countries, Lee and Shin (2004) found that risk-sharing is enhanced under monetary union.

In this sense, a higher degree of exchange rate volatility may contribute to a lower degree of financial integration in East Asia. Since we restricted our sample primarily to the period since 1999 in the studies of cross-border assets, exchange rate volatility in the euro area is completely eliminated. In contrast, most of East Asia chose to float their exchange rates after the crisis in 1997–8, contributing to higher volatilities. In this regard, Kim, Kim and Wang (2005) and Kim (2004) investigated the exchange rate arrangements in East Asian countries before and after the currency crisis. They found that many East Asian countries adopted a free floating after the Asian crisis, based on both *de jure* and *de facto* measures. On the other hand, a similar logic may apply to the results of risk-sharing estimates using longer sample periods since European countries are more eager to stabilize the intra-European exchange rate, for example, through the ERM.

Another special feature after the financial crisis is that East Asia had accumulated a substantial amount of dollar reserve assets. East Asia, with a 'fear of floating' against the US dollar, has intervened in the foreign exchange market so as to moderate excessive volatility of exchange rates and maintain the competitiveness of export sectors. The East Asian economies tended to hoard their reserves in low-yielding US treasuries and other dollar-denominated financial assets. This tendency of East Asia to invest in dollar-denominated assets may have had a negative impact on regional integration.

After the Asian crisis, the leaders of Japan, South Korea, China, and ASEAN member countries pursued financial and monetary cooperation, to ward off future financial crises. In May 2000, these countries met at the annual meeting of Asian Development Bank in Chiang Mai, Thailand, and announced their intention to cooperate in four principle areas: monitoring capital flows, regional surveillance, swap networks, and training personnel. ('Chiang Mai

Initiative' refers specifically to the swap arrangements.) Since then there have been various efforts and steps to promote financial and monetary cooperation. Swap arrangements can be regarded as a risk-sharing tool at the regional level, although current analysis does not comprise it. In addition, further developments in financial and monetary cooperation among these countries are likely to help to enhance regional financial market integration in East Asia.

7.5 Concluding Remarks

It is often claimed that the level of financial market integration within East Asia is relatively low. Based on the gravity model of cross-border portfolio asset and bank claim holdings, we have found some evidence of regional financial integration. However, East Asian countries tend to be relatively more linked to the global markets than integrated with one another, particularly compared to Europe. The consumption risk-sharing model also indicates that East Asia tends to have weaker regional risk-sharing arrangements, but stronger global risk-sharing arrangements than Europe.

A subsequent question raised by our results is what has caused this low level of financial integration. We have inquired into hypotheses that can explain the differing experiences in East Asia and Europe. Weak incentives for portfolio diversification within East Asia, the low degree of development and deregulation of financial markets, and the instability of monetary and exchange rate regimes are considered the main causes of low financial integration within East Asia. One critical issue was exactly what role each factor plays in the regional and global financial integration process. Investigation of this issue, which can be conducted by extending the gravity framework with additional data, will shed light on what policies are needed to strengthen financial integration in the region.

Another important question is the extent to which countries should pursue regional integration along with global integration. Although increased regional financial integration, given the extent of global integration, can be beneficial in many ways, it is unclear what constitutes the optimal degree of regional integration relative to global integration. For instance, regional financial market integration helps to share country-specific risks, but it can also transmit regional shocks and thus increase the vulnerability of the national economy. Furthermore, regional financial integration may substitute for global integration and thus lower national welfare. In subsequent research, we plan to pursue these important and interesting questions.

References

Altug, S. and Miller, R. (1990), 'Household Choices in Equilibrium,' *Econometrica* 82: 1177–98.

Anderson, J. E. (1979), 'A Theoretical Foundation for the Gravity Equation,' *American Economic Review*, 69: 106–16.

Asdrubali, Pierfederico, and Kim, Soyoung (2003), 'Incomplete Risksharing and Incomplete Intertemporal Consumption Smoothing,' Working Paper, Korea University.

Bekaert, G., and Harvey, C. (1995), 'Time-varying World Market Integration,' *Journal of Finance*, 50: 403–44.

Bergstrand, J. H. (1985), 'The Gravity Equation in International Trade: Some Microeconomic Foundations and Empirical Evidence,' *Review of Economics and Statistics*, 67: 474–81.

Blanchard, Olivier, and Giavazzi, Francesco (2002), 'Current Account Deficits in the Euro Area: The End of the Feldstein–Horioka Puzzle?' *Brookings Papers on Economic Activity*, 2: 147–86.

Buch, C. (2002), 'Are Banks Different? Evidence from International Data,' *International Finance*, 5(1): 97–114.

____ (2003), 'Information and Regulation: What Drives the International Activities of Commercial Banks?' *Journal of Money, Credit, and Banking*, 35 (6): 851–70.

Canova, F. and Ravn, M. (1996), 'International Consumption Risk sharing,' *International Economic Review*, 37: 573–601.

Cochrane, J. H. (1991), 'A Simple Test of Full Consumption Insurance,' *Journal of Political Economy*, 99: 957–76.

Crucini, M. J. (1999), 'On International and National Dimensions of Risk Sharing,' *Review of Economics and Statistics*, 81: 73–84.

____ and, Hess, G. D. (2000), 'International and Intranational Risk Sharing,' in G. D. Hess and E. van Wincoop (eds.), *Intranational Macroeconomics* (Cambridge: Cambridge University Press), 37–59.

Chelley-Steeley, P. L. and Steeley, J. M. (1999), 'Changes in the Comovement of Europan Equity Markets,' *Economic Inquiry*, 37: 473–88.

Danthine, J.-P., Giavazzi F., and von Thadden, E.-L. (2000), 'European Financial Markets after EMU: a First Assessment,' Working paper, Centre for Economic Policy Research, Discussion Paper 2413.

Eichengreen, Barry and Luengnaruemitchai, Pipat (2004), 'Why Doesn't Asia have Bigger Bond Markets?' Paper presented at The Korea University/BIS Conference on Asia Bond Market Research, Seoul, March 21–3.

____ and Park, Yung Chul (2005a) 'Why Has There Been Less Financial Integration in Asia than in Europe?' Working paper, University of California, Berkeley.

____ ____ (2005b), 'Financial Liberalization and Capital Market Integration in East Asia,' The EU Center of the University of California, Berkeley and the Ford Foundation.

Evenett, S. J. and Keller, W. (2002), 'On Theories Explaining the Success of the Gravity Equation,' *Journal of Political Economy*, 110 (2): 281–316.

Fratzscher, M. (2001), 'Financial Market Integration in Europe: On the Effects of EMU on Stock Markets,' European Central Bank, Working Paper 48.

Hess, Gregory D. and Shin, Kwanho (1998), 'Intranational Business Cycles in the US,' *Journal of International Economics*, 44: 289–313.

Jeanneau, S. and Micu, M. (2002), 'Determinants of International Bank Lending to Emergent Market Countries,' BIS Working Papers, No. 112.

Jeon, Jongkyon, Oh, Yonghyup, and Yang, Doo Yong (2005), 'Financial Market Integration in East Asia: Regional or Global?' Korea Institute for International Economic Policy.

Keil, Manfred W., Phalapleewan, Amnat, Rajan, Ramkishen S., and Willett, Thomas D. (2004), 'International and Intranational Interest Rate Interdependence in Asia: Methodological Issues and Empirical Results,' Claremont Graduate University Working Paper.

Kim, Soyoung (2004), 'What is Learned from a Currency Crisis, Fear of Floating or Hollow Middle? Identifying Exchange Rate Policy in Recent Crisis Countries,' Working Paper, Korea University.

—— Kim, Sunghyun H., and Wang, Yunjong (2004), 'Regional Versus Global Risk Sharing in East Asia,' *Asian Economic Papers*, 3: 182–201.

—— —— —— (2005), 'Fear of Floating in East Asia,' in Y. Oh, D. R. Yoon, T. D. Willet (eds.), *Monetary and Exchange Rate Arrangement in East Asia* (Seoul: Korea Institute for International Economic Policy), 229–49.

—— —— —— (2006), 'Financial Integration and Consumption Risk Sharing in East Asia,' *Japan and the World Economy*, 18: 143–57.

Lane, Philip R. and Milesi-Ferretti, Gian Maria (2003), 'International Financial Integration,' *CEPR Discussion Papers*, 3769.

Lee, Jong-Wha and Shin, Kwanho (2004), 'Exchange Rate Regimes and Economic Linkages,' Working paper, Korea University.

—— —— and Park, Y. (2004), 'A Currency Union in East Asia,' in *Monetary and Financial Integration in East Asia: The Way Ahead*, vol. 2, edited by Asian Development Bank (Basingstoke and New York: Palgrave Macmillan), 139–76.

Lewis, Karen K. (1996), 'What Can Explain the Apparent Lack of International Consumption Risk Sharing?' *Journal of Political Economy*, 104: 267–97.

—— (1999), 'Trying to Explain Home Bias in Equities and Consumption,' *Journal of Economic Literature*, 37: 571–608.

McCauley, Robert, Fung, San-Sau, and Gadanecz, Blaise (2002), 'Integrating the Finances of East Asia,' *BIS Quarterly Review* (December): 83–95.

Mace, B. J. (1991), 'Full Insurance in the Presence of Aggregate Uncertainty,' *Journal of Political Economy*, 99: 928–56.

Obstfeld, M. (1994), 'Are Industrial-Country Consumption Risks Globally Diversified?' in L. Leiderman and A. Razin (eds.), *Capital Mobility: The Impact on Consumption, Investment and Growth* (Cambridge: Cambridge University Press).

Obstfeld, M. (1995), 'International capital mobility in the 1990's', in: P. Kenen (ed.), *Understanding Interdependence: The Macroeconomics of the Open Economy* (Princeton: Princeton University Press), 201–61.

Park, Yung Chul and Bae, Kee-Hong (2002), 'Financial Liberalization and Economic Integration in East Asia,' Unpublished manuscript, Korea University.

Portes, Richard and Rey, Helene (2005), 'The Determinants of Cross Border Equity Flows,' *Journal of International Economics*, 65 (2): 269–96.

Rose, Andrew K. (2000), 'One Money, One Market: The Effect of Common Currencies on Trade,' *Economic Policy* 30.

——— and Spiegel, Mark (2004), 'A Gravity Model of International Lending: Trade, Default and Credit,' *IMF Staff Papers*, 51: 50–63.

Spiegel, Mark M. (2004), 'Monetary and Financial Integration: Evidence from Portuguese Borrowing Patterns,' Federal Reserve Bank of San Francisco, Working Paper 2004-07.

Townsend, R. M. (1994), 'Risk and Insurance in Village India,' *Econometrica*, 62: 539–91.

World Bank (1997), 'Private Capital Flows to Developing Countries: The Road to Financial Integration,' World Bank.

Yildrim, Canon (2003), 'Informational Asymmetries, Corporate Governance Infrastructure and Foreign Portfolio Equity Investment,' Mimeo, Tilburg University.

8

Determinants of Liquidity in the Thai Bond Market

Akkharaphol Chabchitrchaidol and Sakkapop Panyanukul[1]
Bank of Thailand

8.1 Introduction

The Thai bond market saw significant growth in the years following the Asian financial crisis in 1997. The authorities recognized the need for deep and liquid bond markets, and the important role these markets play in enhancing financial market resilience during times of stress. In particular, markets for government securities can help to create a robust and efficient financial system. While steps have been taken to ensure basic bond market infrastructure has been put in place in the Thai context, the lack of liquidity remains a major obstacle to market development. Market participants realized that market liquidity cannot be taken for granted, even in normal times, with the market having been subject to periods where a sell-off in bonds had an adverse effect on liquidity.

This paper identifies and analyzes the key determinants of liquidity in the Thai bond market as measured by bid-ask spreads. We draw upon the results of this analysis to suggest ways to improve liquidity in the secondary market. The paper also considers policy actions the government and central bank

[1] This paper represents a joint collaborative effort between the Bank of Thailand and the Bank for International Settlements (Asian Representative Office) in improving research on bond markets in Thailand. The authors are grateful to Titanun Mallikamas for his useful advice and comments from the beginning of this project. Thanks go to Robert McCauley, Eli Remolona, and Amporn Sangmanee, who have acted as advisors on this project. Special thanks are due to Corinne Ho for her helpful and extensive comments and suggestions, as well as to participants at a Seminar at the HKIMR, the Bank of Thailand and the University of California, Berkeley. The views expressed herein are those of the authors and not necessarily those of the Bank of Thailand.

can take to ensure that these key determinants are achieved, and provides recommendations for the authorities' role in creating an environment which best facilitates a liquid secondary market.

The following section gives a brief overview of the structure of the bond market in Thailand. Section 8.3 discusses how to measure and interpret bond market liquidity, in particular the use of bid–ask spreads as a proxy for market liquidity. Section 8.4 discusses the theoretical and empirical framework used in the study, and the rationale behind it. Section 8.5 summarizes the empirical results from the estimations. Section 8.6 draws implications for policy, both for the Ministry of Finance in its capacity as an issuer of bonds, as well as for the Bank of Thailand in its role in safeguarding stability in the Thai financial system.

8.2 Overview of the Thai Bond Market

8.2.1 *Background of Thailand's Bond Market: Prior to 1997*

Prior to the economic crisis in 1997, the function of financial intermediation fell almost entirely on commercial banks. Funds were mobilized mainly through deposits through the banking sector. Direct financing through the domestic bond market—both for the public and private sector—was relatively scarce, leading to small and underdeveloped markets in government and corporate bonds.

The underdevelopment of Thailand's bond market was attributed to nine consecutive years of fiscal surplus between 1988 and 1996, which in turn meant that the Thai government had little incentive or need to issue any regular or substantial amount of government bonds. The limited supply of government bonds inhibited the development of a risk-free benchmark against which private issuers could price their bonds. This contributed to difficulties in development of the corporate bond market.

With benefit of hindsight, it was recognized that the lack of a proper bond market—and the resulting imbalance from over-reliance on bank lending—was a factor that contributed to and perpetuated the 1997 financial and economic crisis. The crisis resulted from the practice of borrowing and rolling over short-term US dollar loans from foreign banks to finance longer-term investments with revenues in Thai baht. This dual mismatch became problematic once creditors lost confidence in the Thai economy and refused to continue lending. With limited financing alternatives to bank loans, businesses in Thailand faced a severe liquidity crunch as the banking sector curtailed their lending operations amid rising NPL ratios and increasing recapitalization needs. This intensified the

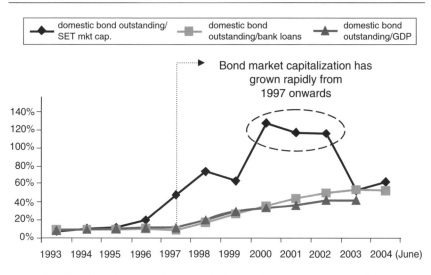

Figure 8.1: Bond market capitalization relative to the stock market, bank loans, and GDP

Source: BOT.

economic slowdown as the normal channels of funding did not function effectively.

8.2.2 Thailand's Bond Market After 1997

Recognizing the imbalance in the Thai financial system, the authorities made a great deal of effort to try to redress this problem. Efforts to develop the domestic bond market were given an extra boost partly due to the need to fiscalize the cost of post-crisis financial sector restructuring, as well as the need to find an alternate funding source to reduce the reliance on bank intermediation and external financing.

The bond market grew rapidly since 1997. Figure 8.1 shows the ratios of domestic bonds outstanding to stock market capitalization, bank loans, and GDP. All three ratios have been on an increasing trend. Domestic bond market capitalization surpassed stock market capitalization during 2000–2, as indicated in the dotted circle. Figure 8.1 also shows that although bank loans still dominate the bulk of financing in the country, the share of bond financing has increased steadily.

Despite the considerable growth in terms of size, the ratio of the Thai bond market to GDP, at about 40 percent, still remains small compared to those in industrial countries—which generally have debt market to GDP ratios above

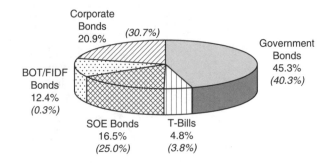

Figure 8.2: Bond outstanding by instruments as of June 2004

Note: Number in parentheses represents corresponding figures in 2000.
Source: ThaiBDC.

100 percent. Local bond markets in the EMEAP[2] economies (excluding Japan) are equivalent to about 50 percent of GDP (Jiang and McCauley 2004). Emerging countries with debt markets comparable in size to industrial countries include Malaysia and Korea. On average, the ratio of bonds outstanding to GDP is about one third for emerging countries.

8.2.3 *Thai Bond Market Profile*

Figure 8.2 shows the distribution of the various types of bonds outstanding in the Thai bond market. The Thai bond market is currently dominated by public debt securities, which account for more than two-thirds of the total outstanding bonds in the market. Though the corporate bond market has grown since the crisis, its development is still handicapped by the lack of quality issuers and of a reliable benchmark yield curve. This issuer characteristic differs from many bond markets in other Asian countries (with exception of Hong Kong) where corporate issues account for a large portion of domestic debt issuance.

The Bank of Thailand acts as a fiscal agent and registrar of government securities as well as collecting and disseminating data on bond holders. Commercial banks are the largest holders of government bonds (see Figure 8.3 below for a profile of holders of government securities); however, they have reduced their investments in the bond market in the past few years, given their inclination to increase credit extension to the private sector. Insurance firms, another significant player in the government bond market, are mainly buy-and-hold investors. These players tend to hold long-term bonds, which they match to their liabilities, reducing the amount of *free-floating* bonds in the market available for trading.

[2] EMEAP economies include Australia, China, Hong Kong SAR, Indonesia, Japan, Korea, Malaysia, New Zealand, Philippines, Singapore, and Thailand.

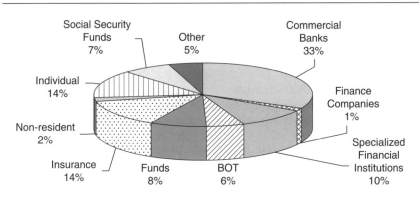

Figure 8.3: Profile of government securities holders as of September 2004
Source: BOT.

Both government and corporate bonds are traded 'over the counter (OTC),' with institutional investors—including banks, mutual funds, provident funds, the Government Pension Funds, and insurance companies—as the main investors in bonds. In 2004, some corporate bond issues have been listed in a newly established exchange market to allow access by retail and individual investors. Going forward, authorities are promoting the establishment of an electronic trading platform (ETP) for all types of bonds to facilitate trade and reduce transaction costs in bond trading.

The majority of trading takes place between institutional investors, with two thirds of trading accounted for by inter-dealer trading. Categorized by type of security, government bonds are the most actively traded securities, accounting for approximately 80–90 percent of total trade. Dealers (financial institutions holding a debt securities license granted by the SEC) are required to report all bond transactions to Thai Bond Dealing Centre.[3] Thai BDC monitors compile and disseminate prices to the public at the end of day. Prices disseminated by Thai BDC are used as market reference.

8.3 Determinants and Measuring Market Liquidity

There is a great deal of literature on the importance of bond market liquidity and the various determinants of liquidity, with somewhat varying conclusions from market to market. Borio (2000) describes the increasing interest in liquidity as following naturally from the increased need for an efficient financial system. In particular, liquidity is an important factor underpinning the smooth

---

[3] The Thai Bond Dealing Centre (Thai BDC) was established in 1998 under the Securities and Exchange Commission (SEC) Act B.E. 2535 as an organized secondary market for bonds. The primary roles of the Thai BDC are to disseminate information on the bond market as well as to facilitate the operation of the secondary market for bond trading.

functioning of the financial system and conditioning the daily activities of economic agents, including pricing, trading, and risk management.

There are many ways in which liquidity can be defined and measured. The Committee on the Global Financial System (CGFS 1999) broadly defines a liquid market as a market where participants can rapidly execute large-volume transactions with a small impact on prices. However, the concept of liquidity can be further elaborated in a number of dimensions. These include:

(1) **tightness**, or how far transaction prices diverge from mid-market prices; this can generally be measured by the bid-ask spread; the lower the spread, the higher the liquidity;

(2) **depth**, denoting either the volume of trades possible without affecting prevailing market prices or the amount of orders on the order books of market-makers at a given time;

(3) **resiliency**, referring to the speed with which price fluctuations resulting from trades are dissipated, or the speed with which imbalances in order flows are adjusted; and

(4) **immediacy**, referring to the time that passes between the placing of a market order and its execution (Upper 2001).

8.3.1 Determinants of Market Liquidity

The Committee on the Global Financial System (CGFS 1999) looks at the importance of liquidity for central bank policies and comes up with a list of factors bearing on market liquidity, ranging from product design, market microstructure—including trade execution systems, transactions costs, and transparency of markets—to market participants' behavior, including the degree of heterogeneity of market participants in their views and risk profiles, as well as the effect of self-fulfilling expectations.

Theory suggests a number of determinants that have an effect on bond market liquidity. The CGFS divides these factors into three broad categories including product design, market microstructure, and the behavior of market participants. Mares (2002) supports the view that fragmentation of the market—in particular the degree of substitutability of instruments and the outstanding amount of fungible assets in the market—plays an important role in determining liquidity. Other factors that affect liquidity include holdings by government accounts and other investors who do not trade actively, the amounts outstanding of benchmark issues, taxes, arrangements for repurchase, as well as clearing and settlement practices.

Macroeconomic factors may also play a role in determining market liquidity (Mohanty 2002). In particular, the size of an economy tends to correlate positively with the size of the bond market—with a small market limiting the feasible range of marketable instruments and their effective tradability. In addition, economies of scale may also play a role, with a minimum turnover required in order for market-makers to function smoothly and cost-effectively. Mohanty refers to the European experience, which seems to suggest that bond markets became deeper after the adoption of a common market and currency. McCauley and Remolona (2000) suggest that debt markets require a minimum aggregate threshold size (roughly 100–200 billion USD in mature markets in industrial countries) in order to maintain liquidity.

Borio (2000), however, points out that the factors determining liquidity, or their degree of significance, can differ substantially during periods of market stress. Past periods of market turbulence seem to indicate that counterparty risks and cash liquidity constraints have important negative effects on bond trading. Consequently, arrangements for dealing with counterparty risk as well as the performance of risk management systems also have important effects on the dynamics of market liquidity. While keeping this in mind, this paper will focus on the determinants of liquidity under more normal circumstances in a developing bond market.

8.3.2 *Measuring Market Liquidity*

A number of approaches have been taken to measure bond market liquidity. D'Souza and Gaa (2004) suggest a number of measures for liquidity, including bid-ask spreads, volatility, trading volume and frequency, as well as quote size and frequency. While trading volume is an intuitive and widely cited measure of market liquidity—with an established positive link with liquidity—one drawback is that it is also associated with price volatility, which tends to be negatively related to market liquidity. This becomes especially apparent during times when the market is under stress. In addition, trading volume has no direct relation with any of the four dimensions of liquidity mentioned earlier. For example, large trades may still occur in the face of low market liquidity (in terms of tightness, depth, resiliency, and immediacy) if traders have a need to trade, such as for hedging purposes. Trade frequency, or the number of trades observed per unit of time, is another indirect measure of liquidity. However, as with trading volume, while higher trading frequency may reflect a more liquid market, it may also be associated with increased price volatility, which is in turn associated with reduced liquidity.

A more commonly used measure of market liquidity is the bid-ask spread, or the difference between the best bid and offer prices. Not only is data for this measure easily available, bid–ask spreads reflect the tightness aspect of liquidity in the bond market. In practice, a market that has very low transaction costs is characterized as liquid; in this sense, the bid–ask–spread is a relatively direct measure of market liquidity. The bid–ask spread directly measures the cost of executing a 'small'[4] trade, and being a major part of trading costs, they are commonly used as an indicator of the quality of market functioning.

In a study of liquidity in the US Treasury Market, Fleming (2001) identifies the bid-ask spread as one of the most appropriate liquidity indicators due to its high degree of correlation with other measures, such as price impact and benchmark/non-benchmark yield spreads. D'Souza, Gaa, and Yang (2003) also find evidence that bid-ask spreads are one of the most appropriate indicators of liquidity, consistently exhibiting the expected relationship with price volatility and other liquidity measures.

However, Fleming (2001) suggests that a drawback of the bid-ask spread is that bid and offer quotes are only good for limited quantities and periods of time. The spread therefore only measures the cost of executing a single trade of limited size. Despite its drawbacks, the bid–ask spread remains the most commonly used and most appropriate measure of market liquidity.

8.4 Theoretical Framework and Statistical Methodology

8.4.1 Basic Model and Rationale

A standard approach to study the impact on liquidity is to estimate an equation of bid–ask spreads (BAS), controlling for the effect of trading volumes and yield volatility (VOL(X)).

The basic least squares equation to be estimated is as follows:

$$BAS_t = \alpha + \beta_1 VOL(X) + \beta_2 \sqrt{Volume} + \beta_3 (Dummy) + \varepsilon_t \tag{1}$$

Higher volume or lower volatility is expected to be associated with lower bid-ask spreads, an indication of better market liquidity. While this can be explained intuitively, it is also supported by market microstructure theory, which will be discussed in greater detail.

Volatility is expected to have a positive relation with bid-ask spreads (a negative impact on liquidity). Intuitively, an increase in volatility poses higher risks, which need to be compensated directly through a higher bid-ask spread.

Trading volume is also an intuitive and widely cited measure of market liquidity. When there is a high degree of liquidity, resulting from a high level of demand for trades, the spread between bid and offer prices will narrow. The opposite occurs when sellers and buyers are more reluctant to trade. Buyers are likely to bid lower prices, as they would require a higher return to compensate for the increased risk resulting from the lack of liquidity, namely the liquidity risk premium. On the other hand, sellers are likely to set a higher offer price

---

[4] A 'small' trade can be defined as the minimum quote size specific to each market. In the case of Thailand, this quote size is set at 20 million baht.

for the same reason. The result is a bid–ask spread that is wider than in times of normal liquidity. In our estimation, trading volume enters our estimation as a square root in order to scale down the impact of volume on bid–ask spreads. At high levels of trading volume, any marginal increments in trading have a much smaller, limited effect on bid–ask spreads.

Formal studies in market microstructure theory have identified three main causes that may affect liquidity in financial markets (Upper 2001). These include order processing costs, inventory control considerations, and adverse selection problems.

Order-processing costs include exchange fees and taxes as well as costs of handling transactions. However, given that these costs should be fairly constant in the short run, they are unlikely to determine short-term changes in liquidity.

Inventory control considerations arise mainly from uncertainty about order flows as well as uncertainty about future prices and valuation of the portfolio, leading to uncertainty in the size of the inventory that dealers need to keep on hand. The inventory cost component needs to compensate dealers for holding less than fully diversified portfolios (Krinsky and Lee 1996). High volatility increases the risk of holding inventory by these dealers, leading them to quote larger bid–ask spreads to compensate for such risks. On the other hand, increased trading in the market, according to this theory, should lead to lower bid–ask spreads as inventory risk for dealers is reduced, suggesting a positive relation between volatility and spreads and a negative relation between trading volume and spreads, consistent with our intuitive predictions above.

Adverse selection problems arise when a group of investors—known in the literature as the 'informed' traders—have private information on the value of an asset not currently reflected in prices. 'Informed' traders will want to trade only if the current ask price they face is below—or the bid price above—the fundamental value of the asset.

The adverse selection theory introduces two sets of hypotheses. Under the first hypothesis, higher trading volume—which signals the presence of 'informed' traders—results in increased spreads (Easley and O'Hara 1992). In this case, increased trading volume signals to the dealer that an information event has occurred. Since the dealer or market maker will always make a loss from dealing with 'informed' traders, he has to recoup these losses from other investors by charging a larger bid–ask spread for his trades, leading the dealer to widen the spread in response to the unusually high number of trades. Under this hypothesis, a higher trading volume will lead to higher spreads.

Under the second hypothesis, higher trading volume reflects an increase in liquidity trading (by the uniformed), therefore signaling higher overall market liquidity (Harris and Raviv 1993). Under this scenario, dealers will interpret that a volume shock is due to a change in the demands of 'liquidity' traders (such as through mutual fund redemption, for example), and would not be expected to decrease liquidity and have little to no effect on bid–ask spreads.

Existing models of adverse selection of this type, however, have mainly looked at liquidity in equity markets, partly due to fact that data are more easily available due to the nature of exchange-traded equity markets. Existing models are based on the assumption that some investors have superior information on the pay-off of the asset, which is unlikely to be the case for government bonds, where cash flows are perfectly known (Lee, Mucklow, and Ready, 1993). While it is unclear which of these two scenarios are more appropriate in our case, it is clear that volatility and trading volume are two of the main factors which will play a role in determining spreads—and hence, liquidity—and are therefore included in our model.

We have included a dummy variable in our model to take into account an apparent structural increase in bid–ask spreads since mid 2001. In May 2001, the removal of Bank of Thailand governor (Chatu Mongkol Sonakul), who had established inflation targeting explicitly as the central bank's main policy objective, raised concerns about new governor's willingness to adhere to this framework. At the time, markets expected the new governor (Pridiyathorn Devakula) to be more biased towards exchange rate stability, possibly at the expense of price stability. This was seen as leading to greater uncertainty about interest rate policy, which would have an effect on government bond yields. After this episode, several other events may have exerted an influence. These include uncertainty of supply issuance to fiscalize losses incurred by the Financial Institutions Development Fund (FIDF) through financial system restructuring, which persists to the present day.[5] Another event that negatively affected liquidity is the massive sell-off of mutual funds invested in fixed income markets in late 2003. A chronology of events affecting the average bid–ask spreads in the bond market in the period between September 1999– October 2004 is summarized in Figure 8.4 below.

8.4.2 Data

The study covers the period from September 1999 to October 2004. September 1999 is the earliest date in which information on Thai bond trading started to be systematically compiled by the ThaiBDC. Data used for the study include

[5] The FIDF incurred over 1.4 trillion baht of losses in its restructuring of the financial sector after the 1997 crisis. Of this, 655 billion baht has been fiscalized through issuance of loan bonds, which are tradable by institutional investor (approx. 47% of total losses), as well as 395 billion baht of saving bonds (28%), targeted at retail investors. It is still unclear how the remaining 25% of losses currently held by the FIDF will be fiscalized, over what time frame, and in what form.

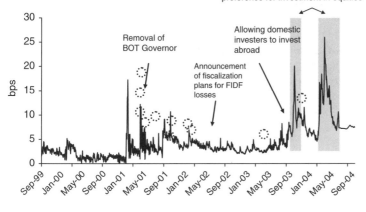

Figure 8.4: Events affecting the bid–Ask spread (September 1999–October 2004)

Note: Auction dates where bid-to-cover ratios are less than one are denoted by the dotted circles .
Source: ThaiBDC, BOT.

daily data on bid-ask spreads (end-day *indicative* averages) of government bonds with maturity of more than one year, data on trading volume (daily traded amount), and data on volatility (based upon end-day quoted yields). Analysis is conducted on the most highly traded bond in the sample period, the LB08DA[6] issue.

The ThaiBDC began to construct a ThaiBDC Government Bond Yield curve in 1998, based on actual executed yields on all government loan bonds. However, since 1999, this yield curve has been adjusted and is now based on average bid yields of government loan bonds, based indicatively, quoted by the Bank of Thailand's nine primary dealers for government bonds. These primary dealers are required to send quotes of both bid yields and offer yields for trades with a minimum size of 20 million baht to the ThaiBDC at the end of each working day (16.00 hours). The Government Bond Yield Curve is constructed and published daily on the ThaiBDC's website.

Trading volume comprises daily data on outright transactions compiled by the ThaiBDC. Data is required to be submitted to the ThaiBDC from dealers within fifteen minutes after a trade is executed. Most trades in the debt securities market are executed in the Over-the-Counter (OTC) market, which operates daily from 9.00 hours to 16.00 hours.

[6] The LB08DA issue is a government bond that was first issued on December 8, 1998, with a 10-year maturity. The outstanding amount for this government bond is 50 billion baht, which is the largest outstanding amount of all tradable government bonds. The selected individual issue (LB08DA) represents a large proportion of trading volume in the market contributing to an average 20% of total trading volume over the study's time period.

8.4.3 *How Data Enters the Estimation*

Data on bid–ask spreads are compiled by the ThaiBDC and are calculated as the difference between bid and ask yields. They are measured in basis points. Data on trading volume, measured in millions of baht, are also compiled by the ThaiBDC and enter into the estimation as is.

A data series for volatility (VOL(X)) is generated based on a rolling daily standard deviation of yield changes over a period of X observations (working days) measured in percent. There are different ways to calculate volatility. The simple approach is as follows:

$$VOL(X)_t = \sqrt{\frac{1}{x}\sum_{i=1}^{x}(YLD_{t-(i-1)} - \overline{YLD_t})^2} \qquad (2)$$

Where X = window width (in number of days)

YLD_t = bond yield at date t

$\overline{YLD_t}$ = average bond yield over the x days to date t

Yield volatility is modeled using varying values of X, ranging from one week (five working days) to six months (126 working days). Given that there are various ways to calculate yield volatility, we proceed later in our estimations to model volatility to take into account other factors which play a role in determining volatility.

As mentioned earlier, we include a dummy variable to allow for an apparent structural widening of bid–ask spreads that we believe to have started around the time of the change of Bank of Thailand Governor in May 2001. The dummy is set to zero before this date, and one thereafter, to capture the effect on markets from the perceived change in policy direction as well as other various effects on the bid–ask spread that cannot be captured by trading and volatility variables.

In entering data into the estimation, we use data for the most widely traded bond, the LB08DA issue. Following this estimation, we repeat the procedure at the aggregate level. Data at the aggregate level are generated using a similar process, using an average of data on all Thai Government bonds with maturity of more than one year, while we use the ten-year interpolated yield (THY10) as a proxy for market yields, as the majority of government bonds in the past have been issued with maturities of around ten years. Details of how these data are generated can be found in Annex 1.

Tables 8.1–8.7 provide summary statistics for the bid–ask spread, trading volume, volatility, and Thai bond yield over a five-year period (1999–2004). Table 8.1 in the annex summarizes some basic statistics for the bid–ask spread. Figures 8.12–8.16 plot the time series for these data.

Table 8.1a: Summary statistics (LB08DA) 1999–2004

99–04	Average	Maximum	Minimum	Standard deviation
BAS (bps)	3.12	30.00	0.25	2.92
Trading Volume (millions of THB)	500.64	4,474.18	0.67	524.34
VOL5 (%)	4.37	38.29	0.12	4.27
VOL21 (%)	12.31	56.76	0.67	8.96
LB08DA Yield (%)	4.01	7.88	1.60	1.63

Table 8.1b: Summary statistics (aggregate level) 1999–2004

99–04	Average	Maximum	Minimum	Standard deviation
BAS (bps)	4.38	25.96	0.06	3.38
Trading Volume (millions of THB)	3,306.93	14,455.30	4.97	2,154.78
VOL5 (%)	4.42	35.46	0.57	4.18
VOL21 (%)	13.04	57.76	0.86	9.71
THY10 (%)	5.19	8.02	2.35	1.37

Table 8.2a: Summary statistics (LB08DA) 1999

1999	Average	Maximum	Minimum	Standard deviation
BAS (bps)	1.10	2.00	0.50	0.47
Trading Volume (millions of THB)	118.86	432.32	8.79	133.64
VOL5 (%)	0.91	4.21	0.21	0.95
VOL21 (%)	1.97	3.58	0.67	0.77
LB08DA Yield (%)	7.85	7.88	7.82	0.02

Table 8.2b: Summary statistics (aggregate level) 1999

1999	Average	Maximum	Minimum	Standard deviation
BAS (bps)	2.72	4.57	1.61	0.61
Trading Volume (millions of THB)	1,271.51	3,867.93	4.97	842.04
VOL5 (%)	1.08	3.77	0.09	0.91
VOL21 (%)	2.38	4.38	0.86	0.93
THY10 (%)	7.96	8.02	7.85	0.04

Table 8.3a: Summary statistics (LB08DA) 2000

2000	Average	Maximum	Minimum	Standard deviation
BAS (bps)	0.99	5.00	0.25	0.67
Trading Volume (millions of THB)	820.85	3,336.38	31.76	685.01
VOL5 (%)	3.26	13.78	0.12	2.76
VOL21 (%)	9.39	28.88	1.88	6.99
LB08DA Yield (%)	6.30	7.81	5.15	0.85

Table 8.3b: Summary statistics (aggregate level) 2000

2000	Average	Maximum	Minimum	Standard deviation
BAS (bps)	1.68	5.18	0.06	1.00
Trading Volume (millions of THB)	3,868.99	9,432.70	139.21	1,868.56
VOL5 (%)	3.30	14.34	0.24	3.10
VOL21 (%)	10.65	34.62	1.52	7.98
THY10 (%)	6.58	7.90	5.57	0.69

Table 8.4a: Summary statistics (LB08DA) 2001

2001	Average	Maximum	Minimum	Standard deviation
BAS (bps)	1.76	10.00	0.50	1.24
Trading Volume (millions of THB)	647.11	2,952.35	12.79	585.42
VOL5 (%)	7.59	38.29	0.35	6.01
VOL21 (%)	21.95	56.76	4.84	10.64
LB08DA Yield (%)	5.03	6.29	3.44	0.72

Table 8.4b: Summary statistics (aggregate level) 2001

2001	Average	Maximum	Minimum	Standard deviation
BAS (bps)	3.91	17.28	0.08	2.50
Trading Volume (millions of THB)	3,490.36	14,455.30	417.01	2,367.51
VOL5 (%)	6.07	35.46	0.25	5.71
VOL21 (%)	20.41	57.76	2.95	13.02
THY10 (%)	5.53	6.66	3.77	0.67

Table 8.5a: Summary statistics (LB08DA) 2002

2002	Average	Maximum	Minimum	Standard deviation
BAS (bps)	3.08	8.50	0.50	1.81
Trading Volume (millions of THB)	632.26	4,474.18	2.64	512.09
VOL5 (%)	3.73	13.77	0.22	2.62
VOL21 (%)	10.20	22.41	1.27	4.93
LB08DA Yield (%)	3.80	4.83	2.66	0.66

Table 8.5b: Summary statistics (aggregate level) 2002

2002	Average	Maximum	Minimum	Standard deviation
BAS (bps)	3.53	6.98	2.10	0.79
Trading Volume (millions of THB)	4,393.35	10,977.25	806.94	1,862.78
VOL5 (%)	4.15	14.70	0.20	2.87
VOL21 (%)	12.08	27.20	1.08	6.00
THY10 (%)	4.79	6.08	3.61	0.72

Table 8.6a: Summary statistics (LB08DA) 2003

2003	Average	Maximum	Minimum	Standard deviation
BAS (bps)	3.54	25.00	1.00	2.82
Trading Volume (millions of THB)	317.27	1,741.15	0.67	268.09
VOL5 (%)	4.64	28.73	0.31	4.66
VOL21 (%)	12.46	43.95	2.78	8.71
LB08DA Yield (%)	2.32	3.91	1.60	0.46

Table 8.6b: Summary statistics (aggregate level) 2003

2003	Average	Maximum	Minimum	Standard deviation
BAS (bps)	4.72	20.07	1.98	3.06
Trading Volume (millions of THB)	3,357.31	13,239.29	73.50	2,241.77
VOL5 (%)	4.68	26.12	0.28	3.89
VOL21 (%)	13.31	39.35	1.64	8.20
THY10 (%)	3.46	5.10	2.35	0.75

Table 8.7a: Summary statistics (LB08DA) 2004

2004	Average	Maximum	Minimum	Standard deviation
BAS (bps)	6.42	30.00	2.50	3.94
Trading Volume (millions of THB)	169.63	1,533.00	2.10	206.03
VOL5 (%)	3.29	19.72	0.35	3.06
VOL21 (%)	9.74	28.49	2.35	6.86
LB08DA Yield (%)	2.97	3.51	2.18	0.41

Table 8.7b: Summary statistics (aggregate level) 2004

2004	Average	Maximum	Minimum	Standard deviation
BAS (bps)	9.14	25.96	4.60	3.89
Trading Volume (millions of THB)	1,801.57	7,778.66	79.80	1,278.62
VOL5 (%)	5.31	26.80	0.69	4.65
VOL21 (%)	10.74	37.16	2.01	8.07
THY10 (%)	4.85	5.22	3.92	0.30

8.5 Empirical Results

8.5.1 *Empirical Results using Least Squares Estimation*

In our initial estimation based on equation (1), BAS for our LB08DA was regressed on a constant, a volatility term, trading volume of the LB08DA issue, as well as a dummy variable.

Results indicate that all explanatory variables are highly significant, with trading volume negatively related with spreads, while volatility as well as the dummy having a positive impact on BAS, as expected (Table 8.8). However, the Durbin-Watson statistic indicates serial correlation in the error term. Adding a lagged term for the BAS to account for this persistence improves the Durbin Watson statistic and results in a slight improvement in goodness of fit.

However, further investigation using an ARCH LM test for autoregressive conditional heteroskedasticity (ARCH) in the residuals indicates heteroskedasticity in our data, possibly leading to inefficient estimators. When OLS is applied to heteroskedastic models, it is no longer a minimum variance estimator. The variances and standard errors are understated. Serial correlation in this case will also lead to biased estimators.

In this case, an EGARCH[7] specification may be preferred to OLS. This process of refining our empirical model, covered in Sections 8.5.1–8.5.3, is summarized in Figure 8.5 below.

8.5.2 *Empirical Results using EGARCH Estimation*

A variation of equation (1) was estimated using an EGARCH process in place of least squares, while keeping the same explanatory variables. The distinctive feature of using an EGARCH estimation is that it recognizes that variance of the error term is not constant, and therefore attempts to keep track of the fluctuations in variance through time by including past values in the explanation of future variances.

Given the characteristics of a financial variable, it has been suggested that it may be more appropriate not to restrict our specification of the variance of the error term. Using an EGARCH model allows greater flexibility in modeling volatility of the error term through asymmetric shocks to volatility.

Under the EGARCH(1,1) model, the variance equation is given by:

$$\log(\sigma_t^2) = \omega + \beta \log(\sigma_{t-1}^2) + \gamma \frac{\mu_{t-1}}{\sqrt{\sigma_{t-1}^2}} + \alpha \left[\frac{|\mu_{t-1}|}{\sqrt{\sigma_{t-1}^2}} - \sqrt{\frac{2}{\pi}} \right] \tag{3}$$

---

[7] The functional form of the EGARCH model has several advantages compared to that of the simple GARCH model. The exponential form that is used for the conditional variance σ_t^2 guarantees that σ_t is always positive. This permits a wide range of variance effects that are not restricted by non-negativity constraints on the parameters.

Table 8.8: Regression results on BAS (individual, LB08DA issue)

Specification (Expected sign)	Constant	Dummy (+)	Trading volume (Square Root) (−)	Volatility (+)	Lagged BAS	MA(1)	Durbin Watson/R^2
8.1 LS with VOL(21)	0.01411***	0.02682***	−0.00069***	0.04274***	—	—	0.8018/0.2479
8.2 LS with VOL(21) and lagged term	0.00561**	0.01036***	−0.00026***	0.01387*	0.61697***	—	2.3212/0.5337
8.3 EGARCH (1,1) with VOL(21)	0.00115	0.00147***	0.00000	−0.00163	0.94971***	0.69222***	1.7677/0.5843
8.4 EGARCH (1,1) with VOL(5)	0.00123*	0.00141***	0.00000**	0.00010	0.94770***	−0.70209***	1.7492/0.5843
8.5 EGARCH (1,1) with modeled volatility (VOLEG08)	0.0010	0.00170***	−0.00004*	0.02033**	0.94154***	−0.66378***	1.8387/0.5956

Significance levels: *(10%), **(5%), ***(1%).

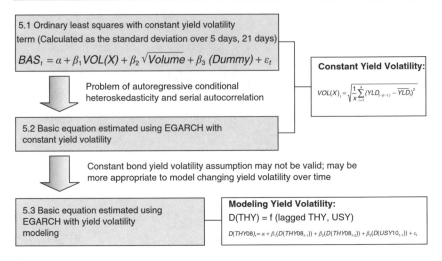

Figure 8.5: Refining the empirical model

As mentioned above, the EGARCH model has an advantage over the GARCH model as it permits a wide range of variance effects that are not restricted by non-negativity constraints on the parameters—since we model the $\log(\sigma_t^2)$, then even if the parameters are negative, σ_t^2 will be positive. In addition, the EGARCH model takes into account the 'leverage effects,' whereby BAS levels may be correlated with changes in volatility of the BAS (depending on direction of change).

In addition to the existing explanatory variables, a one-day lag of the BAS was added to the list of explanatory variables in order to take into account the persistence of the BAS. The BAS, as with many financial variables, tends to exhibit a high degree of persistence based on recent past values. Table 8.8 summarizes regression results on the LB08DA bond using various specifications, which will be interpreted in Section 8.6. Estimation using EGARCH yields better fit than our original OLS specification.

8.5.3 *Modeling Volatility*

However, given the nature of bond yield volatility, which is unlikely to remain constant over extended periods, our previous constant yield volatility assumption (where yield volatility was represented as the sample of standard deviation over a number of days) may not be valid; it may be more appropriate to model yield volatility in such a way that allows it to change over time. Using an EGARCH model to estimate yield volatility allows for the variance of the error term to change continuously with the passage of time.

Table 8.9: EGARCH model for volatility (individual, LB08DA issue) (VOLEG08)

Specification	Constant	D(THY08(-1))	D(THY08(-2))	D(USY10(-1))	Durbin Watson/ R^2
EGARCH(1,1)	−0.00264	0.32152***	-0.04956*	0.12357***	1.9868/0.1161

Significance levels: *(10%), **(5%), ***(1%).

We begin by estimating the historical yield of the LB08DA issue (THY08) based on lagged values of itself. D(THY08) is the difference of yield on LB08DA from the previous day, using end-of-day quoted yields. In addition, given the market's perception that Thai and US interest rates tend to move together, they closely monitor movements in the US Treasury market in their pricing and trading decisions. We therefore introduced lagged interpolated yields of ten year US treasuries, which is considered a benchmark tenor in the US market, as an additional explanatory variable.[8]

We estimate volatility using the following specification, with results shown in Table 8.9:

$$D(THY08)_t = \alpha + \beta_1(D(THY08_{t-1})) + \beta_2(D(THY08_{t-2})) + \beta_3(D(USY10_{t-1})) + \varepsilon_t \tag{4}$$

We use this specification to estimate a new data series for yield volatility (VOLEG08), which we plug back into our main regression equation in place of our original data series for yield volatility, VOL(X). This results in much improved estimates for our main equation (see Table 8.8), which is free from statistical problems faced in earlier regressions. Coefficients from our estimation have the expected signs, while the Durbin-Watson statistic is much improved at 1.8387, allaying our concerns of serial correlation. We proceed to discuss results in the next section based on this model EGARCH model for BAS and the above EGARCH model for volatility.

8.5.4 *The Final Equation*

The process above leads us to a final equation as follows:

$$BAS_t = 0.0010 + (0.00170^{***})Dummy_t - (0.000043^*)\sqrt{Volume_t}$$

$$+ (0.02033^{**})Volatility_t + (0.94154^{***})BAS_{t-1} - (0.66378^{***})MA(1) \tag{5}$$

where volatility is modeled as follows:

$$D(THY08)_t = -0.00264 + (0.32152^{***})(D(THY08_{t-1}))$$

$$- (0.04956^*)(D(THY08_{t-2})) + (0.12357^{***})(D(USY10_{t-1})) \tag{6}$$

---

[8] A one-day lag for US yields is used in order to account for time difference between trading days between the US and Thai markets

Significance levels: *(10%), **(5%), ***(1%)

Our final equation (equation (5)) sees a marginal improvement in goodness of fit, compared to earlier specifications. All explanatory variables in equation (5) are significant and have the expected signs. Results also suggest that there is a high degree of persistence in the bid-ask spread; in other words, 94 percent of the previous day's bid-ask spread contributes to the present-day's bid ask spread.

As theory suggests, equation (5) shows a positive relationship between volatility and bid–ask spread. In this case, a 1 percent increase in volatility results in a 2.0 basis point increase in the bid–ask spread. Results also show a significant, negative relationship between volume and the bid–ask spread, although at much smaller magnitude. In addition, the dummy variable has a small and positive impact on bid-ask spreads.

Equation (6) suggests that movements in Thai Bond yields arise mainly from past yields changes in the Thai market as well as a spillover effect from yield changes in the US Bond Market. In particular, a 1 basis point change in the previous day's yield results in a 0.32 basis point change in present yields, while a 1 basis point change in the previous day's yield in US yields results in 0.12 basis point change in present yields.

AGGREGATE LEVEL REGRESSION

In order to test if these results are robust in the government bond market overall, we repeat the above methodology for the market as a whole. We calculate average bid–ask spreads for the whole market for government bonds with maturity over one year. Trading volume is calculated as the aggregate of all outright trades of government bonds. Volatility is calculated using the same methodology as for the LB08DA issue, but using interpolated ten-year Thai government bond yields (THY10). Details of these calculations and the methodology can be found in Annex 1.

Table 8.10 summarizes regression results at the aggregate level using various specifications, while Table 8.11 shows the regression results of volatility modeling. Using the same processes as those of LB08DA leads us to the a final equation as follows:

$$BAS_t = 0.00056 + (0.00120^{***})Dummy_t - (0.00001)\sqrt{Volume_t}$$

$$+(0.04204)Volatility_t + (0.97755^{***})BAS_{t-1} - (0.16280***)MA(1) \quad (7)$$

where yield volatility is modeled as follows:

$$D(THY10)_t = -0.00136 + (0.39925^{***})(D(THY10_{t-1}))$$

$$+(0.00729)(D(THY10_{t-2})) + (0.13598^{***})(D(USY10_{t-1})) \quad (8)$$

Significance levels: *(10%), **(5%), ***(1%)

Table 8.10: Regression results on average BAS (aggregate of all tradable Government Bonds)

Specification (Expected sign)	Constant	Dummy (+)	Trading volume (Square Root) (−)	Volatility (+)	Lagged BAS	MA(1)	Durbin Watson/ R^2
10.1 LS with VOL(21)	0.04513***	0.03175***	−0.00061***	0.07789***	—	—	0.3423/0.3452
10.2 LS with VOL(21) and lagged term	0.00340*	0.00297***	0.00004	0.00484	0.91107***	—	2.3928/0.8828
10.3 EGARCH (1,1) with VOL(21)	0.00017	0.00097*	0.00000	0.03389	0.98264***	−0.20021***	2.1576/0.8874
10.4 EGARCH (1,1) with VOL(5)	0.00059	0.00133***	0.00000	−0.00986**	0.97666***	−0.16085***	2.2308/0.8868
8.5 EGARCH (1,1) with modeled volatility (VOLEG)	0.00056	0.00120***	−0.00001	0.04204	0.97755***	−0.16280***	2.1692/0.8916

Significance levels: *(10%), **(5%), ***(1%)

Table 8.11: EGARCH model for volatility (aggregate level)

Specification	Constant	D(THY10(-1))	D(THY10(-2))	D(USY10(-1))	Durbin Watson/R^2
EGARCH(1,1)	−0.00136	0.39925***	0.00729	0.13598***	2.1443/0.1538

Significance levels: *(10%), **(5%), ***(1%)

The regression results at aggregate level (equation (7)) yield broadly similar results to the LB08DA estimation in equation (5), in terms of sign and magnitude. However, both volume and volatility are no longer significant at the aggregate level. This is because the estimation using data at the individual issue level is likely to better show sensitivity and responsiveness to market factors and conditions and does not suffer the drawbacks of loss information through aggregation or averaging level variables.

8.6 Implications for Policy

8.6.1 *Dummy Variable*

Our dummy variable has remained consistently significant throughout our regressions. As a proxy for structural changes that occurred during our sample period, we interpret its significance to mean that actions and announcements by the authorities play an important role in determining spreads, with market uncertainty of public policy—such as how fiscalization of FIDF losses will occur, widening bid-ask spreads. With this in mind, the authorities can help to reduce bid-ask spreads by ensuring that any potentially sensitive announcements are effectively communicated with market stakeholders. In addition, the authorities should clearly announce plans regarding auctions and new issuances, and strictly commit to these plans if possible, in order to ensure smooth market movements and avoid market confusion.

8.6.2 *Volatility*

On the policy side, the fact that volatility has an impact on bid-ask spreads, and hence liquidity, mean that ways to safeguard against excessive volatility should be encouraged. One way to do so is to create a vibrant derivatives market which would allow effective hedging of interest rate risks, as well as credit risks. Other tools for risk management in the bond market that may be helpful include the development of a more active and well-functioning private repurchase market as well as short-selling transactions. Mares (2002) highlights the role of a highly liquid futures market to generate liquidity for the cash market—not only for bonds deliverable against futures contracts but also for the rest of the yield curve. In addition, Mares finds that if a dealer can properly and rapidly hedge any bond, that dealer will be more likely to enter into transactions on any of these bonds.

Market liquidity can further be boosted by permitting market participants to short-sell a security and at the same time enabling them to borrow the shorted securities temporarily from its owner with a contractual obligation to redeliver at a later date, possibly through the private repo market (Mohanty 2002). Mohanty finds a general consensus among central banks that short selling can have an important stabilizing influence on bond markets, as market volatility was generally higher when participants were unable to make short sales. In this regard, many industrial countries have relaxed restrictions on domestic and cross-border securities transactions in the 1990s, such as allowing short-sale transactions. Several countries have also developed a 'when-issued' market[9] as a first step in introducing a short selling facility.

The development of a private repurchase market is also an important step in improving market infrastructure. The private repo market could provide a link between the money market and bond market. The private repo is also a tool for market participants to hedge their position and manage liquidity (both bond and cash positions) more effectively. Liquidity in the secondary bond market will be substantially improved once the well-functioning private market is put in place.

Another way to reduce volatility is through widening of investor and market participants. A greater variety and diverse set of participants will make the market more resilient to shocks, such as the recent sell-off by mutual funds, or to unanticipated changes in interest rates, as well as enable smooth dissipation of market shocks. An increase in market participants will also diversify players' risk profiles, reducing the chances of a one-way market. Heterogeneity of market participants in terms of transactions needs, risk assessments, and investment horizons enhances market liquidity, as flows received by diverse players will offset each other instead of adding to each other (Mares 2002). One way to increase competition is to allow the entry of foreign banks and securities firms into the finance sector to create a level playing field (Shih 1996). Shih cites Taiwan's capital market as a model of development whereby foreign banks and securities firms were allowed entry into the local financial sector. A large investor base also generates incentives for financial innovation, leading to greater market dynamism and lower transaction costs.

---

[9] A 'when-issued' market refers to the market for forthcoming 'on-the-run' securities (most recently issued note or bond of a given initial maturity).

Table 8.12: Effect of outstanding issuance on trading volume (TRADE)[+]

Specification	Constant	Outstanding[++]	Dummy for Issuance	Time to Maturity (TTM)	Durbin Watson/ R^2
LS	−7432.120	0.967100**	27095.42***	237.0885	2.0903/0.5072

Significance levels: *(10%), **(5%), ***(1%)
[+] **TRADE** refers to the annualized trading volume of each individual issue in 2004
[++] **Outstanding** refers to the free-float amount of 25 issues of government loan bonds as of November 2004 excluding holding by Bank of Thailand as well as insurance companies, who generally buy and hold to maturity.

8.6.3 *Trading Volume*

Trading volume itself is likely to be affected by various factors. The model uses a simple cross-section regression of annualized trading volume in 2004 against 'free-float' issues, time to maturity, and an auction dummy (equal to one if there is an auction in that particular issue, and zero otherwise). The main factors which have an impact on trading volume in the market for Thai Government bonds include whether or not an issue is auctioned in any particular year as well as the size of outstanding bonds in the market for each issue.

ISSUE SIZE

Issue size has an important and significant contribution to trading volumes in the market for Thai Government bonds. In the following analysis, the actual tradable amount of bonds (free float) available in the secondary market was considered, excluding the amount of bonds held by the Bank of Thailand as well as insurance companies. These bonds are mostly 'buy and hold' and are not traded in the secondary market.

Results (Table 8.12) suggest that the amount of free-floating bonds has a positive relation to the amount of trading volume in the secondary market for each individual issue. In particular, there is almost a one-to-one effect of free float outstanding to trading; in other words, a one unit increase in 'free-float' outstanding bonds available for trade results in a 0.97 units increase in trading volume for that issue. This relation is plotted in Figure 8.6, below.

This has clear implications for policy. In order to increase the amount of outstanding bonds of particular issues to improve liquidity for these issues, the government may consider taking a series of steps, starting with a *bond buy-back program* for various issues that have a small outstanding size. These can then together be *reissued* in more sizeable auctions at tenors which are favored by the market. In other words, debt of different maturities can be 'lumped together' to create fewer maturities, as suggested by McCauley and Remolona (2000). This may include reopening of issues.

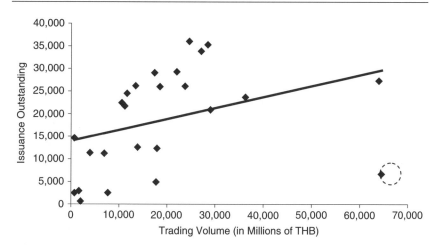

Figure 8.6: The relationship between trading volume and issuance outstanding of the Government Bond in 2004

Note: Dotted circle refers to the LB09NC issue (five-year government bond) which was only recently auctioned in November 2004; annualized trading volume for this issue will therefore be noticeably larger than other issues.

Source: ThaiBDC, BOT.

A second way to enhance liquidity is through more frequent and systematic issuance in the primary market. This reissuance will also increase trading volume in the market through the effect of new auctions as mentioned above, leading to the related improvement in liquidity. McCauley and Remolona (2000) suggest a few methods of *creating size*, for governments worried about generating too much public debt or in a stage of fiscal surplus. The first, as mentioned above, is through 'lumping' together different types of debt. This puts emphasis on gross issuance in specific securities by concentrating issuance in fewer maturities and by buying back illiquid issues. This debt can then be reissued to consolidate maturities to develop a benchmark. They also find that preferred maturities in industrial countries are at two, five, ten, and thirty years. Inoue (1999) also finds concentration on a few important maturities to avoid market fragmentation to be preferable to large number of maturities with small issue sizes, with industrial countries generally concentrating on issuance of four to seven maturities. For governments with a fiscal surplus—and corresponding shrinking debt levels, authorities may consider 'overfunding', with extra proceeds from borrowing channeled to alternative choices for investment. Mohanty (2002) reports the use of bond conversion, outright repurchase (also know as 'coupon pass') and reverse auctions to buy back less liquid securities and replace them with new liquid instruments in Canada and Singapore.

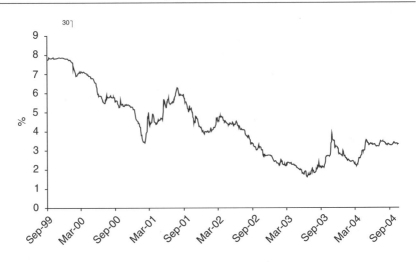

Figure 8.7a: Bid–ask spread for ten–year Treasury issued in 1998

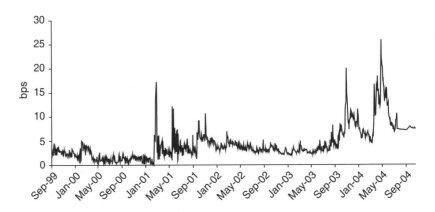

Figure 8.7b: Bid–ask spread for ten–year Treasury issued in 1998
Source: ThaiBDC.

It is worth noting that developing benchmarks through the methods mentioned above are important not only for developing a risk-free yield curve but also for reducing the servicing cost to government. Goldstein and Folkerts-Landau (1994) find that savings to the government from selling benchmark issues are estimated to be in the order of 5–15 basis points in developed countries.

Trading volume of LB08DA

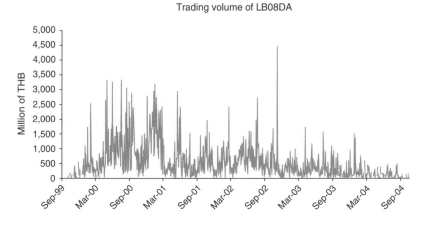

Figure 8.8a: Trading volume for ten–year Treasury issued in 1998

BOND HOLDING

The impact of 'free-float' issues in the market on trading also implies that there are policy implications for bond holding by institutions, including the central bank. While the Bank of Thailand already does its best to ensure that its bond holding has minimal impact on market liquidity, it still holds a sizeable portion of bonds in the market.

In this regard, the Bank of Thailand could consider means to free up these bonds if needed by market participants to support liquidity, such as through a bond-lending facility to support the market-making function of primary dealers, for instance. This can be done in addition to the currently existing Securities Position Adjustment Facility (SPAf), which has been in implementation since the beginning of 2004.[10] This would effectively be an enhancement of the current SPAf in terms of lending amount, number of issues available for borrowing, and more flexible terms of lending (i.e. longer borrowing horizon).

Encouraging repurchase transactions (repos) in general should help contribute to secondary market liquidity by allowing market participants to borrow against their securities portfolios, generally below the unsecured borrowing rate. In particular, encouraging interbank-repos in government bonds would help promote liquidity. Another main buy-and-hold player in the bond market is insurance companies, who also have a substantial holding of government bonds in their portfolios. These companies should be

---

[10] The SPAf allows nine primary dealers for outright transactions to borrow four issues of benchmark bonds to support their market-making functions.

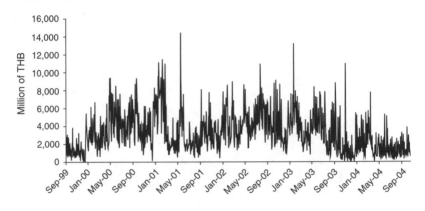

Figure 8.8b: Trading volume for all Thai Government Bonds with residual maturity of at least one year
Source: ThaiBDC.

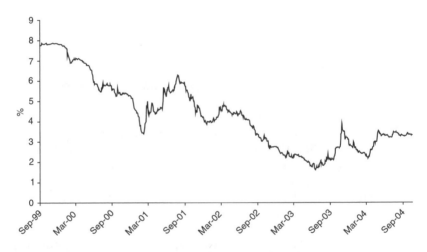

Figure 8.9a: Historical yield of ten–year Treasury issued in 1998

encouraged to lend out their bonds to more active players in the secondary market.

AUCTIONS

In the case of Thailand, auctions of government bonds are conducted using an American auction procedure, and are open to dealers as well as end investors in the primary market. Given the relatively small demand compared

228

Figure 8.9b: Interpolated yield for Thai Government Bond with ten–year maturity
Source: ThaiBDC.

to each issue size, large issues are auctioned in smaller lots over a number of weeks. In addition, to increase the outstanding size of any particular issue, the government, from time to time, auctions additional bonds of the same issue, which has the same effect as a 'reopening' of bond issues.

Using a dummy variable indicating whether or not a particular issue is auctioned or reopened in that year, we find that the fact that there is an auction (or reopening) has a positive impact on trading volume in that year. This may be due to the fact that new issuances are clearly priced at auction, while older issues may lack price transparency due to lack of trading, leading to preference for newer issues. In addition, most auctions are allotted to dealers (mainly primary dealers), which then are sold to end-investors, most of whom are institutional investors. This contributes to greater activity in the secondary market and increased trading volumes. Estimation results in Table 8.12 show that for issues where an auction took place in 2004, trading volume for that particular issue increased significantly by 27,095 million THB.

Aside from frequency of auctions, authorities must make sure that they choose an auction technique that improves the price discovery process, given the informational asymmetries between sellers and buyers.

8.7 Conclusion

Thailand's bond market has developed significantly over the past ten years, and has provided the economy with an alternative source of finance, in addition to traditional equity finance and bank loans. The primary market continues to be dominated by government securities, with a much smaller proportion of issuance going to corporate bonds.

The Thai authorities have focused their efforts on development of the market for government bonds, in the belief that a well-functioning and liquid market for government bonds would lay the foundation for development of a corporate bond market. Doing so requires a liquid secondary market for government bonds, which provides a reliable yield curve that could facilitate pricing. To this extent, numerous steps have been taken to enhance liquidity, by creating a sound framework for the bond market, reducing volatility, and enhancing trading volume, for instance. But the role of authorities in such a pursuit is limited, as many of the factors mentioned above are only likely to come about as a result of market development, increased participation, increased sophistication of players, and possibly a larger size of the economy.

But in the meantime, what the authorities can do is take the necessary measures to ensure that the existing bond market is able to function as smoothly as possible. This is reflected in the various initiatives by authorities to improve transparency in the way bonds are scheduled for issuance and auctioned in the primary market, and the way they are traded in the secondary market. These efforts may have led to a concentration of liquidity in a few benchmark issues, while other issues, particularly towards the longer end, remain quite illiquid. However, this may not necessarily represent a market failure, as arguably, liquidity in a few key tenors is all that is needed for pricing. Liquidity in the other, less-traded issues may naturally dissipate soon after their allocation in the market is done.

Annex 1

At the aggregate level, we calculate average bid–ask spread data as the average of bid–ask spreads of each issue (based upon indicative yields of government bonds traded each day), as follows:

$$BAS_t = \frac{\sum_{i=1}^{n} BAS_{it}}{n} \qquad (9)$$

where n is the number of individual government bond issues available at time t.

Trading volume is calculated as the aggregate of all outright trades of government bonds at time t, as follows:

$$TRADE_t = \sum_{i=1}^{n} TRADE_{it} \qquad (10)$$

Yield volatility is calculated based on equation (2), where YLD is the ten-year interpolated yield.

References

Borio, Claudio (2000), 'Market Liquidity and Stress: Selected Issues and Policy Implications,' *BIS Quarterly Review* (November): 38–48.

Chabchitrchaidol, Akkharaphol and Permpoon, Orawan (2002), 'Development of the Thai Bond Market,' *BIS Papers No. 11—The Development of Bond Markets in Emerging Economies*, June-July.

Chordia, Tarun, Sarkar, Asani, and Subrahmanyam, Avanidhar (2003), 'An Empirical Analysis of Stock and Bond Market Liquidity,' *Federal Reserve Bank of New York Staff Reports*, No. 164, March.

Committee on the Global Financial System (1999), 'Market Liquidity: Research Findings and Selected Policy Implications,' Bank for International Settlements.

D'Souza, Chris and Gaa, Charles (2004), 'The Effect of Economic News on Bond Market Liquidity,' *Bank of Canada Working Paper* 2004–16, May.

—— —— and J. Yang (2003), 'An Empirical Analysis of Liquidity and Order Flow in the Brokered Interdealer Market for Government of Canada Bonds,' *Bank of Canada Working Paper*, No. 2003–28.

Easley, David and O'Han, Maureen (1992), 'Time and the Process of Security Price Adjustment,' *Journal of Finance*, 47 (2): 577–605.

Fleming, M. (2001), 'Measuring Treasury Market Liquidity,' *Federal Reserve Bank of New York Staff Report*, No. 133.

—— and Remolona, Eli M. (1997), 'What Moves the Bond Market?' *Federal Reserve Bank of New York Research Paper*, No. 9706, February.

Goldstein, M. and Folkerts-Landau, D. (1994), 'International Capital Markets: Developments Prospects, and Policy Issues,' *International Monetary Fund*.

Harris, Milton and Raviv, Artur (1993), 'Differences of Opinion Make a Horse Race,' *Reviews of Financial Studies*, 6 (3): 473–506.

Inoue, H. (1999), 'The Structure of Government Securities Markets in G10 Countries: Summary of Questionnaire Results,' *Report of a Study Group Established by the Committee on the Global Financial System*, May.

Jiang, G. and McCauley, R. (2004), 'Asian Local Currency Bond Markets,' *BIS note*, April.

—— Tang, Nancy, and Law, Eve (2002), 'Electronic Trading in Hong Kong and its Impact on Market Functioning,' *BIS Papers* No. 12, August.

Jovanovic, Boyan and Rousseau, Peter L. (2001), 'Liquidity Effects in the Bond Market,' *NBER Working Paper Series*, Working Paper 8597, November.

Krinsky, Itzhak and Lee, Jason (1996), 'Earnings Announcements and the Components of the Bid–Ask Spread,' *The Journal of Finance*, 51 (4), September.

Lee, Charles M. C., Mucklow, Belinda, Ready, Mark J. (1993), 'Spreads, Depths, and the Impact of Earnings Information: An Intraday Analysis,' *The Review of Financial Studies*, 6 (2): 345–74.

McCauley, Robert and Remolona, Eli (2000), 'Size and Liquidity of Government Bond Markets,' *BIS Quarterly Review*, November.

A. Chabchitrchaidol and S. Panyanukul

Mares, Arnaud (2002), 'Market Liquidity and the Role of Public Policy,' *BIS Papers* No. 12, August.

Mohanty, M. S. (2002), 'Improving Liquidity in Government Bond Markets: What Can be Done?' *BIS Papers No. 11—The Development of Bond Markets in Emerging Economies*, June-July.

Shih, Y. C. (1996), 'The Changing Financial System in Taiwan,' *BIS Policy Papers*, No. 1 (December).

Upper, Christian (2001), 'How Safe was the "Safe Haven"? Financial Market Liquidity During the 1998 Turbulences,' *BIS Papers* No. 2.

9

Is East Asia Safe from Financial Crises?[1]

Charles Wyplosz
Graduate Institute of International Studies and CEPR

9.1 Introduction

Almost a decade after East Asia underwent its financial crisis, the scars have not healed. Growth is often significantly lower than it used to be, most countries are still accumulating massive stocks of foreign exchange reserves, and discussions continue to build up collective defense mechanisms. The fear that a crisis could hit again is clearly prevalent throughout the region. Crises can never be ruled out, of course, nor can they often be predicted. But are East Asian countries vulnerable to yet another crisis?

The 1997–8 crisis was spectacular in many respects. It moved slowly from one country to another. It affected the most economically successful countries. With the possible exception of Thailand, standard vulnerability indicators were not sending warning signals. Indeed, the Asian crisis led to the development of a third generation of self-fulfilling currency crisis models (Chang and Velasco 1999; Krugman 1999). It was followed by highly contentious IMF programs that were larger and more intrusive than ever before (Radelet and Sachs 1998; Feldstein 1998; De Gregorio *et al.* 1999), leading to calls for reform (Feldstein 1998; Williamson 2001) that were eventually heeded (Independent Evaluation Office 2003).

The crisis also hit countries that were not historically crisis-prone, as Table 9.1 shows. The table measures the incidence of currency crises. For each country, incidence is calculated as the number of crises observed—using an exchange market pressure index—during the sample period divided by the number of years of observation. The regional incidence index is the unweighted average of national incidence indices. The regions are ranked

[1] I am grateful to Yung Chul Park for asking the question in the paper's title as well as for many enlightening discussions of the Asian crisis.

Table 9.1: Average Incidence of currency crises

East Asia	South Asia	Europe	Others	Africa	South America
0.0802	0.1 019	0.1025	1.1225	0.1481	0.1766

Source: <http://econweb.rutgers.edu/bordo/>.

Notes: The sample period is either 1880–1997 or 1971–97 and it includes 56 countries. 'Others' include: Australia, Canada, Egypt, Israel, New Zealand, Turkey, and the USA.

from the least to the most crisis-prone. East Asia stands out as the least crisis-prone, by far. Removing the fateful year 1997 would drive down the incidence index for East Asia much further.

This chapter examines whether East Asia remains vulnerable to financial crises. To start with, Section 9.2 reminds us that this question would have received a negative answer even as late as in 1996. Then, Section 9.3 describes how the East Asian countries have endeavored since 1998 to protect themselves from a re-run of the traumatic events that are still haunting them. In particular, it argues that the spectacular build-up of foreign exchange reserves reduces, but does not eliminate, the odds of a crisis. Based on the three generations of crisis models, Section 9.4 seeks to identify the remaining vulnerabilities. The last section wraps up the previous conclusions and examines the policy options.

9.2 Was the 1997 Crisis Special?

The Asian crisis took most observers by surprise. This is documented in Table 9.2, which lists various crisis indicators as available in 1996. The first two columns display the probability of a crisis—defined as a change in an exchange market pressure index in excess of three standard deviations—occurring over the following two years, as estimated by two risk-assessment models developed at the IMF. The first index, KLR, based on Kaminsky, Lizondo, and Reinhart (1998), weighs a wide range of crisis indicators according to their signal-to-noise performance. The second index, DCSD, is based on Berg and Patillo (1999), which uses a probit analysis. The crisis probabilities are not negligible, especially those produced by the DCSD indicator. Note, however, that the two sets of risk assessment differ markedly from country to country. For instance, DCSD was issuing concerned signals for Taiwan, Thailand, and Malaysia while KLR put much lower probabilities for these countries, worrying instead about the Philippines.

How did markets react to these contradictory signals? The last three columns indicate that they were not particularly concerned. The third column reports spread on local dollar-denominated government bonds (the maturity

Table 9.2: Crisis risk assessments (1996)

Country[1]	KLR[2]	DCSD[3]	Spred[4] 1997 Q1	Rating[5] 1997 Q1	EIU 1997 Q1 Currency Risk[6]
Korea, Rep. of	22	24	50	18	22
Thailand	20	40	51	25	42
Indonesia	16	32	109	43	38
Malaysia	14	39	37	20	36
Zimbabwe	19	n.a.	n.a.	n.a.	58
Philippines	34	14	165	55	36
Taiwan Province of China	23	46	n.a.	n.a.	12

Source: Berg, Borensztein and Pattillo (2005).

Notes: Based on KLR, DCSD, Bond Spread, Credit Rating, and the Economist Intelligence Unit (EIU) forecasts.

[1] Countries that suffered a crisis in 1997 are in bold. The countries are ordered by severity of crisis.

[2] Probabilities of currency crisis over a 24-month horizon, from average KLR model for 1996.

[3] Probabilities of currency crisis over a 24-month horizon, from average of 1996 DCSD results.

[4] The spread is expressed in basis points. It refers to the difference between the yield on US dollar-denominated foreign government eurobonds and the equivalent maturity US treasury bonds.

[5] Average of S&P and Moody's ratings, each converted to a numerical rating ranging from 100 (S&P SD) to 0 (S&P AAA or Moody's Aaa). A lower number means a better rating.

[6] Currency risk: 'Scores and ratings assess the risk of a devaluation against the dollar of 20 percent or more in real terms over the two-year forecast period,' following EIU.

is not reported). The spreads are well within the normal range of emerging market bond spreads. The fourth column shows average ratings from two agencies, ranging from 0 (no risk) to 100 (extreme risk). The last column indicates the probability of a 20 percent real devaluation as estimated by *The Economist Intelligence Unit.* Given that nominal depreciation rates over 1997–8 ranged from a minimum of 62 percent (Philippines) to more than 500 percent (Indonesia), the markets profoundly underestimated what was to happen. Note that exchange rate pressure on the Thai baht started to rise in 1996.

Why then did the crises come as a surprise? The traditional macroeconomic indicators were not suggesting any cause for concern, as Table 9.3 shows. Inflation was high relatively to the US but generally not different from what it had been in the past. Budgets were in slight surplus. Current accounts were in deficit, especially so in Thailand, but they were easily financed by capital inflows. Growth was high, a continuation of the rates observed over the previous decade, which had earned East Asian countries the nickname of economic dragons.

Of course, after the crisis, it transpired that the capital accounts were leading to dangerously open positions in foreign currencies. Few observers had noticed this situation and, indeed, the third generation of currency crisis models was invented in response to this realization. It may well be that some astute observers had signaled the looming danger, but they were not heard in Washington, Wall Street, or the City.

Table 9.3: Macroeconomic indicators (1996)

	Indonesia	Korea	Malaysia	Philippines	Thailand
Inflation	8.0	4.9	3.5	7.5	5.8
Budget balance	1.2	−4.2	0.7	0.3	0.9
Growth rate	7.8	4.9	10.0	5.8	5.9
Current account	−3.4	−4.2	−4.4	−4.8	−8.1
Overal balance of payments	2.0	4.9	2.5	5.2	1.2

Source: International Financial Statistics, IMF.
Note: Budget balance, current account, and overall balance of payments as percent of GDP.

Unpredictability does not mean that the crisis was unjustified, though. It may be that those who try to predict crises look at the wrong indicators. This is, indeed, the sense in which the Asian crisis was special. Yet, already previously, large open currency positions had represented a lethal vulnerability; this happened in Chile in 1983 as documented in De Gregorio *et al.* (1999), but the lessons had not been adequately taken on board.

In the end, the crisis has taught us many lessons.[2] First, apparently minor vulnerabilities can turn into a major source of concern and eventually trigger financial crises. Second, financial liberalization does not mix well with rigidly fixed exchange rates; this conclusion has led to the two-corner strategy, according to which the only stable foreign exchange regimes are very hard pegs or freely floating rates. Third, even when there exist restrictions to capital mobility, the currency composition of assets and liabilities matters a great deal. Fourth, contagion is a very serious issue, which points to financial market imperfections. Finally, predicting financial crises is a daunting undertaking. Some crises—first-generation crises, created by macroeconomic imbalances—can be foreseen if not dated *ex ante*; other crises—those that occur because underlying vulnerabilities may emerge as a cause of concern in financial markets—may or may not happen; we know those that occurred but how many more could have occurred and did not?

9.3 Crisis Prevention in East Asia

Even though they quickly recovered from the crisis, East Asian countries have dedicated massive efforts to avoid the recurrence of such a traumatic event (Park, 2001). Although the measures taken very significantly differ from one country to another, a number of common features emerge.

[2] See, among many others, Eichengreen and Bordo (2001); Frankel (1999); Park and Song (1999); Rodrik (1998); Wyplosz (2002); and Independent Evaluation Office (2003).

9.3.1 *Structural reforms*

The crisis revealed that a number of economic and political arrangements, which had been previously seen as key factors in the highly successful catch-up phase of the two preceding decades, turned out to be vulnerabilities. The general reason is that East Asia's strategy of trade and financial integration rested to a significant degree on an alliance between governments, banks, and large corporations. Early on, this alliance worked well. It allowed for the mobilization of resources and provided support to dynamic entrepreneurs. Over time, the growing size of these companies, along with their integration into the world economy, made them more vulnerable to reversals of fortune. Guaranteed state and banking support made matters worse. It made these companies less alert to the risks that they were taking. It also proved insufficient when the tide unexpectedly reversed; by then, the companies were too big for bail-outs and yet too big to fail.

Under pressure from creditors and the IMF, corporate restructuring was undertaken in the midst of the crisis. It included a deep overhaul of the banking systems that were in effect bankrupt. The costs were huge but, as the contrast with Japan's lost decade shows, it contributed to a quick resumption of growth, although at a slower pace than before. As growth resumed, though, the appetite for restructuring declined and external pressure to that effect could be resisted. The restructuring process slowed down; quite often it even stopped. The links between government, banks, and large corporations have been lessened but still survive in a number of countries. An indirect indication of this evolution is the size of stock markets, as measured by capitalization. Table 9.4 shows that, ignoring the special cases of Singapore and Hong Kong, stock markets remain somewhat undersized in most Asian countries.

9.3.2 *Exchange Rate Regimes*

A key lesson from the crisis was that exchange rate pegging is dangerous when capital controls are removed. By the time they were hit, many East Asian countries had maintained some limited restrictions on capital movements, but these controls were too light to provide effective protection, except for China whose currency is non-convertible and Malaysia, which promptly reintroduced capital controls. In the aftermath of the crisis, under pressure from the IMF, the process of financial integration accelerated. Full capital mobility is not complete everywhere yet, but is generally high.

Under these conditions, a high degree of exchange rate flexibility is required in order to reduce the risk of currency crises. A classification of exchange rate regimes is presented in Figure 9.1.[3] According to this classification Malaysia

---

[3] This is a *de facto* interpretation of the exchange regime, as opposed to the *de jure* regime reported to the IMF. For a detailed explanation, see Levy-Yeyati and Sturzenegger (2005). For an alternative classification, see Reinhart and Rogoff (2004).

Table 9.4: Stock market capitalization (2004)

Rank	Country	US$ millions	Rank	Country	Percent GDP
1	United States	16,323,509	1	Hong Kong	519.8
2	Japan	5,844,722	2	Switzerland	230.3
3	United Kingdom	2,865,243	3	South Afica	206.1
4	Euronext	2,441,261	4	Singapore	202.4
5	Germany	1,194,517	5	Luxembourg	158.3
6	Canada	1,177,518	6	Malaysia	153.5
7	Spain	940,673	7	Taiwan	145.6
8	Hong Kong	861,463	8	United States	139.1
9	Switzerland	826,041	9	United Kingdom	134.3
10	Italy	789,563	10	Japan	125.2
11	Australia	776,403	11	Chile	124.2
12	China	447,720	12	Australia	122.1
13	South Africa	442,526	13	Canada	118.7
14	Taiwan	441,436	14	Sweden	107.6
15	Korea	389,473	15	Finland	99.6
16	Sweden	376,781	16	Spain	95.4
17	India	363,276	17	Euronext	78.8
18	Brazil	330,347	18	Israel	77.1
19	Singapore	217,618	19	Thailand	71.4
20	Finland	183,765	20	Denmark	63.7
21	Malaysia	181,624	21	Ireland	63.2
22	Mexico	171,940	22	Greece	59.8
23	Denmark	155,233	23	Korea	57.3
24	Norway	141,624	24	Norway	55.8
25	Greece	121,921	25	Brazil	54.7
26	Chile	116,924	26	Malta	53.5
27	Thailand	115,390	27	India	53.0
28	Ireland	114,086	28	Italy	47.4
29	Turkey	98,299	29	New Zealand	44.7
30	Israel	90,158	30	Germany	44.6
31	Austria	87,776	31	Philippines	33.2
32	Indonesia	73,251	32	Turkey	32.5
33	Poland	71,547	33	Austria	30.2
34	Luxembourg	50,144	34	Hungary	28.4
35	New Zealand	43,731	35	Indonesia	28.4
36	Argentina	40,594	36	Poland	28.4
37	Hungary	28,630	37	Argentina	26.5
38	Philippines	28,602	38	China	26.0
39	Colombia	25,223	39	Colombia	25.7
40	Sri Lanka	3,657	40	Mexico	25.4

Source: World Federation of Exchanges, <http://www.world-exchanges.org/>, *International Financial Statistics* and Taiwan Statistics.

Note: The US figure combines NYSE, Nasdaq and American; the Japanese figure combines Tokyo and Osaka.

and the Philippines were *de facto* floating in 1995, the year before the crisis, but they tightened their regimes in 1996. The other crisis countries were operating a mixed regime (Indonesia and Thailand) or moving toward fixity (Korea). Since the crisis, formally or informally, most of the East Asian countries have adopted a basket—mostly including the dollar, the euro, and the yen; some include the renminbi—to which they more or less loosely peg their currencies. Yet, the figure suggests that the currencies of Indonesia and

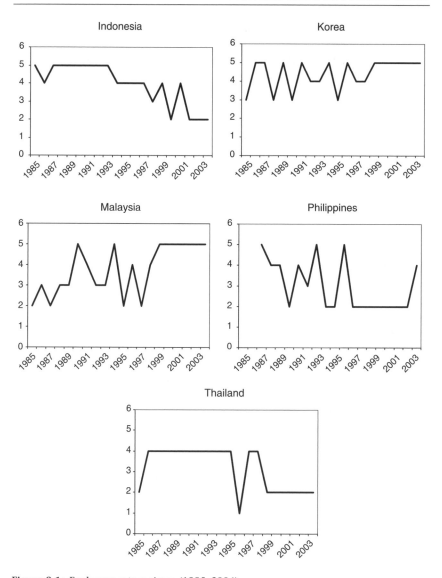

Figure 9.1: Exchange rate regimes (1985–2004)

Note: 1 = inconclusive; 2 = float; 3 = dirty; 4 = dirty/crawling peg; 5 = fixed.
Source: Update of Levy-Yeyati and Sturzenegger (2005).

Thailand are *de facto* floating, while the other three countries have moved toward more fixity.[4]

[4] More recently, Korea has reestablished a fair degree of flexibility, although it remains to be seen how this will translate into *de facto* behavior.

For countries that have expressed fear of crisis, the prevalence of pegs, even quite soft, may be surprising. One interpretation is that free floating clashes with the export-led strategy that has long prevailed in the region. With export competitiveness at the heart of their growth strategy, East Asian countries also exhibit fear of overvaluation. The trade-off between these two fears has been sharpened by the emergence of China as a regional economic power. One response has been to implicitly tie the currencies to the renminbi or to otherwise stabilize the effective nominal or real exchange rates. The growing role of basket pegs, advocated by Williamson (1999), is a manifestation of fear of overvaluation. Even if China were to move toward exchange rate flexibility, the other Asian countries are likely to continue keeping a close eye on their renminbi exchange rates.

9.3.3 *Foreign exchange rate accumulation*

Having rejected the free-float option, the East Asian countries have turned to foreign exchange reserve accumulation to reduce the risk of speculative attacks. The reserve build-up can also be seen in the context of another legacy from the 1997–8 crisis, fear of the IMF. To varying degrees, all countries share the view that the IMF conditions, imposed at the apex of the crisis, were ill-designed and excessively coercitive. As noted above, there is much *ex post* agreement, including at the IMF, that the same conditions would not be applied in a re-run of the crisis. Still, the East Asian countries are unwilling to test that hypothesis and are determined to avoid calling up the IMF again in the event of financial market turbulence. Foreign exchange reserves, even if they are costly to accumulate and hold, are seen as an insurance against such a risk.

The impressive reserve build-up in six Asian countries is shown in Figure 9.2. The data refer to gross reserves, ignoring gross liabilities, which explains the apparent stability of the stock of international assets at the time of the crisis in all countries except Indonesia and Thailand. This means that the accumulation of net reserves has been even faster since the crisis.

Table 9.5 further documents the process by looking at the ratio of reserves to GDP and showing the ranking among all IMF member countries. In absolute terms, China is the largest world holder of gross reserves; as a percentage of GDP, Singapore tops the world league, just ahead of Hong Kong. On either measure, all Asian countries have moved up the ladder between 1995 and 2004.

The costs of investing such large amounts of wealth in presumably low-yielding assets—little is known about portfolio management in most countries—are significant. As noted above, these costs can be seen as an insurance premium, but is the insurance likely to deliver? No one knows but the case of Thailand provides an indication to what the answer could

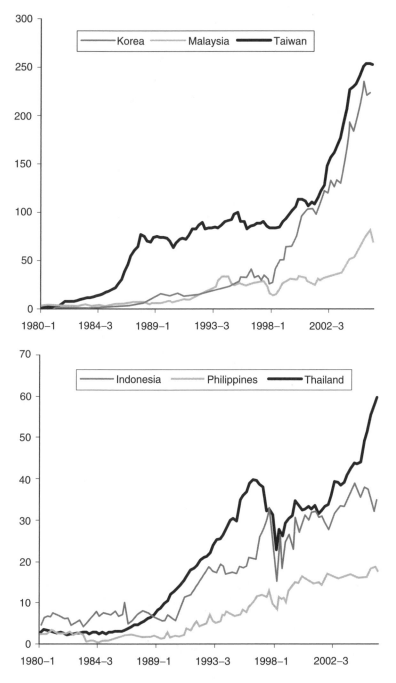

Figure 9.2: Gross foreign exchange reserves (US$ billions)
Source: *International Financial Statistics*, IMF and Central Bank of Taiwan.

Table 9.5: Gross foreign exchange reserves

| | Per cent of GDP | | | | | | US $billions | | | | | |
| | 1995 | | | 2004 | | | 1995 | | | 2004 | | |
Rank	Country	Reserves	Rank	Country	Reserves	Rank	Country	Reserves	Rank	Country	Reserves
2	Singapore	82.9	1	Singapore	101.2	4	China	79.86	1	China	567.37
8	Hong Kong	37.7	2	Hong Kong	70.1	5	Singapore	68.67	2	Korea	199.12
12	Malaysia	27.9	4	Malaysia	56.4	9	Hong Kong	48.68	5	Hong Kong	116.19
21	Thailand	21.4	10	China	33.0	13	Thailand	37.32	6	Singapore	108.77
42	Philippines	14.2	12	Thailand	30.4	15	Korea	32.92	10	Malaysia	66.69
44	China	14.0	14	Korea	29.3	16	Malaysia	25.47	13	Thailand	49.23
67	Indonesia	11.4	39	Philippines	18.7	24	Indonesia	19.41	17	Indonesia	38.50
116	Korea	6.3	53	Indonesia	14.9	45	Philippines	7.92	32	Philippines	16.12

Source: *International Financial Statistics*, IMF.

be. Before the crisis, Thailand ranked fifteenth in terms of the reserves to GDP ratio and thirteenth in absolute size of its gross reserves stock. It ran down 43 percent of its stock during the crisis and yet could not avoid a deep devaluation. Would its current stock, 50 percent larger than in 1995, do a better job should speculation hit again? This is quite unlikely.

In fact, no matter how large they are, reserve stocks do not provide a fool-proof guarantee that speculative attacks can be beaten back. The following simple model, borrowed from Jeanne and Wyplosz (2003), explains why. It portrays four types of agents: a domestic central bank, domestic private banks, bank depositors, and international investors. Bank deposits are liquid in the sense that they can be withdrawn in period 1, the short run, while long term assets are held for the long run, i.e. period 2. The model creates both a liquidity and a currency mismatch in the banks' balance sheets by assuming that the only bank deposits D^* in dollars are liquid, while bank assets A are in long-term bonds denominated in the local currency, say the won. In order to pay back depositors who wish to withdraw their funds in period 1, banks must sell their won bonds in exchange for dollars.

This double mismatch is introduced to create the possibility that a bank run can occur under some conditions. We assume that all banks are identical; consequently, depositors run on the whole banking sector or do not run at all. Let P^* be the dollar price in period 1 of a won bond due to mature in period 2. If i is the nominal won interest rate and S_1 is the won/dollar exchange rate, $P^* = 1/[(1 + i)S_1]$. With these definitions, a bank run occurs when $P^*A < D^*$. In such an event, we assume that the banks sell their won bonds for dollars, and then they collapse. On the contrary, there is no run if $P^* A \geq D^*$ and we safely move to period 2.

In addition to banks and depositors, we consider N identical investors endowed with W_1^* dollars at the beginning of period 1. They decide whether to invest in dollar or in won-denominated bonds. If they invest B in won-denominated bonds and $W_1^* - (B/S_1)$ in dollar-denominated bonds, their wealth in period 2 will be $W_2^* = (1 + i^*)W_1^* + \rho\,(B/S_1)$, where $\rho = i - i^* - (s_2\text{-}s_1)$ is the excess return on won bonds, and $s_t = \ln(S_t)$ is the log deviation of the exchange rate from an arbitrary base level S. Note that investors can hold short won positions i.e. B can be negative. If each investor maximizes a mean-variance utility function such as $U = E(W_2^*) - (a/2)Var(W_2^*)$, where a is a measure of risk aversion, her demand for domestic bonds is:

$$\frac{B}{S_1} = \frac{i - i^* - [E(s_2) - s_1]}{a\,Var(s_2)} \tag{1}$$

We now consider the central bank's policy. The bank enters period 1 with a stock R_0^* of foreign exchange reserves in dollars. In period 1, the balance-of-payments identity is:

$$R^* - R_0^* = CA + N\frac{B}{S_1} - \delta P^* A \tag{2}$$

where R^* is the end-of-period 1 stock of foreign exchange reserves, CA is the period 1 current account (taken to be exogenous) and δ is a bank run indicator: $\delta = 1$ indicates a bank run and $\delta = 0$ no bank run, for reasons explained shortly. The bank decides on i and s_1 under the constraint that $R^* \geq 0$, in order to keep the exchange rate fixed. Its preferences are presumed to be lexicographic. Its priority is to avoid a bank run; when this is achieved, it sets the interest rate and the exchange rate so as to maximize its other objectives.[5] This priority can be expressed as:

$$R^* \geq 0 \text{ and } P^* A \geq D^* \tag{3}$$

However, if a bank run occurs, the central bank is assumed to be committed to support the banking system by selling its reserves in order to provide the dollars needed to pay back the depositors. Thus, in the event of a bank run, the central bank sells to its banks an amount $P^* A$ of its reserves.

Finally, we assume that the second period exchange rate S_2 depends on whether or not the banking sector has collapsed in period 1. Other things equal, a banking collapse tends to depreciate the domestic currency, which is exogenously set to be equal d if the banking system has collapsed in period 1, and to 0 if not.

The central bank's problem is captured by (3). The central bank can always reduce the threat of a bank run by raising $P^* = 1/[(1+i)S_1]$, i.e. by lowering the interest rate or appreciating the exchange rate. But, in doing so, the central bank reduces the demand for domestic bonds, as (1) shows, and therefore its stock of foreign exchange reserves R^*, see (2). Thus it is possible for the two objectives in (3) to be mutually inconsistent.

The Appendix shows that if $R_0^* > R_0^{*sup}$ the central bank will set $i + s_1 \leq x$ and avoid a bank run. If $R_0^* < R_0^{*inf}$, there is a bank run and the central bank runs out of reserves, hence a currency collapse follows. For $R_0^{*inf} \leq R_0^* \leq R_0^{*sup}$, we have a situation of multiple equilibria, with or without a bank run, depending on whether or not depositors coordinate on a run. The thresholds x, R_0^{*inf} and R_0^{*sup} are shown in the Appendix.

This is nothing else than the familiar case of multiple bank-run equilibria (Diamond and Dybvig 1983) in an international setting. It carries three important implications. First, the stock of reserves does matter. Indeed, if $R_0^* > R_0^{*sup}$ a bank run and currency collapse can be ruled out. The knowledge that the central bank has enough resources to thwart a bank run is enough to reassure

---

[5] The central bank can decide on both i and s_1 because interest rate parity does not hold, a consequence of investors' risk aversion.

domestic depositors and international investors and prevent a speculative attack.

Second, what matters is the initial stock of reserves R_0^*, not the reserves being accumulated. Once depositors and international investors become suspicious, the central bank does not have any good option left. If it tries to solve the banking problem it creates an exchange rate problem, and conversely. This would seem to vindicate the strategy of East Asian central banks.

Third, the question is how big is R_0^{*sup}? Obviously, this stylized model cannot provide a reliable guide to answer that question, but one observation is important. When risk aversion becomes very low, i.e. when a becomes arbitrarily small and domestic and foreign bonds become close substitutes,[6] (3) implies that both R_0^{*inf} and R_0^{*sup} become arbitrarily large. In that case, the required amount of accumulated foreign exchange reserves is virtually unbounded. This latter result indicates that there is no guarantee that the strategy of the East Asian central banks provides iron-clad insurance. In particular, the deepening financial integration of East Asia into world markets can be seen as raising the thresholds.

The interpretation of this latter conclusion is clear. As a central bank intervenes on the foreign exchange market and sells its reserves, international investors—some of whom may well be home-based—interpret the declining reserve stock as a signal of growing vulnerability. Consequently they take increasingly large negative open positions in domestic bonds—B becomes negative—which, according to (2) accelerates the loss of reserves in an ever-deepening vicious circle. It is not just the assets of the banking system—$\delta P^* A^*$ in (2) with $\delta = 1$—that the central bank must underwrite, but the whole amount of potential speculative capital. Given the size of international financial markets, the situation can quickly become desperate. Even an IMF rescue may prove insufficient, as the 1997–8 crisis made abundantly clear. Put differently and starkly, the view that East Asian countries are now immune to speculative attacks thanks to their asset stocks is illusory. No matter how much they accumulate, they remain vulnerable.

9.3.4 Monetary Cooperation

Ever since the project of an Asian Monetary Fund was strongly opposed from outside in the midst of the crisis, East Asian countries have sought to strengthen monetary cooperation. The 2000 Chiang Mai Initiative has allowed the pooling of $35.5 billion of foreign exchange reserves, in line with the reserve accumulation process. The 2003 Asian Bond Market Initiative aims at developing a regional market for Asian currency bonds. Recently, the

---

[6] Note that (1) implies that expected excess returns $E(\rho)$ become arbitrarily small.

Asian Development Bank has proposed the creation of an Asian Currency Unit (ACU) that would underpin the bond-market project.

The striking feature of these efforts is that they stay well short of effective monetary cooperation. Each country seems to regard the others as competitors as much as partners. This is in line with the growth-led strategy and its emphasis on using the exchange rate as a key development tool. In effect, as previously noted, the adoption, formal or informal, of currency basket targeting is an efficient way of guaranteeing that regional bilateral exchange rates remain stable. Mimicry seems to deliver most of what Asian countries wish. Unsurprisingly the appetite for deeper cooperation, which would require some loss of sovereignty, is limited.

What mimicry does not deliver, though, is a protection against currency and financial crises. An implication of Section 9.3.3 is that reserve pooling can help but not eliminate the risk of crisis. The ABM initiative may eventually contribute to boosting resilience to shocks. The ACU proposal is not adding much to the existing web of baskets[7] unless it is a step towards a European-style Exchange Rate Mechanism on the way to a monetary union. Deep political differences preclude such an evolution in the foreseeable future. Indeed, in spite of countless conferences and statements, the Asian countries have never created the kind of supranational institution that could embody a deep cooperation process and receive whatever elements of national sovereignty countries are willing to forego.

9.4 How Vulnerable Are the Asian Countries?

In order to examine the potential vulnerabilities of the Asian countries, this section follows the logic of the exchange crisis literature, distinguishing among the three generations of models.

9.4.1 First Generation: Macroeconomic Vulnerabilities

The first generation of exchange crisis models deals with crises that are caused by macroeconomic vulnerabilities and are therefore predictable, for example in Russia in 1998 and in Argentina in 2001. Krugman (1979) and Flood and Garber (1984) emphasize budget deficits that must eventually be money-financed, but a broader array of factors would also include monetary policy indiscipline, overvalued exchange rates and contagion from crises in important trading partners.

The East Asian countries are known for their prudent macroeconomic policies. As Table 9.3 shows, macroeconomic factors generally did not play a major

[7] Park and Wyplosz (2004) show that the precise definition of these baskets makes no significant difference.

Table 9.6: Macroeconomic Indicators (2005)

	Indonesia	Korea	Malaysia	Philippines	Taiwan	Thailand
Inflation	5.9	3.0	2.4	6.5	1.7	3.5
Budget balance	−0.8	−2.8	−3.1	−3.6	−4.9	0.0
Growth rate	5.5	4.1	5.7	5.0	4.2	5.6
Current account	2.1	3.9	10.2	3.0	6.8	2.3
Overal balance of payments	0.1	5.7	0.0	−1.8	—	3.5

Source: *Asian Economic Outlook* 2005, Asian Development Bank.

Note: Overall balance of payments are from *International Financial Statistics* and concern 2004.

role in the 1997–8 crisis; this is indeed why these crises were not predicted. Table 9.6 further shows that the situation remains broadly similar in 2005, except that the current account deficits observed in 1996 have been replaced by surpluses while, on the other hand, most countries now exhibit negative budget balances, a mild source of concern.

9.4.2 Second Generation: Non Financial Vulnerabilities

The second generation models emphasize non-financial conditions that may abruptly sour in a way that becomes unmanageable by the authorities. Obstfeld (1986) has shown how crises can be self-fulfilling in such a situation. If, facing a speculative attack, the authorities are unable to adopt defensive measures, such as raising the interest rate or tightening fiscal policy, two outcomes are possible. If the markets believe that a crisis is likely, they will attack the currency and will be vindicated by the authorities' inability to react. On the other hand, if the markets are not particularly concerned, the situation may gradually improve without any crisis.

There is no standard list of potential culprits in this case. Large public debts, low growth, and high unemployment rates are believed to have played a role in Europe and Argentina, for instance. Political weakness may also prevent governments from displaying firmness when and if needed. The diffuse and imprecise description of what may be a vulnerability means that it is practical to evaluate this source of crisis. One can note that some Asian countries (Korea, Malaysia, Thailand) exhibit relatively large external debts.[8]

9.4.3 Third Generation: Financial Vulnerabilities

The third-generation interpretation, developed in the wake of the Asian crisis, is a variant of the second one. Third-generation crises are also of the self-fulfilling variety. What distinguishes them is that the vulnerabilities—which

[8] When is 'large' too large? For an attempt to deal with this question, see Reinhart *et al.* (2003).

may or may not provoke a crisis—originate in the financial sector. At the root of financial vulnerabilities are mismatches between assets and liabilities, whether they are held by financial institutions or the non-financial sector, and whether they concern the public or the private sectors. Mismatches refer both to the currency composition and to the maturity structure of assets and liabilities.

Evidence on both kinds of mismatches is fragmentary. Some aggregate data are produced by the BIS, but they conceal many crucial details. Bleakley and Cowan (2003) provide measures of maturity mismatch in non-financial corporations for a number of emerging market countries, including the crisis countries of East Asia. Although they mostly cover the 1990s, their conclusion is that maturity mismatch is not significant. Whether this conclusion applies to the financial and public sectors is apparently not known. Certainly, large public debts can be seen as source of maturity mismatch.

Goldstein and Turner (2004) produce a synthetic indicator of currency mismatch. This indicator, shown in Figure 9.3 for the pre-crisis year (1995) and for the latest available year (2002), is negative when the country has a short foreign currency position and it is scaled by the share of foreign currency debt in total debt. Brazil is added as a comparator. Except for Indonesia and

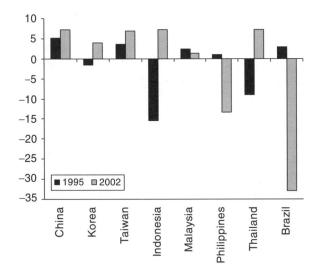

Figure 9.3: Currency mismatch indicator

Note: When negative, the indicator is $\frac{NCA}{X}\frac{D^\$}{D}$, when positive it is $\frac{NCA}{M}\frac{D^\$}{D}$, where *NCA* is the country net foreign currency assets, *X* and *N* are exports and imports, respectively, *D* is the country's external debt and $D^\$$ is foreign currency-denominated debt.

Source: Goldstein and Turner (2004).

Thailand, the currency mismatch, as reported by this indicator, was negligible (Korea) or non-existent.[9] The figure shows that, as of 2002, the situation has further improved throughout the region, with the exception of the Philippines. Inasmuch as this indicator is reliable, currency mismatch is not a major source of vulnerability.

9.5 Conclusions: Unanswerable Questions and Policy Implications

This section starts by asking the questions that we would like to answer but that we really cannot with any degree of certainty. It then goes on to raise some policy issues that cannot be resolved conclusively either. The sad truth is that, in spite of years of active and innovative research and the gradual production of new data sets, we still know much too little. Maybe the more depressing conclusion is that each major crisis provides us with new insights so that we will need many more crises to be able to provide firmer answers to vitally important questions. Economics is not an experimental science, yet we learn mostly through experiments.

Question 1: Is East Asia safe from financial crises? A rigorous answer must be negative. No country that, in one way or another, pegs its exchange rate is ever safe. Accidents happen and, when compounded with pre-existing vulnerabilities, they can suddenly and radically alter the economic situation. This is, after all, one lesson from the Asian crisis.

Question 2: Is a financial crisis in Asia likely in the coming years? The likelihood of a major crisis is low, but it is far from zero. Much progress has been made to deal with the vulnerabilities that have been identified so far, but vulnerabilities—some of which may not have been identified yet—remain. The massive accumulation of foreign exchange reserves is raising the threshold at which markets would trigger speculative attacks, but the threshold is still well within reach.

Question 3: Would letting the exchange rate freely float remove the specter of a financial crisis? Exchange rate targets, whether fixed or fuzzy, and whether officially announced or not, offer themselves to speculative pressure. Removing this magnet is a significant step towards lessening the risk of a crisis. Yet, in the end, there is little difference between a collapsing pegged exchange rate system and a freely falling currency.

Because so many vulnerabilities exist, many of which may have not yet been identified as such, most countries face the risk of self-fulfilling attacks. This is one reason behind the popularity of the two-corner strategy. It does not mean, though, that all countries should adopt corner exchange rate

---

[9] As it adds the currency position of banks and non-banks, the indicator can hide sectoral mismatches.

regimes. The argument in favor of corner strategies must be balanced against other arguments. The Asian countries have generally decided to remain 'in the middle' for reasons associated with their development strategies. They have decided to trade off the benefits from an export-led strategy, based on exchange rate stability and external competitiveness, against the probability of renewed speculative attacks. If the probability is low enough, which we do not know, the choice is reasonable.

Accumulating foreign exchange reserves is one way of bringing the probability down. As noted in Section 9.3.3, this can work, although it would be wrong to assume that even very large reserve stocks fully eliminate the threat of successful attacks. It is easy to imagine how a domestic financial accident or serious political turmoil could precipitate a currency crisis. One vulnerability of the current situation is that several countries seem to believe that they are now protected from a currency crisis. It would be sad if such a misguided perception acted as a disincentive to continue removing existing vulnerabilities.

Should a crisis occur, it need not be devastating. One lesson from financial turmoil in the developed countries—the European currency crisis of 1992–3 and the sharp fall of the Nasdaq in 2000—is that economies can be made resilient. Adequate financial market regulation, labor market flexibility, and, of course, a healthy macroeconomic situation all contribute to alleviate and abbreviate the impact of a financial crisis.

A general vulnerability to financial crises is part and parcel of the process of liberalization and integration into world markets. It is usually considered that this process is a positive one, at least in the long run. Yet, in the shorter run, it tends to be associated with crises that foster deep recessions. Does that mean that financial liberalization should be resisted? The logical answer has to be negative on the ground that permanent gains eventually outweigh temporary costs.[10] Yet, the mounting evidence that financial liberalization only enhances growth for countries that have reached a sufficient degree of development[11] suggests that delaying this step may bring about gain without pain.

Finally, the East Asian countries have sought to strengthen monetary cooperation partly to forge a common defense mechanism against speculative attacks. Recent initiatives have gone further than symbolism but remain well short of an arrangement that would indeed make a significant contribution. At this stage, repelling speculative attacks remains largely a national responsibility.

---

[10] Kaminsky and Reinhart (1999) find that financial liberalization is the most reliable predictor of twin (currency and banking) crises while Wyplosz (2002) and Kaminsky and Schmukler (2003) identify systematic boom and bust cycles in the aftermath of financial liberalization. Taking into account the occurrence of crises, Tornell, Westermann, and Martinez (2004) conclude in favor of financial liberalization, in contrast with Rodrik (1998).

[11] See Edwards (2001) and Kose, Prasad, and Terrones (2005).

Appendix 9.1: Proof of (3)

Using (2) and log-linearizing around S, conditions (3) can be rewritten as:

$$R_0^* + CA + N\frac{i + s_1 - i^* - \delta d}{a\,\mathrm{var}(s_2)} - \delta P * A \geq 0 \text{ and } i + s_1 \leq x = \ln\left(\frac{A}{SD^*}\right) \tag{3'}$$

where $\ln P^* \approx -i - s_1$.

A no bank-run equilibrium occurs when (3') is satisfied for $\delta = 0$, i.e. when:

$$R_0^* \geq N\frac{i^* - x}{a\,\mathrm{var}(s_2)} - CA = R_0^{*\,\mathrm{inf}}$$

A bank-run equilibrium occurs when (3') is not satisfied for $\delta = 1$, i.e. when:

$$R_0^* < D^* + N\frac{i^* + d - x}{a\,\mathrm{var}(s_2)} - CA = R_0^{*\,\mathrm{sup}}$$

References

Berg, Andrew, Borensztein, Eduardo, and Pattillo, Catherine (2005), 'Assessing Early Warning Systems: How Have They Worked in Practice?' *IMF Staff Papers,* 52: 462–502.

—— and Pattillo, Catherine (1999), 'Predicting Currency Crises: The Indicators Approach and an Alternative,' *Journal of International Money and Finance,* 18: 561–86.

Bleakley, Hoyt and Cowan, Kevin (2003), 'Maturity Mismatch on the Pacific Rim: Crises and Corporations in East Asia and Latin America,' LAEBA Working Paper No. 20.

Chang, Roberto and Velasco, Andres (1999), 'Liquidity Crises in Emerging Markets: Theory and Policy,' in B. Bernanke and J. Rotemberg (eds.), *NBER Macroeconomics Annual 1999* (Cambridge, MA: MIT Press), 11–58.

De Gregorio, José, Eichengreen, Barry, Ito, Takatoshi, and Wyplosz, Charles (1999), *An Independent and Accountable IMF: Geneva Reports of the World Economy* 1 (London: CEPR).

Diamond, Douglas and Dybvig, P. (1983), 'Bank Runs, Deposit Insurance, and Liquidity,' *Journal of Political Economy,* 91: 401–19.

Edwards, Sebastian (2001), 'Capital Flows and Economic Performance: Are Emerging Economies Different?' NBER Working Paper 8076.

Eichengreen, Barry and Bordo, Michael (2001), 'Crises Now and Then: What Lessons from the Last Era of Financial Globalization?,' University of California at Berkeley.

Feldstein, Martin (1998), 'Refocusing the IMF,' *Foreign Affairs* (March/April): 20–33.

Flood, Robert and Garber, Peter (1984), 'Collapsing Exchange Rate Regimes: Some Linear Examples,' *Journal of International Economics,* 17: 1–13.

Frankel, Jeffrey A. (1999), 'Ten Lessons Learned from the Korean Crisis.' Unpublished MS, Harvard University.

Goldstein, Morris and Turner, Philip (2004), *Controlling Currency Mismatches in Emerging Economies* (Washington, DC: Institute for International Economics).

Jeanne, Olivier and Wyplosz, Charles (2003), 'The International Lender of Last Resort: How Large Is Large Enough?', in M. P. Dooley and J. A. Frankel (eds.), *Managing Currency Crises in Emerging Markets* (Chicago: University of Chicago Press), 119–24.

Kaminsky, Graciela, Lizondo, Saul, and Reinhart, Carmen M. (1998), 'Leading Indicators of Currency Crises,' *IMF Staff Papers* 45: 1–48.

—— and Carmen, Reinhart (1999), 'The Twin Crises: The Causes of Banking and Balance-of-Payments Problems,' *American Economic Review* 89: 473–500.

—— and Schmukler, Sergio (2003), 'Short-Run Pain, Long-Run Gain: The Effects of Financial Liberalization,' NBER Working Paper 9787.

Kose, M. Ayhan, Prasad, Eswar S., and Terrones, Marco E. (2005), 'How Do Trade and Financial Integration Affect the Relationship Between Growth and Volatility?' IMF Working Paper WP/05/19.

Krugman, Paul (1979), 'A Model of Balance-of-Payments Crises,' *Journal of Money, Credit, and Banking,* 11: 311–25.

—— (1999), 'Balance Sheets, the Transfer Problem and Financial Crises,' in P. Isard, A. Razin, and A. Rose (eds.), *International Finance and Financial Crises: Essays in Honor of Robert Flood,* (Dordrecht: Kluwer Academic Publishers), 31–44.

Independent Evaluation Office (2003), 'Report on the Role of the IMF in Recent Capital Account Crises,' IMF.

Levy-Yeyati, Eduardo and Sturzenegger, Federico (2005), 'Classifying Exchange Rate Regimes: Deeds vs. Words,' *European Economic Review,* 49 (6): 603–35.

Obstfeld, Maurice (1986), 'Rational and Self-Fulfilling Balance of Payments Crises,' *American Economic Review,* 76 (1): 72–81.

Park, Yung Chul (2001), 'East Asian Dilemma: Restructuring Out or Growing Out?' *Princeton Essays in International Economics,* 233.

—— and Song, Chi Young (1999), 'The East Asian Financial Crisis: A Year Later,' in W. C. Hunter, G. G. Kaufman, and T. H. Krueger (eds.), *The Asian Financial Crisis: Origins, Implications, and Solutions,* (The Federal Reserve Bank of Chicago and IMF), 207–10.

—— and Wyplosz, Charles (2004), 'Exchange Rate Arrangements in East Asia: Do They Matter?' in Yonghyup Oh, Deo Ryong Yoon, and Thomas D. Willett (eds.), *Monetary and Exchange Rate Arrangements in East Asia* (Seoul: Korea Institute for International Economic Policy), 129–60.

Radelet, Steven and Sachs, Jeffrey (1998), 'The East Asian Financial Crisis: Diagnosis, Remedies, Prospects,' *Brookings Papers on Economic Activity,* 1: 1–90.

Reinhart, Carmen and Rogoff, Kenneth (2004), 'The Modern History of Exchange Rate Arrangements: A Reinterpretation,' *Quarterly Journal of Economics,* 119: 1–48.

—— —— and, Savastano, Miguel A. (2003), 'Debt Intolerance,' *Brookings Papers on Economic Activity,* 1: 1–74.

Rodrik, Dani (1998), 'Who Needs Capital-Account Convertibility?' in S. Fischer *et al.* (eds.), *Should the IMF Pursue Capital-Account Convertibility? Princeton Essays in International Finance,* 207.

Tornell, Aaron, Westermann, Frank, and Martinez, Lorenza (2004), 'The Positive Link Between Financial Liberalization, Growth and Crises,' NBER Working Paper 10293.

Williamson, John (1999), 'The Case for a Common Basket Peg for East Asian Currencies,' in S. Collignon, J. Pisani-Ferry, and Y. C. Park (eds.), *Exchange Rate Policies in Emerging Asian Countries* (London: Routledge).

Williamson, John (2001), 'The Role of the IMF: A Guide to the Reports,' *Policy Brief* 00–5, Institute for International Economics, Washington, DC.

Wyplosz, Charles (2002), 'How Risky is Financial Liberalization in the Developing Countries?' *Comparative Economic Studies,* 44: 1–26.

10

Chinese Macroeconomic Management: Issues and Prospects

Yu Yongding
Institute of World Economics and Politics, Chinese Academy of Social Sciences

10.1 Introduction

Despite all sorts of talk about China's overheating, soft landing and hard landing, the country's economic situation has never been so good. In 2006 China's growth rate was 10.7 percent, while inflation was 1.5 percent. This is the fifth year of high growth and low inflation in a row.[1] China's average annual growth rate since 1979 is more than 9.6 percent. It is fair to say that China has grown faster for longer than any country in history. As a result, China has become the fourth largest economy in the world. In terms of the purchasing power parities, China has already been the second largest economy in the world for many years.

Although, on average, China's annual growth rate is high and its inflation is modest, it had never been able to maintain a growth rate above 9 percent and an inflation rate below 5 percent more than two years in a row. Over the past twenty-five years, the Chinese economy has been characterized by large fluctuations (Figure 10.1). China has experienced roughly three economic cycles since 1981. The latest cycle started in 1996 and ended in 2002. Usually, growth is driven by a high growth rate of fixed asset investment (Figure 10.2), and high inflation follows growth with a lag of 4–5 quarters.

To bring inflation under control, the government uses tight monetary and fiscal policy to cool down the economy. As a result, economic growth slows down, leading to higher unemployment and/or deflation. When inflation is

---

[1] In this paper statistics for 2006 have been added at the time of publishing.

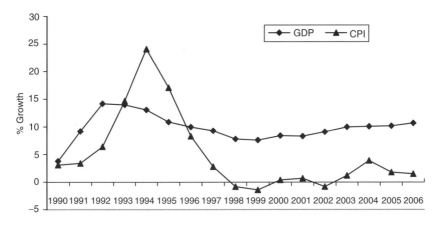

Figure 10.1: China's economic growth and inflation, 1990–2006
Sources: Statistical Year Book, various issues, National Bureau of Statistics.

under control, the government uses expansionary monetary and fiscal policy to reflate the economy. In response, the economy bottoms out and a new cycle begins. Over the past 25 years the Chinese economy has shown a clear 'stop-go' pattern.

The first part of this paper provides a historical review of China's conducting of monetary policy since the later 1990s. The second section then discusses China's fiscal policy briefly. The third section finally, is about China's growth prospects in 2006. Lastly, concluding remarks are provided.

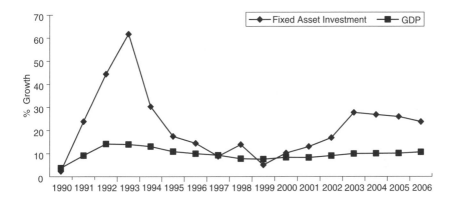

Figure 10.2: Fixed asset investment and GDP growth, 1990–2006
Sources: Statistical Year Book, various issues, National Bureau of Statistics.

10.2 China's Monetary Policy

Officially, the objective of monetary policy is to maintain the stability of currency values so as to promote economic growth. The stability of currency value means both price stability and exchange rate stability. Therefore, there are three explicit objectives for China's macroeconomic policy: growth (employment), price stability, and exchange rate stability. There is another implicit objective: structural adjustment. Macroeconomic policy is used to adjust the relative speeds of components of aggregate demand. For example, monetary policy may be used to slow the growth of fixed asset investment, while the overall growth rate of the economy is assumed at a desirable level. In practice, the number-one objective is to guarantee a minimum growth rate of 8 percent. The number two objective is to keep the inflation rate around 3 percent. Up until recently, a trade-off between growth and inflation existed (Figure 10.3). However, in China's current economic cycle, after three years' high growth, there is still no sign of rising inflation. Economists and decision-makers are puzzled by this new phenomenon. Has something fundamental changed? Or is it just that the lag has lengthened, creating the possibility that, if actions aimed at inflation prevention are not taken in a timely fashion, inflation will be out of control sooner or later?

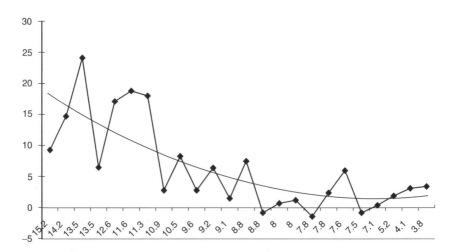

Figure 10.3: The trade-off between growth and inflation

Note: The vertical axis represents inflation and horizontal represents growth. The data cover the period of time from 1980 to 2002.

The third objective is to maintain the stability of the exchange rate of the RMB that previously was pegged to the US dollar and now is geared to a basket of currencies. When capital control was still effective, the PBOC did not need to worry about the impact on the exchange rate when implementing monetary policy. Following the gradual liberalization of capital account, exchange rate stability and the other two objectives have become more and more difficult to reconcile.

China's monetary policy was shaped under the influence of monetarism in the early 1980s. According to monetarist orthodoxy, the authorities should fix the growth of the money supply at a rate that is consistent with a non-accelerating rate of inflation. It is understood that the inflation rate will accelerate with a lag after growth has reached its full potential. According to historical experience, when the growth rate is above 10 percent, inflation surpasses 10 percent with a four-five quarters' lag, and when the growth rate is above 9 percent the inflation rate surpasses 5 percent. When the growth rate reaches 10 percent, the government will therefore tighten monetary policy. When the growth rate reaches 9 percent, the government will become very nervous and ready to tighten. On the other hand, when the economy is in a downturn and the growth rate has fallen below 8 percent, the government will adopt an expansionary policy to stimulate the economy. If while the growth rate has dropped to 9 percent, the inflation rate is still high, it is very difficult for the decision-makers to judge whether the inflation rate will fall further, without the further tightening of policy. For example, in 1997, when the growth rate was dropping and overcapacity was prevalent, the government was reluctant to simulate the economy, for fear that inflation would rebound. Only when it was already too late were actions taken to shift economic policy from contractionary to expansionary. Perhaps the government's failure to shift policy direction until it was too late explains why China then entered a period of deflation. In early 2003, the government found numerous pieces of evidence indicating a heating up of the economy, but it was uncertain whether the economy had turned around and a tight policy should be adopted. As a result, the government refrained from taking strong action for the fear of harming the recovery which was in its initial stage. Only later, when the authorities were convinced that a turnaround had happened, were actions taken. Even so, due to the existence of conflicting signals the government was still cautious in its tightening. Until now, it has kept its options open, and no drastic actions have been taken in either direction.

When the course of action has been decided, monetary policy will often be the first instrument to be used to achieve the policy goal of tightening or loosening. In the process of implementation, there are two key variables: the monetary base (high-powered money, HPM) and the monetary multiplier. The authorities control the monetary base (reserves plus currency) directly, and through a monetary multiplier control the money supply (Allsopp and Vines 2000). After a monetary policy decision has been taken, an immediate question is how changes in the money supply will influence the real economy. It is assumed that changes will influence the real economy via transmission mechanisms such as the portfolio balance mechanism, the wealth transmission mechanism, the credit availability mechanism, and the expectations transmission mechanism (Pierce and Tysome 1985).

Until now the intermediate target of monetary policy has been the growth rate of money supply rather than a benchmark interest rate. Each year, the PBOC sets a target for the growth of the money supply. However, this is just a reference target. More often than not, the PBOC fails to hit it. When the objective is to tighten the money supply in the face of the heating up of the economy, the actual growth rate of the money supply tends to be above target. When the objective is to loosen the money supply in the face of a cooling down, the actual growth rate of money supply tends to be below target. In recent years, the PBOC has set a target of 16 percent for the growth of broad money. However, the growth rate of M2 has been persistently higher than target. The PBOC's missing the target can be attributed to the endogeneity of the money supply. Under different circumstances, monetary policy can become ineffective in different ways. In China, the ineffectiveness of monetary policy is attributed to the breakdown of the above-mentioned two key links in the money-supply process and the collapse of the transmission mechanism.

To hit the target for money supply by manipulating the monetary base, the PBOC carries out open market operations (OMOs). The financial instruments traded in open market operations are government bonds, central government bills, and financial policy bills. China has a relatively well-developed money market consisting mainly of the inter-bank money market and the inter-bank government bond market where repurchasing and inverse repurchasing (to reduce liquidity) are conducted.

From the balance sheet of the central bank (Table 10.1), it can be seen that reserve money can be controlled by changing the quantity of various entries. The most important component of the reserve money consists of two parts: mandatory reserves and excess reserves. The latter are used for settlement with other commercial banks in the accounts of the central bank. In China, the entries that are commonly targeted for changes include: loans to commercial banks (re-lending), government bonds, and, more recently, central bank bills.

Early in the process of reform and opening up, the most frequently used measure to control the monetary base was to change central bank re-lending to commercial banks. When the economy was overheating, the central bank

Table 10.1: The PBOC's assets-liability sheet by the end of 2005 (Billion CNY)

Liabilities		Assets	
Currency	2585	Loans to the banking system	782
Bankers' deposits	3839	Loans to the government	29
Reserves			
Excess reserves			
Government deposits	753	Foreign exchange reserves	6214
Central bank bills	2030		
Other liabilities		Other assets	
Own capital	22	Government bonds	
Total liabilities	10368	Total assets	10368

Sources: *Quarterly Bulletin*, the People's Bank of China (PBOC), Q3, 2005.

would reduce loans to commercial banks, and vice versa. Until 1998, the amount of bonds the central bank could trade in OMOs was limited, because the large-scale issuance of government bonds only started in the middle of that year as a component of the policy package relating to the economy. In 1999 following the development of the money and bond markets and increase in the issuance of government bonds, transactions in government bonds between the central bank and financial institutions through OMOs totaled 707.6 billion yuan, a threefold increase over the previous year. The net increase in the monetary base resulting from OMOs was 192 billion yuan, which constituted 52 percent of the increase in the then existing monetary base (Genyou 2001: 15).

Since the middle of the 1990s, the increase in foreign exchange reserves has become one of the most important contributing factors to the increase in reserve money (or HPM). Open market operations have been carried out to sterilize the increase in reserve money caused by the increase in foreign exchange reserves by selling government bonds held by the PBOC. However, while China's accumulation of foreign exchange reserves began to speed up after 2001, due to the so-called twin surpluses (Figures 10.4 and 10.5), the economy has shown signs of overheating. Owing to the enormous scale of OMOs aimed at neutralizing the expansionary impact of the increase in foreign exchange reserves, in just a couple of years, the PBOC sold all the government bonds it had accumulated as a result of the previous OMOs aimed at stimulating the economy. In 2003, the PBOC found that it had to create a new instrument, central bank bills, to mop up the liquidity.

There is no fundamental difference between OMOs aimed at changing monetary base and OMOs aimed at sterilization. The difference is that the latter is more passive than the former. We can artificially call OMOs aimed

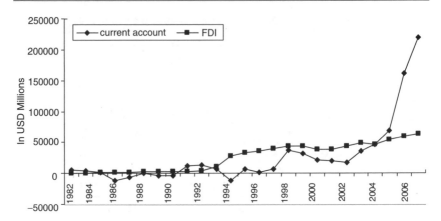

Figure 10.4: China's twin surpluses, 1982–2006

Note: Current Account of 2006 is forecasted.

Sources: Data from 1982 to 2004 from IMF statistics, 2005–6 from *Statistical Year Book* and *Statistics Bulletin of National Bureau of Statistics* (various issues), *Statistics Bulletin of SAFE*.

at reducing liquidity created by the increase in foreign exchange 'reserve sterilization' and OMOs that exceed sterilization 'normal OMOs'.

As a result of large-scale sterilization, in a short period of three years total central bank bills issued reached more than 2 trillion Yuan RMB (see Table 10.1). In contrast, total government bonds were just 3 trillion Yuan RMB after ten years' issuance. Most central bank bills are short-term bills of

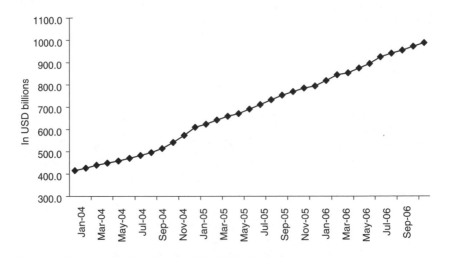

Figure 10.5: China's accumulation of foreign exchange reserves

Sources: *Statistical Year Book*, various issues, National Bureau of Statistics; *Statistics Bulletin*, State Administration of Foreign Reserve.

three months. The burden of rolling-over for the central bank is horrendous, as it becomes increasingly difficult to attract commercial banks to buy the central bank bills. The rising share of low-yielding bills in banks' total assets has an unfavourable impact on the banks' performance, while the banks want to record a good performance at a time of initial public offering (IPO). Consequently, the central bank has to give up the attempt to sterilize fully the increased liquidity caused by the rise in foreign exchange reserves. As a result, the monetary base expands at much higher speed than the PBOC wishes.

The question to which this points is whether sterilization can be implemented without limit. Theoretically, as long as the interest rates paid by the central bank on its bills are lower than corresponding interest rates on American assets, say, the yields of treasury bills, the central bank should be able to carry on with sterilization, and hence maintain effective control of the monetary base. However, there are several obstacles to the continuation of one-way sterilization. Other things being equal, the sale of central bank bills will push up interest rates in money markets, which in turn will invite more capital inflows and place more pressure on the RMB, hence creating the need for more sterilization. Second, when the overall financial conditions are tight, commercial banks may refuse to buy the low-yield central bank bills due to the existence of better options. Yields of the central bank bills will be bid up, and the central bank may incur operational losses. Third, in cases where the commercial banks have to buy more low-yielding central bank bills, commercial bank profitability will fall, which will have a long-term negative impact on the banking system. Fourth, in order to sell central bank bills, the central bank may be tempted to force commercial banks to buy. As a result, not only will the profitability of commercial banks be compromised, but the whole process of financial reform will suffer a setback.

As long as the stability of the exchange rate is one of the central bank's key objectives, sterilization through OMOs cannot carry on indefinitely. Are there other measures available to mop up the liquidity, which at the same time will not lead to an increase in interest rates in money market?

Another measure that has been taken to mop up the liquidity is changing reserve requirements (Table 10.2). By raising reserve requirements, liquidity can be frozen. On September 1, 2003, the PBOC raised the reserve requirements from 6 percent to 7 percent. As a result, commercial banks were forced to reduce their excess reserves, and 150 billion CNY excess reserves were frozen against a backdrop of about 4.3 trillion of total reserve money. The rise in reserve requirements led to a higher multipliers and lower growth rate of broad money and credits. In fact, the increase in reserve requirements was the first important measure taken by the PBOC, since the Chinese economy bottomed out from the deflation that began in

Table 10.2: Adjustment of reserve requirements

Time	Adjustment	Purposes
1985	Unified to 10%	
1987	12%	Tightening money supply
1988	13%	Tightening money supply
1998 (03/21)	8%	Reforming the requirement system
1999 (11/21)	6%	Increasing money supply
2003 (09/21)	7%	Tightening money supply
2004 (04/21)	7.5%	Tightening money supply
2006 (06/16)	8.0%	Tightening money supply
2006 (07/21)	8.5%	Tightening money supply
2006 (11/3)	9.0%	Tightening money supply
2007 (01/05)	9.5%	Tightening money supply

Source: People's Bank of China, <http: www. pbc.gov.cn>

1997. On April 21, 2004, the PBOC again raised the reserve requirements by 0.5 percent.

In a market economy, the central bank will typically hesitate to change reserve requirements, because the measure is too drastic and clumsy. However, this does not seem to be a problem for China. Though the rise of reserve requirements will cause problems for commercial banks, the latter can adapt to the new situation. The simplest way is by shifting a portion of excess reserves into mandatory reserves. Future intervention by the PBOC in the foreign exchange market is expected to satisfy the need for excess reserves, thanks to the continuous increase in foreign exchange reserves. What is in question is the effectiveness of this policy instrument, rather than its negative impact on the smooth functioning of the banking system.

The most important condition for the second link in the money-supply process is the stability of the multiplier. However, this condition, more often than not, cannot be met with China's fragile financial system. Over the past decade, the monetary multiplier has varied between 3 and 4. These variations are caused by institutional factors that are beyond the control of the monetary authorities. Chinese banks have accumulated a huge amount of non-performing loans (NPLs). As a result, commercial banks have become more concerned about loan safety than profitability and reluctant to lend during periods of deflation. In contrast, when commercial banks are able to reduce their non-performing loans and increase capital adequacy, which is often in boom periods they become more ready to extend loans to enterprises, especially when they are pressurized by the local governments to lend. In other words, the multiplier is subject to the influence of institutional factors that are undergoing change. The multiplier

Table 10.3: Changes in interest rates since 1995

Time of adjustment	Reserve deposits	Excess reserve deposits	Re-lending (loans to banks)				Redis-count	Bank Loans 1 year	Deposits 1 year
			1 year	6 months	3 months	20 days			
1996.05.01	8.82	8.82	10.98	10.17	10.08	9	**	10.98	9.18
1996.08.23	8.28	7.92	10.62	10.17	9.72	9	**	10.98	7.47
1997.10.23	7.56	7.02	9.36	9.09	8.82	8.55	**	8.64	5.67
1998.03.21	5.22		7.92	7.02	6.84	6.39	6.03	7.92	5.22
1998.07.01	3.51		5.67	5.58	5.49	5.22	4.32	6.93	4.77
1998.12.07	3.24		5.13	5.04	4.86	4.59	3.96	6.39	3.78
1999.06.10	2.07		3.78	3.69	3.51	3.24	2.16	5.85	2.25
2001.09.11							2.97		
2002.02.21	1.89		3.24	3.15	2.97	2.70	2.97	5.31	1.98
2003.12.20		1.62							
2004.03.25			3.87	3.78	3.6	3.33	3.24		
2004.10.29								5.58	2.25
2005.03.25		0.99							
2006.04.28								5.85	

Source: The PBOC <http://www.pbc.gov.cn>

often changes in pro-cyclical ways, contrary to the wishes of monetary authorities.

Many enterprises' demands for loans are also subject to the influence of institutional factors. In 1998, despite the fact that the central bank lowered reserve requirements for commercial banks from 13 percent to 8 percent and made excess reserves voluntary, in the fourth quarter of 1998 all major banks' actual reserve ratios were above 15 percent. This showed that commercial banks did not need more funds. They would rather let unneeded funds lay idle earning low interest in the vaults of the central bank. After 2003, when the PBOC began to tighten the money supply by lowering the rate of growth of the monetary base, various methods were used by commercial banks to neutralize the impact so as to maintain a high growth of bank loans.

In developed countries, 'the most important control instrument of the central bank is a short-term interest rate and that this influences the behavior of commercial banks by determining the price at which they lend' (Allsopp and Vines 2000: 7). Interest rate policy is also an important instrument of monetary policy in China. Since 1999 the inter-bank money market has assumed an increasingly important role in influencing the liquidity and interest rate structure of the economy. However, despite interest rate liberalization, the so-called ripple-effect of a change in a benchmark interest rate is far from perfect, due to the fragmentation of the money market. Furthermore, there is still no benchmark interest rate equivalent to the Fed funds rate in the US, bank rate in England, and the overnight call rate in Japan. Though a few key short-term inter-bank interest rates are determined by market forces and can be influenced by the PBOC, these rates cannot influence the whole interest rate structure automatically. Important interest rates that have direct impact on the economy are those on household savings deposits and bank loans to enterprises. Bank loans to individuals such as mortgages are a very recent phenomenon. Starting in May 1996, in order to prevent the economy from stumbling, the central bank began to lower interest rates. From 1996 to 1999, the central bank lowered interest rates seven times (Table 10.3). In particular, between July 1997 and November 1998, it cut rates on one-year loans to financial institutions (re-lending rate) four times. Before the first rate cut on May 1, 1996, the interest rate on one-year savings deposits was 9.18 percent. After seven cuts, the rate fell to 2.25 percent.

The most important instance of using the interest rate instrument to slow down the economy developed on October 29, 2004, when the PBOC decided to raise interest rates on loans extended and deposits received by commercial banks. Interest rates on one-year deposits and loans were raised by 0.27 percentage point from 1.98 percent to 2.25 percent and 5.31 percent to 5.58 percent, respectively. This was the first time in nine years that the PBOC had raised interest rates. Bands were set to allow interest rates on bank loans and deposits to fluctuate. In fact, commercial banks had obtained autonomy over the interest rates they charged on loans as long as those rates were not lower than benchmark rates on loans decided by the PBOC. On the other hand, commercial banks have the autonomy to charge interest rates on deposits as long as those rates are not higher than the benchmark interest rates on deposits decided by the PBOC. In January 2004 the PBOC announced a further widening of the bands on bank loans and deposits. Commercial banks are allowed to charge interest rates between 1.7 times and 0.9 times that of the benchmark loan interest rates. Because there was strong demand for loans by enterprises, there should have been an increase in the interest rates which were liberalized. The failure of interest rates to serve as regulators of financial resources is attributable to institutional factors. Big state-owned enterprises have enough liquidity anyway and lack a strong need for bank loans. On the other hand, they were the targeted consumers of commercial banks, and banks wished to provide them with credits even with low interest rates. Although small and middle-sized enterprises needed credits desperately, commercial banks were reluctant to provide them due to riskness of the loans. Banks would not extend loans to them, no matter how high the interest rates were. As a result, the disequilibrium in the loan market persisted. In the formal market, rates were low. In the curb market, rates were high. Owing to the failure to achieve equilibrium in the credit market via changes in interest rates, the efficiency of financial resources allocation was compromised.

It is worth emphasizing that interest rates are still a very important policy instrument. At least, they are important in terms of public perception. In March 2005, the PBOC raised the benchmark interest rates on mortgages to slow down the growth of loans to real estate developers, and the resulting uproar showed that the measure does indeed bite.

On several occasions, while the PBOC has raised interest rates on loans or adopted measures to tighten financial conditions, it has lowered the rate on excess reserves. By doing so, commercial banks are given an incentive to reduce their deposits at the central bank. As a result, the effect of monetary tightening is offset by the increase in liquidity in money markets. One important motivations behind this policy is to push down interest rates in the money market so as to discourage capital flowing in from abroad in response to expectations of RMB revaluation and make the central bank bills more attractive for the commercial banks.

In summary, there are three major problems for the effectiveness of China's monetary policy. The first problem is conflicts between multiple objectives. The objective of maintaining the stability of the exchange rate constrains the policy aimed at controlling overheating. The second problem is there are too many intermediate targets. China needs to make a choice between the growth of broad money and benchmark interest rates. According to Poole's theory, it is impossible to use two intermediate targets at the same time. The third problem is that China needs to further liberalize its money and credit markets so as to obtain a benchmark interest rate equivalent to the Fed funds rate or call rate. Without an effective inter-bank overnight loan rate, it is impossible to change the cost of bank lending, when the decision is made to use a benchmark interest rate as an intermediate target.

10.3 Fiscal Policy

Fiscal policy has played a significant role in the past eight years in maintaining the growth of China's economy. Government expenditures were concentrated in building infrastructure, reforming state-owned enterprises, developing the social security system, science and technology, education, agriculture, and development of the Western regions. That has led to rapid increases in tax revenues relative to the increase in interest payments. As a result, China's fiscal position has improved rather than deteriorated.

After ten years of expansionary fiscal policy, China has accumulated large debts. The debt has increased from 4.9 billion Yuan in 1981 to more than 3 trillion Yuan in 2005. However, officially, China's debt/GDP ratio is still less than 20 percent. Many economists argue that if we take into consideration so-called contingent liabilities, China's debt/GDP ratio is much higher, perhaps as high as 100 percent. The government's ability to repay debts is also much higher than it appears. However, whether China's fiscal position is sustainable depends on the dynamics of the debt/GDP ratio. Two factors determine the dynamic path of the debt/GDP ratio: the growth rate and the budget deficit/GDP ratio. As long as China can maintain a relatively high growth rate of 7–8 percent and a budget deficit/GDP ratio of less than 3 percent, the debt balance/GDP ratio will converge to a limit of less than 40 percent. Incorporating contingent liabilities into the debt balance would merely influence the initial position of the debt/GDP ratio, and it would not change the limit to which the ratio converges.

The dynamic path of the debt/GDP ratio can be derived as follows. By definition, the budget deficit and debt balance have the following relationship:

$$\frac{dZ}{dt} = G \tag{1}$$

Where Z and G are debt and budget deficit. Changes in debt balance over GDP ratio can be expressed as:

$$\frac{dz/dt}{z} = \frac{d(Z/GDP)/dt}{Z/(GDP)} = \frac{dZ/dt}{Z} - \frac{d(GDP)/dt}{GDP}$$

z is the debt over GDP ratio. Combining the above two relationships, we have:

$$\frac{d(Z/GDP)/dt}{Z/GDP} = \frac{dZ/dt}{Z} - \frac{d(GDP)/dt}{GDP} = \frac{G/GDP}{Z/GDP} - \frac{d(GDP)/dt}{GDP} = \frac{g}{z} - n$$

namely:

$$\frac{dz/dt}{z} = \frac{g}{z} - n \tag{2}$$

g is budget deficit over GDP ratio; n is growth rate of GDP.

The solution for this differential equation is:

$$z = \frac{g}{n} + C_1 e^{-nt} \tag{3}$$

Assume that when t(0) = 0, z = 0.12; g = 0.02, n = 0.071, and C_1 = −0.16. The solution of the equation then takes the form of:

$$z = 0.28 - 0.16e^{-0.07t} \tag{4}$$

Equation (4) shows that as long as China can maintain a growth rate of 7 percent and a budget deficit/GDP ratio of 2 percent, the debt/GDP ratio will converge to a limit of less than 28 percent.

Therefore, there is nothing inherent that will cause a fiscal crisis. This was an analysis that I first made eight years ago, when some economists were

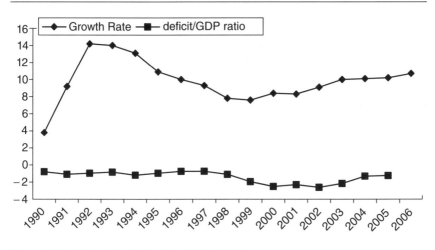

Figure 10.6: China's fiscal situation, 1990–2006
Sources: Statisticsal Year Book, various issues, National Statistics Bureau.

predicting that China was going to face a fiscal crisis due to its huge contingent liabilities in the from of non-performing loans and unpaid pensions. As long as the government can avoid making fatal mistakes in macroeconomic policy and economic restructuring so as to maintain a decent growth rate and a relatively low budget deficit, the fiscal position will remain sustainable. This leaves ample room to use expansionary fiscal policy to counterbalance any negative impact on growth by a tight monetary policy. Indeed due to the high growth rate over the past four years, China's fiscal situation has been improved steadily (Figure 10.6).

10.4 Growth Prospects

In 2006, China was able to maintain a high growth rate while keeping inflation under control. Investment is strong; exports have maintained strong momentum, and there is no sign of inflationary pressure. On the whole the situation is very good.

However, there are uncertainties. First, overcapacity in many industries is worsening. Will this lead to deflation, or are fears of deflation just hype? Second, what will the local governments' economic policy be, while waiting for a change of government at the provincial level over the next few years? Third, what will be the lagged impact on inflation of the high growth of GDP and of the high growth rate of the money supply over the past several years? Fourth, what will be the US policy towards China? Fifth, what will be the external knocks China has to face? Will be there another oil price hike?

At the time of writing, it seems that on the whole, the growth momentum of the Chinese economy has weakened since early 2005. According to historical experience, there are three indicators that can be used to measure economic temperature. The first is the growth rate of net exports. In the past, whenever net exports becomes an important contributor to GDP growth, the economy is suffering from lack of domestic demand and will ultimately slow down. The second is the price level. All major price indexes fell in 2005. In 2005, the fall in the CPI was 1.8 percent. The across-board fall of price indexes indicated that the economy was slowing down. Third is the growth of profitability of enterprises. Usually, profitability is a leading indicator of the strength of domestic demand. Faced with a fall in profitability, enterprises cut back production and investment. The worsening economic situation in turn leads to an accelerating fall in profitability, creating a downward spiral. In 2005, the growth rate of profitability fell quite significantly. Although, on the surface, the fall was something like 20 percent, if profits from oil, coal, and fuel, and a few other raw-materials based sectors are excluded, the overall growth rate of profits of the economy was only—7 percent or even lower. The fourth is the presence of bottlenecks. In recent years, the Chinese economy has been characterized by the prevalence of so-called bottlenecks, but the situation has improved since 2005. The shortage of electricity eased in 2005. According to the National Development and Reform Commission (NDRC), the supply of and demand for electricity was basically in balance in 2006. The disappearance of bottlenecks in electricity, coal, gasoline, transportation and basic materials such as steel usually is not only the result of the increase in supply but also the result of the slackening of demand. More than 80 percent of products enumerated by the Ministry of Commerce are in oversupply. Based on past experience, it is safe to say that the Chinese economy is slowing down. However, the slowdown is not that dramatic. Sporadic rebound cannot be ruled out.

According to official estimates, in 2005 the growth rate of GDP was 10.2 percent. The contributions to GDP growth made by investment, consumption and net exports were 36.1 percent, 38.1 percent, and 25.8 percent, respectively. However, these statistics seem questionable. The contribution of net exports almost certainly is underestimated. According to foreign experts, the contribution made by net exports should be around a third of the total growth (Figure 10.7).

Assuming that China runs a US\$ 100 billion trade surplus in 2006,[2] the contribution of net exports to GDP growth will be zero, due to the high base

---

[2] In 2006, despite appreciation of the RMB, China's trade surplus registered a record of \$170 billion. Many Chinese economists hold that this figure was inflated by capital inflows disguised as a trade surplus by overinvoicing exports and underinvoicing imports.

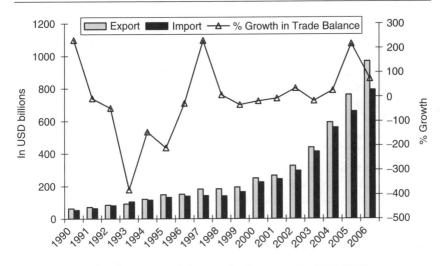

Figure 10.7: Exports, imports, and the growth of net exports, 1990–2006
Sources: Statistical Year Book, various issues, National Bureau of Statistics.

in 2005. If this is the case, other things being equal, China's growth rate in 2006 will drop to 7 percent, which is a growth rate equivalent to recession by China's standard. Furthermore, if the growth rate of net exports turns out to be high, this implies the worsening of China's external balance (too large a current account surplus). If the growth rate of net exports drops significantly because of external conditions or government policy aimed at rebalancing the economy, the growth rates of other components of domestic demand must rise significantly. What are the potential candidates? Investment? Not very likely, because growth rate of profits of enterprises is falling. According to the National Bureau of Statistics, in 2005 loss-making state-owned enterprises recorded the second largest losses in the history. The total losses amounted to 102.6 billion RMB, an increase of 56.7 percent over the previous period. In the first two months in 2006 losses have increased further compared with the same period of last year.[3]

According to the National Bureau of Statistics, four factors contributed to the increase in losses. First, production costs rose significantly due to increases in prices of energy and raw materials. Among thirty-nine major industries, in

[3] This analysis turns out to be wrong, according to the most recent statistics (late 2006), Chinese enterprises' profitability has increased significantly, though the profits were concentrated in a few monopolistic state-owned enterprises. As a result, China's fixed asset investment in 2006 was still very strong. Due to the stronger than expected growth rates of fixed assets investment and net exports, China's GDP growth rate was higher in 2006 than in 2005.

269

twenty-nine the increase in costs surpassed the increase in the sales revenues and half suffered from falling profitability. The automobile, chemical, and electronic industries suffered the greatest falls in profitability.

Second, price controls over a few resource products and public goods, such as gasoline, caused producers such as oil refineries suffering huge losses. The oil refinery industry registered a loss of 22 billion RMB in 2005.

Third, overcapacity contributed to the losses or falls in profitability in industries which had experienced the investment upsurge since 2003. Among these are steel, electrolyte aluminum, ferroalloy, coke, calcium-carbide, automobiles, and copper smelting. The profits of the steel, ferroalloy, coke, cement, and automobile industries fell by 9.1 percent, 94 percent, 77 percent, 68 percent, and 40 percent respectively. Eighty percent of electrolyte aluminum enterprises made losses. Fourth, the lack of property rights for core technology was an important contributing factor to the fall in profitability of state-owned enterprises. Communication equipment, computers, and other electronic equipment manufacturers made only a 3.1 billion RMB profit, a fall of 62.1 percent over the previous year. The mobile phone industry suffered losses of 1.6 billion RMB. The Chinese mobile phone makers' market share contracted from 60 percent in 2004 to 40 percent in 2005.

The government hopes that increased household consumption will promote growth in 2006. But without an increase in public expenditure, it is not very likely that the consumption demand will increase significantly. Therefore, fiscal policy should be more expansionary both for structural reasons and for the maintenance of macroeconomic stability. Monetary policy does not have much room for play in 2006. The PBOC has to reduce appreciation pressure on RMB. Therefore, there is not much space for the PBOC to raise interest rates or tighten the money supply. Investors expect that the RMB exchange rate will appreciate by 3 percentage points. Whether these market expectations are right or wrong, the PBOC must keep its benchmark interest rates about 3 percentage points lower than the Fed funds rate. Capital controls are leaky. Sterilization has become a heavy burden for the PBOC. Hence US interest rates will cap China's interest rates in 2006. On the other hand, the growth rate of the money supply exceeds its target. Cheap credits will worsen resource allocation and economic efficiency and hence damage both long-run growth and short-run economic stability. One important danger in 2006 is that because fiscal policy is tight and slow to respond to the slowdown of the economy, the PBOC has to maintain an unjustifiably loose monetary policy in order to maintain a growth rate as high as 9 percent, which in turn feeds asset bubbles, worsens resource allocation, and damages China's long-term stability.

10.5 The Recent Anomaly

Recent data releases have surprised many observers. The following are the main economic figures in the first quarter of 2006:

- GDP growth rate 10.2 percent higher than in the same period of 2005.
- Growth rate of fixed asset investment of 27.7 percent, 4.9 percentage points higher than in the same period of 2005.
- Growth rate of social consumption of 12.8 percent; the real growth is 12.2%, 0.3 percentage points higher than in the same period of 2005.
- Trade surplus: 23.3 billion US dollars; a growth of 41.4 percent; the growth of exports is 197.3 billion US dollars; a growth rate of 26.6 percent; the corresponding figures for imports are 174 billion US dollars and 24.8 percent.
- Increase in the number of construction projects (for the first two months in 2006)
  - In-process construction projects: 39.8 percent
  - Newly started construction projects: 33.4 percent
  - Growth rate of profits of large-scale industrial enterprises: 21.3 percent.

Three things are surprising. The first is Chinese enterprises' ability to defy the odds in maintaining high growth of investment. The declining growth of profitability has failed to slow the growth of investment by enterprises. The second is the rapid growth of net exports, despite the revaluation of RMB. The third is that while the growth rate has been rising persistently, inflation has shown no signs of accelerating.

As for the first surprise, there are three points to make. First, one still cannot be sure whether the resurgence of investment is temporary or permanent. A high growth rate of investment is not sustainable, without the support of profitability. Why has investment momentum been restored when there is prevalent overcapacity? The rebound of fixed asset investment seems to be attributable to non-economic factors as well as economic ones. In the first year of the eleventh Five-Year Plan and on the eve of changes of government at provincial level, the incentive to invest is too great to resist, as long as there is financing. In fact, commercial banks that were flush with liquidity in 2005 were in a rush to extend loans, which should have been extended in 2005, at the beginning of 2006, due to favourable factors, both internal (lower NPLs and higher capital adequacy) and external (strong demand for loans).

Second, it is doubtful whether China can maintain a growth rate of net exports comparable with their growth in 2005, considering the turbulence of the world economy, worsening global imbalances, and rising protectionism.

Third, the relationship between growth and inflation is changing. While the growth rates of the economy were 9.1 percent, 10 percent, 10.1 percent, and 9.9 percent respectively from 2002 to 2005, inflation rates were −0.8 percent, 1.2 percent, 3.9 percent, and 1.8 percent respectively in the same period of time. In the first quarter of 2006 while the growth rate of GDP was 10.1 percent, CPI inflation eased to 0.8 percent YoY in March, down from 0.9 percent in February. However, it is dangerous to be complacent: if the growth rate of money supply is too high, even though the inflation rate is not high, something must be wrong. Now investment in real estate development is speeding up again, as are housing prices in many areas including Beijing. All this augurs mounting inflationary pressure.

10.6 Concluding Remarks

In 2006, China's economic situation was good. The Chinese economy was able to maintain a growth rate in excess of 9 percent without causing serious problems of price stability. However, China needs to slow the growth of fixed asset investment initiated by local government and supported by loose monetary policy. But the authorities should also be on guard against a significant slowdown of the growth rate. The right combination should be a tight monetary policy and loose fiscal policy. A tighter monetary policy will cause two problems. First, the growth rate may fall. Fiscal policy can be used to counteract this danger. As mentioned earlier, China's fiscal position is strong, and it is possible for China to use an expansionary fiscal policy for years to come. Second, the pressure of appreciation of the RMB may increase as a result of tighter monetary policy and higher interest rates. The multiple objectives of China's monetary policy and its inability to use an effective intermediate target have handicapped the PBOC's ability to implement a relatively tight monetary policy effectively. To raise the effectiveness of macroeconomic control so as to provide an environment conducive for China's structural adjustment while maintaining the macroeconomic stability, further reform of the policy regime is pressing.

References

Allsopp, C. J., and Vines, D. (2000), 'The Assessment: Macroeconomic Policy,' *Oxford Review of Economic Policy*, 16: 1–32.

Dornbusch, R., and Helmers, F., and Leslie, C. H. (1988), *The Open Economy* (Oxford: Oxford University Press).

Genyou, Dai (2001), 'China's Monetary Policy: Retrospect and Prospect,' *World Economy and China*, No. 3.

Lardy, Nicholas (1998), *China's Unfinished Economic Revolution* (Washington, DC: Brookings Institute Press).

Lee, Jang-Yung (1996), 'Implications of a Surge in Capital Inflows: Available Tools and Consequences for the Conduct of Monetary Policy,' IMF Working Paper 96/53.

Mishkin, Frederic S., and, Eakins, Stanley G. (1998), *Financial Markets and Institutions* (Reading, MA: Addison Wesley).

Pierce, D. G., and Tysome, P. J. (1985), *Monetary Economics: Theories, Evidence and Policy*, 2nd edn. (London: Butterworth & Co.).

Yu, Yongding (2000*a*), 'China's Deflation during the Asian Financial Crisis, and Reform of the International Financial System,' *Asian Economic Bulletin*, 17(2, August): 163–74.

—— (2000*b*), 'An Analytical Framework for Analyzing China's Fiscal Stability,' *World Economy (Shijie Jingji)*. 3–12

—— (2001), 'China's Macroeconomic Outlook,' *World Economy and China*, 9 (1) pp. 3–13.

—— (2002), 'The Dynamic Path of M2-GDP ratio in China,' *The World Economy (Shijie Jingji)*, 12: 3–11

—— (2004), 'How to Analyze China's Macroeconomic Situation,' *International Economic Review (Guoji Jingji Pinglun)*, 3: 5–9

—— and Li, Jun (2000), 'China's Current Fiscal Situation,' in Guoguang Liu, Luoling Wang, and Jingwen Li (eds.), *Outlook of the Chinese Economy, Spring Blue Book, 2000* (Beijing: The Publishing House of Documentation of Social Sciences), 49–72.

—— —— and Liang, Cong (2001), 'On China's Proactive Fiscal Policy,' in Guoguang Liu, Luoling Wang, and Jingwen Li (eds.), *Outlook of the Chinese Economy, Spring Blue Book, 2001* (Beijing: The Publishing House of Documentation of Social Science), 15–41.

—— and Zhang, Yanqun (1999), 'An Analysis of Monetary Policy and Its Prospect,' in Gssuoguang Liu, Luoling Wang, and Jingwen Li. (eds,). *Outlook of the Chinese Economy, Spring Blue Book, 1999*. (Beijing: The Publishing House of Documentation of Social Sciences), 40–62.

11

The Chinese Approach to Capital Inflows: Patterns and Possible Explanations

Eswar Prasad and Shang-Jin Wei[1]
International Monetary Fund

11.1 Introduction

China has in many ways taken the world by storm. In addition to its swiftly rising prominence in the global trading system, where it now accounts for over 6 percent of total world trade, it has also become a magnet for foreign direct investment (FDI), overtaking the United States (in 2003) as the number one destination for FDI.

It was not always thus. China's integration with the global economy began in earnest only after the market-oriented reforms instituted in 1978. Capital inflows, in particular, were minimal in the 1970s and 1980s, impeded by capital controls and the reluctance of international investors to undertake investment in a socialist economy with weak institutions and limited exposure to international trade. All of this changed in the early 1990s, when FDI inflows surged dramatically on account of the selective opening of China's capital account as well as the rapid trade expansion that, in conjunction with China's large labor pool, created opportunities for foreign investors. These

[1] We are grateful to Jahangir Aziz, Ray Brooks, Michael Dooley, Sebastian Edwards, Mark Wright, and participants at the NBER Capital Flows Conference, the Stanford China Conference, a conference at the Graduate Institute of International Studies (Geneva), and a seminar at the China Center for Economic Research for helpful comments and suggestions. We are indebted to members of the IMF's China team, from whose work we have drawn extensively. We owe a particular debt to Qing Wang, who provided many useful suggestions and comments. Ioana Hussiada provided excellent research assistance. This is a revised and updated version of a paper that is forthcoming in an NBER volume on capital flows edited by Sebastian Edwards.

inflows have remained strong ever since, even during the Asian crisis of the late 1990s.

Given China's status as a global economic power, characterizing the nature and determinants of China's capital inflows is of considerable interest for analytical reasons as well as for understanding the implications for the regional and global allocation of capital. Our primary objective in this study is to provide a detailed descriptive analysis of the main aspects of capital inflows into China. Given the degree of interest in China and the relative paucity of data, we aim to provide a benchmark reference tool for other researchers, including some critical perspectives on the numbers that we report.

Section 11.2 presents a detailed picture of the evolution of China's capital inflows. A feature of particular interest is that China's capital inflows have generally been dominated by FDI, which, for an emerging market, constitutes a preferred form of inflows since FDI tends to be stable and associated with other benefits such as transfers of technological and managerial expertise. An interesting aspect of these inflows is that, contrary to some popular perceptions, they come mainly from other advanced Asian countries that have net trade surpluses with China, rather than from the United States and Europe, which constitute China's main export markets. As for other types of inflows, China has limited its external debt to low levels, and non-FDI private capital inflows have typically been quite limited, until recently.

In Section 11.3, we examine the evolution of the balance of payments and dissect the recent surge in the pace of accumulation of international reserves. A key finding is that, while current account surpluses and FDI have remained important contributors to reserve accumulation, the dramatic surge in the pace of reserve accumulation during 2001–4 is largely attributable to non-FDI capital inflows. We provide analytical perspectives on the costs and benefits of holding a large (and growing) stock of reserves. There has also been considerable international attention focused recently on the issue of the currency composition of China's massive stock of international reserves (which is now second only to that of Japan). Despite data constraints, we attempt to shed what light we can on this issue, both by carefully examining a popular source of data for China's holding of US securities and by calculating the potential balance of payments implications of reserve valuation effects associated with the depreciation of the US dollar in recent years.

Section 11.4 discusses the broader composition of China's capital inflows in the context of the burgeoning literature on financial globalization. Notwithstanding the recent surge of non-FDI inflows, FDI remains historically the dominant source of inflows into China. The literature on the benefits and risks of financial globalization suggests that China may have benefited greatly in terms of improving the risk-return trade-offs by having its inflows tilted so much toward FDI.

Whether this composition of inflows is a result of enlightened policies, the structure of institutions, or plain luck is an intriguing question. In Section 11.5, we examine various hypotheses that have been put forward to explain why China has its inflows so heavily tilted toward FDI. In this context, we provide a detailed description of China's capital account restrictions and how these have evolved over time. While controls on non-FDI inflows as well as tax and other incentives appear to be proximate factors for explaining the FDI-heavy composition of inflows, other factors may also have contributed to this outcome. It is not straightforward to disentangle the quantitative relevance of alternative hypotheses. We argue, nonetheless, that at least a few of the hypotheses—including some mercantilist-type arguments that have been advanced recently—are not consistent with the facts.

11.2 The Chinese Pattern of Inflows and Some International Comparisons

11.2.1 *The Evolution of Capital Inflows*

Gross capital inflows into China were minuscule before the early 1980s. After 1984, the 'other investment' category, which includes bank lending, increased significantly and accounted for the largest share of total inflows during the 1980s (Figure 11.1). FDI rose gradually from the early 1980s to early 1991 and then rose dramatically through the mid-1990s. During the 1990s, FDI has accounted for the lion's share of inflows. It is interesting to note that FDI inflows were only marginally affected during the Asian crisis. Figure 11.2 provides some more detail on the evolution of the main components of the capital account, both in terms of gross outflows and inflows. Note that all components other than FDI show sharp increases in outflows in the period immediately after the Asian crisis, with the subsequent recovery in net inflows of these components taking two to three years to materialize. Recent data indicate that, after remaining in a range of around $50 billion during 2002-3, gross FDI inflows increased to almost $68 billion in 2005.

From a cross-country perspective, China's net capital inflows are of course large in absolute magnitude but hardly remarkable relative to the size of the economy. Before the Asian crisis, many of the other 'Asian Tigers' had significantly larger inflows relative to their GDP (Figure 11.3, top panel). What is striking, however, is that, except for Singapore, the share of FDI in total inflows is clearly the highest for China. Its total net inflows as a share

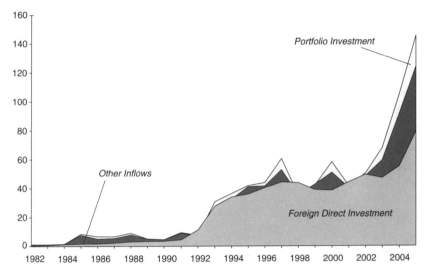

Figure 11.1: Level and composition of gross capital inflows, 1982–2005 (in US$ billions)

of GDP rank among the highest across all emerging markets after the Asian crisis, especially since many of the Asian Tigers were no longer the darlings of international investors (Figure 11.3, lower panel). While net inflows dropped sharply across all emerging markets after the late 1990s, the interesting thing to note is that most of the inflows that did come into the emerging markets after 1999 took the form of FDI.

China's average net inflows, and the share of FDI in those inflows, look quite similar during the periods 1990–6 and 1999–2005. Since FDI is clearly the main story in the context of China's capital inflows, we now turn to a more detailed examination of these flows.

11.2.2 Foreign Direct Investment

Over the past decade, China has accounted for about one-third of gross FDI flows to all emerging markets and about 60 percent of these flows to Asian emerging markets (Figure 11.4, top panel). Even excluding flows from Hong Kong SAR to China from these calculations (on the extreme assumption that all of these flows represent 'round-tripping' of funds originating in China—this point is discussed further below), China's share in these flows to emerging markets is substantial (Figure 11.4, lower panel). The shares spike upward during the Asian crisis and, more recently, in 2002, when

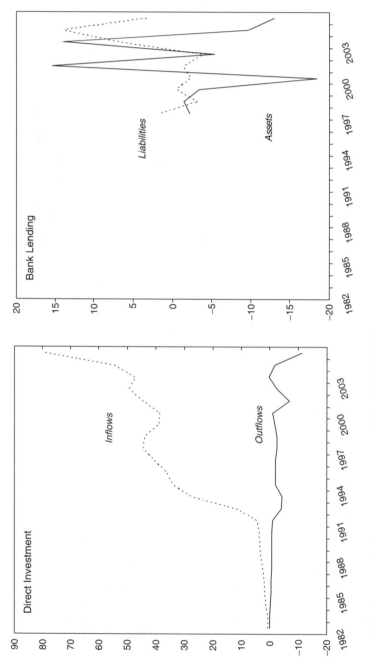

Figure 11.2: Gross capital flows by component, 1982–2005 (US$ billions)

Source: CEIC database

Note: Scales differ across the four panels of this figure.

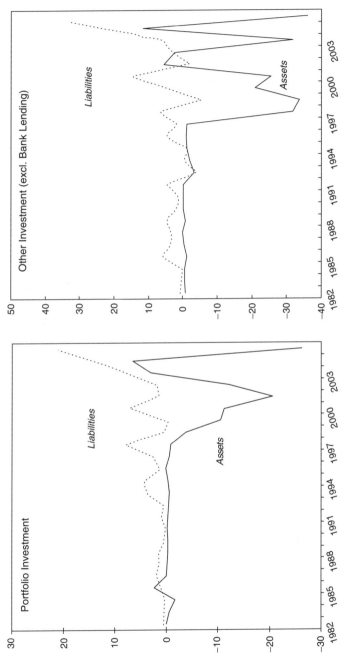

Figure 11.2: *(cont.)*

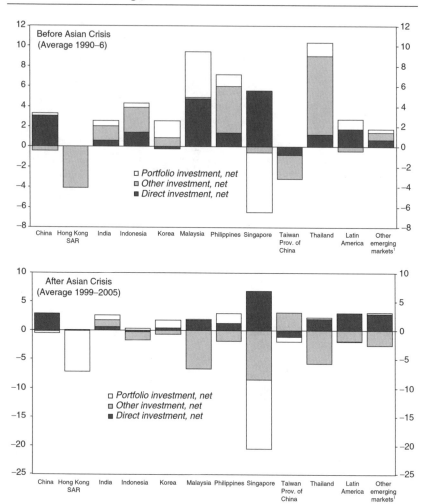

Figure 11.3: Asian economies and emerging markets: net capital flows, 1990–2005 (% of GDP)

Source: World Economic Outlook database.

Note: Average for emerging markets in EMBI+ index, excluding Latin America and Asian countries.

weaknesses in the global economy resulted in a slowdown in flows from industrial countries to most emerging markets other than China. With the pick-up in flows to emerging markets in 2003, there has been a corresponding decline in China's share, even though flows to China remained essentially unchanged.

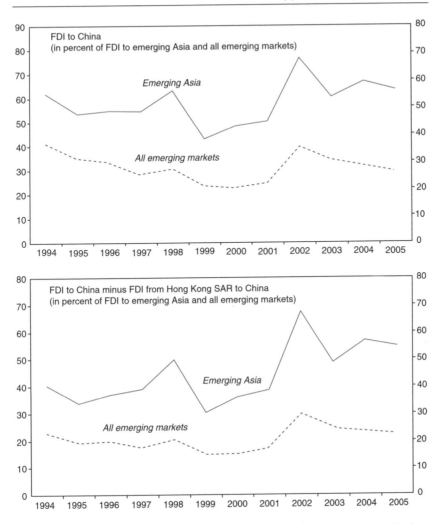

Figure 11.4: China's Share of Foreign Direct Investment Inflows to Emerging Markets, 1994–2005

Source: World Economic Outlook database, CEIC database, and authors' calculations.

Note: This figure uses data on gross FDI flows. The bottom panel excludes gross FDI flows to China originating from Hong Kong SAR from both the numerator and denominator of the two ratios shown.

Where are China's FDI inflows coming from? Table 11.1 shows the share of utilized FDI by source country. Some aspects of the results are worth noting. First of all, the share of Hong Kong SAR has declined steadily over the past decade, from 58 percent in 1994 to 30 percent in 2005. One of the concerns in interpreting FDI data for China is that a significant portion of these flows

Table 11.1: FDI inflows by source country (% share)

	1994	1995	1996	1997	1998	1999	2000	2001	2002	2003	2004	2005
Total	100	100	100	100	100	100	100	100	100	100	100	100
Hong Kong SAR	58.2	53.4	49.6	45.6	40.7	40.6	38.1	35.7	33.9	33.1	31.3	29.8
Virgin Islands	...	...	...	...	8.9	6.6	9.4	10.8	11.6	10.8	11.1	15.0
Japan	6.1	8.2	8.8	9.6	7.5	7.4	7.2	9.3	7.9	9.4	9.0	10.8
Korea	2.1	2.8	3.3	4.7	4.0	3.2	3.7	4.6	5.2	8.4	10.3	8.6
United States	7.4	8.2	8.2	7.2	8.6	10.5	10.8	9.5	10.3	7.8	6.5	5.1
European Union—15	...	...	...	...	...	11.1	11.0	8.9	7.0	7.3	7.0	8.6
Taiwan Province of China	10.0	8.4	8.3	7.3	6.4	6.4	5.6	6.4	7.5	6.3	5.1	3.6
Singapore	3.5	4.9	5.4	5.8	7.5	6.6	5.3	4.6	4.4	3.8	3.3	3.7
Australia	0.6	0.6	0.5	0.7	0.6	0.0	0.8	0.7	0.7	1.1	1.1	1.1[1]
Western Samoa	...	...	...	...	0.3	0.5	0.7	1.1	1.7	1.8	1.9	2.2
Macao SAR	...	...	...	...	0.9	0.8	0.9	0.7	0.9	0.8	0.8	0.8[1]
Others	12.0	13.4	16.0	19.3	14.7	6.5	6.7	7.9	8.9	9.2	12.6	10.9

[1] Data for these regions for 2004 and 2005 are not available, so the same share has been assumed as in 2003.
Sources: CEIC database and CEIC China database.
Note: This table is based upon data for utilized (rather than contracted) FDI.

could potentially represent round-tripping to take advantage of preferential tax treatment of foreign investment relative to domestic investment. Much of this round-tripping is believed to take place through Hong Kong SAR. While it is difficult to estimate the extent of round-tripping, the declining share of Hong Kong SAR in total inflows at least suggests that the magnitude of round-tripping as a share of total FDI inflows may have been declining over time. On the other hand, the shares of small economies like the Virgin Islands and Western Samoa, which have risen over the past few years, could now be accounting for some of these round-tripping flows.[2]

Asian economies account for a substantial fraction of China's FDI inflows. For instance, over the period 2001–5, five Asian economies—Hong Kong SAR, Japan, Korea, Taiwan Province of China, and Singapore—together account for about 60 percent of FDI inflows. That a lot of China's FDI comes from these relatively advanced Asian economies suggests that these flows do bring the usual benefits associated with FDI, including transfers of technological and managerial expertise. The other interesting point to note is that—contrary to the widespread perception of large direct investment flows from western industrial economies to China—the United States and the European Union (EU) economies together accounted for only 14 percent of total inflows in 2005, and even that is down from a share of 22 percent in 1999–2000. Even if one were to assume that half of the reported FDI inflows from Hong Kong SAR are accounted for by round-tripping and that all of the share of the Virgin Islands in fact represents flows originating in the United States, the share of

[2] A more likely possibility is that those could be flows from sources such as Japan, Taiwan Province of China, and the United States that are channeled through such offshore financial centers in order to evade taxes in the source countries.

Table 11.2: Utilized FDI by sector (% share)

	1998	1999	2000	2001	2002	2003	2004	2005 Jun
Primary sector	1.4	1.8	1.7	1.9	1.9	1.9	1.8	1.2
Extraction industries	1.3	1.4	1.4	1.7	1.1	0.6	0.9	0.5
Manufacturing	56.3	56.1	63.5	65.9	69.8	69.0	71.0	71.1
o/w Textile	3.4	3.4	3.4	4.1	5.6	4.1	3.3	3.4
Chemicals and raw materials	4.3	4.8	4.4	4.7	6.0	4.9	4.9	5.4
Medicine	0.8	1.7	1.3	1.3	1.7	1.4	1.1	0.8
Ordinary machinery	2.1	2.4	2.6	2.8	3.2	2.9	3.0	3.3
Special use equipment		1.3	1.3	1.7	2.5	2.3	3.0	3.0
Electronics and communication equipment	5.3	7.8	11.3	15.1	20.0	11.9	13.7	14.1
Utilities	6.8	9.2	5.5	4.8	2.6	2.4	1.9	3.2
Construction	4.5	2.3	2.2	1.7	1.3	1.1	1.3	0.7
Transport and telecommunication services	3.6	3.8	2.5	1.9	1.7	1.6	2.1	2.1
Distribution industries	2.6	2.4	2.1	2.5	1.8	2.1	1.2	1.5
Banking and finance		0.2	0.2	0.1	0.2	0.4	0.4	0.5
Real estate	14.1	13.9	11.4	11.0	10.7	9.8	9.8	8.8
Development and Operations	12.0	11.7	10.7	10.2	9.9	9.5	8.2	8.4
Social services	6.5	6.3	5.4	5.5	5.6	5.9	5.9	5.9[1]
Hotels	1.1	1.8	1.1	1.0	0.9	0.9	0.6	0.4
Health care, sports and social welfare	0.2	0.4	0.3	0.3	0.2	0.2	0.1	0.0
Media and broadcasting	0.2	0.2	0.1	0.1	0.1	0.1	1.6	1.4
Scientific research services	0.1	0.3	0.1	0.3	0.4	0.5	0.5	0.6
Other	2.4	1.9	3.6	2.3	2.5	4.2	1.5	2.5

[1] Assumed the same share as in 2003 as the definition of this category has changed.
Source: CEIC database.

the United States and the EU in China's total FDI inflows would be about 30 percent, a large but hardly dominant share.

To which parts and regions of China's economy are FDI inflows being directed? Table 11.2 shows that about two-thirds of these flows have been going into manufacturing, with real estate accounting for about another 10 percent. Within manufacturing, the largest identifiable share has consistently gone to electronics and communication equipment. The share of manufacturing has risen by 15 percentage points since 1998, largely at the expense of the shares of utilities, construction, transport and telecommunication services, and real estate. Since the industries with declining FDI shares are largely focused on non-traded goods, the evolution of this pattern of FDI seems to be consistent with the notion that these inflows have been stimulated by China's increasing access (both actual and anticipated) to world export markets following its accession to the World Trade Organization (WTO).

The regional distribution within China of utilized FDI inflows has shown some changes over time (Table 11.3). Guangdong Province has typically accounted for about one-quarter of FDI inflows, consistent with its proximity to Hong Kong SAR and its reputation as an exporting powerhouse, but its share fell by 10 percentage points from 1995–7 to 2004. The big winner over the past few years has been Jiangsu Province (next to Shanghai), which

Table 11.3: Foreign direct investment inflows into China by Region (% of total FDI inflows)

	Average 1995–2004	Average 1995–7	Average 2000–4	2004
Guangdong	24.2	27.0	21.2	16.5
Jiangsu	15.2	12.8	16.9	14.8
Shanghai	8.7	8.8	9.1	10.4
Fujian	8.1	9.9	6.4	3.2
Shandong	7.8	6.2	9.9	14.3
Beijing	3.9	3.4	3.9	4.2
Zhejiang	5.0	3.4	6.7	9.5
Tianjin	4.0	4.8	3.2	2.8
Liaoning	5.1	4.3	6.2	8.9
Hebei	1.9	2.0	1.5	1.2
Guangxi	1.3	1.8	0.8	0.5
Hubei	2.3	1.7	2.7	2.9
Hainan	1.3	2.1	0.8	0.2
Hunan	1.8	1.7	1.9	2.3
Jiangxi	1.4	0.8	2.0	3.4
Henan	1.2	1.4	1.0	0.7
Anhui	0.8	1.2	0.7	0.7
Sichuan	0.9	1.0	0.9	0.6
Heilongjiang	0.9	1.4	0.7	0.6
Jilin	0.7	1.0	0.5	0.3
Shaanxi	0.7	1.0	0.6	0.2
Chongqing	0.6	0.9	0.5	0.4
Shanxi	0.5	0.4	0.4	0.1
Inner Mongolia	0.5	0.2	0.7	0.6
Yunnan	0.3	0.3	0.2	0.2
Quizhou	0.1	0.1	0.1	0.1
Gansu	0.1	0.2	0.1	. . .
Qinghai	. . .	. . .	0.1	. . .
Ningxia	. . .	. . .	0.0	. . .
Xinjiang	. . .	0.0	0.0	. . .

Source: CEIC database.

increased its share from 12 percent in 1995–7 to 25 percent in 2003, thereby displacing Guangdong from the lead position.[3] However, Jiangsu's share fell back to 15 percent in 2004. This has come at the expense of the relative shares of provinces such as Fujian, Tianjin, Hebei, and Hainan. Except for Fujian, however, the other provinces didn't have large shares to begin with.

Another phenomenon of some interest is the increase in FDI outflows from China. As China intensifies its trade linkages with other Asian economies, anecdotal evidence suggests that its FDI outflows have increased significantly

[3] In the early 1980s, Guangdong was heavily promoted as a leading experimental lab for market-oriented reforms, in part due to its proximity to Hong Kong SAR. By contrast, the reform of the Yangtze River Delta region (especially Jiangsu, Shanghai, and Zhejiang) was held back in the 1980s. Shanghai was a key provider of revenue to the central government and, since the experiment with a market economy was considered as being risky, central planning features were largely retained there until the late 1980s. Once it was clear that the market economy experiment was working well, reforms in Shanghai went into full swing.

in recent years. This phenomenon has been actively encouraged by the Chinese government as part of its policy of gradual capital account liberalization. Since 2001, some steps have been taken each year to ease restrictions on FDI outflows. However, while it is true that FDI outflows have risen sharply from the mid-1990s to 2005, total outflows are still modest, amounting to only about $7 billion in 2005 (Table 11.4). Many of these outflows have indeed gone to other Asian economies, especially Hong Kong SAR. The United States has, over the past decade, accounted for about 8 percent of China's FDI outflows. More recently, the Chinese government has encouraged FDI outflows to countries in Asia and Latin America in order to ensure more reliable sources of raw materials (for instance, by purchasing mining operations) and upstream products for processing in China.[4]

11.2.3 External Debt

Unlike some other emerging markets, China has been quite cautious about taking on external debt (Figure 11.5). There has been little sovereign borrowing until very recently and, as a matter of policy, enterprises have been discouraged from taking on external debt. As a consequence, notwithstanding the significant increase in the absolute amount of external debt since the mid-1980s, the ratio of external debt to GDP has remained relatively stable at around 15 percent since the early 1990s.

However, it is not just the level of external debt but also the maturity structure of this debt that has been shown to be associated with currency and financial crises. As discussed earlier, countries that have more short-term debt relative to long-term debt tend to be more susceptible to such crises. On this score, one noteworthy development is that the share of short-term debt in China's total external debt has risen significantly, from 9 percent in 2000 to 56 percent in 2005 (Figure 11.6 and Table 11.5).[5] This level is close to the threshold that some studies have identified as posing a high risk of crises. However, this increase could appear more dramatic than warranted since this ratio appears to have bottomed in 2000. Furthermore, a significant part of the increase in the relative importance of short-term debt since 2001 can be accounted for by the surge in trade credits. Trade credits constituted 32 percent of total external debt in 2003, up from 13 percent in 2001 (Table 11.5).[6]

---

[4] Official reports note that the cumulative amount of outward FDI as of the end of 2004 was $37 billion, which does not seem to match the annual data shown in this table. Based on anecdotal and other evidence, however, the upward trend in FDI outflows is incontrovertible even if the magnitudes may be suspect.

[5] The ratio of short-term external debt to GDP has risen from 1.2 percent to 7.0 percent over this period.

[6] One cautionary note about the trade credit data in the external debt statistics is that they are partly estimated from data on imports. Consequently, they do not always match the balance of payments data on trade credits (discussed below), which are based on sample surveys. But the broad trends revealed by these two sources are similar.

Table 11.4: Total outward foreign direct investment (top ten countries with the highest average % share between 2001 and 2004)

	1995	1996	1997	1998	1999	2000	2001	2002	2003	2004	2005	Average (1995–2000)	Average (2001–4)
Total amount (USD mn)	110.0	290.0	200.0	260.0	590.0	551.0	785.0	2701.0	2850.0	5500.0	6920.0		
Hong Kong SAR	18.9	39.9	4.0	4.9	4.1	3.2	25.6	13.2	9.3	17.4		12.5	16.4
United States	22.0	2.0	0.0	9.9	13.7	4.2	6.8	5.6	4.0	2.6		8.6	4.7
Thailand	60.7	1.7	0.0	0.3	0.3	0.6	15.5	0.1	1.7	0.5		10.6	4.5
Republic of Korea	3.5	0.1	0.0	0.4	0.0	0.8	0.1	3.1	6.8	11.0		0.8	5.3
Vietnam	1.8	0.7	0.3	0.9	1.1	3.2	3.4	1.0	0.3	0.4		1.3	1.3
Australia	0.9	0.3	0.0	-0.1	0.3	1.8	1.3	1.8	1.2	4.2		0.5	2.1
Cambodia	0.0	7.9	6.1	2.3	5.6	3.1	4.4	0.2	1.2	1.8		4.2	1.9
Brazil	0.5	0.6	13.7	0.6	0.1	3.8	4.0	0.3	0.0	0.1		3.2	1.1
Russia	0.1	0.0	0.8	1.0	0.6	2.5	1.6	1.3	11.9	2.0		0.8	4.2
Yemen	0.0	0.0	0.0	0.0	0.0	2.0	2.7	0.0	0.0	0.4		0.3	0.8

Source: CEIC China database.

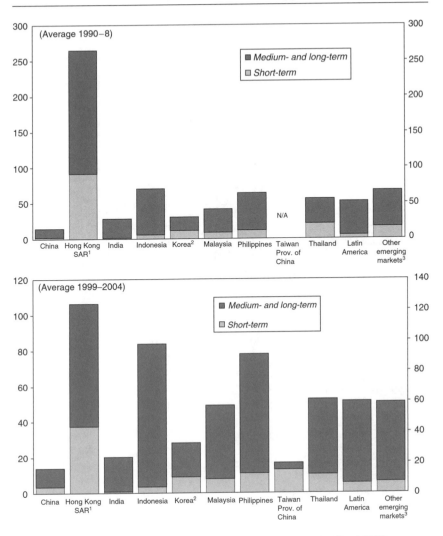

Figure 11.5: External debt: cross-country comparison, 1990–2004 (% of GDP)

Source: World Economic Outlook database, CEIC database, and joint BIS–OECD–IMF–WB statistics on external debt. Includes private sector debt.

[1] Average for Hong Kong SAR consists of data between 1996 and 1998.
[2] Average for Korea consists of data between 1994 and 1998.
[3] Average for emerging markets in EMBI+ index, excluding Latin America and Asian countries.

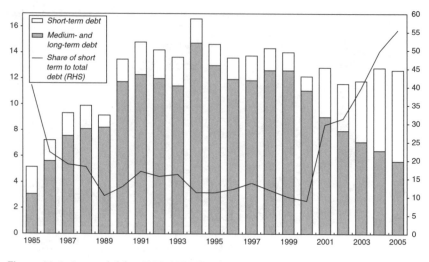

Figure 11.6: External debt, 1985–2005 (% of GDP)
Source: CEIC.

While trade credits often have short maturities, they do not pose the same type of risks as other short-term borrowing since they tend to be closely linked to subsequent export receipts.

In short, while the stock of debt is in itself not a source of concern, the maturity structure and composition of this debt bears careful observation.[7]

11.3 International Reserves[8]

11.3.1 *Recent Developments*

A different perspective on China's capital inflows is provided by examining the evolution of the balance of payments and the stock of international reserves. Table 11.6 shows that China's gross international reserves have risen sharply over the past decade, from well below $50 billion during 1990–3 to $897 billion at the end of 2005.[9]

---

[7] The World Bank's 2003 *Global Development Finance Report* (pp. 136–9) indicates that, in recent years, about 70 percent of China's outstanding long-term external debt has been denominated in US dollars, and about 15 percent has been denominated in Japanese yen. Data on the currency composition of short-term external debt are not available in this report.

[8] Some of the analysis in this section draws upon work done by members of the IMF's China team.

[9] These figures include the $45 billion used to recapitalize two state commercial banks in 2003, the additional recapitalization in 2005, and foreign exchange swaps in 2005. To

Table 11.5: External debt

	1995	1996	1997	1998	1999	2000	2001	2002	2003	2004	2005
Total											
(in billions of US dollars)	106.6	116.3	131.0	146.0	151.8	145.7	170.1	168.5	193.6	247.5	281.0
(in percent of GDP)	14.6	13.6	13.7	14.3	14.0	12.2	12.8	11.6	11.8	12.8	12.6
By Maturity											
(in percent of total debt)											
Short-term[1]	11.2	12.2	13.8	11.9	10.0	9.0	29.7	32.5	39.8	45.6	55.6
Medium and long-term debt	88.8	87.8	86.2	88.1	90.0	91.0	74.2	72.0	62.3	54.4	44.4
By Type											
(in percent of total debt)											
Registered external debt	...	...	...	...	...	...	87.3	84.6	81.1	79.7	67.7
Trade credit	...	...	...	...	...	...	12.7	15.4	18.9	20.3	32.3
Registered External Debt by Debtor[2]											
(in percent of registered external debt)											
Public and publicly guaranteed	29.2	28.8	27.5	28.5	31.2	33.6	33.5	34.8		18.4	17.3
Chinese-funded enterprises	11.0	10.6	10.2	10.6	9.7	9.3	7.6	6.9	4.9	3.3	2.4
Chinese-funded financial institutions	33.5	29.6	25.3	23.3	22.7	20.5	20.2	22.0	21.2	36.2	33.8[3]
Chinese-funded non financial institutions	10.8	9.7	8.5	6.6	5.3	3.9	2.9	3.0	2.7	...	...
Foreign-funded enterprises	2.1	3.2	5.3	6.3	...	...	23.7	22.9	24.1	24.5	26.6
Foreign-funded financial institutions	...	...	...	...	...	...	11.5	10.4	13.3	17.4	19.3[3]
Other	13.5	18.1	23.2	24.6	31.2	32.7	0.5	0.0	0.2	0.1	53.7

[1] Assumes original maturity through 2000 and remaining maturity from 2001 onwards.

[2] Effective June 2004, loans from foreign governments that are assumed by policy banks were reclassified under debt of Chinese-funded financial institutions (rather than debt of government departments). Furthermore, in 2004, the outstanding external debt of government departments decreased but that of Chinese-funded financial institutions increased by US$18.7 billion. This accounts for the sharp shift in the shares of these two categories in 2004.

[3] As of September 2005.

Sources: CEIC, Chinese authorities, and author's calculations.

Notes: Maturity structure is based on classification by residual maturity of outstanding debt.

In 2004, gross reserves rose at an even faster pace than in previous years, reaching $619 billion at the end of the year, according to official figures. However, it is necessary to add the $45 billion used for bank recapitalization at the end of 2003 to this stock in order to allow for comparability of the stock levels in 2003 and 2004 (these adjusted figures are reported in Table 11.6). Thus, we arrive at an increase of $206 billion, or an average of about $17.2 billion a month, during 2004 (compared to $162 billion, or about $13.5 billion a month, during 2003). Similarly, in 2005, adjusting official

understand the evolution of the capital account, it is relevant to include that figure in the calculations.

Table 11.6: Balance of payments (US$ billions)

	1997	1998	1999	2000	2001	2002	2003	2004	2005
Gross International Reserves	143.4	149.8	158.3	168.9	218.7	295.2	457.2[1]	663.9[1]	896.9[2]
Increase in international reserves	35.7	6.4	8.5	10.5	47.3	75.5	162.0[1]	206.7	233.0[2]
Current account balance	29.7	29.3	21.1	20.5	17.4	35.4	45.9	68.7	160.8
Merchandise trade balance	46.2	46.6	36.0	34.5	34.0	44.2	44.7	59.0	134.2
Capital account balance	23.0	−6.3	5.2	2.0	34.8	32.3	97.8	110.8	89.0
FDI, net	41.7	41.1	37.0	37.5	37.4	46.8	47.2	53.1	67.8
Errors and omissions, net	−17.0	−16.6	−17.8	−11.9	−4.9	7.8	18.4	27.0	−16.8
Non-FDI capital account balance (including errors and omissions)	−35.6	−64.0	−49.6	−47.4	−7.4	−6.7	69.0	84.9	4.4

[1] Reserves data for 2003–4 include the $45 billion used for bank recapitalization at the end of 2003. This amount is added to non-FDI capital inflows.
[2] Reserves data for 2005 include the $45 billion used for bank recapitalization at the end of 2003, as well as additional $15 billion recapitalization in April 2005, $5 billion in Sept 2005 recap, and $6 billion fx swap. These amounts are added to non-FDI capital inflows.
Sources: CEIC, PBC, SAFE, and authors' calculations.

figures for bank recapitalization yields a reserve accumulation figure of $233 billion for the year, or about $19.5 billion a month.

It is instructive to examine the factors underlying changes in the pace of reserve accumulation over time. After registering relatively small changes over the period 1985–93, reserve accumulation rose sharply and averaged $30 billion a year over the period 1994–7. This was largely due to a strong capital account, which in turn reflected robust FDI inflows on the order of $30–40 billion a year. Interestingly, the errors and omissions category was significantly negative over this period (averaging about minus $15 billion a year), suggesting that unofficial capital outflows were occurring at the same time that significant FDI inflows were coming in through official channels.

Reserve accumulation then tapered off during 1998–2000, the years right after the Asian crisis. A sharp rise in outflows on other investment and large negative errors and omissions together offset much of the effect of continued robust FDI inflows and a strong current account, the latter reflecting an increase in the trade surplus.

The subsequent sharp increase in reserves since 2001 is noteworthy, particularly because it was accompanied by a sustained export boom and the possibility—according to a number of observers and analysts—that the renminbi may have become significantly undervalued over this period.[10] It is

[10] There is a considerable range of opinions about the degree of undervaluation of the renminbi. IMF (2004) and Funke and Rahn (2004) conclude that there is no strong evidence that the renminbi is substantially undervalued. Goldstein (2004) and Frankel (2004), on the other hand, argue that the renminbi may be undervalued by at least 25–30 percent. Market analysts have a similar broad range of views.

Table 11.7: A Decomposition of the recent reserve buildup (US$ billions)

	Average 1998–2000 (1)	Average 2001–3 (2)	Change (2)–(1)	Average 2001–4 (3)	Change (3)–(1)	Average 2001–5 (4)	Change (4)–(1)
Foreign reserve increase	8.5	80.0	71.5	122.9	114.4	144.9	136.4
Current account balance	23.7	32.9	9.2	41.8	18.2	65.6	42.0
Capital account balance	0.3	40.0	39.7	68.9	68.6	72.9	72.6
FDI, net	38.5	43.8	5.3	46.1	7.6	50.5	11.9
Errors and omissions, net	−15.4	7.1	22.5	12.1	27.5	6.3	21.7
Non-FDI capital account balance (including errors and omissions)	−53.6	3.3	57.0	35.0	88.6	28.8	82.5

Sources: CEIC, PBC, and authors' calculations.

instructive to compare the factors underlying the accumulation of reserves in 2001–4 relative to 1998–2000.

Table 11.7 shows that the average annual increase in foreign exchange reserves during 2001–4 was an order of magnitude higher than during 1998–2000. The current account surplus was on average larger in the latter period, but it does not account for much of the increase in the pace of reserve accumulation since 2001. Similarly, while FDI inflows are an important contributor to reserve accumulation, there is little evidence of a major increase in the pace of these inflows in the latter period. The most significant increase is in non-FDI capital inflows (including errors and omissions), which swung from an average of minus $53.6 billion in 1998–2000 to $35.0 billion in 2001–4, a turnaround of $89 billion on an annual basis. Errors and omissions, in particular, changed from an average of minus $15.4 billion in the first period to $12.1 billion in the second.

This decomposition is significant as it shows that much of the increase in the pace of reserve accumulation during 2001–4 is potentially related to 'hot money' rather than a rising trade surplus or capital flows such as FDI that are viewed as being driven by fundamentals. The trade balance has shot up since then, rising to $134 billion in 2005 (see Table 11.6). The decomposition in Table 11.7 (last two columns) shows that the trade balance played a much bigger role in the reserve accumulation for 2001–5 relative to 1998–2000.

To better understand recorded non-FDI capital inflows, we examine more detailed information from capital and financial account transactions. Table 11.8 shows how the main items changed from 2000 to 2004. Of the total increase of $154 billion in the capital and financial account over this period, the increases in net FDI inflows and net portfolio flows account for $16 billion and $24 billion, respectively. This leaves a substantial portion, about $114 billion, to be explained by other capital flows.

Similarly, the large switch in the errors and omissions category could potentially be indicative of unrecorded capital flows into China, stimulated by the prospect of an appreciation of the renminbi against the US dollar. In this context, it is worth trying to investigate in more detail where the unrecorded flows are coming from, how much larger could they be in the absence of capital controls, and how much money may try to find its way around the capital controls. Anecdotal evidence suggests that the money flowing in is primarily accounted for by a reversal of outflows from Chinese households and corporates that took place during the 1990s to evade taxes or to avoid losses associated with a possible depreciation of the renminbi. It is difficult to answer precisely the question of how much such money is outside of China and could potentially come back into the country.

We take a simple and admittedly naive approach of adding up errors and omissions and portfolio flows and labeling the total as 'hot money' that could potentially switch directions within a short time horizon. Figure 11.7 shows the amount of such hot money flows over the past two decades.[11] The lower panel shows that the cumulative amount of errors and omissions since the early 1990s is quite large, peaking at about $150 billion, and the recent swing has reversed at best a small part of this flow. Under this interpretation, there could potentially be significant amounts of further inflows if there continues to be a strong expectation of an appreciation of the renminbi.

An alternative, and more benign, possibility is that the errors and omissions category may in part reflect an accounting issue.[12] China's officially reported holdings of foreign bonds are not marked to market in terms of exchange rate valuations while the stock of international reserves on the People's Bank of China's (PBC's) balance sheet does reflect these currency valuation effects. This implies, for instance, that any changes in the dollar value of reserve holdings could end up in the balance of payments under the errors and omissions category.[13] In the absence of published data on the currency composition of foreign exchange reserves, it is widely believed that a substantial fraction of China's foreign exchange reserve holdings is in US treasury bonds, with the remainder in government bonds denominated in euros and other currencies.[14] Given the recent large swings in the value of the US dollar,

[11] Capital flight through underinvoicing of exports or overinvoicing of imports may not show up in the errors and omissions or any other part of the balance of payments statistics. Net errors and omissions may also understate unrecorded capital flows to the extent that there are offsetting unrecorded flows on current and capital account transactions, or even among transactions within each of these categories. Gunter (2004) estimates that capital flight during the 1990s may have been greater than suggested by such crude estimates.

[12] The calculations below are based upon unpublished work by Ray Brooks.

[13] China does not report its international investment position, which would clarify this matter.

[14] There has been a great deal of recent interest in the share of Chinese official reserve holdings accounted for by US dollar-denominated instruments, particularly treasury bonds. The recent depreciation of the US dollar has fueled speculation that China has been diversifying away from US dollar bonds into other currencies.

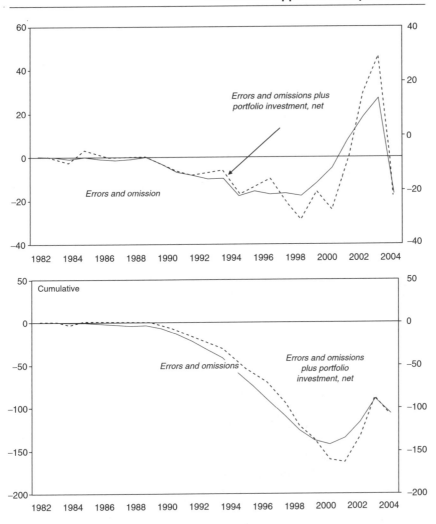

Figure 11.7: Errors and omissions and portfolio investment, net for 1982–2005 (US$ billions)

Source: CEIC and World Economic Outlook database.

however, even modest holdings of reserves in instruments denominated in other major currencies could have a significant quantitative impact on the dollar value of gross reserves.

Table 11.9 shows the effects of some simple simulations to illustrate how large these valuation effects could potentially be. For instance, in panel 1, we assume that 80 percent of China's foreign reserve holdings are in

Table 11.8: Capital flows under the financial account (US$ billions)

	2000			2004			Change in Balance
	Balance	Credit	Debit	Balance	Credit	Debit	(2004 less 2000)
Financial Account	2	92	90	156	343	188	154
Direct Investment	37	42	5	53	61	8	16
Inward	38	41	2	55	61	6	17
Outward	−1	1	2	−2	0	2	−1
Portfolio Investment	−4	8	12	20	20	1	24
Assets	−11	0	11	6	7	0	18
Equity Securities							
Debt Securities							
Liabilities	7	8	0	13	14	0	6
Equity Securities							
Debt Securities							
Other Investment	−32	42	74	83	262	179	114
Assets	−44	5	49	47	51	4	91
Trade Credit	−13	0	13	−16	0	16	−3
Loans	−18	0	19	−10	0	10	9
Currency and Deposits	−6	1	7	20	21	1	26
Other Assets	−6	3	10	52	30	−22	59
Liabilities	12	37	25	36	211	175	24
Trade Credit	18	18	0	19	19	0	0
Loans	−2	12	15	14	175	161	16
Currency and Deposits	0	0	0	2	15	13	2
Other Liabilities	−3	7	10	2	3	1	5

Source: CEIC database.

US-dollar-denominated instruments, with the remainder in euro-denominated instruments. This calculation suggests that, in 2003, roughly $16 billion, representing about 85 percent of the errors and omissions amount for the year, could be accounted for by valuation changes on the stock of reserves. In 2004, valuation changes could account for about $11 billion of unrecorded capital inflows although, in the absence of full balance of payments data at this stage, one cannot tell how this fits into the broader picture. But, as a share of the total change in reserves, valuation effects are clearly going to be a lot less important in 2004 than in 2003, both because the underlying exchange rate changes were smaller and the change in reserves was larger in 2004. The appreciation of the dollar in 2005 of course works in the reverse direction.

The remaining panels of this table show how the results change under different assumptions about (i) the share of reserves held in US-dollar-denominated bonds and (ii) the other G-3 currencies in which the remainder of the reserves are held. The results generally seem to confirm the possibility that errors and omissions in recent years may, to a significant extent, reflect currency valuation effects rather than unrecorded capital inflows. This is clearly an issue that bears further investigation in the future.

Table 11.9: Possible effects of valuation changes on reserves

Year	Foreign Exchange Reserves USD bn	Increase/Decrease in Reserves Due to Foreign Exchange Rate Change			Errors and Omissions USD bn	Exchange Rates			
		Euro	Yen	Total	USD bn	USD/Euro		USD/Yen* 100	
						Beginning of Period	End of Period	Beginning of Period	End of Period
Assumed composition of reserves: 80% U.S. dollars and 20% euros									
2000	165.6	-2.4		-2.4	-11.9	1.00	0.93		
2001	212.2	-2.2		-2.2	-4.9	0.93	0.88		
2002	286.4	10.4		10.4	7.8	0.88	1.04		
2003	403.3	16.1		16.1	18.4	1.04	1.25		
2004	609.9	10.8		10.8	24.3[1]	1.25	1.36		
Assumed composition of reserves: 90% U.S. dollars and 10% euros									
2000	165.6	-1.2		-1.2	-11.9	1.00	0.93		
2001	212.2	-1.1		-1.1	-4.9	0.93	0.88		
2002	286.4	5.2		5.2	7.8	0.88	1.04		
2003	403.3	8.1		8.1	18.4	1.04	1.25		
2004	609.9	5.4		5.4	24.3[1]	1.25	1.36		
Assumed composition of reserves: 70% U.S. dollars, 20% euros, and 10% Japanese yen									
2000	165.6	-2.4	-1.8	-4.2	-11.9	1.00	0.93	0.98	0.87
2001	212.2	-2.2	-2.7	-4.9	-4.9	0.93	0.88	0.87	0.76
2002	286.4	10.4	2.9	13.3	7.8	0.88	1.04	0.76	0.84
2003	403.3	16.1	4.3	20.5	18.4	1.04	1.25	0.84	0.93
2004	609.9	10.8	2.7	13.5	24.3[1]	1.25	1.36	0.93	0.97

Sources: IFS, CEIC, Datastream, and authors' calculations.

Notes: Foreign exchange reserves shown in the second column are end-of-year stocks. In this table, we do not include the US$45 billion used for bank recapitalization at end-2003 to the reserve stock numbers for 2003 and 2004. In principle, any currency valuation changes on that amount should affect the balance sheets of the banks to whom those reserves were transferred. Thus, the currency valuation effects would matter for the net international investment position but not for official reserves.

[1] Errors and omissions data for 2004 are based on very preliminary estimates (see notes for Table 6).

11.3.2 *Implications of the recent reserve buildup*

The fact that China's capital inflows over the past decade have been dominated by FDI is a positive outcome. As documented above, however, non-
FDI capital inflows have accounted for much of the recent surge in the pace
of reserve accumulation. This raises a question about whether, from China's
domestic perspective, the continued rapid build-up of reserves is desirable.

The literature on the optimal level of reserves (see, e.g., Aizenman and
Marion 2004 and references therein) does not provide a clear-cut way of
answering this question. The usefulness of a large stock of reserves is essentially that, especially for a country with a fixed exchange rate system, it can
help to stave off downward pressures on the exchange rate. The trade-off
results from the fact that developing-country reserves are typically held in
treasury bonds denominated in hard currencies. The rate of return on these
instruments is presumably lower than that which could be earned by physical
capital investment within the developing country, which would typically
have a scarcity of capital. In addition, the capital inflows that are reflected in
reserve accumulation could increase liquidity in the banking system, creating
potential problems in a weakly supervised banking system as banks have an
incentive to relax their prudential standards in order to increase lending.
Sterilization of capital inflows to avoid this outcome could generate fiscal costs
as the rate of return on domestic sterilization instruments is typically higher
than that earned on reserve holdings.

China, however, appears to be a special case in some respects. China's
low (controlled) interest rates imply that, since its reserve holdings are
believed to be held primarily in medium- and long-term industrial-country
treasury instruments and government agency bonds, there are in fact net
marginal *benefits* to sterilization. This is of course enabled by domestic financial repression—with no effective competition for the state-owned banking
sector—and capital controls.[15] Furthermore, with domestic investment rates
of around 40 percent (supported mainly by domestic saving, which is an
order of magnitude larger than FDI inflows), capital scarcity is apparently not
a concern, and it is not obvious that the marginal return on investment is
higher than the rate of return on reserve holdings, particularly in the likely
scenario in which the allocation of capital remains the sole prerogative of an
improving but still inefficient state banking system.[16]

Commonly used reserve adequacy indicators provide one way of assessing
the insurance value provided by reserve holdings (Figure 11.8). China's reserve
holdings provide comfortable coverage of its imports, more so than most

---

[15] This suggests that there are implicit costs to these sterilization efforts. However, determining the incidence of these costs is not straightforward; much of these costs is presumably
borne by depositors in the state banks in the form of low real returns on their deposits.

[16] See Boyreau-Debray and Wei (2004) for evidence of low returns to lending by state banks.

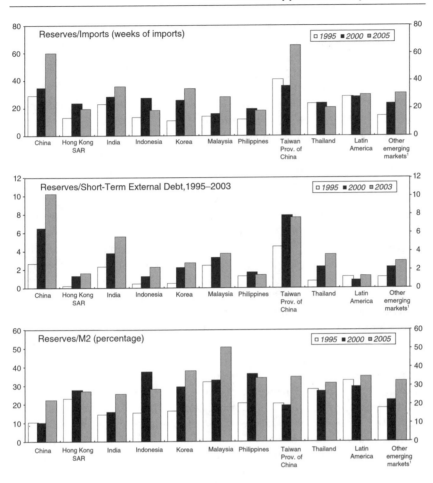

Figure 11.8: Reserve adequacy indicators, 1995–2005

Source: IFS, DOT, WEO, and Joint BIS/IMF/OECD/World Bank Statistics of External Debt.

Note: In the top panel, end-of-year reserves are shown as a ratio to the number of weeks' worth of imports in that year. Data for remaining panels are also based on end-of-year figures.

[1] Average for emerging markets in EMBI+ index, excluding Latin America and Asian countries.

other emerging markets. The stock of reserves at the end of 2005 accounted for about sixty weeks', worth of imports in that year, significantly above the corresponding figures for most other emerging markets. In terms of reserve coverage of short-term external debt, China outperforms virtually every other emerging market, with its reserves amounting to more than ten times short-term external debt (in 2003).[17] One aspect where China's position looks less

[17] Figure 11.8 uses Bank for International Settlements (BIS) data on external debt that are, in principle, comparable across countries. Based on official Chinese data, reserves amount to

favorable relative to other emerging markets is the reserve coverage of the monetary base, which is a useful indicator of reserve adequacy in the context of a currency peg. Reflecting the high degree of monetization of the Chinese economy (the ratio of M2 to GDP at end-2004 was about 1.9), reserves cover only about 20 percent of M2.

In addition to providing a buffer to stave off any future downward pressures on the fixed exchange rate, the high level of reserves has been cited as necessary to cushion the financial sector from external shocks. Reported non-performing loans (NPLs) in the banking system amounted to about 30 percent of GDP in 2003 (see Prasad *et al.* 2004), similar in magnitude to the stock of reserves, suggesting that the present level of reserves could be used to finance a bailout of the banking system if the need should arise. Indeed, the recapitalizations of three of the major state commercial banks using reserves is indicative of the intention of the Chinese authorities to use reserve holdings to help strengthen the books of state banks. However, there are concerns that deficiencies in accounting practices and the reporting of non-performing loans (NPLs) could mean that their true level is higher than the reported numbers. Furthermore, the rapid expansion of credit in recent years has contributed to an investment boom that could result in a new wave of problem loans in the future if the surge in investment results in excess capacity being built up in some sectors (Goldstein and Lardy 2004). This could justify maintaining a high level of reserves.[18]

One risk associated with maintaining a high level of reserves, however, is the vulnerability of the balance sheet of the PBC to changes in the industrial-country treasury yield curve. An upward shift in the yield curve could significantly reduce the mark-to-market value of Chinese holdings of industrial-country treasury instruments.[19] Similarly, an appreciation of the currency relative to, e.g., the US dollar could lead to a fall in the renminbi value of dollar-denominated treasury bond holdings. Since the primary sterilization instrument in China—central bank bills—is denominated in renminbi, this would lead to a net capital loss in domestic currency terms. Interestingly, this suggests that, at least on this dimension, the costs of a move toward greater exchange rate flexibility (which, under present circumstances, is expected to lead to some appreciation of the renminbi in the short run) could increase as

about six times the stock of short-term external debt, still above comparable ratios in almost all other emerging markets.

[18] Preliminary indications are that the reported ratio of NPLs to GDP has declined in 2004, but this may partly be attributable to the transfer of some NPLs off the books of state commercial banks.

[19] One could argue that these notional capital losses in mark-to-market terms should not be of concern if the Chinese authorities' intention is to hold the bonds to maturity. This argument has validity only so long as the reserves do not need to be liquidated before maturity.

the stock of reserves rises.[20] It could also increase the incentive to diversify out of dollar assets and into other hard currencies.

To summarize, there is no clear evidence that the build-up of reserves in China has significant direct sterilization costs, although it could have some efficiency costs and also expose the balance sheet of the PBC to some exchange rate and capital risks, at least on a mark-to-market basis.

11.4 Viewing China's Capital Inflows through the Prism of the Literature on Financial Globalization[21]

It has long been an article of faith among economists that international capital flows allow for a more efficient global allocation of capital. For capital-poor developing countries in particular, financial integration (with world capital markets) is seen as a key to moving onto a high growth path. In addition, financial integration in theory provides enhanced possibilities for consumption smoothing through better sharing of income risk across countries. Those developing countries that subscribed to this logic by liberalizing their capital accounts starting in the mid-1980s—a group that has come to be known as the emerging markets—captured a lion's share of the net capital flows from industrial to developing economies that took place over the subsequent decade. Capital account liberalization proved, however, to be a mixed blessing, with many emerging markets suffering debilitating financial and balance of payments crises in the late 1990s. But do the crises by themselves imply that financial integration is not advisable for developing countries? A closer look at the evidence is in order.

11.4.1 *Financial Integration and Growth*

In theory, there are a number of channels through which capital inflows can help to raise economic growth in developing countries. These include direct channels such as augmentation of domestic savings, lower cost of capital, transfer of technology, and development of the domestic financial sector. Indirect channels include the inducements for better domestic policies offered by capital account openness and the promotion of specialization of production. Theory drives one inexorably to the conclusion that financial integration *must* be good for growth.

---

[20] A related point is that if the accumulation of reserves continues apace, the potential capital loss from any appreciation would grow over time, suggesting that an earlier move toward exchange rate flexibility would be preferable from this narrow perspective (if such a move was regarded as being inevitable). In any event, we doubt if this factor will play a significant role in influencing the timing of a move toward greater flexibility.

[21] The discussion in this section draws on Prasad, Rogoff, Wei, and Kose (2003).

The empirical evidence, however, paints a far more sobering picture. It is true that emerging markets as a group have posted much higher growth on average than other developing economies over the past two decades. Notwithstanding the painful crises that many of them experienced, these countries have done far better overall in terms of raising per capita incomes. However, this does not by itself imply a causal relationship. Indeed, while there is a considerable divergence of results among different studies, the weight of the evidence seems to tilt toward the conclusion that it is difficult to find a strong and robust causal link once one controls for other factors that could affect growth (Prasad, Rogoff, Wei, and Kose (2003) provide an extensive survey of this literature). There is of course an element of endogeneity here—financial integration could induce countries to have better macroeconomic policies and improve their institutions, and this effect would not be picked up in a regression framework. However, there is at best mixed evidence that financial integration induces a country to pursue better macroeconomic policies (Tytell and Wei 2004). More research is needed on this question, but the bottom line is that it is difficult to make a *prima facie* case that financial integration provides a strong boost to growth in emerging markets.

11.4.2 *Financial Integration and Volatility*

As for volatility, economic theory has the strong implication that access to financial markets—either at the household or national level—must be welfare-enhancing from a consumption-smoothing perspective. So long as aggregate shocks (at the relevant level of aggregation) are not dominant in explaining variations in household or national income growth, financial markets should improve welfare by providing a mechanism that allows individual economic units to share their idiosyncratic income risk. The reason countries (and households) like to do this, of course, is to smooth their consumption growth and reduce the otherwise necessarily close linkage of national consumption growth to national income growth and its intrinsic volatility. While some countries may not be able to take full advantage of such risk-sharing opportunities (e.g. due to problems of monitoring and moral hazard), access to international financial markets should improve their welfare—in terms of reducing consumption volatility—at least marginally.

The reality for emerging markets is starkly different. Recent research suggests that, for these countries, the ratio of consumption growth volatility to output growth volatility in fact increased on average in the 1990s, precisely during the key period of financial globalization (Kose, Prasad, and Terrones 2003). Note that this result cannot simply be ascribed to the fact that some of these countries experienced crises during this period. In principle, a country should be able to do no worse than having its consumption growth as volatile as its income growth. Formal regression analysis controlling for a variety of other determinants of volatility and growth suggests the existence of a non-linearity in the relationship between the degree of financial integration and the relative volatility of consumption growth.[22]

An increase in financial integration from a low to a medium level tends to be associated with a rise in the relative volatility of consumption growth. At one end of the spectrum, for countries with very limited access to international financial markets, consumption growth tends to be about as volatile as income growth.[23] At the other end, industrial countries, which tend to be highly integrated into global financial markets, appear to be able to take advantage of financial openness to effectively reduce their relative consumption growth volatility. For emerging markets, the problem of course is that international investors are willing to provide capital when times are good. These countries often lose access to international capital markets precisely when times are bad (see, e.g., Kaminsky, Reinhart, and Végh 2004). Thus, sadly, it is precisely those countries that dip their toes into the waters of financial globalization that appear to be penalized by the procyclical nature of their access to world capital markets.

The situation appears bleak. Developing countries need external capital to grow. But is financial integration just 'snake oil'—delivering at best weak growth effects and exposing countries to higher volatility? The answer, it turns out, depends.

11.4.3 *The Composition of Capital Inflows Matters*

A large literature shows that it is not just the degree of financial openness, but the composition of capital inflows, that determines the quality of a developing country's experiences with globalization (see Prasad, Rogoff, Wei, and Kose 2003, for a survey and additional references for the points made below). For instance, FDI inflows tend to be far less volatile than other types of inflows. In particular, FDI appears to be less subject to sharp reversals than other types of inflows, particularly bank lending.[24] External debt, on the other hand, clearly increases vulnerability to the risks of financial globalization. In particular, debt crises are more likely to occur in countries where external debt is of relatively short maturity (see, e.g., Frankel and Rose 1996; and Detragiache and Spilimbergo 2001).

The problem, of course, is that the composition of inflows as well as related matters such as the maturity structure of external debt are not entirely

---

[22] In this subsection, the term 'relative' volatility of consumption growth should always be taken to mean its volatility relative to that of income growth.

[23] Even in a closed economy, of course, the existence of investment opportunities should allow for some degree of intertemporal smoothing of national consumption.

[24] See Wei (2001). The evidence that net FDI flows to emerging markets are less volatile than portfolio flows is weaker (see Dooley, Claessens, and Warner 1995; Wei 2001).

under the control of developing-country governments. Countries with weak macroeconomic fundamentals are often forced to rely more on external debt and end up having little choice but to borrow at short maturities. Financial integration can in fact aggravate the risks associated with weak macroeconomic policies. Access to world capital markets could lead to excessive borrowing that is channeled into unproductive government spending, ultimately increasing vulnerability to external shocks or changes in investor sentiment. In addition, lack of transparency has been shown to be associated with herding behavior by international investors, which can destabilize financial markets in an emerging market economy. Furthermore, a high degree of corruption tends to adversely affect the composition of a country's inflows, making it more vulnerable to the risks of speculative attacks and contagion effects.

Thus, the apparently negative effects of globalization appear to be related to a particular kind of threshold effect. Only countries with good institutions and sound macroeconomic policies tend to have lower vulnerability to the risks associated with the initial phase of financial integration and are able to realize its full benefits.

11.4.4 The Right Composition of Inflows for China

From a number of different perspectives, China is a prototypical developing country that is best served by FDI rather than other types of inflows. In the context of the above discussion on the benefits and potential risks of financial globalization, the dominance of FDI in China's capital inflows implies that it has been able to control the risks and get more of the promised benefits of financial integration than many other emerging markets that have taken a less cautious approach to capital account liberalization.

FDI may have served China well in other ways also. Given the low level of human capital and technical expertise in China, FDI could serve as a useful conduit for importing technical and managerial know-how (Borensztein, De Gregorio, and Lee 1998). Furthermore, the state-owned banking system is inefficient at allocating credit. This system has improved over time, particularly with the much-heralded end of the directed policy lending that these banks were forced to undertake until the late 1990s. However, most bank credit still goes to the public sector, especially since, with the controls on lending rates that existed until end-October 2004, banks were not able to price in the higher risk of lending to new and/or small firms in the private sector (see Dunaway and Prasad, 2004). As the experiences of some of the Asian crisis countries have shown, a weakly supervised banking system that is allowed to raise funds abroad and channel them into the domestic economy can generate serious imbalances. Thus, restrictions on bank borrowing from abroad can serve a useful purpose.

With a fixed exchange rate, openness to other types of financial flows, which tend to be less stable and are subject to sudden stops or reversals, would be less advisable. For instance, external borrowing by banks could cause instability in exchange markets and would have at best dubious effects on growth. Substantial opening of the capital account would also be inadvisable in this context, suggesting that the sort of selective opening that China has pursued may have some advantages (see Prasad, Rumbaugh, and Wang 2005).

11.5 What Explains the Composition of China's Capital Inflows?

China appears to have benefited from a pattern of capital inflows heavily tilted toward FDI. A key question is how China has attained such a composition of its inflows, one that many emerging markets aspire to but that few achieve. Some context is important before addressing this question. Earlier work by Wei (2000c) suggests that the size of FDI inflows into China relative to its GDP size and other 'natural' determinants is not unusually high. If anything, China seems to be an underperformer as a host of FDI from the world's five major source countries. In more recent years, with the continued rise in FDI, China may have become a 'normal' country in terms of its attractiveness as a destination for FDI.

One explanation for the composition of China's capital inflows is that it is the result of a pragmatic strategy that has been adjusted over time through trial and error. The pattern in the 1980s and early 1990s could well have reflected a combination of inertia and luck, with the post-1997 pattern reflecting the scare of the Asian financial crisis. Indeed, at the beginning of the reform period in the late 1970s and early 1980s, there were few capital inflows of any kind.

The early stage of reform sought to import only the type of foreign capital that was thought to help transmit technical and marketing know-how; hence the policy enunciated as 'welcome to FDI, but no thank you to foreign debt and portfolio flows.' Export performance and foreign exchange balance requirements were initially imposed even on foreign-invested firms. The restrictions on FDI were relaxed step by step, together with certain 'supernational treatment' (of incentives) for foreign-owned enterprises and joint ventures. Over time, the government also started to relax restrictions on foreign borrowing by corporations (and took steps to expand the B–, H–, and N–shares markets). The government declared in the mid-1990s that it intended to implement capital account convertibility by 2000.

The psychological impact of the subsequent Asian financial crisis was profound. Several countries that China had regarded as role models for its own development (especially Korea) went into deep crises in a very short period of time. It was a common perception among policymakers in China that the swings in the non-FDI part of international capital flows had played a crucial role in the process. In this sense, the Asian financial crisis caused a rethinking of the Chinese approach to capital inflows. The idea of capital account liberalization by 2000 disappeared and in its place rose the notion that the higher the level of foreign exchange reserves the better in order to avoid painful crises.

11.5.1 *Incentives and Distortions Affecting FDI*

A more traditional explanation for the composition of China's capital inflows is that the unusually high share of FDI could reflect a simultaneous policy mix of discouraging foreign debt and foreign portfolio inflows as well as providing incentives for FDI.[25] Indeed, the existence of tax benefits for FDI has meant that, until recently, the playing field was in fact tilted in favor of foreign-funded firms. This was conceivably a part of an enlightened policy choice, which included restricting other types of inflows using capital controls.

Since China promulgated laws governing foreign investment at the start of the reform, the government has offered generous tax treatment to foreign firms. In the first two years that a foreign-invested firm makes a profit, it is exempt from corporate income tax. In subsequent years, foreign companies are subject to an average corporate income of 15 percent, less than half the normal rate of 33 percent paid by Chinese companies.

Tax exemptions and reductions constitute only one aspect of government incentives favoring FDI. To capture these incentives more comprehensively and to place the Chinese FDI regime in a cross-country comparative context, we now make use of the description of the legal FDI regimes for forty-nine countries in 2000 constructed by Wei (2000*b*), who in turn relied on detailed, textual descriptions prepared by PricewaterhouseCoopers (PwC) in a series of country reports entitled 'Doing Business and Investing in China' (or in whichever country that may be the subject of the report). The 'Doing Business and Investing in . . . ' series is written for multinational firms intending to do business in a particular country. These reports are collected in one CD-ROM titled 'Doing Business and Investing Worldwide' (PwC, 2000). For each country, the relevant PwC country report covers a variety of legal and regulatory issues of interest to foreign investors, including 'Restrictions on foreign investment and investors' (typically chapter 5), 'Investment incentives' (typically chapter 4), and 'Taxation of foreign corporations' (typically chapter 16).

To convert the textual information in these reports into numerical codes, we read through the relevant chapters for all countries that the PwC series covers.

---

[25] Tseng and Zebregs (2002) discuss other factors that may have helped to attract FDI, such as market size, infrastructure, and the establishment of open economic zones, which have more liberal investment and trade regimes than other areas.

PwC (2000) contains information on incentives for FDI in the following four categories:

a. Existence of special incentives to invest in certain industries or certain geographic areas;
b. Tax concessions specific to foreign firms (including tax holidays and tax rebates, but excluding tax concessions specifically designed for export promotion, which are in a separate category);
c. Cash grants, subsidized loans, reduced rent for land use, or other non-tax concessions, specific to foreign firms; and
d. Special promotion for exports (including existence of export processing zones, special economic zones, etc.).

For each category of incentives, we then created a dummy variable, which takes the value 1 if a particular type of incentive is present. An overall 'FDI incentives' variable can then be constructed as the sum of the above four dummies. This variable takes a value of zero if there is no incentive in any of the categories, and 4 if there are incentives in all of them.

Of the forty-nine countries for which one can obtain information, none has incentives in all four categories. The median number of incentives is 1 (mean = 1.65). China is one of the only three countries that have incentives for FDI in three categories—the other two countries being Israel and Egypt. Therefore, based on this information, we might conclude that China offers more incentives to attract FDI than most countries in the world.

Of course, legal incentives are not the only things that matter for international investors. To obtain a more complete picture, one also has to look at legal restrictions. The same PwC source also offers information, in a standardized format, on the presence or absence of restrictions in four areas:

a. Existence of foreign exchange control (this may interfere with foreign firms' ability to import intermediate inputs or repatriate profits abroad);
b. Exclusion of foreign firms from certain strategic sectors (particularly national defense and mass media);
c. Exclusion of foreign firms from additional sectors that would otherwise be open in most developed countries;
d. Restrictions on foreign ownership (e.g. they may not be permitted 100 percent ownership).

We generated dummy variables for each category of restrictions and created an overall 'FDI restriction' variable that is equal to the sum of those four dummies. This variable takes the value of zero if there is no restriction in any category, and 4 if there are restrictions in all of them.

The median number of restrictions is 1 (mean = 1.69). Interesting, China is one of only five countries in the sample that place restrictions on FDI in all four categories. Different restrictions and incentives may have different effects on FDI, so they cannot be assigned equal weights. Notwithstanding this caveat, in terms of the overall legal regime, it is not obvious that China makes for a particularly attractive FDI destination (as of 2000).[26]

So far, we have been discussing explicit incentives and restrictions that are written into laws and regulations. Of course, there can be many other implicit incentives or restrictions that are nonetheless an important part of the overall investment climate in the mind of potential investors. For example, corruption and bureaucratic red tape raise business costs and are implicit disincentives for investment. Statistical analyses by Wei (2000a,b,c) suggest that these costs are economically as well as statistically significant.

To sum up, while the Chinese laws and regulations offer many legal incentives to attract FDI, they should be placed in context along with implicit disincentives as well as explicit legal restrictions in order to form a more complete assessment of the overall investment climate.

11.5.2 A Mercantilist Story

Another hypothesis for explaining China's pattern of capital inflows is that encouragement of FDI inflows is part of a mercantilist strategy to foster export-led growth, abetted by the maintenance of an undervalued exchange rate (see papers by Dooley, Garber, and Folkerts-Landau, 2004a,b; henceforth, DFG). The basic idea here is that, with a large pool of surplus labor and a banking system that is assumed to be irremediably inefficient, a more appropriate growth strategy for China is to use FDI to spur 'good' investment in the export sector and to maintain an undervalued exchange rate in order to maintain export competitiveness. To support this equilibrium, China allows manufacturers in its export markets (the US market in particular) to bring in FDI and take advantage of cheap labor to reap substantial profits, thereby building a constituency in the United States to inhibit any action to force China to change its exchange rate regime. In addition, China's purchases of US government securities as a part of its reserve holdings acts as a 'collateral' or insurance policy for foreign firms that invest in China.

While this is an intriguing story, the facts do not support it. For instance, most of the FDI inflows into China have come from countries that are exporting to China rather than importing from it (see section II). Furthermore, it is worth noting that (i) China chose not to devalue in 1997–8, even though that would have increased its exports; (ii) the massive build-up of foreign exchange

[26] The regression analysis in Wei (2000b and 2001) suggests that these FDI incentives and restrictions variables explain a part of the cross-country variation in inward FDI.

reserves is a relatively recent phenomenon; and (iii) for much of the past two decades up to 2001, the Chinese currency was likely to be overvalued rather than undervalued according to the black market premium. Even if one were to accept the DFG approach as a sustainable one, there is a conceptual question of whether it is the right approach. To take just one aspect, the sheer size of domestic saving (more than $500 billion a year) eclipses FDI (at about $45–50 billion a year, an order of magnitude smaller). Hence, writing off the domestic banking sector and focusing solely on FDI-led growth can hardly be regarded as a reasonable strategy. In short, while the DFG story is a seductive one and has many plausible elements, it does not appear to be a viable overall approach to fostering sustainable growth in China.[27]

11.5.3 *Institutions and Governance*

A different possibility, suggested by the work of Yasheng Huang (2003), is that the dominant share of FDI in China's inflows over the past decade reflects deficiencies in domestic capital markets. In particular, private firms have faced discrimination relative to state-owned enterprises, both from the banking system (in terms of loan decisions by state-owned banks) and the equity market (in terms of approval of stock listings). As a result, private firms have taken advantage of pro-FDI policies in an unexpected way and used foreign joint ventures to acquire needed capital in order to undertake investment. Foreign investors have presumably been willing to go along because they are appropriately compensated by their Chinese partners in the form of profit shares, even in cases where the foreign investors may have no particular technological, managerial, or marketing know-how to offer. If the Chinese financial system had no such discrimination in place, much of the foreign investment in the form of joint ventures might not have taken place. In this sense, the deficiency of the domestic financial system may have artificially raised the level of inward FDI.

This is an interesting hypothesis and may well explain part of the inward FDI in the 1980s. However, there is some mismatch between this hypothesis and the data, especially in terms of the time-series pattern of FDI inflows. On the one hand, inward FDI has been increasing at a rapid rate—indeed more than half of the cumulative stock of inward FDI can be accounted for by recent inflows over the period 1998–2003. This hypothesis would require a financial system ever more discriminatory against private firms. On the other hand, domestic banks have become increasingly willing to make loans to non-state firms. Similarly, in the equity market, both the absolute number and the relative share of the non-state-owned firms in the two stock exchanges have

---

[27] Roubini (2004) and Goldstein and Lardy (2005) present broader arguments against the DFG story.

been rising. Therefore, it seems to us that Huang's hypothesis is unlikely to be a major part of the explanation for the rapid rise in inward FDI in recent years.

Governance, which includes various aspects of public administration, is another potentially important determinant of the composition of inflows. Unlike other types of inflows, FDI that is used to build plants with joint ownership by Chinese entrepreneurs provides foreign investors with the best possibility of being able to successfully negotiate the bureaucratic maze in China. However, this is somewhat at odds with recent literature that has examined the role of weak institutions (high level of corruption, lack of transparency, weak judicial system, etc.) in affecting the volume and patterns of capital inflows. Low levels of transparency tend to discourage international portfolio investment (Gelos and Wei 2004). Weak public governance—especially rampant insider trading—tends to exacerbate stock market volatility, further discouraging foreign portfolio inflows (Du and Wei 2004). High corruption also tends to discourage FDI (Wei 2000c). However, taken together, these factors are unlikely to explain the particular composition of the Chinese capital inflows, since weak public governance by itself should tend to tilt the composition away from FDI and toward foreign debt (Wei and Wu 2002a).

It is not straightforward to empirically disentangle the various hypotheses that we have reviewed above for explaining why China gets more FDI than other types of inflows. In our view, the nature of the capital controls regime and the incentives for FDI appear to have played a big part in encouraging FDI inflows. But the story is not quite that straightforward, since one would expect a counteracting effect from factors such as weak governance, legal restrictions on investment by foreigners, and poor legal infrastructure and property rights. Furthermore, it is useful to keep in mind that FDI inflow figures may have been artificially inflated by the incentives for disguising other forms of inflows as FDI in order to get around capital account restrictions and to take advantage of tax and other policies favoring FDI.

11.6 Concluding Remarks

In this paper, we have provided an overview of China's capital inflows and analyzed the composition of these inflows in the context of a rapidly burgeoning literature on financial globalization. We have also examined a number of hypotheses for explaining China's success in attracting FDI inflows. Further research will be needed to disentangle the competing explanations for this phenomenon, but there is little evidence that mercantilist stories are the right answer. Understanding the reasons for China's success in tilting inflows toward FDI is important, especially as China continues its integration into the world financial market and becomes more exposed to the vagaries of these markets. China has done well so far in managing the risks associated with financial globalization, but major challenges remain to ensure that continued integration with financial markets does not worsen the risk-return trade-off.

11.7 References

Aizenman, Joshua and Marion, Nancy (2004), 'International Reserve Holdings with Sovereign Risk and Costly Tax Collection,' *The Economic Journal*, 114 (July): 569–91.

Borensztein, Eduardo, De Gregorio, José, and Lee, Jong-Wha (1998), 'How Does Foreign Direct Investment Affect Growth?' *Journal of International Economics*, 45 (June): 115–35.

Boyreau-Debray, Genevieve and Wei, Shang-Jin (2004), 'Pitfalls of a State-Dominated Financial System: Evidence from China,' CEPR Discussion Paper No. 4471 (United Kingdom: Centre for Economic Policy Research).

Detragiache, Enrica and Spilimbergo, Antonio (2001), 'Crises and Liquidity—Evidence and Interpretation,' IMF Working Paper 01/2 (Washington, DC: International Monetary Fund).

Dooley, Michael P., Claessens, Stijn, and Warner, Andrew (1995), 'Portfolio Capital Flows: Hot or Cold?' *World Bank Economic Review*, 9 (1): 53–174.

—— Folkerts-Landau, David, and Garber, Peter (2004a), 'The Revived Bretton Woods System: The Effects of Periphery Intervention and Reserve Management on Interest Rates and Exchange Rates in Center Countries,' NBER Working Paper 10332 (March), (Cambridge, MA: National Bureau of Economic Research).

—— —— —— (2004b), 'Direct Investment, Rising Real Wages and the Absorption of Excess Labor in the Periphery,' NBER Working Paper 10626 (July), (Cambridge, MA: National Bureau of Economic Research).

Du, Julan and Wei, Shang-Jin (2004), 'Does Insider Trading Raise Market Volatility?' *The Economic Journal*, 114 (498): 916–42.

Dunaway, Steven and Prasad, Eswar (2004), 'Interest Rate Liberalization in China,' Op-ed article in *International Herald Tribune*, December 3.

Frankel, Jeffrey A. (2004), 'On the Renminbi: The Choice between Adjustment under a Fixed Exchange Rate and Adjustment under a Flexible Rate.' Manuscript, Kennedy School of Government (Cambridge, MA: Harvard University).

—— and Rose, Andrew K. (1996), 'Currency Crashes in Emerging Markets: Empirical Indicators,' CEPR Discussion Papers, 1349.

Funke, Michael and Rahn, Jorg (2004), 'Just How Undervalued is the Chinese Renminbi,' *The World Economy*, forthcoming.

Gelos, Gastos R. and Wei, Shang-Jin (2005), 'Transparency and International Portfolio Positions,' *Journal of Finance*, forthcoming.

Goldstein, Morris (2004), 'Adjusting China's Exchange Rate Policies,' Institute for International Economics Working Paper 04/126 (Washington: Institute for International Economics).

Goldstein, Morris and Lardy, Nicholas R. (2004), 'What Kind of Landing for the Chinese Economy?' Policy Briefs in International Economics, No. PB04-7 (Washington: Institute for International Economics).

____ ____ (2005), 'China's Role in the Revived Bretton Woods System: A Case of Mistaken Identity.' Manuscript (Washington: Institute for International Economics).

Gunter, Frank R. (2004), 'Capital Flight from China,' *China Economic Review*, 15: 63–85.

Hausmann, Ricardo and Fernandez-Arias, Eduardo (2000), 'Foreign Direct Investment: Good Cholesterol?' IADB Working Paper No. 417 (Washington: Inter-American Development Bank).

Huang, Yasheng (2003), *Selling China—Foreign Direct Investment During the Reform Era* (Cambridge: Cambridge University Press).

IMF (2004), 'People's Republic of China: Article IV Consultation—Staff Report,' (Washington: International Monetary Fund). Available on the web at <http://www.imf.org>.

Kaminsky, Graciela, Reinhart, Carmen, and Végh, Carlos (2004), 'When It Rains, It Pours: Procyclical Capital Flows and Macroeconomic Policies,' in Mark Gertler and Kenneth Rogoff (eds.), *NBER Macro Annual 2004* (Cambridge, MA: National Bureau of Economic Research).

Kose, M. Ayhan, Prasad, Eswar S., and Terrones, Marco E. (2003), 'Financial Integration and Macroeconomic Volatility,' *IMF Staff Papers*, 50: 119–42.

Lane, Philip R. and Milesi-Ferretti, Gian Maria (2001), 'The External Wealth of Nations: Measures of Foreign Assets and Liabilities for Industrial and Developing Nations,' *Journal of International Economics*, 55: 263–94.

Mody, Ashoka and Murshid, Antu Panini (2005), 'Growing Up With Capital Flows,' *Journal of International Economics*, 65: 249–66.

Prasad, Eswar, Rogoff, Kenneth, Wei, Shang-Jin, and Kose, M. Ayhan (2003), *The Effects of Financial Globalization on Developing Countries: Some Empirical Evidence*, IMF Occasional Paper No. 220 (Washington, DC: International Monetary Fund).

Prasad, Eswar (ed.), Barnett, Steven, Blancher, Nicolas, Brooks, Ray, Fedelino, Annalisa, Feyzioglu, Tarhan, Rumbaugh, Thomas, Singh, Raju, Jan, and Wang, Tao (2004), *China's Growth and Integration into the World Economy: Prospects and Challenges*, IMF Occasional Paper No. 232 (Washington, DC: International Monetary Fund).

Prasad, Eswar and Rajan, Raghuram (2006), 'Modernizing China's Growth Paradigm,' *American Economic Review*, 96 (2, May): 331–6.

____ Rumbaugh, Thomas, and Wang, Qing (2005), 'Putting the Cart Before the Horse? Capital Account Liberalization and Exchange Rate Flexibility in China,' IMF Policy Discussion Paper 05/1 (Washington, DC: International Monetary Fund).

PricewaterhouseCoopers (2000), 'Doing Business and Investing Worldwide,' (CD-Rom).

Roubini, Nouriel (2004), 'BW2: Are We Back to a New Stable Bretton Woods Regime of Global Fixed Exchange Rates?' Nouriel Roubini's Global Economics Blog (October 8) at < http://www.roubiniglobal.com/archives/2004/10/are_we_back_to.html>.

Tseng, Wanda and Zebregs, Harm (2002), 'FDI in China: Lessons for Other Countries,' IMF Policy Discussion Paper 02/3 (Washington, DC: International Monetary Fund).

Tytell, Irina and Wei, Shang-Jin (2004), 'Does Financial Globalization Induce Better Macroeconomic Policies.' Unpublished manuscript (Washington, DC: International Monetary Fund).

Wei, Shang-Jin (2000a), 'How Taxing is Corruption on International Investors?' *Review of Economics and Statistics*, 82 (1, February): 1–11.

—— (2000b), 'Local Corruption and Global Capital Flows,' *Brookings Papers on Economic Activity*, 2: 303–54.

—— (2000c), 'Why Does China Attract So Little Foreign Direct Investment?' in Takatoshi Ito and Anne O. Krueger (eds.), *The Role of Foreign Direct Investment in East Asian Economic Development*, (Chicago: University of Chicago Press), 239–61.

—— (2001), 'Domestic Crony Capitalism and International Fickle Capital: Is There a Connection?' *International Finance*, 4 (1): 15–45.

—— and Wu, Yi (2002), 'Negative Alchemy? Corruption, Composition of Capital Flows, and Currency Crises,' in Sebastian Edwards and Jeffrey Frankel (eds.), *Preventing Currency Crises in Emerging Markets*, (Chicago: University of Chicago Press), 461–501.

12

Do China's Capital Controls Still Bind?

Guonan Ma and Robert N. McCauley[1]
Bank for International Settlements

12.1 Introduction

Divergent interpretations of the interaction of monetary and foreign exchange policies in China often form on different assumptions regarding the efficacy of capital controls. At one extreme is the view that capital controls merely change the form of capital flows without altering their magnitude. On this interpretation, pegging the exchange rate or closely managing its path implies that China imports its monetary policy and lacks control over domestic short-term interest rates. At the other extreme is the view that capital controls are still effective or binding enough to allow short-term interest rates to be set domestically, even though the exchange rate is managed.

Different views of the status quo also inform the interpretation of the likely results of further liberalization of capital flows. Again, at one extreme, this would just unevenly lower transactions costs and thereby alter the mix of cross-border capital flows, but without necessarily affecting their total volume. On this interpretation, capital account liberalization might be of interest to specialists in international finance, but not to those who follow the Chinese macroeconomy. At the other extreme, capital account liberalization would influence both the scale and composition of capital flows and ultimately force a choice between exchange rate management and an independent monetary policy.

[1] The authors wish to thank participants of the Seoul 'China and Emerging Asia: Reorganizing the Global Economy' conference of May 11–12, 2006 and the Bellagio 'New Monetary and Exchange Rate Arrangements for East Asia' conference of May 22–7, 2006 for their comments. Special thanks go to Yu Yongding and George M. von Furstenberg. The views expressed are the authors' and not necessarily those of the Bank for International Settlements.

This chapter examines both price and flow evidence to determine how effective China's capital controls have been in the past and remain at present. We put the analysis of prices first because it provides the most telling evidence on the question. Our basic conclusion is that sustained interest rate differentials argue that Chinese capital controls have continued to bind, despite the responsiveness of cross-border flows to price signals in an increasingly open economy. With capital controls still binding, future liberalization is likely to proceed incrementally rather than to leapfrog, in order to accommodate a shifting balance of exchange-rate, and financial- and monetary-stability objectives.

In what follows, Section 12.2 describes the increasing openness of the Chinese economy to cross-border flows as background for both price and flow analysis to follow. Then Section 12.3 reviews and updates the price evidence that capital controls are still binding. In particular we test whether onshore and offshore renminbi interest rates are substantially the same. In this we recognize the practical difficulty of drawing appropriate comparisons given the low level of development of money markets in China. Section 12.4 examines the gap between renminbi and US dollar short-term interest rates during the period of *de facto* dollar pegging of the renminbi between the mid-1990s and July 2005, arguing that these rates converged soon after China's inflation had fallen from double-digit levels in the early 1990s. Section 12.5 demonstrates the responsiveness of various measures of capital flows to interest-rate differentials and exchange-rate expectations. Section 12.6 discusses challenges to China's capital account liberalization. The last section concludes.

12.2 Growing cross-border flows in China

One factor conditioning the efficacy of capital controls is the size of external flows. The past two decades have witnessed a rapid rise in China's cross-border flows on both the current and capital accounts. As a share of GDP, China's gross cross-border flows more than quintupled to above 120 percent in 2005 from less than 20 percent in 1982 (Figure 12.1), with a noticeable acceleration in the 1990s. Also, notwithstanding the remarkable expansion of the gross current account flows, China's capital account flows have been gaining relative importance.[2] In 2005, gross capital account flows represented

---

[2] Lane and Milesi-Ferretti (2006) find that China's stock of international assets and liabilities has barely kept pace with the global stock, in contrast to China's growing share of global GDP and international trade. They compare asset/liability stocks to GDP flows, while we compare two types of international flows. On our measure, China's financial integration is outpacing its trade integration.

As a percentage of GDP

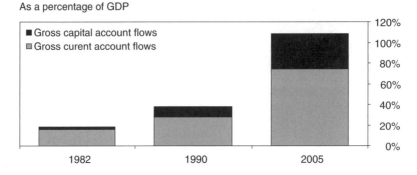

Figure 12.1: China's gross cross-border flows[1]

[1] Defined as the sum of debit and credit flows on China's balance of payments, excluding errors and omissions.
Source: CEIC.

one third of China's total gross cross-border flows, compared with just 13% in 1982 and 25% in 1990.[3]

The backdrop of growing cross-border flows suggests that the Chinese economy has grown more open and integrated into the global economy and thus more prone to influence from global markets. In particular, much larger external flows point to more opportunities to avoid and evade capital controls.

Growing trade and financial openness, however, does not support an immediate conclusion about the efficacy of capital controls. In particular, even large and highly responsive cross-border flows may limit without gutting capital controls, just as small and stable flows need not imply effective controls. A more direct and stringent test of capital control effectiveness is whether substantial cross-border arbitrage opportunities persist for a considerable period of time. Such a test, based not on flows but on onshore and offshore prices, can also indicate how effectiveness has varied over time. When price and flow measures are consistent with each other, one may arrive at an easy conclusion regarding capital mobility, but when they point in different directions, price evidence should be given more weight. In what follows, we examine both measures but put more weight on the price measures in gauging the degree of capital mobility.

[3] Gross capital account flows are likely underestimated relative to gross current account flows because some capital flows take the form of current account transactions in order to avoid official restrictions (see below). Also, most reported bank-related gross flows represent changes between two dates and do not capture any intervening gross flows.

12.3 Price test of capital mobility: onshore and offshore renminbi yields

This section analyses the combination of onshore renminbi interest rates, offshore US dollar rates, and non-deliverable forward (NDF) exchange rates to test for capital mobility between China and the offshore financial markets. The null hypothesis is that there are no substantial differences between renminbi interest rates onshore and those implied by the offshore NDFs in conjunction with US dollar Libor.[4] We interpret the evidence as supporting the alternative hypothesis of there being an economically substantial gap between on- and offshore renminbi yields. Acceptance of this hypothesis favours the view that capital controls in China have so far remained substantially binding.

12.3.1 *Measuring onshore and offshore renminbi yield differentials*

Especially in the case of relatively undeveloped money and foreign exchange markets, instruments must be chosen carefully to perform this test. Care must be exercised in the dimensions of maturity, credit, and liquidity. Ideally, one wants to compare instruments of identical maturity, issued by the same private parties, usually banks, and enjoying the same liquidity. An appropriate comparison would be between the yields on large US dollar certificates of deposit in New York versus yields on US dollar deposits posted in London by the top-rated banks that report to the British Bankers Association (BBA). Such a comparison of strictly bank rates often is based on the three-month maturity that is representative of both domestic and offshore yields. In the case of China, the challenge has come from getting a reasonable match between a representative renminbi money-market yield, on the one hand, and the NDF rate, on the other. In particular, the interbank renminbi money-market trades with greatest liquidity at very short maturities—overnight to seven days—whereas the NDF market trades with greatest liquidity at the three-month to one-year tenors.

Ma, Ho, and McCauley et al. (2004) traded off these considerations and chose to compare the three-month China interbank-offered rate (Chibor) yield to the three-month NDF. This comparison stretched to a relatively long maturity in the domestic money market, on the one hand, and took a relatively short maturity in the offshore market, on the other. Here, we update the earlier analysis with a different pair of instruments. In particular, we compare the weekly auction rates for People's Bank of China (PBC) one-year bills available since 2004 to the one-year NDF. This choice compares liquid

---

[4] For related literature on capital mobility and controls, see Frankel (1992), and Otani and Tiwari (1981). Capital controls are also discussed in the contexts of liberalization sequence (Frankel 2004; and Prasad *et al.* 2005) and financial contagion (Kawai and Takagi 2001).

Table 12.1: Credit default swap rates for People's Republic of China and British Bankers Association's Libor Panel Banks (at the one-year maturity in 2004–6, in basis points)

Issuer	Low	High	Average
People's Republic of China	5.383	27.556	11.161
US dollar Libor panel members:			
Bank of America	2.737	24.586	6.764
Barclays	5.000	9.000	6.867
Citibank	1.913	15.500	4.675
HBOS	1.832	9.000	4.459
HSBC	2.213	9.776	4.187
JP Morgan Chase	1.250	23.000	4.896
Lloyds	1.919	6.517	3.390
BMTU	6.844	63.000	19.018
Norinchukin	5.835	19.976	9.433
Rabobank	3.439	11.881	5.910
Royal Bank of Scotland	2.650	6.201	3.972
Royal Bank of Canada	2.000	11.383	5.081
UBS	1.919	7.325	3.497
WEST LB	2.833	22.833	6.885
Average across banks	*3.027*	*17.141*	*6.360*

Source: Markit.

instruments in both markets, although it introduces a possibly confounding credit difference between the sovereign bill and the bank NDF or deposit.

Liquidity across the two markets matches well at the one-year tenor. The PBC issued CNY 1.2 trillion (about $150 billion) of its one-year bills in 2005 out of a total bill issuance of CNY 2.8 trillion, for an average weekly issuance of about $3 billion equivalent.[5] In January–March 2006, issuance ranged between CNY 40 and CNY 120 billion per week. In the NDF market, the one-year is reportedly the most traded maturity.

With regard to credit, comparing sovereign and bank yields onshore and offshore, respectively, is problematic in principle, but in practice it does not skew the comparison substantially. Credit default swaps suggest that the credit standing of China attracts an insurance payment of only a handful of basis points more than that of the major international banks that form the Libor panel (Table 12.1). Since in the period 2004–6, offshore renminbi rates were lower than the onshore PBC bill yield, the mixing of sovereign and bank credit does favor the finding that capital controls are effective. But as we shall see below, the scale of the yield difference dwarfs the five-basis-point credit difference.

Before examining the data, it might be useful to consider a particular example of an arbitrage transaction at the one-year tenor by a multinational firm with a profitable operation in China. Since September 2003, the offshore

[5] *China Money* (2006), 2: 76.

speculative demand to be long in renminbi has given the treasurer of such a firm a strong incentive in effect to hold renminbi onshore and to sell them forward offshore (i.e. lending renminbi onshore and borrowing them offshore). One way of constructing such a position is for the affiliate in China *not* to convert renminbi into dollars in order to remit a dividend to its parent outside China. Instead the funds are retained in renminbi and invested in the Chinese money market. The yield on the one-year deposit is proxied by the PBC bill rate (one can think of a bank taking the funds in trust and investing in the PBC bill). Thus, renminbi funds have been lent onshore.

Simultaneously, the affiliate borrows dollars at one-year Libor, replacing the cash flow of the unpaid dividend from China, and sells renminbi one year forward against US dollars, say to a hedge fund. This combination of dollar borrowing and forward position amounts to borrowing renminbi offshore and converting the proceeds into dollars, and the rate of interest paid is (by construction) the relatively low NDF-implied renminbi yield. At the end of the year, the renminbi invested onshore can be sold for dollars at the then-prevailing spot exchange rate that is also used to determine any profit or loss on the NDF, leaving the firm with the arbitrage gain between the interest rate in the Chinese money market and the lower offshore yield. Thus, by *lagging* a current dollar payment, namely the profit repatriation, the firm has in effect acquired a long renminbi position and locked in a gain by selling it offshore.[6]

12.3.2 *Onshore-offshore renminbi yield differentials based on three-month Chibor*

As noted, our earlier analysis compared a domestic interest rate, the so-called three-month Chibor, to the offshore renminbi rate implied by three-month NDFs and dollar Libor. We found significant differences. Figure 12.2 compares the three-month yield gap for the renminbi with Asian peers for the periods of 1999–2001 and 2002–4. The absolute value of the gap between renminbi yields onshore and offshore averaged 250–300 basis points in the five years to early 2004. This placed China in the middle of our sample, with smaller differentials than those seen in the Philippines and India, on the one hand, but larger differentials than those in Taiwan (China), and Korea, on the other. The narrowing of the differentials in 2002–4 was in fact less evident in the case of China than for most of the other Asian currencies. A gap of 250–300 basis points is very wide compared to the onshore-offshore differential of 20

[6] An opposite case could be considered for the earlier period in the wake of the Asian crisis. A multinational firm with operations in China could profit from a short-onshore, long-offshore renminbi position. If it could borrow renminbi onshore, it could accelerate dollar payments to an affiliate abroad, which could buy renminbi forward against dollars offshore.

Guonan Ma and Robert N. McCauley

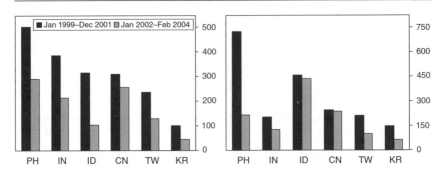

Figure 12.2: Average absolute onshore–offshore yield Spreads

Note: PH = Philippines; IN = India; ID = Indonesia; CN = China; TW = Taiwan (China); KR = Korea.
Source: Ma, Ho, and McCauley (2004).

to 30 basis points observed for the yen before capital controls were lifted in the early 1980s (Otani and Tiwari 1981).

The evolution of the renminbi yield gaps over the period from late 1998 through early 2006 is also quite informative. The gap averages 310 basis points in absolute value but goes through several phases (Figure 12.3). In the period from the Asian financial crisis through early 2001, the weight of offshore positioning on the renminbi was in the direction a weakening renminbi, resulting in higher yields offshore. This was consistent with China's foreign exchange reserves growing more slowly than would be suggested by the reported current account surplus and net direct investment inflows (see below). Then followed a period of smaller differences that saw offshore rates below those onshore but with a gap less than 150 basis points.

In basis points

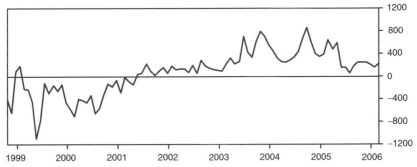

Figure 12.3: The onshore less offshore CNY yields, based on three-month Chibor
Note: onshore less offshore yield.
Source: Bloomberg; PBC, authors' own estimates.

With the intensification of public pressure from trading partners on the renminbi's exchange rate policy in September 2003, however, offshore yields dropped substantially below their onshore counterparts. Reserve growth far exceeded the pace that could be explained by the current account and direct investment balances (see below). The average onshore/offshore yield gap widened to more than 360 basis points during January 2003 to April 2006. The gap reached a peak value of fully 800 basis points in mid-2005 when the implied offshore yield fell well below zero. But since the July 2005 policy change, the yield gap has narrowed markedly to less than 200 basis points.

The principal message based on the three-month tenor of the Chibor and CNY NDF is that the estimated onshore/offshore gap in the renminbi yields has been substantial, persistent and consistent with prevailing market pressures. In other words, hitherto, China's capital controls have prevented sufficient cross-border arbitrage to equalize onshore and offshore short-term yields.

12.3.3 *Onshore-offshore renminbi yield differentials based on PBC bills*

The above finding that offshore renminbi yields have traded below those onshore over the past two years is confirmed by another test based on a newly available and more liquid benchmark money-market yield in renminbi in China. As noted above, the introduction of a weekly auction of PBC bills in early 2004 has provided an alternative basis for comparison of domestic renminbi money-market yields with the renminbi yields implied by the NDFs traded offshore. The one-year maturity makes for a good match, with most PBC bills issued at this maturity and the one-year NDF being the most actively traded. This more telling and updated test, covering the two years between April 2004 and April 2006, produces a much smoother estimate of the yield gap, consistent with better liquidity in both markets.

The updated test based on trading in liquid market segments offers further evidence of binding controls. The gap averages 300 basis points based on the one-year PBC bill, compared to an average of 350 basis points based on the three-month Chibor over the same period. Both updated estimates exceed the average of 280 basis points calculated for the earlier period of 1999–2004 and suggest two distinct phases since April 2004. Before the July 2005 policy move, the gap was wider and more volatile, reacting to policy comments and market rumours. The absolute average spread for this first phase was around 400 basis points on both estimates. Since the July 2005 policy shift, the yield gap has shrunk to less than 200 basis points based on three-month Chibor and to around 100 basis points based on the one-year PBC bill.

It is remarkable that the narrowing of the onshore-offshore interest differential occurred in the wake of the July 2005 policy change that many observers found to be more modest than expected. This resulted from the Chinese

In basis points

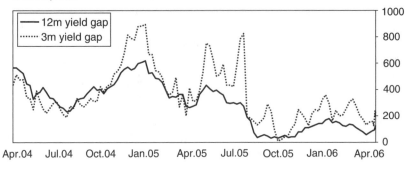

Figure 12.4: Onshore less offshore NDF-implied yields

Note: weekly data; 12-month (3-month) NDF, one-year PBC bill yield (3-month Chibor) and 12-month (3-month) Libor.

Source: People's Bank of China, Bloomberg, BIS estimates.

authorities' managing to combine a movement of the spot exchange rate with descriptions of their policy intentions in a way that left the one-year NDF broadly unchanged (Figure 12.5). This case of 'inelastic expectations' stands in contrast to the frequent experience of exits from a pegged exchange rate regime that have moved expected exchange rates even further away from the spot exchange rate. The Chinese authorities' 'solemn declaration' that another jump in the exchange rate was not contemplated seems to have been accepted by market participants who often scoff at such statements. Indeed, the dispersion of near-term views on the renminbi's exchange rate, as measured by the volatility of the three- or six-month NDFs traded offshore, declined.

How should this recent convergence of offshore to onshore renminbi yields be interpreted? Those observers with a prior conviction that capital controls cannot long remain effective in the presence of growing cross-border flows can read the reduction of the onshore-offshore renminbi interest rate differential as demonstrating the waning effectiveness of capital controls. This possibility is supported to some extent by the flow evidence to be discussed in the next section.

We propose an alternative interpretation. In early 2005, the Chinese authorities prepared for the exchange rate regime shift by widening the renminbi-dollar interest differentials, reducing the one-year PBC bill rate to about 1 percent even as US dollar one-year Libor rose. Technically, the PBC bill rate was guided lower both by reducing the PBC interest rate on excess reserves, which sets the floor for interbank rates, from 1.62% to 0.99% in February 2005, and by scaling back open market operations to drain liquidity in the following months. The roughly 3 percent excess over the official onshore yields in June and early July 2005 (Figure 12.4) thus incorporates the offshore

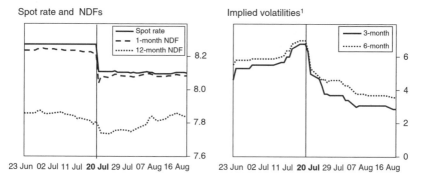

Figure 12.5: Exchange rate, NDFs, and implied volatilities of the Renminbi[2]

[1] The vertical lines indicate last closing prices before the announcement.
[2] In percent.
Source: Bloomberg; HSBC; national data.

renminbi yields of about −2 percent, due to positioning in anticipation of an appreciation. Since the regime change, the one-year PBC bill rate has been guided up from 1 to about 2 percent, while US policy rates have increased even more. This has opened up a 3.5 percent gap between US and renminbi yields. At the same time, the Chinese authorities have suggested a 3–4 percent annual appreciation through statements and the pace of the spot crawl. The consistency of such exchange rate expectations and the dollar-renminbi interest rate differential keeps onshore and offshore renminbi rates not far out of line. We see the narrowing of the onshore and offshore renminbi yield differential as the outcome of a particular policy conjuncture between China and the United States rather than as a forced outcome of the weight of money.

In sum, one might go so far as to say that the normalization of US interest rates has allowed the Chinese authorities to use covered interest rate parity as an operating guide for the combination of their money-market interest rate and exchange rate policies during the transition towards greater currency flexibility. One possible consideration might be to lessen the policy burden on capital controls, which have been binding but not watertight. Should the US interest rate cycle reverse dramatically or China raise interest rates sharply, market pressure could build up once more, again putting capital controls to the test.

12.4 Price measures: tests of uncovered interest parity

The failure of the onshore and offshore renminbi yields to equalize through cross-border arbitrage indicates that capital controls bite. This in turn points to a degree of monetary independence in China. This section addresses this

321

In basis points

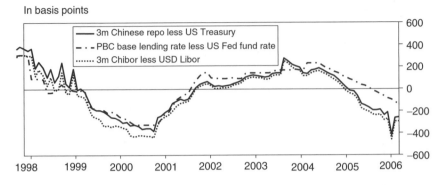

Figure 12.6: Domestic CNY yields less US dollar yields
Source: CEIC.

question directly by first assessing the gap between short-term yields in China and the United States and then by comparing the difference between short-term interest rates in these two economies and that between the United States and the euro area.

12.4.1 *Interest rate differentials in a period of de facto fixed exchange rates*

China and the United States went through very distinct interest rate cycles during 1996–2006, despite the *de facto* dollar peg of the Chinese renminbi until July 2005. Figure 12.6 reveals sizable and sustained albeit varying differentials between short-term renminbi yields in China and the US dollar yields in the United States and the United Kingdom. Yield differentials, whether measured in terms of policy rates or short-term money-market rates, have generally been 100 basis points or more in absolute value. In sum, experience between the tightening of the peg to the dollar in 1997 and its loosening in mid-2005 suggested that the Chinese monetary authorities could still set a somewhat independent domestic policy (even in the face of capital flows responsive to the resulting yield gap, as shown below).

Cheung, Chinn, and Fujii (2003) fit autoregressive models to the short-term interest rate differential between China and the United States and find that 'the lagged uncovered interest differential variables are positively significant and indicative of strong persistence... If monies are free to move across markets, arbitrage can generate profits based on the pattern of persistent deviation and help restore the parity. However, this kind of arbitrage activity is quite difficult, especially in the short run, given the prevailing capital controls in the PRC.'

Another finding of Cheung *et al.* (2003) has been read by Eichengreen (2004) as indicating that the capital controls have become less effective over time. In particular, Cheung *et al.* report a statistically significant downtrend in the interest rate differential over the sample period January 1996 to May 2002.[7] Eichengreen's interpretation is weakened, however, if the result depends on data from the early to mid-1990s. Recall that China experienced a bout of moderately high inflation, reaching 20 percent, in 1994–5, triggering a draconian tightening by the authorities. The one-month Chinese interbank rate remained at double digit levels in 1995–7 and was 6 percent to 8 percent throughout 1998. Only after the Asian financial crisis had delivered sharp deflationary shocks to the Chinese economy through its appreciation of the effective exchange rate of the renminbi did Chinese policymakers cut interest rates repeatedly.

Thus, if one divides the 1996–2005 period into two equal subsamples, the results point to policy convergence based on inflation convergence in the earlier period rather than any ongoing attenuation of the effect of capital controls. As the regression results in Appendix 12.1 show, the trend that Cheung *et al.* (2003) identify characterizes China's period of pronounced disinflation in 1996–2000 when the Chinese authorities generally tightened capital controls in order to shield the economy from the shocks of the Asian crisis. In 2000–5, when China considerably deepened its participation in the global economy and controls were generally relaxed, the estimated trend convergence of short-term interest rates drops from 100 basis points a year to 15 basis points per year, and the trend loses its statistical significance. If closer financial integration forces interest rate convergence given exchange rate stability, it is hard to account for the lack of convergence in the more recent years.

Thus, the distinct interest rate cycles in China and the US support the idea that China's capital controls have bound sufficiently to offer policymakers some degree of short-term monetary autonomy under a *de facto* dollar peg. The observed convergence of policy rates in the 1990s owed more to inflation convergence than weaker capital controls. Indeed, Granger causality tests suggest that of the three interest rate pairs shown in Figure 12.6, none of the causality runs from the US rate to the Chinese rate. Indeed, the null hypothesis that the three-month Chinese repo yield does not cause the three-month US Treasury bill yield cannot be rejected! Rather than happenstance, the inflation and interest rate convergence in 1996–2000 can be seen as reflecting the dollar peg's provision of a useful *medium-term* monetary anchor through traded goods prices.[8] However, what matters is that in the context

---

[7] The authors caution: 'there is a subtlety involved in using parity conditions to evaluate the level of integration. When a parity condition is rejected, then...diminutions of deviations may be due either to greater economic integration, greater convergence of economic policies, or both' (Cheung *et al.* 2003: 6). We incline to policy convergence.

[8] Robert Mundell and Ron McKinnon have long stressed the importance of the renminbi's *de facto* dollar peg as a credible nominal anchor. It remains, however, an empirical question

Table 12.2: Interbank rate differentials: Renminbi–dollar and Euro–dollar (bps)

	One-week		Three-month	
	Chibor/Libor	Euribor/Libor	Chibor/Libor	Euribor/Libor
Av. of absolute difference	160.47	143.45	166.64	144.56
Max of the differential	173.36	190.04	213.16	166.81
Min of the differential	−429.58	−281.50	−439.01	−284.07
Standard deviation	181.39	156.60	194.88	157.37
Correlation coefficient	0.32	0.58	0.21	0.60

Note: The interbank market offer rates are Chibor for the renminbi, Libor for the US dollar and Euribor for the euro; monthly data from January 1999 to March 2006.
Source: CEIC.

of low inflation in both countries, capital controls have permitted Chinese interest rate policy to diverge from that of the Federal Reserve in the short term, notwithstanding the exchange rate linkage.

12.4.2 *Relative monetary independence*

It might be objected that the yield differentials just considered are not wide enough to indicate monetary independence. This objection suggests the usefulness of a benchmark. How do the differentials between the domestic renminbi yields and global dollar yields compare to those between the euro and dollar yields? The euro area, after all, is another large economy, but one with a flexible exchange rate and an open capital account. Any similarity in dollar and euro yields cannot reflect the exchange rate policy of the euro area (unlike, say, any similarity in US and Hong Kong dollar yields).

The differentials between Chibor and Libor are no narrower than those between Euribor and Libor (Table 12.2). Indeed, at both the seven-day and three-month maturities, the average differentials between Chibor and Libor are wider than those observed between Euribor and Libor. While the range of the yield differentials between the Chibor and Libor is much wider than those between Euribor and Libor, this might be attributed to the lack of development and consequent volatility of the Chinese money market.

More tellingly, for the period under consideration, Euribor and Libor exhibit greater positive co-movement than do Chibor and Libor. These results hold as well across split samples. Thus, the evidence from interbank market yields suggests that China, with a fixed exchange rate and continued capital controls,

as to how much of the inflation convergence should be attributed to this anchor as opposed to strong-arm Chinese macro controls. The US Fed tightened aggressively from 1994 to mid-1995 when the renminbi was first stabilized against the US dollar. In the following three years, the Fed eased somewhat while Premier Zhu Rongji took forceful measures to control domestic inflation until the Asian crisis delivered strong deflationary shocks to the Chinese economy.

does not import its interest rate policy from the United States to any greater extent than the euro area. This observation is consistent with the view that capital controls in China remain binding.[9]

12.5 Flow evidence on effectiveness of capital controls

Flow measures provide useful indications of cross-border interactions between the onshore and offshore markets, giving indirect evidence of capital mobility. However, there are two qualifications to using flow evidence to gauge the efficacy of capital controls. First, the intensity of capital controls over different types of capital flows may vary. Thus capital mobility could differ across types of capital flows. Adapting the analysis to such differences, however, is made difficult by more restricted flows in effect taking the form of less restricted flows. Second, observed flow measures of capital mobility cannot address the question of how large a flow is required to equalize the associated prices. Thus, such evidence needs to be combined with discussion of price measures. Our flow evidence suggests that while China's capital-account controls are not watertight, with certain cross-border flows responding to market conditions, these flow measures do not challenge the main findings that capital controls are still substantially binding.

12.5.1 A discriminating regime of capital controls

China's capital control regime discriminates among different cross-border flows. Given a large trade sector, the current account convertibility commitment in 1996 and the WTO entry in 2001, China's current account has been quite open. Even with respect to the capital account, controls apply only to a quarter or so of the IMF categories (Prasad and Wei 2005). Welcoming and encouraging foreign direct investment (FDI) has been a long-held policy, and movements on this account and in associated trade credit have the potential to arbitrage on- and offshore yields. Outward direct investment, to be discussed below, has until recently been tightly regulated and thus has provided little scope for such arbitrage. Portfolio flows and most external debts have been tightly controlled. However, authorized banks have been allowed to transact cross-border to accommodate decisions of onshore non-bank depositors and borrowers, including those depositing and borrowing in foreign currency.

[9] This is a much harder test than a benchmark based on US dollar and Hong Kong dollar yields, since Hong Kong has a dollar-based currency board and no capital controls. Appendix 12.2 shows that these HKD/USD benchmarks would be even more advantageous to our arguments. The USD/HKD yield pairs exhibit narrower and more stable differentials and much higher correlations than do the Chibor/Libor or Euribor/Libor pairs.

Hence care must be taken in both devising and interpreting flow measures when gauging the efficacy of capital controls. For instance, large FDI inflows need not suggest ineffective capital controls, although they may provide scope for arbitrage transactions. Conversely, a lack of bank flows may only indicate the combined response to currency expectations and relative yields. We discuss a variety of such flow measures below, in order of the complexity of their construction.

12.5.2 Cross-border flows under the current account

As investors respond to market pressure, remaining capital controls may entice some capital flows to circumvent official regulations via a large and liberalized current account. Two particular current receipts and payments give such evidence. They are rising net inward remittance transfers and flattening dividend/interest payments in recent years. Both point to the possibility that avoidance and evasion of capital controls are distorting the current account.

Remittance inflows, predominantly private, more than tripled between 2001 and 2005, suggesting capital inflows from Chinese residents' overseas relatives (Figure 12.7). In 2005, net current transfers reached $25 billion, up from $8 billion in 2001 and represented some 15 percent of China's current account surplus. With outward current transfers rising only to $2.5 billion in 2005 from $0.6 billion in 2001, much of the jump in net transfers apparently was driven by rising inward current transfers. The Chinese government, which had traditionally encouraged such dollar inflows, moved in late 2004 to require banks to report unusually large remittance inflows and the related dollar sales, with a threshold of daily conversion of dollars into the renminbi in excess of $10,000 per transaction (SAFE 2004). This new reporting requirement remains effective to date.

In billions of US dollars

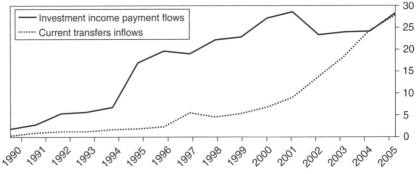

Figure 12.7: Investment income and current transfers flows of China
Source: CEIC.

The other flow measure is the suspiciously weak current investment income payments by multinational firms and other foreign investors in China.[10] Outward dividend and interest remittances by foreign companies operating in China have flattened since 2001 at around $25 billion per annum, after quintupling between 1995 and 2000 (Figure 12.7). This is rather puzzling even given the decline in dollar yields after 2000, considering that both of China's foreign equity liability and external debts appeared to have doubled during this episode. At the same time, most Chinese companies listed at the Hong Kong Stock Exchange recorded stronger corporate profits. These oddly stagnant current account outflows could be a possible sign of disguised capital inflows into China. As discussed earlier, there are strong incentives for foreign firms to delay converting their renminbi profits onshore into dollars even if they cover this long renminbi position through offshore NDFs.

These unusual cross-border flows in recent years suggest that capital inflows could occur through a liberalized current account, especially after the authorities tightened controls on incoming capital. If we assume that recorded remittance inflows overstated, and recorded investment income outflows understated, their respective true 2005 levels by one-third, capital inflows into China through the more liberalized current account could have exceeded $16 billion or 10 percent of the reported $160 billion current account surplus.[11]

12.5.3 *Foreign currency bank deposit flows*

Changes in foreign currency deposits held by Chinese households and firms with banks in China respond to changing market conditions and give rise to cross-border flows through the banking system.[12] Figure 12.8 shows that onshore foreign currency deposits held by Chinese residents have tracked exchange rate expectations. Appendix 12.3 shows that they respond to interest rate differentials as well. As a share of total bank deposits, dollar deposits rose in 1999 and 2000 when offshore speculation of renminbi depreciation prevailed, reaching a peak of 8 percent. Since then, appreciation expectations have led to a trend decline in the ratio (and sometimes even absolute declines of dollar deposits) to less than 4.5 percent of total bank deposits by the end of 2005.

Such flows do not directly shed light on the issue of the efficacy of capital controls, because Chinese residents, although subject to constraints in their

[10] According to the IMF guidelines, multinationals' profits are accounted for as current-account outflows regardless of whether they are paid out as interest and dividends or accompanied by offsetting capital inflows as in the case of retained earnings. In China's case, however, the actual accounting treatment of retained earnings is not clear.

[11] There could also be under- and overinvoicing of exports and imports in response to market conditions.

[12] See McCauley and Mo (2000), and Ma and McCauley (2002a, 2002b, 2003 and 2004a).

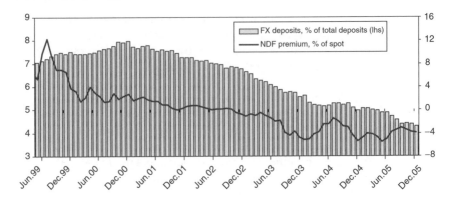

Figure 12.8: Onshore foreign currency deposits and exchange rate expectations

Note: Total deposits include both renminbi and foreign currency deposits; 12-month NDF. A negative premium indicates expectations of appreciation.

Source: CEIC; PBC; Bloomberg; authors' own estimates.

initial dollar acquisition, are permitted to hold foreign currency deposits onshore. Similarly, the Chinese banking sector is authorized to offset domestic surpluses or deficits in dollars with cross-border deposits or borrowing from global banks. Nevertheless, these permitted cross-border flows could help reduce the effectiveness of the remaining capital controls. The main point is that they have not been large enough to eliminate the onshore/offshore renminbi yield gaps.

12.5.4 *Net flows of errors and omissions*

Cross-border flows under 'errors and omissions' in the balance of payments can be seen as a general measure of unrecorded capital flows and often have been cited in the literature on China's capital flight (Jin and Li 2005; and Song 1999). This residual fluctuated sharply in response to market conditions, from an annual outflow of $15 billion during the 1995–9 period of high inflation, the Asian financial crisis and expectations of renminbi depreciation to an inflow averaging $20 billion in 2003–4 amid expectations of renminbi appreciation (Figure 12.9). Of this latter period, Prasad and Wei (2005) write 'that, given the apparent one-way bet on the renminbi, the fact that these flows are not larger than they are suggests that capital controls may be at least partially effective.'

While often interpreted as indicating the direction of unrecorded capital flows, errors and omissions should be interpreted with caution. In particular, the errors and omissions in China's balance of payments could have captured valuation changes of the official foreign exchange reserves (positive when the dollar falls against major currencies, leading to an errors and omission inflow),

In billions of US dollars

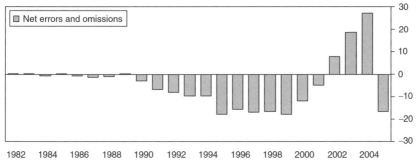

Figure 12.9: Net errors and omissions on China's BoP
Source: CEIC.

which have nothing to do with capital controls or capital mobility. Thus, the surprising net outflows under errors and omissions in 2005 partly resulted from dollar strength (Prasad and Wei 2005).

In sum, various flow measures point to both current account and capital account flows responding to market conditions and thus suggest limits to the effectiveness of China's capital controls. However, some of these capital flows are permitted, while others can take place only by circumventing regulations. Hence, the existence of large capital flows is not sufficient evidence of capital controls being so leaky as to be ineffective. What is most striking, though, is that, despite the obvious limits on the ability of capital controls to prevent very substantial cross-border flows, sizable onshore-offshore yield gaps have persisted, as have very distinct US–China interest rate cycles.

12.6 Challenges to capital account liberalization

Whether China's capital controls still bite have important implications for future liberalization. The current effectiveness may condition the pace and sequence of decontrol. On the one hand, if controls are largely ineffective and non-binding, the task of further liberalization would be relatively simple and the effect would be mostly on the recorded composition of capital flows, with more implications for financial stability than for monetary policy. If, on the other hand, capital controls remain substantially binding, future liberalization still poses real challenges to policymakers, potentially affecting both the scale of capital flows and their composition, and with important implications for monetary policy.

China's sophisticated capital control regime has two important features. First, capital controls are intended to be tighter for cross-border flows thought to be more volatile than for more stable flows. Second, the regulatory regime over time has shifted from one biased against outflows toward one managing two-way cross-border capital flows in a more balanced fashion. Looking ahead, Chinese policymakers face two related challenges in liberalizing the capital account. First, is setting up rules to manage potentially highly variable short-term capital flows such as portfolio and deposit flows. As noted above, China's current account openness has already made it more difficult to control such short-term flows, while China's ample foreign exchange liquidity makes it easier to accept their inherent volatility. The second challenge is to open up additional channels for permitted capital outflows and to put in place a regulatory framework to deal with the associated risks (Ma and McCauley 2003). This section discusses three such liberalization measures: easier outward direct investment, further relaxation of the 'QFII' and 'QDII' schemes, and freer conversion of renminbi deposits into dollars for overseas uses.

12.6.1 *Outward direct investment*

Since 2001, China has experimented with a policy of promoting overseas direct investment by Chinese companies. The previous discouragement of such outflows was in contrast to the long-pursued policy of encouraging inflows of foreign direct investment. The result of this policy bias is the order of magnitude difference between an estimated $610 billion of direct investment liability and the corresponding $55 billion of such assets in China's end-2005 international investment position. As of June 2006, the government had scrapped foreign exchange quotas for outward investment, simplified approval and annual review processes, allowed all profits to be reinvested abroad, and improved access to offshore guarantees issued by Chinese banks. This policy shift intends to promote outflows to lessen the external surplus, to secure access to natural resources overseas and to encourage the growth of selected large Chinese companies. Outbound direct investment by Chinese companies rose from less than $2 billion in 2004 to $11 billion in 2005.

However, with capital controls still binding, the impact of this policy shift on China's capital account could extend in effect well beyond the category of direct investment itself, if the experience in other Asian economies offers any guidance. With an expanded overseas presence, treasurers of Chinese companies could more readily manage their financial and currency exposure with large-scale transactions spanning both their onshore and offshore operations. Such enhanced ability to engage in cross-border arbitrage would tend to weaken controls on other types of capital flows and foreign exchange activities (such trade credit and covered forward trading). The Korean experience before and during the Asian financial crisis suggests that inter-office trade credit flows, debts incurred by overseas subsidiaries and cross-guarantees all afforded Korean conglomerates extra degrees of freedom in the face of various official restrictions (Cho and McCauley 2003). Thus, Chinese policymakers need to be aware about the potential for restricted transactions to occur in effect within the intra-corporate accounts of Chinese-based multinationals.

12.6.2 *Qualified institutional investor schemes*

China has attempted to institutionalize the management of two-way portfolio flows under the so-called 'qualified foreign institutional investors' (QFII) and 'qualified domestic institutional investors' (QDII) schemes. The former regulates portfolio inflows while the latter manages outflows. Both schemes involve pre-approval procedures, quota management, foreign exchange conversion rules, instrument restrictions, and intensive reporting requirements.

Before the QFII scheme was first implemented in 2003, foreign investors could not invest in local equity and bonds onshore, with the sole exception of a tiny foreign-currency-denominated B-share market. Until the QDII scheme, non-bank Chinese residents were prohibited from directly investing in overseas securities, while banks could invest their own dollar liquidity in fixed income instruments. Resident issues of both equity and debt securities in offshore markets must also go through a rigorous approval process.[13] Nonresident issuers found it impossible to tap the onshore markets before the two special IFC and ADB renminbi bond issues in 2005.[14] Thus, measured two-way portfolio flows are effectively regulated and their variation can be expected to shed little light on the efficacy of capital controls (hence their exclusion from the last flow measure examined above).

QUALIFIED FOREIGN INSTITUTIONAL INVESTORS SCHEME (QFII)

The QFII scheme was initially introduced as an attempt to boost the domestic stock markets.[15] As of May 2006, the investment quota for the QFII scheme had reached a cumulative $7 billion, divided among some forty QFII investors.[16] The total QFII investment amounts to around 1 percent of China's

---

[13] Examples include the so-called H-shares issued by Chinese companies at the Hong Kong Stock Exchange and international bonds issue by China Development Banks. Beside H-shares, Chinese companies have also sought listing in other international stock exchanges such as New York Stock exchange (N-shares), London Stock Exchange (L-shares) and Singapore Stock Exchange (S-shares).

[14] IFC and ADB issued so-called renminbi-denominated 'panda bonds' worth RMB 1.13 billion and RMB 1 billion, respectively, in China in 2005.

[15] The Chinese A-share stock market had been languishing for several years and currently is still undergoing a wrenching overhaul as the authorities address the majority of shares that are held off-market by the state.

[16] QFII players have access only to exchange-listed local currency securities in China (A-shares, local currency convertible bonds, treasury and mutual funds) but could not directly participate in China's interbank bond and money markets. The China Index Bond Fund of the ABF2 family has been the first ever QFII allowed into the interbank bond market. Global banks do have access to the interbank bond and money markets through their domestic branches, however.

stock market capitalization. This compares with some 40 percent of foreign ownership in the Korean stock markets and 7 percent in Taiwan in 2002. In India, foreign institutional investors own 6 percent of the total stock-market capitalization but represent nearly 18 percent for the top 200 companies listed in the Bombay Stock Exchange (CEIC database). The Asian experience provides overwhelming evidence that foreign portfolio investors in Asia are more interested in equity securities than in local debt securities, either because of portfolio considerations or of market impediments to investing in local fixed-income instruments.

There is room for further relaxing China's QFII scheme. Domestically, there is a need to expand the role of institutional investors in the retail-dominated Chinese stock markets. This need is all the more pressing in view of the prospect of massive public share offerings in the coming years as the overhang of state shares is resolved. In the end, however, such QFII arrangements can be seen as no more than transitional measures in the process of capital account liberalization. For example, a similar QFII scheme in Taiwan, China (hereafter Taiwan) was established in 1992 and abolished in 2003 as the authorities gained experience and confidence, not least as a result of their large holdings of international reserves.

QUALIFIED DOMESTIC INSTITUTIONAL INVESTOR (QDII) SCHEME

In April 2006, the PBC formally announced a QDII scheme that will permit Chinese individuals and companies to invest in overseas securities. The new scheme comprises three key elements. First, Chinese individuals and institutions can, via authorized banks and subject to quotas, convert their renminbi bank deposits into dollars onshore for investing in overseas 'fixed-income' products. Second, Chinese individuals and institutions can, via authorized securities companies and fund managers and subject to quotas, invest dollar deposits now held onshore into overseas securities including equity shares.[17] Third, authorized domestic insurers can convert their renminbi funds into dollars to invest in overseas bond and money-market instruments, subject to certain prudential requirements.

The QDII scheme is designed to manage portfolio outflows via licensed banks and fund managers and with the aid of investment quota and instrument restrictions. Through the scheme, Chinese private-sector investors will gain institutionalized access to international financial markets. The timing of the introduction of the QDII scheme seems comfortable, since it permits some autonomous cross-border portfolio flows needed for a more market-based renminbi exchange rate, and helps to hold down the rapid foreign

---

[17] As discussed in Ma and McCauley (2002b), the Chinese government opened up the foreign currency denominated B-share market to Chinese residents already holding dollar deposits onshore.

reserve build-up at the PBC.[18] As will be discussed below, the Chinese resident investment in foreign equity could potentially reach as high as $150 billion in a few years.

Looking forward, the QFII and QDII schemes may interact to shape the liberalization process. While accelerated portfolio inflows via a bigger QFII window may spur further relaxation of the QDII scheme that caps portfolio outflows, a more liberalized QDII channel may potentially invite even more capital inflows. Thus, these two schemes are likely to expand the trend for two-way gross portfolio flows, allow volatile net portfolio flows in response to market conditions, and thereby make capital controls less binding. In sum, policymakers need to anticipate the possibility that further liberalization of the currently still binding controls may lead to increased volatility in cross-border flows.

12.6.3 *Generalized Liberalization of resident deposit conversion*

As the QDII scheme evolves, China's capital decontrol may eventually progress to a stage where Chinese households and companies are free to convert their bank deposits between local and foreign currencies and move their funds across the border, for whatever purposes. Conceptually, there could be two distinct liberalization phases. First, Chinese residents might be allowed to freely convert renminbi and foreign currency bank deposits onshore. Second, Chinese residents might be allowed to transfer foreign or local currency funds across the border via the banking sector without restrictions.

As already discussed, foreign currency deposits in China have been sensitive to both relative yields and exchange rate expectations (Appendix 12.3). If China's capital controls currently remain binding, policymakers need to assess the potential for instability arising from freer switching of bank deposits between renminbi and foreign currency. Onshore currency conversion of bank deposits will have ramifications for cross-border bank flows, since a change in the difference between onshore dollar deposits and dollar loans in the Chinese banking sector tends to result in a net cross-border interbank flow. These cross-border transactions in turn show up in the positions of international banks *vis-à-vis* Chinese banks as reported to the BIS (Ma and McCauley, 2002b).

Our discussion focuses mostly on the first liberalization phase. An important step in this direction was the April 2006 announcement of a $20,000 ceiling on free conversion of renminbi into foreign currency by Chinese individuals per person per year. On the reasonable assumption that 10 million

---

[18] The QDII scheme has operated informally on a trial basis since late 2005 and involved China's National Social Securities Fund and some selected Chinese insurers. Market analysts predict the initial QDII quota to be modest—within a range of $2 billion to $10 billion in 2006, compared to the foreign reserves of $870 billion.

Table 12.3: Ratio of foreign currency deposits to total deposits (2000–5)[1]

	China	India	Korea	Taiwan	Indonesia	Hong Kong
Mean	6.63	2.89	4.22	5.27	18.10	46.48
Max	8.02	3.42	7.59	6.38	23.50	48.30
Min	4.30	2.31	2.79	3.38	14.67	44.37
St Dev (annualized)[2]	0.84	0.32	0.92	0.70	2.53	1.67
FC deposits ($bn)[3]	161.57	3.97	18.63	45.27	19.22	249.31

[1] Percent; total deposits include both local and foreign currency deposits; monthly data.
[2] Annualized standard deviation of monthly changes in the percentage share.
[3] End of 2005.
Source: CEIC; authors' estimates.

wealthier Chinese residents could take full advantage of this quota, the annual onshore switching of renminbi into dollars could reach $200 billion a year or 12 percent of the total renminbi household savings deposits as of 2005. This still partial liberalization thus allows much more than 5 percent diversification upon liberalization envisioned by Goldstein (2004).

This possible shift under the $20,000 ceiling can be usefully compared to other Asian benchmarks for both the level and variation of foreign currency deposits (Table 12.3). At one extreme, the share of foreign currency deposits is nearly half of the overall deposits in Hong Kong's liberal banking sector. At the other extreme, 'deposit dollarization' represents no more than 3 percent of the total deposits in India's restricted banking system. China's ratio rests in the middle, comparable to that of Taiwan and Korea. In the case of Indonesia, on the other hand, the recent history of high inflation may partly explain its relatively high share of dollar deposits in its onshore banking system. We think that Taiwan, where remaining controls on resident purchases of dollars essentially do not bind, may be the most relevant case for China—the ceilings of Taiwanese individuals and companies converting their NT dollars into US dollars are, respectively, US$5 million and US$50 million a year.

What could be expected to happen to the average ratio of foreign currency deposits in China were restrictions on converting renminbi deposits into foreign currency to be eliminated? While the Hong Kong example suggests that a sum could be switched that is the same order of magnitude as China's foreign exchange reserves, the Taiwanese example suggests that not much would happen.[19]

---

[19] In Hong Kong's case, for example, the high dollar portion may simply be a by-product of its status as a free international financial center as well as possibly a wealth effect. See Lai and Shi (2003). Moreover, most of the foreign currency held in Hong Kong is held in US dollars, which for a generation has shown little volatility against the Hong Kong dollar. To some extent, US dollar holdings may reflect deposit-pricing strategies of Hong Kong banks in offering better yields on large, US dollar deposits to more price-sensitive clients.

Variation in the foreign currency deposit share could be a source of instability in cross-border capital flows. As restrictions on currency conversion are eased, one would expect the holding of foreign currency deposits by residents to be more responsive to market interest rate differentials and exchange rate expectations.[20] A regime of liberal currency switches of bank deposits thus might not only raise the average dollar share but make foreign currency deposits less sticky and thus raise their volatility. This volatility of the foreign currency deposit share, as measured by annualized standard deviation of monthly changes in the share, ranges from 0.3 to 2.5 percentage points for the selected Asian markets (Table 12.3). The economy with a highest standard deviation is Indonesia, where much of the variation must reflect valuation changes from the volatile rupiah exchange rate rather than the flows that are of interest to policymakers.

Going beyond these summary statistics, Taiwan's case again provides the basis for a more relevant stress test since its foreign exchange regulations are essentially non-binding. A very large shift to foreign currency holdings took place in the latter half of the Federal Reserve's previous tightening cycle in April-December 2000. Taiwan's foreign currency deposit share rose by 3.7 percentage points on an annual basis. If we take this episode as a stress test for China, a rise of 4 percentage points in the foreign currency deposit share would imply a conversion of renminbi into dollar deposits on the scale of some $130 billion per annum. This sum is below the aforementioned scenario of $200 billion annual dollar purchase and well covered by China's current foreign reserve holding of $870 billion, even given the potential claims represented by short-term external debt of around $100 billion. Hence, whether one considers a theoretical maximum or a worst case from a neighboring economy, China's new liberalization measure of conversion of renminbi into dollars would not appear to pose an excessive liquidity risk.

Nevertheless, two implications of such a scenario are worth exploring. First, as Chinese residents switch renminbi into dollars and the banks sell dollars for renminbi, the PBC could well be on the other side of the market selling dollars to banks. Other things being equal, Chinese banks might add the proceeds to their offshore interbank deposits or holdings of dollar securities. This would entail a shift of China's external assets from the official sector to the banking system, amounting to the privatization of China's official dollar holdings. Thus the dollar exposure would be more evenly distributed across the economy rather than concentrated in the official sector. Second, an abrupt shift from renminbi to dollar deposits could pose challenges to monetary policy-making. Since dollar deposits are excluded from the current

---

[20] See Fung and McCauley (2001), and Ma and McCauley (2002*a* and 2002*b*). Other factors such as exchange rate volatility as well as confidence in the local financial system may also potentially affect the observed variation of the foreign currency deposit share.

Chinese M2 measure, this shift would slow down M2 growth, other things being equal. Should this deceleration of M2 be taken seriously and resisted with lower policy rates? Or should this measured M2 weakness be discounted as a reflection of portfolio shift bearing no message about future growth? Once this broad question is answered, monetary operations would need to take into account any foreign exchange market intervention accommodating the initial deposit shift as well as the gap between reserve requirements on renminbi and foreign currency deposits.

Beyond easing the switching of deposits onshore between currencies is policy governing the transfer of foreign or local currency funds offshore through the banking sector. Thus, the next guidepost in the capital account liberalization process could be a gradual relaxation of regulations over cross-border movements of bank deposit. On the one hand, an immediate question is when to liberalize foreign-currency bank deposit outflows. In some way, the newly introduced QDII scheme has already opened the door, allowing the $160 billion in foreign currency accounts to flow into foreign securities, including equities. On the other hand, cross-border renminbi flows could be allowed to take place only in phases. Renminbi bank inflows from abroad should not be an issue for the time being, since offshore renminbi funding is strictly prohibited, except the limited special arrangement of renminbi bank deposits in Hong Kong (HKMA 2006). Similarly, renminbi bank outflows could for the time being only be contemplated *vis-à-vis* Hong Kong. Further down the road, with offshore renminbi deposits outside of Hong Kong and offshore renminbi loans, the issue of internationalizing the renminbi may come into view.

12.7 Conclusion

We find that China's capital controls remain substantially binding. They prevent the equalization of onshore renminbi yields and those implied by offshore NDFs. We also find that the observed convergence of short-term interest rates between China and the United States was more characteristic of the mid- to late-1990s than of the years since. China's short-term interest rate setting seems no more imported from the United States than that of the euro area.

That said, capital flows between China and the rest of the world do respond to interest rate differentials and to expected exchange rate changes. With interest rates favouring the dollar and expectations of exchange rate appreciation contained, recent reserve growth has owed more to underlying current account and direct investment flows than to speculative capital flows. For now, the Chinese authorities may find it convenient to take the burden off the capital controls by signaling a rate of appreciation against the dollar that is broadly consistent with the interest rate differential. How long this stance will continue to be convenient in view of the changing interest differentials will determine when the effectiveness of capital controls will again be tested in a major way. Finally, our findings may also help shed light on how policymakers in China may pace the country's ongoing capital account liberalization.

Appendix 12.1

We estimate the following equation relating Sino-American interbank interest rate differentials to a time trend using monthly data for the sample period of January 1996 and July 2005. We test the hypothesis that the observed convergence of interest rates between the US and China varied over time. The sample period is evenly split into two sub-periods: (1) 01/1996 to 10/2000, and (2) 11/2000 and 07/2005. The time trend is negative and statistically significant in the first period. But it was statistically insignificant in the second period. We read this as suggesting that the observed convergence in the first period was driven more by converging inflation and policy cycles in the two economies than diminishing effectiveness of capital controls in China.

$$I_t = 6.212D_1 + 1.585D_2 - 0.086T_1 - 0.012T_2$$
$$(17.73) \quad (4.48) \quad (-8.32) \quad (-1.15)$$
$$\text{Adj } R^2 = 0.59; DW = 0.175; LLF = -192.8$$

Where
I_t = the absolute value of the differential of one-month Libor and Chibor
D_1 = dummy variable for the period of January 1999 to October 2000
D_2 = dummy variable for the period of November 2000 to July 2005
T_1 = linear trend variable for the period of January 1999 to October 2000
T_2 = linear trend variable for the period of November 2000 to July 2005

Appendix 12.2

Hibor and Libor Differentials

	One-week Hibor/Libor	Three-month Hibor/Libor
Av of absolute difference	54.1	47.0
Max of the differential	71.2	99.7
Min of the differential	−222.8	−213.0
Standard deviation	54.8	58.9
Correlation coefficient	0.965	0.965

Note: Monthly average from January 1999 to March 2006.
Source: CEIC.

Appendix 12.3

We estimate the following two equations relating the share of foreign currency bank deposits to interest rate differentials and exchange rate expectations using monthly observations for the sample period of June 1999 to December 2005. We test the hypotheses that, as a share of total bank deposits, foreign currency holdings respond to both dollar/renminbi yield differential and expected CNY/USD exchange rate changes. In regression (1), the null hypothesis of a unitary coefficient for the lagged dependent variable is rejected. When one treats (1) as a partial adjustment model, on the reasonable interpretation of still-binding foreign exchange controls in China, the long-run effect for the relative yield and currency expectations is 0.864 and 0.409, respectively.

$$F_t = 0.108 + 0.019R_t + 0.009E_t + 0.978F_{t-1}$$
$$(1.24) \quad (2.11) \quad (1.97) \quad (73.31)$$

Adj R^2 = 0.994; DW = 2.109; LLF = 84.41   (1)

$$\Delta F_t = -0.033 + 0.018R_t + 0.005E_t$$
$$(-3.39) \quad (1.98) \quad (1.15)$$

Adj R^2 = 70.196; DW = 2.091; LLF = 83.05   (2)

Where
F_t = the share of foreign currency deposits in total bank deposits, adjusted for valuation effects after July 2005
ΔF_t = the first difference of F_t
R_t = the interest rate differential (onshore USD minus CNY 12-month rate)
E_t = CNY NDF premium or discount as a share of the spot rate

References

Cheung, Yin-Wong, Chinn, Menzie D., and Fujii, Eiji (2003), 'The Chinese Economies in Global Context: The Integration Process and its Determinants', *NBER Working Paper* No. 10047, October.

Cho, Yoonje, and McCauley, Robert N. (2003), 'Liberalising the Capital Account without Losing Balance: Lessons from Korea', in 'China's Capital Account Liberalisation: International Perspectives', *BIS Papers*, no. 15 (April): 75–92.

Eichengreen, Barry (2004), 'Chinese Currency Controversies.' Paper presented at the Asian Economic Panel of Hong Kong, April.

Frankel, Jeffrey (1992), 'Measuring International Capital Mobility: A Review,' *American Economic Review*, 82(2): 197–202.

Frankel, Jeffrey (2004), 'On the Renminbi: The Choice between Adjustment under a Fixed Exchange Rate and Adjustment under a Flexible Rate.' Paper presented at the High-Level Seminar on Foreign Exchange System, Dalian, China, 26–7 May.

Fung, Ben and McCauley, Robert N. (2001), 'Analysing the Growth of Taiwanese Deposits in Foreign Currency,' *BIS Quarterly Review* (September): 49–56.

Goldstein, Morris (2004), 'Adjusting China's Exchange Rate Policies.' A discussion paper of Institute for International Economics presented at the IMF seminar on China's foreign exchange rate system, Dalian, 26–7 May.

Hong Kong Monetary Authority (2006), 'Hong Kong's Renminbi Business Two Years On,' *HKMA Quarterly Bulletin* (March): 38–43.

Jin, Lou and Li, Zinai (2005), 'A Study of the Efficacy of China's Capital Controls,' *World Economy*, 8 (August): 22–31 (in Chinese).

Kawai, Masahiro and Takagi, Shinji (2001), 'Rethinking capital controls,' draft paper.

Lai, Kitty and Shi, Joanna (2003), 'Factors Influencing the Share of Hong Kong Dollar Deposits in Total Deposits,' *HKMA Quarterly Bulletin* (September): 15–22.

Lane, Philip and Milesi-Ferrantti, Gian Maria (2006), 'The External Wealth of Nations Mark II: Revised and Extended Estimates of Foreign Assets and Liabilities, 1970–2004,' *IMF Working Paper*, no 06/69.

Ma, Guonan, Ho, Corrinne, and McCauley, Robert N. (2004), 'The Markets for Non-deliverable Forwards in Asian Currencies', *BIS Quarterly Review* (June): 81–94.

____ and McCauley, Robert N. (2002*a*), 'Following Chinese Banks' Foreign Currency Liquidity', *BIS Quarterly Review* (June): 18–19.

____ ____ (2002*b*), 'Rising Foreign Currency Liquidity of Banks in China,' *BIS Quarterly Review* (September): 67–73.

____ ____ (2003), 'Opening China's Capital Account amid Ample Dollar Liquidity', in 'China's Capital Account Liberalisation: International Perspectives', *BIS Papers*, no. 15 (April): 25–34.

____ ____ (2004*a*), 'Tracing China's Foreign Exchange Liquidity,' *BIS Quarterly Review* (March): 26–7.

____ ____ (2004*b*), 'Effectiveness of China's Capital Controls: Some Empirical Evidence.' Paper presented at the Second KIEP–PRI seminar 'Financial Independence and Exchange Rate Regimes in East Asia,' Tokyo, December.

McCauley, Robert N. and Mo, Y. K. (2000), 'Foreign Currency Deposits of Firms and Individuals with Banks in China,' *BIS Quarterly Review* (August): 35–9.

Otani, Ichiro and Tiwari, Siddharth (1981), 'Capital Controls and Interest Rate Parity: The Japanese Experience 1978–81,' *IMF Staff Papers* (December): 793–815.

Prasad, Eswar, Rumbaugh, Thomas, and Wang, Qing (2005), 'Putting the Cart before the Horse? Capital Account Liberalization and Exchange Rate Flexibility in China,' *IMF Policy Discussion* Paper, PDP/05/01, January.

Prasad, Eswar and Wei, Shang-Jin (2005), 'The Chinese Approach to Capital Inflows: Patterns and Possible Explanations,' *IMF Working Papers*, no. 05/07, April.

Song, Wenbin (1999), 'A Study of China's Capital Flight: 1987–1997,' *Economic Research*, No. 5, May (in Chinese).

State Administration of Foreign Exchange (SAFE) (2004), 'Reporting Rules by Financial Institutions on Unusually Large Foreign Exchange Transactions,' October, Beijing.

13

Impact of Financial Services Trade Liberalization on Capital Flows: The Case of China's Banking Sector[1]

Li-Gang Liu
Hong Kong Monetary Authority

Elvira Kurmanalieva
National Graduate Institute for Policy Studies, Tokyo, Japan

13.1 Introduction

China is undergoing a process of simultaneous, though gradual, domestic financial liberalization and capital account opening. At the same time, its financial sector is also experiencing increased foreign competition, as the country has already started to allow considerable foreign participation in its domestic financial sector. 2007 will be a watershed year because China will have to implement fully its WTO commitments on financial services trade liberalization under the General Agreement on Trade and Services (GATS).

While foreign banks in emerging markets promote efficiency through enhanced competition and skill transfer (Claessens, Demirguc-Kunt, and Huizinga 2001; Committee on the Global Financial System (CGFS) 2004), they also pose challenges to policymakers in managing liberalization pace, upgrading supervisory skills, and conducting monetary policy. Indeed, empirical findings suggest that with more countries embarking upon domestic financial

[1] The first version of this paper was written when the first author was a visiting senior fellow at Research Institute of Economy, Trade and Industry (RIETI), affiliated with the Japanese Ministry of Economy, Trade and Industry. The authors would like to acknowledge helpful comments from Barry Eichengreen, Hans Genberg, Masamachi Kono, Yung Chul Park, Wensheng Peng, Martin Schulz, Hui Tong, Willem Thorbecke, Masaru Yoshitomi, and seminar participants at RIETI, HKMA, and this conference. Vu Hoang Nam provided valuable research assistance. The views expressed here are those of the authors alone.

liberalization, the risk of financial crises has also increased. It was observed that since the 1980s, over two-thirds of the IMF member countries have experienced significant problems in the banking system (Lindgren, Garcia, and Saal 1996). Studies on the relationship between financial liberalization and banking crisis also indicate that financial liberalization raises the probability of a banking crisis (Demirguc-Kunt and Detragiache 1998). Furthermore, in emerging market economies, a banking crisis is usually associated with a balance of payment crisis when the country's capital account is open (Kaminsky and Reinhart 2000).

Because financial services trade liberalization often involves capital flows, foreign participation will complicate the process of domestic financial and capital account liberalization in China. It is hypothesized that foreign bank participation will accelerate both domestic financial and capital account liberalization and in particular, it will make China's capital control regime progressively more ineffective, thus leading to *de facto* capital account liberalization. Without corresponding changes to the exchange rate regime and in the conduct of monetary policy, China may experience inherent policy inconsistencies that could potentially lead to a banking and balance of payment crisis.

This chapter examines these issues in two steps: First, it reports that foreign banks, in spite of their small presence in China, have already played an important role in channeling capital flows in and out of the country. Second, it examines the impact of the liberalization commitments made under the GATS in financial services and especially in the banking sector on international bank loans to developing economies. Specifically, the empirical study hopes to shed light on whether the financial services trade liberalization helps promote bank loans to developing economies.

The chapter proceeds as follows: Section 13.2 provides an updated review of the GATS with a focus on the financial services. Section 13.3 documents the role of foreign banks in channeling capital flows in and out of China. Section 13.4 presents some empirical findings on whether the financial services trade liberalization commitments promote bank loans to emerging market economies. Section 13.5 concludes and discusses implications for policy.

13.2 Financial Services Trade Liberalization Under the GATS

13.2.1 *GATS Rules: An updated review*

Financial services trade liberalization negotiations (FSTLN) under GATS aim at reducing or even totally removing all trade barriers in the financial services sector by allowing foreign financial firms in sectors such as insurance, banking, and securities to enter a host country and enjoy *national treatment*. The GATS, launched in the Uruguay Round in 1986, was not able to reach any agreement until April 1994, several months after the conclusion of the Uruguay Round at the end of 1993 (Kono, *et al.* 1997). Negotiations on financial services were also extended far beyond the Uruguay Round and finally reached an agreement in 1997. In the current and new Doha Round of WTO negotiations, financial services and other services will be a 'built-in' agenda, thus having the benefit of renewed emphasis (Key 2003).

FSTLN specifies general commitments, specific exemptions, and modes of supply of services. These commitments govern modes of financial services supplied, although they may differ from country to country because of the level of commitments and can be phased out over time depending on the initial agreements. However, the general commitments of GATS also apply to FSTLN and they have the following features (Kono *et al.* 1997):[2]

- Most favored nation status (MFN): All liberalization measures must be extended to all WTO members equally.

- Market access and national treatment: WTO member countries cannot discriminate between domestic and foreign firms, except when explicitly indicated at the time of joining the GATS.

- Transparency: Local regulations should be published and made accessible to all.

- Progressive liberalization: Member states agree to increase the number of liberalized sectors and to eliminate exceptions within sectors by committing to future negotiating rounds.

- Dispute settlement mechanism: All commitments are legally binding. States can initiate an arbitration procedure. If found harmed, the country can impose sanctions against the violating country.

However, FSTLN also has some important exemptions:

- Exemption for government services: Activities of the central banks or other government authorities carrying out monetary and exchange rate policies are excluded from GATS.

---

[2] International contestability of markets is based on three pillars: (1) National treatment and market access; (2) Domestic structural reform, and (3) Freedom of capital flows, but the current financial services trade liberalization agreement under the GATS only deals with the first issue, national treatment and market access. The second issue will be a central topic of the Doha Round. The third issue is a concern of the IMF and not a trade liberalization issue (Key 2003).

Table 13.1: Domestic versus international capital flows under GATS: Mode 1

	Loans provided by domestic banks	Loans provided by foreign banks abroad
Loans involve domestic capital only	No financial services trade and international capital flows	Financial services trade only
Loans involve international capital only	International capital flow only	Both financial services trade and international capital flows

Source: Kono and Schuknecht (2000) with author's change of classification.

- Prudential carve-out: This ensures that host-country governments can protect their domestic financial system and participants of the financial system through the application of the host-country prudential standards. These prudential measures in principle do not have to comply with the national treatment, market access commitments, and its most favored nation responsibility (Key 2003).[3] However, the prudential carve-out is not meant to be an overriding exception to a member's obligations, as prudential measures should not be used to avoid a member's obligation or commitments.

- Some non-prudential-related government regulations (e.g. practices related to industrial policy to provide credit to certain industries) are also exempted from the commitments of the GATS unless such policies violate the general commitments as specified above (Kono *et al.* 1997).

Similar to other types of services, FSTLN also covers four modes of supply: cross-border, consumption abroad, commercial presence, and movements of natural persons.

- Mode 1 or cross-border supply: If there is a consumer in country A and a supplier in country B, the service crosses the border to meet the need of the consumer in country A (e.g. a Japanese bank in Tokyo lends to a Chinese firm in Shanghai). Depending on the nature of transactions, this mode of supply in financial services will often involve not only financial services but also capital flows (Table 13.1).

- Mode 2 or consumption abroad: This refers to a scenario in which a consumer in country A has to travel to country B where the service supplier is located in order to conduct a transaction (e.g. a Japanese company opens a bank account with a bank in China (a Japanese, other

[3] Because there is no necessary test of the validity, such 'carve-outs' could be potentially used as restrictions or barriers for foreign entry. In addition, only a sovereign, not a private bank, can bring complains to the WTO dispute panel (Key 2003).

Table 13.2: Domestic versus international capital flows under GATS: Mode 3

	Loans provided by domestic banks	Loans provided by foreign banks in the country
Loans involve domestic capital only	No financial services trade and international capital flows	Financial services trade plus inward FDI
Loans involve international capital only	International capital flow only	Financial services trade plus FDI and international capital flows

Source: Kono and Schuknecht (2000) with author's change of classification.

foreign, or even a domestic Chinese bank) for transactions occurring in China).

- Mode 3 or commercial presence: This refers to a service in country A provided by a supplier in country B that makes place at a permanent place of business located in country A (e.g. a Japanese bank lends firms in China through its branches there) (Table 13.2).

- Mode 4 or movements of natural persons: This refers to a service in country A is provided by country B with personnel imported from country B (e.g. A branch of a Japanese bank draws its management from its headquarters in Tokyo).

Table 13.3 uses commercial bank business as an example to highlight the areas in which foreign bank entry not only brings about financial services trade but also cross-border capital flows. Out of seventeen categories of banking business in Mode 1, only three types of banking business can take place without involving capital flows (financial leasing, provision of financial information, and financial advisory). Only in Mode 3 (commercial presence) can most financial services trade occur so long as foreign capital is not involved. China, given its existing capital controls, does not allow most of the Mode 1 and Mode 2 operations of foreign commercial banks (Table 13.4).

Despite these perceived limitations, FSTLN under GATS is an important step forward in liberalizing the financial service trade worldwide as it provides national treatment to foreign financial firms, promotes transparency of financial regulations, and promises further liberalization in financial services. Similar to foreign direct investment in manufacturing sectors, the impact of foreign participation in a host country may be much larger than one can contemplate based only on the existing WTO rules and regulations.

345

Table 13.3: Financial services trade (FST) and capital flows under different modes of supply (no capital account restrictions)

Category of Banking and other Financial Services Business	Mode1: Cross-border supply Can FST occur without cross-border capital flow?	Mode 2: Consumption abroad Can FST occur without cross-border capital flow?	Mode 3: Commercial Presence Can FST occur without cross-border capital flow?
Acceptance of deposits	N	N	Y
Lending (consumer credit, mortgage, commercial loans)	N	N	Y
Financial leasing	Y	N	Y
Payments and money transmission (credit cards, travellers checks, and bankers drafts)	N	N	Y/N[a]
Guarantees and commitments	N	N	Y
Securities trading			
Money market instruments	N	N	Y
Foreign exchange	N	N	N
Derivatives	N	N	Y/N[a]
Exchange rate and interest rate instruments	N	N	Y/N[a]
Transferable securities	N	N	Y
Other negotiable instruments	N	N	Y
Securities issuance and underwriting	N	N	Y/N[a]
Money broking	N	N	Y
Asset management (pension, fund management, custodial, depository, and trust services)	N		Y/N[a]
Settlement and clearing services for financial assets (securities, derivative products, and other negotiable instruments)	N		Y
Provision and transfer of financial information	Y		Y
Advisory, intermediation and other auxiliary financial services	Y		Y

Source: Adapted from Kono and Schuknecht (2000) and Kireyev (2002) with author's change of classifications
Legend: 'Y' yes and 'N' no.

Note: a, depending whether external fund is involved.

13.3 Foreign Banks in China and their Roles in Channeling Capital Flows

China signed the GATS upon its WTO accession at the end of 2001. Although there is a phase-out period of five years with respect to business scope (local currency vs foreign exchange business), customers (resident vs non-resident, consumers vs firms), and geographic locations (Appendix 13.1), its overall commitments are relatively liberal compared with countries in East Asia and even some OECD economies (Figure 13.1). Even before its WTO commitments, foreign banks have already been allowed to operate

Table 13.4: China's capital control and its effect on financial services trade liberalization

	Details	Comments
Restrictions on Commercial Credits		
By Residents to non-residents	Only authorized by PBOC may lend	Mode 1 allowed but restriction
To Resident from non-resident	Must be Incorporate in the plan for the use of foreign capital, undergo transaction-based examination and subject-SAFE Approval. Foreign-funded enterprises may borrow from non-resident without obtaining approval but must register the borrowing with the SAFE.	Mode 1 allowed but restriction
Financial credits	Restrictions on Commercial Credits Apply	Mode 1 allowed but restriction
Guarantees, securities		
By residents to non-residents	Prior SAFE Approval Required for financing guarantee	Mode 1 allowed but restriction
	Prior SAFE Approval not required for non-financing guarantee but registration with SAFE required	
To resident by non-residents	Foreign fund firms may accept guarantees from foreign institutions	
Provisions and controls specific to commercial banks and other credit institutions		
Borrowing abroad	Same restrictions on commercial credits apply	Mode 1 allowed but restriction
Maintenance of account abroad	Registration with the SAFE is required for domestic banks, domestic non-bank financial institutions and non-financial enterprise	Mode 2 allowed but with restriction
Lending to non-residents (financial or commercial credits)	Same restrictions on commercial credits apply	Mode 1 allowed but restriction
Lending locally in foreign exchange	Lending is subject to review by PBOC and to asset-liability ratio requirements. Borrowers must register the transactions ex post with the SAFE and must obtain a permit from the SAFE to repay principal. Such requirements are no longer required for residents to borrow FX from domestic Chinese financial institutions. But creditor needs to inform SAFE loan and payment structure.	Mode 2 allowed but with restriction
Differential treatment of deposit account of foreign exchange		
Reserve requirement	RR of 7.5% for deposits in RMB for all banks	
	RR of 2% for FX deposits of Chinese funded banks	
	RR of 5% for FX deposits with maturity less than 3 month, 3% for maturity of more than 3 months of foreign funded banks	
	Reserves on foreign currency are not remunerated	
Liquid assets requirement	Asset/liability ratio for FX may not be less than 60%	
Credit controls	Lending to a single borrower may not exceed 10%	

Source: IMF Annual Report on Foreign Exchange Restrictions (2003).

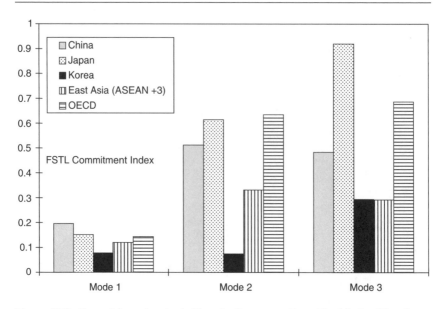

Figure 13.1: Financial services trade liberalization commitment by Mode of Supply

in certain geographic areas with progressively liberalized scope of banking businesses (Table 13.5). However, the opening was relatively modest because such liberalizations were only unilateral and based on the country's own economic needs. They are quite different from the multilateral and the rule-based financial services trade liberalization under the GATS that are supposed to be predictable, transparent, and extended to all members of the WTO.

13.3.1 Foreign Bank Presence in China

Size, entry form, and location: By all measures, foreign banks at present have a relatively small presence in China. Their total asset size is only 1.4 percent of the domestic banking assets (Table 13.6)[4] and their primary form of entry is through branches (Table 13.7). There are 162 foreign bank branches by the end of June 2004, while there are only fourteen foreign subsidiaries. In terms of asset size, subsidiaries are only 6 percent of the total foreign assets in China (Table 13.8). With respect to geographic locations, foreign banks are predominantly located in two coast cities: Shanghai and Shenzhen (Figure 13.2).

Motivation of Entry and Customers: The motivation for foreign banks to enter the Chinese market is no different from the experiences of other countries:

[4] This should be interpreted in relative terms as Chinese banks have increased their lending rapidly in recent years in an attempt to reduce the non-performing loan ratio in spite of foreign banks' increased presence in China.

Table 13.5: Chronology of foreign bank presence in China since 1979

Time	Events	Geographic Location	Business Scope
1979	Foreign Bank Representative Offices were allowed: Japan Export–Import Bank was the first foreign bank to set up a representative office in China.	Yes	Limited to Foreign Exchange Business
1980	31 foreign bank representative offices were established.	Yes	Limited to Foreign Exchange Business
July 1981	Foreign bank business was allowed	Foreign banks can open in 5 special economic zones	Only in foreign exchange business
1982	Hong Kong Nanyang Commercial Bank opened branch in Shenzhen		Only in foreign exchange business
September 1990	Foreign banks were allowed to open in Shanghai	5 special economic zones and Shanghai	Only in foreign exchange business
1992	Foreign banks were allowed to open in two more cities	7 cities including Dalian	Only in foreign exchange business
August 1994	Foreign banks were allowed to open in 11 inland cities including Beijing. Regulations on Foreign Financial Institutions were issued for the first time	23 cities and Hainan Province	Only in foreign exchange business
December 1996 to August 1998	Foreign banks were allowed to do RMB business in limited areas at an experimental basis	RMB business was limited to Shanghai Pudong and Shenzhen	RMB deposit and loans, settlements, guarantees, government bonds, and securities investment
April 1998	Foreign banks were allowed to enter the interbank market		(1) Foreign banks can borrow from central bank up to 100 million for their RMB business-related activities.
July 1999	Foreign Banks are allowed to expand their RMB business	Foreign banks' RMB business in Shanghai and Shenzhen was allowed to expand to their neighboring provinces.	(2) Foreign banks are allowed to syndicated loan business.
			(3) The RMB loans not covered by RMB can be borrowed from Chinese banks.
			(4) Foreign banks can enjoy the same treatment in the interbank market. Maximum borrowing is one time of its operating capital. Up to 100 million can be borrowed with permission of the central bank.
			(5) RMB liabilities to foreign exchange liability ratio increased from 35% to 50%.

(Continued)

Table 13.5: (*Continued*)

Time	Events	Geographic Location	Business Scope
December 2001	China entered WTO and signed the GATS	See Appendix 13.1	See Appendix 13.1
December 2002	Foreign banks are allowed to do RMB business in 5 more cities	RMB business was expanded to Guangzhou, Zhuhai, Qingdao, Nanjing, and Wuhan	See Appendix 13.1
December 2003	Foreign banks are allowed to do RMB business in 4 more cities	RMB business was expanded to Jinan, Fuzhou, Chongqing, and Chengdu	See Appendix 13.1
July 2004	Regulations on Foreign Bank Operation in China Issued by CBRC	Maximum foreign branch and subsidiary operating capitals were lowered to 500 million	See Appendix 13.1
December 2004	Foreign banks are allowed to do RMB business in 5 more cities	RMB business was allowed in Kunming, Beijing, Xiamen, Xian, and Shenyang. Foreign banks are encouraged to set up operations in China's West and Northeast Region.	See Appendix 13.1
December 2006	Foreign bank RMB restrictions no longer subject to geographic and business restriction		See Appendix 13.1

Source: CBRC and WTO, and Huang (2005).

Table 13.6: Foreign bank presence in China (top ten banks by assets in millions of US$)

Rank	Bank Name	Assets
1	HSBC	7570.83
2	Citibank	6700.93
3	Tokyo-Mitsubishi	3333.36
4	Standard Chartered	3032.45
5	Mizuho	2923.57
6	UFJ	2858.42
7	SMBC	2463.76
8	Bank of East Asia	2121.63
9	Deutsche Bank	677.57
10	Dutch Commercial Bank	627.62
	Total Foreign Bank Assets	48050.85
Memorandum		
	Foreign Bank Total Assets as a share of total Chinese Banking assets	1.40%

Source: China Bank Regulatory Commission (2003).

Table 13.7: Foreign financial institutions in China

	Foreign Bank	Subsidiary	Joint Venture Bank	Foreign Finance Company	Total
Subsidiary		14	10	3	27
Branch	162				162
Subsidiary Branch		9	4		13
Sub-Branch	15		1		16
Total	177	9	15	3	218

Data Source: China Bank Regulatory Commission (2004).

Foreign banks follow their customers' FDI activities (Nigh, Cho, and Krishnan 1986).[5] Figure 13.3 shows that foreign bank assets by country or region in China correspond closely to their respective FDI presence in China. The correlation coefficient is quite high at 0.8. As foreign banks follow their firms, it is not surprising that they have mainly lent to their manufacturing FDI firms (Table 13.9).

Funding sources: Over 66 percent of foreign bank loans are made in US dollars (Table 13.9). Local currency or the renminbi (RMB) loans, supported by the increases in RMB deposits, have grown rapidly in recent years. Despite the growth, foreign banks' RMB loans are largely hampered by the restrictions that they are only allowed to do RMB business in some restricted geographic areas and with foreign-affiliated firms. Only recently were they able to deal

---

[5] However, a recent paper by Seth *et al.* (1998) showed that these patterns are not necessarily valid for Japanese and European banks in the US market.

Table 13.8: Comparison of subsidiaries and branches (billions of US dollars)

	Subsidiary	Branch	Total	Subsidiary/Branch Ratio
Assets	2.74	46.30	48.74	0.059
Loans	1.44	21.04	22.40	0.068
Liabilities	1.65	42.40	43.93	0.039
Deposits	0.80	11.97	12.40	0.067
Profitability	0.021	0.20	0.225	0.105
CAR (%)	35.88	8.17	9.68	4.392
NPL	4.92	2.79	2.93	1.763

Data Source: China Bank Regulatory Commission (2004)

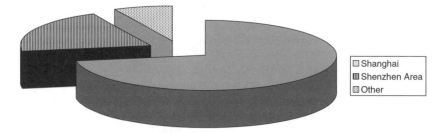

Figure 13.2: Foreign bank concentration in terms of assets by region

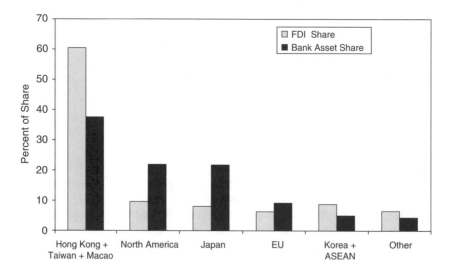

Figure 13.3: Foreign Banks do follow their customers in China (correlation coefficient = 0.81)

Table 13.9: Foreign bank loans by sector (millions of RMB)

Sectors	Total Loans Outstanding	Percent of Total (%)
Manufacturing sector	119,283	55.8
Machinery Sector	12,539	5.9
Electronics Sector	25,969	12.1
Chemical Sector	26,316	12.3
Light Industry Sector	26,622	12.4
Other Manufacturing Sector	27,836	13.0
Real Estate Sector	27,324	12.8
Retail Sector	8,929	4.2
Other Sectors	58,316	27.3
Total	213,851	100.0
Memorandum		
Total Loans in RMB	84,448	33.8
Total Dollar Loan in RMB	165,043	66.2
Total Dollar Loan in Dollar	19,981	

Data Source: China Bank Regulatory Commission (June 2004).

with Chinese firms.[6] Until recently, foreign banks mainly depended upon the interbank market for their RMB loans. But once the restrictions on doing RMB businesses with firms were removed in 2002, their RMB loans were largely matched by their RMB deposits of firms. Foreign banks are much less dependent on the interbank markets for RMB loans (Figure 13.4).

Other than the interbank market, loans of foreign banks not covered by deposits will have to be supported by borrowings from their headquarters. Owing to limited deposit base and the restrictions on borrowing from the interbank market prior to 1998, foreign bank loans until 2000 relied almost entirely on funds from their head offices. Indeed, once they were able to access the interbank markets in China, funds borrowed from headquarters until June 2003 merely met the needs of loans.

It also appears that the net borrowing from head offices of foreign banks follows rather closely expectations of changes in the RMB exchange rate. Because of the expectation of a RMB depreciation during the 1997–8 Asian financial crises, net borrowing of foreign banks from their head offices declined rapidly from over $22 billion in 1997 to $6 billion in 2002. However, since the end of 2002 borrowing from head offices has increased considerably, exceeding US dollar loans extended. This largely reflected expectations of RMB's revaluation. Indeed, direct borrowing from head offices is one of the most important

---

[6] Foreign banks are allowed to engage in the RMB business with both foreign entities and Chinese firms in 18 cities. There are still restrictions for them to deal with deposits of Chinese consumers. However, those restrictions will be removed by the end of 2006.

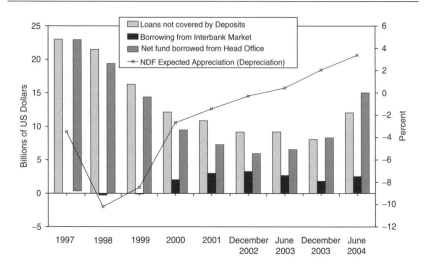

Figure 13.4: Funding source of foreign bank loans in China

channels through which foreign banks can affect China's cross-border capital flows.[7]

13.3.2 *Foreign Banks and China's Cross-Border Capital Flows*

By conventional measures, China has already become a highly open economy, with its total trade exceeding 60 percent of GDP. Capital flows from the lead and lag of its trade alone are estimated at $170 billion (Ma and McCauley 2004). As foreign banks have already been able to deal with joint-venture, foreign-funded, and Chinese firms, they play an active role in intermediating China's capital flows. Table 13.10 shows that foreign-funded firms and foreign banks borrowed over $58.5 billion in 2003, or 20 percent of total Chinese external debt in that year.

Foreign banks, once in China, have certainly opened more channels for cross-border capital flows, thus making China's capital controls more porous. Indeed, foreign banks may have played an active role in intermediating short-term bank loans to China.

LIBOR or HIBOR[8] plus 100 to 200 basis points usually set interest rates on foreign exchange loans and large deposits in China after liberalization in

---

[7] Realizing this, the State Administration of Foreign Exchange (SAFE) issued a new regulation in June 2004 by restricting total amount of foreign banks' short-term borrowing to a quota that is no more than five times of operating capital of a foreign bank branch or subsidiary.

[8] Hong Kong Interbank Offering Rate.

Table 13.10: Chinese external debt data by borrowers

	1998	1999	2000	2001	2002	2003
Central Government	41.6	47.3	48.96	49.8	50.5	52.8
Chinese banks	33.98	34.4	29.84	30	29.1	33.3
Chinese non-bank financial institution	8	6.47	5.72	4.38	4.4	4.3
Chinese firms	15.5	14.7	13.52	11.2	10	7.6
Foreign Funded Enterprises	45.2	47.3	46.5	35.2	33.2	37.8
To Resident by non-residents	..	..	..	17.04	14.5	20.7
Trade Credit				21.6	26.3	36.8
Others	1.76	1.63	1.16	0.88	0.5	0.3
Total	146.04	151.8	145.7	170.1	168.5	193.6

Data source: SAFE website in billions of US dollars
Note: Reclassification of China's foreign indebtedness was made in 2001 in accordance to the International Standards.
(1) Debt of foreign financial institutions are included as domestic debt and at the same time, foreign currency lending of foreign financial institutions to China borrowers are deducted from the total foreign debt.
(2) All trade credits (including 1–3 month) are included in the total foreign debt.
(3) Long-term debt with expected payment within one year is also included as short-term debt.

2000. In the fourth quarter of 2000, the three-month LIBOR rate fell to less than 2 percent, reflecting the Fed's aggressive monetary easing. On the other hand, China's short-term lending rates for RMB loans less than six months were hovering above 5 percent, thus providing arbitrage opportunities for both foreign banks and Chinese banks that have access to the London market. They could borrow from the London market at rate of less than 2 percent and then lend to foreign-funded or joint-venture firms in China or even to Chinese firms after 2002 at LIBOR plus 1 to 2 percent, netting a profit of at least 1 to 2 percent of the lending. Such loans were also welcomed by the firms because they could quickly exchange dollar loans into RMB and save 1–2 percent in interest rate charges relative to what they would have paid had thay borrowed in RMB. Indeed, arbitrage opportunities might explain the reasons why China's short-term loans went up rapidly from around US $20 billion at the end of 1999 to US $38 billion in 2004 (Figure 13.5). As a result, it is not difficult to understand the rationale that prompted the SAFE to issue a regulation on June 21, 2004, setting a limit of short-term external debt of both foreign and domestic banks at no more than five times their operating capital.

The observation in Figure 13.5 is also confirmed by a statistical analysis (Table 13.11). After adjusting for effects of sovereign risk, growth, capital control, and trade balances, China's short-term bank loans are shown to be positively affected by interest rate differentials, measured here by an arbitrage condition, that is, deviations from the interest rate parity condition.[9] In

---

[9] The simple interest rate differentials between LIBOR and the Chinese short-term lending rate (0 to 6 month) are also statistically significant with the right sign.

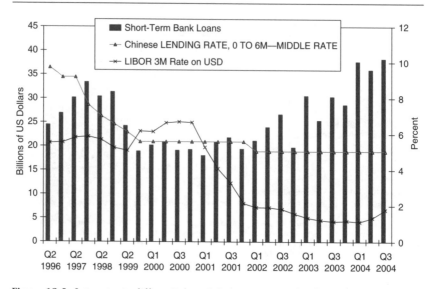

Figure 13.5: Interest rate differentials and short-term capital inflows

addition, capital controls measured by the IMF capital control index are negatively associated with the short-term bank loans. This indicates that capital controls in China are still binding.

Another channel for moving capital in and out of a country is through borrowing from and lending to head offices of foreign bank branches. As Figure 13.4. indicates, foreign banks' net borrowing from their head offices

Table 13.11: Determinants of China's short-term bank loans

Dependent variable: log of short-term bank loans	(1)	(2)	(3)	(4)
Deviations from the Interest Rate Parity Condition	3.643** (2.49)	4.004*** (3.28)	2.499*** (3.91)	2.505** (3.03)
Standard and Poor sovereign rating	0.360*** (7.00)	0.395*** (10.25)	0.381*** (9.59)	0.262*** (1.22)
IMF Capital control index	−1.751*** (2.46)	−1.553*** (3.41)	−1.737*** (3.44)	−1.930*** (3.44)
Trade balance to GDP	−0.014** (1.85)	−0.005 (0.88)	−0.014** (2.39)	0.038*** (0.36)
GDP growth rate	4.540 (1.26)	5.053* (1.53)	6.024** (2.41)	12.773 (0.93)
Tax-equivalent of reserve requirements		−1.886** (4.50)	−0.408 (0.66)	
Constant	5.756*** (5.19)	5.114*** (6.89)	5.356*** (6.42)	6.616*** (3.03)
Sample size	36	36	36	36
Adjusted R-square	0.85	0.88	0.89	0.79
F	51.18	63.44	91.82	30.30
Prob>F	0.0	0.0	0.0	0.0

Note: Signs of ***, **, * represent 99, 95, 90 percent of statistical significance
Numbers in parentheses are Newey–West standard errors

could be driven by two factors. The first factor is related to the amount of local currency available for local currency-lending activities. For example, if foreign banks have full access to the RMB, they will have less incentive to borrow from their head offices and thus fewer capital inflows. This indeed argues for foreign banks to be given access to the local currency in order to meet their local currency-lending needs. In addition, it would also make it easy for the regulatory agency to monitor the funding motives of foreign banks and their transactions with head offices. The second factor is related to exchange rate risk. As Figure 13.4 demonstrated, there appears to be a positive relationship between the amount of foreign currency borrowing from the head offices of foreign bank branches in China and expectations of the exchange rate appreciation calculated using the non-deliverable forward exchange rate.

That observed, the advantage that foreign banks have in arbitraging between the domestic and external market and their access to funds from the head offices will likely make China's capital controls more porous and the existing control regime less effective. As it stands now, foreign bank presence in China is still relatively small. Should foreign banks' operating capital double or even triple, say to US$10 or US$ 15 billion, the maximum short-term foreign exchange debt outstanding per annum under the June 2004 regulations will be around US$50 or $75 billion. As capital flows become large enough, onshore and offshore interest rate differential will disappear, making capital controls ineffective and compromising independence of monetary policy. Furthermore, if coupled with domestic financial liberalization, financial derivatives, often making term structures of capital flows fungible, will pose much greater challenges to the authorities in monitoring short-term capital flows (Garber 2000).

13.4 Impact of Financial Services Trade Liberalization on Bank Loans to Emerging Market Economies: Some Empirical Evidence

The effect of financial services trade liberalization on financial development and stability is a new and evolving topic. Using data from twenty-seven emerging market economies, Kono and Schuknecht (2000) find that financial services trade liberalization reduces distortion and volatility of capital flows to developing countries, thus promoting financial sector stability. Similar findings were obtained by Kireyev (2002). However, Valckx (2002) finds that financial services liberalization is weakly linked to financial instability. On the one hand, more liberal commitments on commercial presence systematically increase the likelihood of banking crises, most likely reflecting the short-run negative effect of increased foreign competition on the host country's financial services market. Bias toward cross-border supply of financial services, on the other hand, increases the probability of a currency crisis because of the increased volatility in capital flows. The findings of these limited studies appear to provide contrasting empirical results: Financial services trade liberalization promotes both financial stability and fragility.

However, the existing literature has not paid much attention to the impact of GATS on international bank loans to developing economies. This study is perhaps one of the first attempts to address this issue by applying a gravity model.[10]

The gravity model approach can be justified on several grounds. First, the well-documented fact that countries of large economic size tend to trade more with each other indicates that economic size is an important determinant of trade credits and finance through international banks. Second, higher per capita income is associated with deeper financial markets, leading to greater international bank loans. Third, information asymmetry may become greater with geographical distance between a lender and a borrower, thereby raising monitoring costs and exerting a negative influence over cross-border bank loans. Fourth, to the extent that the lender country has closer economic, political, and historical ties with a borrower country, international bank loans to the latter tend to be higher. These linkages act as factors that could reduce the problem of information asymmetry and therefore facilitate cross-border banking transactions.

This study also takes into account recent theoretical advances that recognize the importance of the country fixed effect, or the so-called 'multilateral resistance factor,' in empirical applications of the gravity model (Anderson and van Wincoop 2003; Rose 2002; Subramanian and Wei 2003; Eichengreen and Park 2003). The estimating regression equation can then be specified as follows:

$$\log(BL_{ijt}) = \sum_k \beta_k G_{ijt} + \sum_k \lambda_k F_{jt} + \sum_k^{\gamma k} X_{ijt} + \sum_k \delta_k Y_{jt} + \sum_k \varepsilon_k Z_{jt} + \mu_{ijt}$$

BL_{ij} indicates bank loans from developed country i to less developed country j. Vector G_{ijt} represents key gravity variables such as economic size, per capita income, an indicator of economic development, and distance between

---

[10] The theoretical underpinnings of the gravity model and its applications are reviewed by Frankel (1997). See Frankel (1997) for an application to the factors affecting the formation of trade blocs, Kawai and Urata (1998) on the relationship between trade and FDI using Japanese data at the industry level, Portes and Rey (1999) on the determinants of equity flows, Rose and Spiegel (2002) on the effect of a default on sovereign lending on bilateral trade, and Kawai and Liu (2004) on the determinants of bank loans to developing economies.

a lender country i and borrower country j, which could be interpreted as a proxy of information asymmetry. Vector F_{jt} represents country fixed effect of loan recipient economies. Vector X_{ijt} represents variables related to bilateral country linkages, such as the bilateral trade, official development assistance (ODA), and other economic linkage variables such as trade arrangements, common border, colonial ties, and common language. Vector Y_{jt} represents variables for a borrower country j related to its country risk such as macroeconomic and exchange rate volatility variables, institution characteristics such as whether a country has any explicit form of deposit insurance, history of default, and whether the country has a higher level of domestic financial liberalization or capital account opening. Vector Z_{jt} represents variables such as whether a loan recipient economy has signed up on the financial services trade liberalization and in addition, the intensity of the liberalization commitment.

The indexes of financial services trade liberalization are updated using the combined metrics of Matto (2000) and Valckx (2002). Detailed metric specifications of GATS commitments are presented in Appendix 13.2. The indexes are updated to 2003 as more countries have become members of the WTO and have signed the GATS. All gravity variables and some variables in X_{ijt}, Y_{jt}, and Z_{jt} are also in logs, except for dummy variables. Data sources are presented in Appendix 13.3.

13.5 Empirical Results

Table 13.12 presents empirical results. For the panel regression, fixed-effect regression techniques are used to accommodate the recent theoretical advances emphasizing the importance of the multilateral resistance effect when applying the gravity model empirically. We use two indexes of GATS commitments. One is an index that includes all financial sectors (insurance, banking, and other securities), the overall GATS score. The other one is an index that measures the banking sector commitment only, GATS-Bank score.

Gravity Variables: Equations (1) to (4) present panel regression results after adjusting for both time and country fixed effects. The log GDP variables of both a lender and a borrower country, a measure of country or market size, are statistically significant and have the right sign. This indicates that the larger the lending country, the more loans it provides, whereas the smaller the borrower country, the relatively fewer loans it tends to receive at margin. Both lender and borrower countries of higher economic development as indicated by the per capita income do not necessarily make a difference. However,

Table 13.12: Panel regression results (1999–2003)

Log[Distance$_{ij}$]	−0.967 (12.64)**	−0.967 (12.64)**	−0.967 (12.64)**	−0.967 (12.64)**
Log[GDPi]	0.732 (17.18)**	0.732 (17.18)**	0.732 (17.17)**	0.732 (17.17)**
Log[GDPj]	−0.6 (2.58)**	−0.601 (2.59)**	−0.614 (2.76)**	−0.615 (2.76)**
Log[GDPPC$_j$]	−0.201 (1.71)	−0.201 (1.71)	−0.201 (1.71)	−0.201 (1.71)
Log[GDPPCj]	0.358 (0.61)	0.361 (0.62)	0.376 (0.66)	0.378 (0.66)
[Common Borderij]	−0.099 (0.2)	−0.099 (0.2)	−0.099 (0.2)	−0.099 (0.2)
[Common Languageij]	0.761 (6.27)**	0.761 (6.27)**	0.761 (6.27)**	0.761 (6.27)**
[Former Colonyij]	2.632 (13.30)**	2.631 (13.30)**	2.632 (13.30)**	2.632 (13.30)**
Log[Exchange rate Volatilityij]	−0.008 (0.07)	−0.005 (0.04)	0.015 (0.12)	0.019 (0.16)
Log[Bilateral Tradeij]	0.176 (5.25)**	0.176 (5.25)**	0.176 (5.24)**	0.176 (5.24)**
[IMF programme]j	−0.381 (1.11)	−0.302 (0.9)	−0.355 (1.03)	−0.28 (0.83)
[IMF Capital Control Indexj]	−0.04 (0.15)	−0.041 (0.16)	0.032 (0.14)	0.031 (0.14)
Log[Interest rate Differentialij]	0.291 (0.82)	0.293 (0.82)	0.295 (0.83)	0.297 (0.83)
Log[GDP Volatilityj]	−0.002 (-0.04)	0.001 (-0.002)	0.001 (-0.03)	0.003 (-0.07)
Log[Short-Term Debtj]	0.016 (-0.27)	0.017 (-0.28)	0.02 (-0.33)	0.021 (-0.35)
Log[ODAij]	0.203 (10.74)**	0.203 (10.74)**	0.203 (10.74)**	0.203 (10.74)**
Log[Financial Sect. Efficiency Indexj]	−0.043 (0.16)	−0.052 (0.19)	−0.006 (0.02)	−0.013 (0.05)
Log[Fiscal Substainabilityj]	−0.09 (0.37)	−0.084 (0.35)	−0.116 (0.48)	−0.11 (0.46)
Log[Corruptionj]	0.03 (0.16)	0.032 (0.18)	0.029 (0.16)	0.031 (0.17)
Log[GATS-Indexj]	0.03 (0.53)			
LATIN Dummy*Log[GATS-Indexj]			1.234 (7.19)**	
Asia Dummy*Log[GATS-Indexj]			5.261 (-0.5)	
China Dummy*Log[GATS-Indexj]			1.199 (4.27)**	
Offshore Dummy*Log[GATS-Indexj]			0.728 (4.15)**	
Log[GATS-Indexj]*[IMF Capital Control Indexj]	0.073 (1.08)		0.073 (1.09)	
Log[GATS-Bank Indexj]		0.031 (0.53)		
Latin Dummy*Log[GATS-Bank Indexj]				0.084 (1.05)
Asia Dummy*[GATS-Bank Indexj]				5.128 (0.51)
China Dummy*Log[GATS-Bank Indexj]				1.149 (4.26)**
Offshore Dummy*Log[GATS-Bank Indexj]				0.713 (4.16)**
[IMF Capital Controlj]*Log[GATS-Bank Indexj]		0.058 (0.87)		0.059 (0.89)
Borrower Fixed Effect	Yes	Yes	Yes	Yes
Time Effect	Yes	Yes	Yes	Yes
Observations	4057	4057	4057	4057
R-squared	0.78	0.78	0.78	0.78

Note: t statistics are in parentheses. * and ** indicated significant at 5% and 1%, respectively.

the distance between a lender and a borrower, an indicator of information asymmetry, is negatively and statistically significant, thus confirming the notion that the greater the distance between a lender and a borrower, the less information tends to flow between them and therefore the fewer bank loans. A similar result is also found in Kawai and Liu (2004) and Portes and Rey (1999).

Economic Linkages: Although geographic linkage such as whether a lender and a borrower economy share a common border is not important, common languages and whether a recipient county is a former colony of a lender country play a significant and positive role in promoting bank loans from a lender to a borrower. In general, the more trade between a borrower and a lender, the more bank loans go from the lending country to the borrowing country. This demonstrates that bilateral trade flows play a significant role in facilitating bank loans to developing economies. It also confirms empirical observations that trade financing and trade credits facilitate international trade. Here we used lagged bilateral trade figures to avoid the problem of endogeneity. Official development assistance (ODA) also facilitates commercial bank loans to developing economies.

Country Risk Indicators: The model also attempts to capture the effect of country risk on bank loans, as measured by the exchange rate and GDP volatility, fiscal sector sustainability, and short-term debt as a share of foreign exchange reserves. However, these measures do not appear to be statistically significant.[11]

Institutional Quality and History of Default: Similarly, variables that attempt to measure institutional support or guarantee of the borrowing country's banking system such as whether the country has an explicit deposit insurance system, financial sector quality and development, rule of law as measured by the corruption index, and history of default measured by the IMF loan variable do not appear to be relevant here. Interestingly, whether a country has a high or a low degree of capital control does not matter either, which appears to imply that capital control is not an important factor affecting commercial loans to developing economies.

Indexes of GATS Commitments: After adjusting for country characteristics, the study is essentially interested in determining whether a signing up on GATS commitments helps a country to attract more commercial bank loans. The regression results suggest not. This is true for both the GATS index in general and the GATS index in the banking sector in particular.

---

[11] When the country risk measure is replaced with a synthetic country risk rating variable such as the S&P sovereign ratings, a similar result is obtained.

To some extent, such a result is not surprising. Our indexes show that GATS commitments do not necessarily correlate with per capita income. Some small, low-income transition and African economies tend to have quite liberal commitments. However, they do not receive more international bank loans, adjusting for their economic size, market potential, and economic development. But this may not be the case for all developing economies. When the developing-country group is split into sub-regions such as Latin America, ASEAN plus Korea, China, and offshore financial centers, the result is indeed quite different. Making more liberal commitments helps promote more loans to Latin America, China and the offshore financial sector, although it has little effect on the ASEAN countries plus Korea.[12]

Capital Control and GATS Commitments: The result shows that capital controls do not appear to matter for countries that also made liberalization commitments under the GATS.

Robustness Tests: An important problem with our data is missing observations, that is, for some countries gross bilateral flows of bank loans are zero for a given year. As a result, taking a logarithm of zero gives us an invalid value. These observations then have to be dropped. A similar problem is dealing with negative values as banks may wish to disinvest from a country.

One solution is to simply add one to the all observations. This may not be very desirable because adding a one to a small number would have much larger effect than adding one to a large number. We also apply the Box-Cox transformed regressions and the results are quite similar.[13]

13.6 Concluding Remarks

This chapter has examined the impact of financial services trade liberalization on international bank loans to developing economies using both a China country case study and a cross-country panel.

The country case study demonstrates that foreign banks, though still relatively small in size, have already had considerable impact on China's capital

[12] The result for the region may be due to the effect of the 1997–8 East Asian financial crises when a large number of loans was withdrawn from the region.

[13] Although not reported here, the Box-Cox transformation procedure (1964) is also used to treat the missing value problem. The prime aim of the procedure is to make the dependent variable as well as regression residuals approximately unskewed. It is also a useful method to alleviate heteroscedasticity when the distribution of the dependent variable is not known. For situations in which the dependent variable Y is known to be positive, the following transformation can be used: $g(y, \lambda) = \begin{cases} \frac{y^{\lambda}-1}{\lambda} & \text{if } \lambda \neq 0 \\ \ln(y) & \lambda = 0 \end{cases}$

flows via transactions between their branches and head offices and also via arbitraging opportunities between domestic and offshore markets. Indeed, the role of intermediating capital flows played by foreign banks will become even more significant as their total asset size becomes bigger after the barriers to entry are fully reduced.

The findings from the cross-country panel study indicate that the financial services trade liberalization under the GATS promotes bank loans to developing economies strongly though not evenly, depending on country characteristics. Large emerging market economies such as China tend to benefit from further financial services liberalization while small and low-income economies may not necessarily benefit from such liberalization.

Another important finding is that banks loans to developing economies have little to do with the capital controls of a host country, possibly implying that financial services trade liberalization is likely to make controls less effective because of the potential capital flows associated with the presence of foreign banks. Therefore, financial services trade liberalization may lead to *de facto* capital account opening or at least accelerate capital account opening in developing economies.

The study has some important policy implications. On the one hand, foreign bank presence has a spillover effect or demonstration effect on domestic financial institutions, thus promoting efficiency. Foreign bank presence can also help speed up domestic institution building as they bring both human capital and technology needed to the host economy. Thus, foreign banks should be welcome to participate in domestic financial sector.

On the other hand, once emerging market countries with fixed exchange rate regimes and capital controls open up their financial services trade for foreign competition, they may also invite more capital flows to their economies, which in turn will tend to render the existing capital control regime less effective. Large cross-border capital flows will also make interest rate differentials between onshore and offshore disappear. Therefore, they can no longer maintain an independent monetary policy. As the freedom of capital flows increases and if the objective is still to retain an independent monetary policy, the exchange rate regime will have to be made flexible as a result. In the case of China, the potential impact on its capital flows due to financial services trade liberalization will become substantial. This then implies that China's capital controls will become more porous. That said, China's move to a managed floating exchange rate regime in July 2005 was a right sequencing step, given the expected outcome of ongoing financial services liberalization.

Appendix 13.1

China's WTO Commitments adopted from *Report on the Working Party on the Accession of China, October 2001*

Sector or subsector	Market access	National treatment	Additional
B. Banking and other financial services (excluding insurance and securities) Banking services as listed below: a. Acceptance of deposits and other repayable funds from the public; b. Lending of all types, including consumer credit, factoring, and financing of commercial transaction; c. Financial leasing; d. All payment and money transmission services, including credit, charge and debit cards, traveller's cheques and banker's drafts (including import and export settlement); e. Guarantees and commitments; f. Trading for own account or for account of customers: foreign exchange	(1) Unbound except for the following: – Provision and transfer of financial information, and financial data processing and related software by suppliers of other financial services; – Advisory, intermediation and other auxiliary financial services on all activities listed in subparagraphs (a) through (k), including credit reference and analysis, investment and portfolio research and advice, advice on acquisitions and on corporate restructuring and strategy. (2) None (3) A. Geographic coverage: For foreign currency business, there will be no geographic restriction upon accession. For local currency business, the geographic restriction will be phased out as follows: Upon accession, Shanghai, Shenzhen, Tianjin, and Dalian; Within one year after accession, Guangzhou, Zhuhai, Qingdao, Nanjing, and Wuhan; within two years after accession, Jinan, Fuzhou, Chengdu, and Chongqing; within three years after accession, Kunming, Beijing, and Xiamen; Within four years after accession, Shantou, Ningbo, Shenyang, and Xi'an. Within five years after accession, all geographic restrictions will be removed. B. Clients: For foreign currency business, foreign financial institutions will be permitted to provide services in China without restriction as to clients upon accession. For local currency business, within two years after accession, foreign financial institutions will be permitted to provide services to Chinese enterprises. Within five years after accession, foreign financial institutions will be permitted to provide services to all Chinese clients. Foreign financial institutions licensed for local currency business in one region of China may service clients in any other region that has been opened for such business.	(1) None (2) None (3) Except for geographic restrictions and client limitations on local currency business (listed in the market access column), foreign financial institution may do business, without restrictions or need for case-by-case approval, with foreign-invested enterprises, non-Chinese natural persons, Chinese natural persons and Chinese enterprises. Otherwise, none. (4) Unbound except as indicated in Horizontal Commitments.	For financial leasing services, foreign financial leasing corporations will be permitted to provide financial leasing service at the same time as domestic corporations

C. Licensing: Criteria for authorization to deal in China's financial services sector are solely prudential (i.e. contain no economic needs test or quantitative limits on licenses). Within five years after accession, any existing non-prudential measures restricting ownership, operation, and juridical form of foreign financial institutions, including on internal branching and licenses, shall be eliminated. Foreign financial institutions who meet the following condition are permitted to establish a subsidiary of a foreign bank or a foreign finance company in China:

– total assets of more than US$10 billion at the end of the year prior to filing the application. Foreign financial institutions who meet the following condition are permitted to establish a branch of a foreign bank in China:

– total assets of more than US$20 billion at the end of the year prior to filing the application. Foreign financial institutions who meet the following condition are permitted to establish a Chinese-foreign joint bank or a Chinese-foreign joint finance company in China:

– total assets of more than US$10 billion at the end of the year prior to filing the application. Qualifications for foreign financial institutions to engage in local currency business are as follows:

– three years' business operation in China and being profitable for two consecutive years prior to the application, otherwise, none. (4) Unbound except as indicated in Horizontal Commitments

(1) Unbound except for the following:

– Provision and transfer of financial information, and financial data processing and related software by suppliers of other financial services;

– Advisory, intermediation, and other auxiliary financial services on all activities listed in subparagraphs (a) through (k), including credit reference and analysis, investment and portfolio research and advice, advice on acquisitions and on corporate restructuring and strategy.

(2) None

(3) None

(4) Unbound except as indicated in Horizontal Commitments

– Motor vehicles financing by non-bank financial institutions

(1) Unbound

(2) None

(3) None

(4) Unbound except as indicated in Horizontal Commitments.

(cont.)

(Continued)

Sector or subsector	Market access	National treatment	Additional
– Other financial services as listed below: – K. Provision and transfer of financial information, and financial data processing and related software by supplier of other financial services; l. Advisory, intermediation, and other auxiliary financial services on all activities listed in subparagraphs (a) through (k), including credit reference and analysis, investment and portfolio research and advice, advice on acquisitions and on corporate restructuring and strategy	(1) None (2) None (3) None (Criteria for authorization to deal in China's financial services sector are solely prudential (i.e. contain no economic needs test or quantitative limits on licenses). Branches of foreign institutions are permitted. (4) Unbound except as indicated in Horizontal Commitments.	(1) None (2) None (3) None (4) Unbound except as indicated in Horizontal Commitments	
– Securities	(1) Unbound except for the following: - Foreign securities institutions may engage directly (without Chinese intermediary) in B share business. (2) None	(1) None (2) None (3) None	

(3)

a. Unbound, except for the following:

    – Upon accession, representative offices in China of foreign securities institutions may become Special Members of all Chinese stock exchanges.

    – Upon accession, foreign service suppliers will be permitted to establish joint ventures with foreign investment up to 33 percent to conduct domestic securities investment fund management business. Within three years after China's accession, foreign investment shall be increased to 49 percent. Within three years after accession, foreign securities institutions will be permitted to establish joint ventures, with foreign minority ownership not exceeding 1/3, to engage (without Chinese intermediary) in underwriting A-shares and in underwriting and trading of B- and H-shares as well as government and corporate debts, launching of funds.

b. Criteria for authorization to deal in China's financial industry are solely prudential (i.e. contain no economic needs test or quantitative limits on licenses).

(4) Unbound except as indicated in Horizontal Commitments

(4) Unbound except as indicated in Horizontal Commitments

Appendix 13.2

Metrics used to calculate the financial services trade liberalization commitment

Numerical values	Score
No mention in the schedule or not a WTO member	0
Unbound against relevant mode	0.05
No new entry—unbound for new entry	0.1
Discretionary licensing—Economic needs test	
Licensing/Authorization Requirements; acquisition approval—not mentioning terms, conditions, or procedures	0.3
Voting/Ownership <50%	0.35
Limited Commitments	0.4
License/Authorization by supervisor (central bank, association), acquisition approval—with indications or guiding principles	0.5
Minor limitations (grandfathering clause, legal form, number of observations, ownership >50%, types of operations, value of transactions/assets, reciprocity and registration requirements)	0.75
No limitations	1

liberalization Commitments in
A—Insurance services (direct life and non-life insurance, reinsurance, intermediation)
B—Banking services (deposits, lending, money-broking, trading)
C—Securities services (underwriting, settlement, asset management)
D—Other financial services (supply of financial information, payments and settlements)

Mode 1: Cross-border supply
Mode 2: Consumption abroad
Mode 3: Commercial presence

Source: Valckx (2002) and authors' updating calculation.

Appendix 13.3

Data sources and financial commitment index

Variables	Sources
Foreign claims classified by maturity	Bank for International Settlements (BIS)
Border, language, colony, distance	<http://faculty.haas.berkeley.edu/arose/>
Trade balances	IFS
Lending interest rates	IFS
International reserve	IFS
Foreign exchange rate	IFS
External debt	WB–IMF–BIS–OECD
Budget deficit (% of GDP)	World Bank
Inflation rate	World Bank website
GDP, GDP per capita, population, GDP growth rates	World Bank website and World Development Indicators
Financial liberalization scores	WTO website—Financial commitments Kireyev, '*liberalization of Trade in Financial Services and Financial Sector Stability (Analytical Approach)*', August 2002, IMF website
Institution Quality	World Bank/ICRG
Bilateral trade	Direction of Trade

References

Anderson, J. E. and Wincoop, E. van (2003), 'Gravity with Gravitas: A Solution to the Border Puzzle,' *American Economic Review*, 93 (1): 170–92.

Caprio, G. Jr., Honohan, P., and Stiglitz, J. E. (2001), 'Introduction,' in G. Caprio, P. Honohan, and J.E. Stiglitz (eds.), *Financial liberalization: How Far and How Fast?* (London: Cambridge University Press), 3–30.

Claessens, S., Demirguc-Kunt, A., and Huizinga, H. (1998), 'How Does Foreign Entry Affect the Domestic Banking Market?' World Bank Working Paper.

Committee on the Global Financial System (2004), 'Foreign Direct Investment in the Financial Sector of Emerging Market Economies,' Bank for International Settlement, March.

Demirguc-Kunt, A. and Detragiache, E. (1998), 'Financial Liberalization and Financial Fragility,' *IMF Working Paper* 98/83.

_____ Levin, R., and Min, H. G. (1998), 'Opening to Foreign Banks: Issues of Stability, Efficiency, and Growth,' in S. Lee (ed.), *The Implication of the World Financial Market* (Seoul: Central Bank of Korea).

Eichengreen, B., and Park, Y. C. (2003), 'Why Has There Been Less Financial Integration in Asia Than in Europe?' *Research Paper*, University of California, Berkeley.

Frankel, J. (1997). *Regional Trading Blocs* (Washington, DC: Institute for International Economics).

Garber, P. (2000), 'What You See Versus What You Get: Derivatives in International Capital Flows,' in C. Adams, R. E. Litan, and M. Pomerleano (eds.), *Managing Financial and Corporate Distress: Lessons from Asia* (Washington, DC: Brookings Institute Press), 361–83.

Goldberg, L., Dages, G., Kinney, D. (2000), 'Foreign and Domestic Bank Participation In Emerging Markets: Lessons from Mexico and Argentina,' *NBER* Working Paper No. 7714.

Kaminisky, G. and Reinhart, C. (2000), 'The Twin Crises: The Causes of Banking and Balance-of-Payments Problems,' *American Economic Review*, 89 (3), June: 473–500.

Kawai, M. and Liu, L. (2004), 'Determinants of International Commercial Bank Loans to Developing Countries,' *Journal of Japan and International Economies* (forthcoming).

_____ and Urata, S. (1998), 'Are Trade and Direct Investment Substitutes or Complements? An Empirical Analysis of Japanese Manufacturing Industries,' in H. Lee and D. Roland-Holst (eds.), *Economic Development and Cooperation in the Pacific Basin: Trade, Investment, and Environmental Issues* (Cambridge: Cambridge University Press), 251–96.

Key, S. J. (2003), *The Doha Round and Financial Services Negotiations* (Washington, DC: The American Enterprise Institute Press).

Kireyev, A. (2002), 'liberalization of Financial Services Trade and Financial Stability: An Analytical Approach,' IMF Working Paper, WP/02/138.

Kono, M., Low, P., Luanga, M., Mattoo, A., Oshikawa, M., and Schuknecht, L. (1997), 'Opening Markets in Financial Services and the Role of the GATS,' WTO Special Report.

Kono, M., Low, P., Luanga, M., Mattoo, A., Oshikawa, M., and Schuknecht, L. (2000), 'How Does Financial Services Trade Affect Capital Flows and Financial Stability?' in S. Claessens and M. Jansen (eds.), *Internationalisation of Financial Services* (London: Kluwer Law International), 139–76.

Levin, R. (1997), 'Financial Development and Economic Growth: Views and Agenda,' *Journal of Economic Literature*, 35 (June): 688–726.

Lindgren, C -J., Garcia, G., and Saal, M. I. (1996), *Bank Soundness and Macroeconomic Policy* (Washington, DC: International Monetary Fund).

Ma, G. and McCauley, R. (2004), 'Capital Account Liberalization, Monetary Policy and Exchange Rate Regime,' Mimeo, KIEP-PRI Seminar on Financial Interdependence and Exchange Rate Regimes in East Asia, Tokyo.

Matto, A. (2000), 'Financial Services and the WTO: Liberalization Commitments of the Developing and Transition Economies,' World Bank Trade Research Report, 351–86.

Nigh, D., Cho, K. R., and Krishnan, S. (1986). 'The Role of Location-Related Factors in US Banking Involvement Abroad: An Empirical Examination,' *Journal of International Business Studies*, (Fall): 59–72.

Portes, R. and Rey, H. (1999), 'The Determinants of Cross Border Equity Flows,' NBER Working Paper No. 7336 (September).

Rose, A. K. (2002), 'Do We Really Know that the WTO Increases Trade?' *NBER* Working Paper No. 9273.

—— and Spiegel, M. M. (2002), 'A Gravity Model of Sovereign Lending, Trade Default and Credit,' NBER Working Paper, No. 9285.

Seth, R., Nolle, D. E., and Mohanty, S. K. (1998), 'Do Banks Follow Their Customers Abroad?' *Financial Markets, Institutions & Instruments*, 7 (November): 1–25.

Subramanian, A. and Wei, S. (2003), 'The WTO Promotes Trade, Strongly but Unevenly,' *NBER* Working Paper No. 10024.

Valckx, N. (2002), 'WTO Financial Services Trade liberalization: Measurement, Choice, and Impact on Financial Stability,' Research Memo, WO No. 705 (October).

World Trade Organisation (2001), 'Report of the Working Party on the Accession of China,' Addendum, October. Geneva.

14

Why Does China Save So Much?[1]

Charles Yuji Horioka
Osaka University and National Bureau of Economic Research

Junmin Wan
Fukuoka University

14.1 Introduction

China has attracted increasing attention because it is the world's most populous nation and because it has maintained phenomenal rates of economic growth in recent years. For example, the Asian Development Bank now projects that China will attain a growth rate in excess of 9 percent in 2006 for the fifth consecutive year, thereby serving as the engine of growth in the Asian-Pacific region (*Nihon Keizai Shimbun*, evening edition of April 6, 2006, p. 1). Furthermore, China is now the third largest exporter and importer in the world behind the United States and Germany (*Nihon Keizai Shimbun*, morning edition of April 12, 2006, p. 1).

Moreover, there are at least two other reasons for being interested in China. First, China was a socialist economy during the 1949–77 period, but Deng Xiaoping implemented dramatic reforms in 1978, which turned China into a capitalist economy and caused rates of economic growth to skyrocket.[2] Thus, it is of interest to know whether the laws of economics apply in China both

[1] We are grateful to Christopher Carroll, Teh-Ming Huo, Shinsuke Ikeda, Junichiro Ishida, Miki Kohara, Louis Kuijs, Justin Yifu Lin, Ronald I. McKinnon, Masao Ogaki, Hugh Patrick, Etsuro Shioji, Katsuya Takii, Xiaoping Wang, Calla Weimer, Tongsheng Xu, Yaohui Zhao, and participants of the Seoul Conference on 'China and Emerging Asia: Reorganizing the Global Economy,' the Seattle Conference of the Asia-Pacific Economic Association, the Summer Institute of the National Bureau of Economic Research, and the fall meeting of the Japanese Economic Association, seminars at the Osaka School of International Public Policy (OSIPP) of Osaka University, the Asian Public Policy Program of Hitotsubashi University, the China Center for Economic Research of Peking University, and the School of Economics of Jiangxi University of Finance and Economics, and Horioka's graduate seminar for valuable comments.

[2] For example, Lin (1992) finds using province-level panel data that rural reforms raised agricultural growth in China.

before and after the 1978 regime change. Second, China introduced a so-called 'one-child policy' in 1979 as a way of controlling population growth. This is an interesting natural experiment that makes fertility largely exogenous and enables us to assess the impact of the age structure of the population on the household saving rate without worrying about endogeneity issues. Moreover, because the one-child policy was applied more leniently to ethnic minorities, the policy also led to substantial variations among provinces in the age structures of their populations, and this will enable us to more sharply estimate the impact of the age structure of the population on the household saving rate.

Yet another noteworthy aspect of China's economy is its high saving rate. China has had by far the highest overall saving rate in the world since at least 2000, and her saving rate has increased even further since 2000—to nearly 50 percent of GDP. Gross capital formation (investment) is also high in China, but because saving exceeds investment, China has been running a net saving surplus, which translates into a current account surplus, and that surplus has been growing sharply—from 1.9 percent of GDP in 2000 to 3.6 percent in 2004 and a remarkable 7.2 percent in 2005–even though China is investing at a staggering rate of 43–6 percent of GDP and even though China is still relatively poor. This has made China one of the world's largest capital exporters and has exacerbated trade frictions with the United States and other countries. Moreover, China's net saving surplus shows no signs of abating ('A Survey of the World Economy,' *The Economist*, September 24–30, 2005: 13). Thus, the surge in China's saving rate has drastically reshaped global financial flows and relations, and it is therefore important to understand the determinants of, and future trends in, China's saving rate.

In this chapter, we present data on saving rates and related variables in China and conduct an econometric analysis of the determinants of the household saving rate using a life cycle model and panel data on Chinese provinces for the 1995–2004 period from the household survey conducted by the Chinese government.

The paper is organized as follows: in Section 14.2, we conduct a survey of the previous literature; in Section 14.3, we discuss the theoretical link between the age structure of the population and the household saving rate; in Section 14.4, we present data on saving rates and related variables; in Section 14.5, we discuss the estimation model and data sources; in Section 14.6, we discuss the estimation method; in Section 14.7, we present the estimation results; and Section 14.8 is a concluding section.

To preview our main findings, we find that China's saving rate has been high and that it has generally shown an upward trend over time and that the main determinants of variations over time and over space in China's household saving rate are the lagged saving rate, the income growth rate, (in many cases) the real interest rate, and (in some cases) the inflation rate. However, we find that the variables relating to the age structure of the population have the expected impact on the household saving rate in only one of the four samples. These results provide mixed support for the life-cycle hypothesis, which are consistent with the existence of inertia or persistence, and imply that China's household saving rate will remain high for some time to come.

14.2 Literature Survey

In this section, we conduct a selective survey of previous analyses of household saving in China. We focus on two seminal papers—Kraay (2000) and Modigliani and Cao (2004)–but a more comprehensive survey can be found in Kraay (2000). Kraay (2000) uses panel data on Chinese provinces from China's household survey to analyze the determinants of the saving rates of rural and urban households during the 1978–83 and 1984–9 periods and finds that, in the case of rural households, future income growth has a negative and significant impact on their saving rates, that the share of food in total consumption has a negative and significant impact on their saving rates, presumably because households closer to the subsistence level have less ability to save, and that neither the dependency ratio (proxied by the ratio of population to employment) nor future income uncertainty has a significant impact on their saving rates. In the case of urban households, virtually none of the explanatory variables has a significant impact on their saving rates.

Turning to Modigliani and Cao (2004), they conduct a regression analysis of the determinants of the household saving rate using times series data for the 1953–2000 period and find that the long-term growth rate, the reciprocal of the dependency ratio (proxied by the ratio of the employed population to the number of minors), the deviation of growth from the long-term growth rate, and inflation all have positive and significant impacts on the household saving rate.

Thus, the two studies obtain somewhat conflicting results. Kraay (2000) finds that the dependency ratio does not have a significant impact on the household saving rate, whereas Modigliani and Cao (2004) find that it does. Moreover, Kraay (2000) finds that future income growth has a negative and significant impact on the household saving rate, whereas Modigliani and Cao (2004) find that the long-term growth rate and the deviation of growth from the long-term growth rate have a positive and significant impact on the household saving rate.

The current study improves upon these earlier studies in a number of respects: (1) the data are much newer, (2) the dependent variable (the household saving rate) is defined more carefully and includes household investments in real assets, (3) the dependency ratio is defined more carefully and the young dependency ratio and the old dependency ratio are entered separately, (4) we include variables not included by previous authors such as the interest rate and the lagged saving rate, (5) we obtain results for the sample of urban households, the sample of rural households, and the full sample (unlike Kraay (2000), who obtains results only for urban and rural households, and Modigliani and Cao (2004), who obtain results only for the full sample), and (6) we use superior estimation techniques.

14.3 Theoretical Considerations

In this section, we present a brief theoretical discussion of the impact of the age structure of the population on the household saving rate (see Horioka and Wan (2006) for a more rigorous treatment). The life-cycle model, which is one of the most commonly used models in economics, provides an explanation of this relationship. According to this model, people work and save part of the income they earn when they are young and retire and finance their living expenses by dissaving their previously accumulated savings when they become old. Thus, the saving rate of the household sector as a whole will be lower, the higher is the ratio of the number of retirees to the working-age population.

Similarly, it costs parents money to raise and educate their children, but children do not earn any income. Thus, the more children one has, the less able one is to save. Moreover, the more children one has, the more likely it is that one or more of them will provide care and financial assistance during old age and thus the less need there is to save on one's own in preparation for one's retirement. For both reasons, the more children one has, the less one will save, and the more children there are relative to the working-age population, the lower will be the saving rate of the household sector as a whole.

If one defines the 'overall dependency ratio' as the ratio of children and retirees to the working-age population, the higher the dependency ratio is, the lower will be the saving rate of the household sector as a whole, and conversely.

14.4 Data on Saving Rates and Other Related Variables

In this section, we present data on saving rates and other related variables. Figure 14.1 shows data on trends over time in the national gross investment rate (the ratio of national gross investment to GNP or GDP) during the 1952–2004 period because the national accounts of China do not provide data on saving and because saving and investment were more or less equivalent until 1978 because the Chinese economy was a closed economy until then. As can be seen from this figure, the national gross investment ratio has

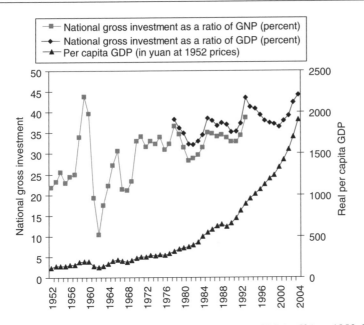

Figure 14.1: National gross investment rate and per capita GDP in China, 1952–2004
Source: China Statistics Yearbook, 1991–2005.

been relatively high throughout the postwar period, fluctuating in the 20–35 percent range during the 1952–77 period (except for a temporary spike in 1958–60 and a temporary dip in 1961–3) and fluctuating in the 28–45 percent range during the 1978–2004 period. Thus, China's investment (saving) rate has been relatively high and has shown an upward trend throughout most of the postwar period.

Turning to demographic data, Figure 14.2 shows data on trends over time in the total population of China and in life expectancy at birth during the 1949–2004 period, and as can be seen from this figure, there has been a steady and pronounced improvement in life expectancy during the past half century (with the exception of the 1958–61 period) from about 40.8 in 1950 to more than 71.96 in 2004. It is this steady and pronounced increase in life expectancy that is the primary cause of the rapid increase in the old dependency ratio (see Figure 14.3).

Next, Figure 14.3 shows data on trends over time in the age structure of the population during the 1949–2004 period, and as can be seen from this figure, there have been pronounced trends in both the young dependency ratio (the ratio of the population aged 0–14 to the population aged 15–59) and the old dependency ratio (the ratio of the population aged 60 or older to the population aged 15–59). The former increased from 0.57 in 1950 to 0.77 in 1964 before starting to decline, falling to 0.28 by 2004 (due in large part to

Figure 14.2: Population and life expectancy in China, 1949–2004

Sources: China Population Statistics Yearbook; 1988–2005, Banister (1987); and US CIA Factbook.

the 'one-child policy' and other population control measures), while the latter increased more or less steadily from 0.13 in 1950 to 0.18 in 2004. Finally, the total dependency ratio (the ratio of the population aged 0–14 or 60 or older to the population aged 15–59) showed more or less the same trends over time as the young dependency ratio, increasing from 0.70 in 1950 to 0.89 in 1964

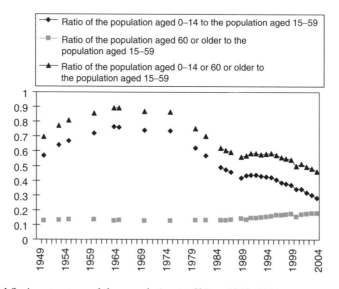

Figure 14.3: Age structure of the population in China, 1949–2004

Sources: China Population Statistics Yearbook, 1988–2005, and World Population Prospects: The 2002 Revision (United Nations).

before starting to decline, falling to 0.46 by 2004 (also due in large part to the 'one-child policy' and other population control measures). The life-cycle model predicts that the age structure of the population will have a significant impact on the saving rate and in particular that the dependency ratios will have a negative impact on the saving rate, and if we compare trends over time in the national gross investment rate (a proxy for the national saving rate) with trends over time in the dependency ratios, it can be seen that the upward trend in the investment (saving) rate during the 1968–2004 period coincides with a downward trend in the young and total dependency ratios during the same period, suggesting that the latter may be a cause of the former.

Looking next at the age structure of China's population in international comparison, China's young dependency ratio was higher than the worldwide level in 1975 (0.74 vs 0.67) but fell at an unprecedented rate due to the one-child policy and other population control measures. As a result, it was far less than the worldwide level by 2005 (0.32 vs 0.46).[3]

By contrast, the old dependency ratio was somewhat lower than the world-wide level in 1975 (0.13 vs 0.16) but has gradually increased due to the steady increases in life expectancy and was just under the worldwide level by 2005 (0.16 vs 0.17).

However, because trends over time in the young dependency ratio have been more pronounced than trends over time in the old dependency ratio, trends in the total dependency ratio mirror trends in the youth dependency ratio: it was just over the worldwide level in 1975 (0.87 vs 0.83) but declined sharply thereafter, falling to far less than the worldwide level by 2005 (0.48 vs 0.63).

The fact that the young and total dependency ratios were formerly relatively high by international standards can explain why China's investment (saving) rate was formerly relatively low by international standards, and the fact that the young and total dependency ratios are now relatively low by international standards can explain why China's investment (saving) rate is now relatively high by international standards.

Figure 14.4 shows data on the income sources of the elderly in China in 2004, and as can be seen from this figure, family support (support from one's children) is the dominant income source for nearly half (47.5 percent) of the elderly in China, making it by far the dominant income source of the elderly. Few, if any, elderly rely on dissaving (which is presumably included in 'other' in Figure 14.4). This may explain why trends over time in the investment (saving) rate and trends over time in the old dependency ratio are not opposite, as predicted by the life-cycle model.

---

[3] The demographic data in this paragraph and the two following paragraphs are based on United Nations data and hence do not coincide precisely with the earlier data.

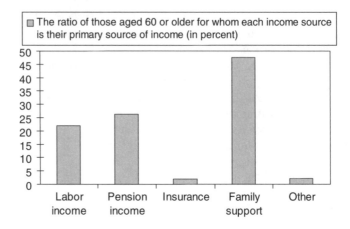

Figure 14.4: The income sources of the aged in China in 2004
Source: China Statistics Yearbook, 2005.

Figures 14.5 and 14.6 show data on urban, rural, and (in the case of Figure 14.6) all households for the 1995–2004 period from China's household survey. First, Figure 14.5 shows the per capita income and consumption of urban and rural households, and as can be seen from this figure, there is a considerable gap between urban and rural households in their per capita income and consumption. For example, for the 1995–2004 period as a whole, the per capita income of rural households was a mere 37.7 percent of that of urban households, and the per capita consumption of rural households was a mere

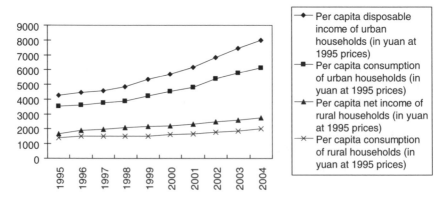

Figure 14.5: Household income and consumption in China, 1995–2004
Source: Author's calculations based on China Statistics Yearbook, 1996–2005.

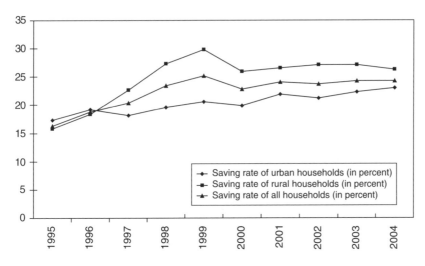

Figure 14.6: Household saving rate in China, 1995–2004

Source: Authors' calculations based on China Statistics Yearbook, 1996–2005.

35.20 percent of that of urban households (see Table 14.1). Moreover, this gap has been increasing over time.[4]

Figure 14.6 shows data on trends over time in the saving rates of urban, rural, and all households, and as can be seen from this figure, the saving rates of the three categories of households are roughly comparable with respect not only to their levels but also with respect to trends over time therein. With respect to the level of the saving rate, the saving rates of all three categories of households fluctuated in the 15.78–30.34 percent range and the saving rates of urban, rural, and all households averaged 20.3 percent, 24.7 percent, and 22.4 percent, respectively, during the 1995–2004 period. The fact that the saving rate of rural households is higher than that of urban households, even though their income levels are lower, is surprising but it could be due to the greater income volatility of rural households, the vast majority of whom are farmers, as a result of which they save more for precautionary purposes, or to the fact that differences in income levels largely reflect differences in price levels, as a result of which the purchasing power of the incomes of urban and rural households are not nearly as different as their incomes *per se*.

Turning to trends over time in the saving rates of urban, rural, and all households, all three showed upward trends until at least 1999 although the saving rates of rural and all households levelled off thereafter. The upward trends in the saving rates of all three categories of households coincide with

[4] Note, however, that these figures do not control for regional differences in price levels and exaggerate the gap between urban and rural areas to the extent that prices are lower in rural areas.

Table 14.1: Household saving rate by province (averages for the 1995–2004 period)

Province	Saving rate (in percent)		
	Urban households	Rural households	All households
Beijing	19.4	27.2	20.8
Tianjin	22.4	43.7	27.6
Hebei	23.5	41.7	35.1
Shanxi	21.7	35.5	28.8
Inner Mongolia	22.5	17.4	20.2
Liaoning	17.6	29.0	21.5
Jilin	19.3	27.7	22.5
Heilongjiang	22.6	31.1	25.6
Shanghai	22.4	19.6	22.1
Jiangsu	23.4	31.0	27.3
Zhejiang	21.9	23.3	23.0
Anhui	21.1	26.7	24.5
Fujian	22.8	26.1	24.7
Jiangxi	25.7	22.6	24.0
Shandong	24.5	30.3	27.5
Henan	22.8	31.9	28.7
Hubei	17.0	24.9	21.0
Hunan	18.5	10.4	13.7
Guangdong	19.4	24.8	21.6
Guangxi	19.6	20.8	20.6
Hainan	22.7	34.5	28.9
Chongqing	10.7	24.4	17.7
Sichuan	16.6	18.2	17.5
Guizhou	19.9	20.3	20.2
Yunnan	19.5	10.0	14.1
Tibet	19.1	31.2	25.1
Shaanxi	15.9	10.9	13.5
Gansu	18.2	21.0	19.6
Qinghai	17.9	16.1	17.2
Ningxia	17.0	17.8	17.4
Xinjiang	22.5	16.6	21.1
Mean	20.3	24.7	22.4

Source: Authors' calculations based on China Statistics Yearbook, 1996–2005 editions, and China Population Statistics Yearbook, 1996–2005 editions.

the downward trends in the young and total dependency ratios, and thus it is possible that the latter are one of the causes of the former. Thus, the evidence presented thus far suggests that the age structure of China's population can explain not only the high level of China's household saving rate but also the upward trend therein.

Table 14.1 shows data on the average saving rates of urban, rural, and all households during the 1995–2004 period by province, and as can be seen from this table, there has been enormous variation among provinces in their saving rates, with the saving rate of urban households ranging from 10.7 percent to 25.7 percent, that of rural households ranging from 10.0 percent to 43.7 percent, and that of all households ranging from 13.5 percent to 35.1 percent.

Finally, Table 14.2 shows data on the age structure of urban, rural, and all households by province during the 1995–2004 period, and as can be seen from this table, there has been enormous variation among provinces in the age structure of their populations. For example, the young dependency ratio ranged from 0.17 to 0.39 for urban households, from 0.18 to 0.52 for rural households, and from 0.18 to 0.48 for all households, the old dependency ratio ranged from 0.07 to 0.18 for urban households, from 0.07 to 0.16 for rural households, and from 0.07 to 0.18 for all households, and the total dependency ratio ranged from 0.29 to 0.48 for urban households, from 0.34 to 0.66 for rural households, and from 0.31 to 0.56 for all households. We will now conduct a regression analysis in Sections 14.5 through 14.7 to see if variations in the saving rate correlate with variations in the age structure of the population.

14.5 The Estimation Model and Data Sources

In Sections 14.5–7, we briefly describe our empirical analysis of the determinants of household saving in China (see Horioka and Wan (2007) for more details). In this section, we discuss the estimation model and data sources we use in our empirical analysis.

The dependent variable we use in our analysis is SR = the household saving rate, defined as the ratio of household saving to household disposable income (net household income in the case of rural households) and where household saving is calculated as household disposable (or net) income minus household consumption.

Following Loayza, Schmidt-Hebbel, and Serven (2000) and Schrooten and Stephan (2005), we estimate a reduced-form linear equation rather than adhering to a particular, narrow structural model, but the theoretical discussion presented in section 14.3 offers guidance regarding what variables should be included as explanatory variables.

Pursuant to the theoretical model in the previous section, we include the following explanatory variables:

(1) SR(-1) = the one-year lag of the saving rate

(2) CHY = the income growth rate, defined as the real rate of growth of per capita household disposable income (net household income in the case of rural households)

(3) RINT = the real interest rate, defined as NINT—INFL, where NINT = the nominal interest rate on one-year bank deposits and INFL = the rate of change of the consumer price index

(4) YOUNG = the young dependency rate, defined as the ratio of the population aged 0–14 to the population aged 15–64

Table 14.2: Age structure of the population by province (average for the 1995–2004 period)

Province	Urban households			Rural households			All households		
	Young dependency ratio	Old dependency ratio	Total dependency ratio	Young dependency ratio	Old dependency ratio	Total dependency ratio	Young dependency ratio	Old dependency ratio	Total dependency ratio
Beijing	0.167	0.123	0.290	0.276	0.125	0.401	0.188	0.123	0.311
Tianjin	0.204	0.136	0.340	0.338	0.109	0.447	0.245	0.127	0.372
Hebei	0.264	0.092	0.357	0.355	0.104	0.459	0.333	0.101	0.435
Shanxi	0.304	0.088	0.392	0.419	0.101	0.519	0.378	0.096	0.474
Inner Mongolia	0.269	0.078	0.347	0.326	0.088	0.414	0.303	0.084	0.387
Liaoning	0.207	0.119	0.325	0.278	0.098	0.375	0.239	0.109	0.349
Jilin	0.216	0.094	0.310	0.280	0.078	0.357	0.248	0.086	0.333
Heilongjiang	0.227	0.080	0.308	0.291	0.068	0.359	0.257	0.075	0.332
Shanghai	0.175	0.185	0.360	0.182	0.160	0.341	0.176	0.181	0.357
Jiangsu	0.236	0.122	0.358	0.328	0.158	0.486	0.287	0.138	0.425
Zhejiang	0.223	0.123	0.347	0.278	0.145	0.423	0.255	0.135	0.390
Anhui	0.300	0.107	0.407	0.396	0.115	0.511	0.369	0.112	0.481
Fujian	0.272	0.103	0.375	0.427	0.119	0.546	0.368	0.110	0.479
Jiangxi	0.303	0.099	0.402	0.428	0.101	0.529	0.388	0.100	0.488
Shandong	0.265	0.100	0.365	0.321	0.130	0.450	0.299	0.117	0.417
Henan	0.290	0.098	0.388	0.407	0.110	0.518	0.381	0.108	0.488
Hubei	0.266	0.092	0.358	0.409	0.111	0.520	0.353	0.103	0.456
Hunan	0.257	0.109	0.366	0.360	0.117	0.477	0.330	0.114	0.444
Guangdong	0.315	0.098	0.412	0.525	0.134	0.659	0.429	0.116	0.545
Guangxi	0.290	0.120	0.410	0.427	0.118	0.545	0.393	0.118	0.511
Hainan	0.342	0.080	0.422	0.486	0.121	0.607	0.436	0.106	0.542
Chongqing	0.231	0.133	0.364	0.356	0.127	0.483	0.305	0.129	0.435
Sichuan	0.255	0.129	0.384	0.355	0.110	0.465	0.321	0.117	0.437

(Cont.)

Table 14.2: (Continued)

Province	Urban households			Rural households			All households		
	Young dependency ratio	Old dependency ratio	Total dependency ratio	Young dependency ratio	Old dependency ratio	Total dependency ratio	Young dependency ratio	Old dependency ratio	Total dependency ratio
Guizhou	0.313	0.101	0.414	0.479	0.092	0.572	0.431	0.095	0.526
Yunnan	0.270	0.111	0.381	0.423	0.095	0.518	0.391	0.098	0.490
Tibet	0.389	0.093	0.481	0.497	0.083	0.580	0.479	0.086	0.565
Shaanxi	0.280	0.107	0.387	0.412	0.095	0.507	0.371	0.099	0.470
Gansu	0.247	0.090	0.337	0.433	0.078	0.511	0.383	0.081	0.465
Qinghai	0.265	0.077	0.342	0.460	0.069	0.529	0.394	0.072	0.466
Ningxia	0.276	0.071	0.347	0.509	0.068	0.577	0.427	0.069	0.496
Xinjiang	0.282	0.075	0.357	0.494	0.074	0.568	0.402	0.075	0.477

Notes: The young dependency ratio is defined as the ratio of the population aged 0–14 to the population aged 15–64. The old dependency ratio is defined as the ratio of the population aged 65 or older to the population aged 15–64. The total dependency ratio is defined as the ratio of the population aged 0–14 or 65 or older to the population aged 15–64.

Source: Authors' calculations based on China Population Statistics Yearbook, 1996–2005.

(5) OLD = the old dependency rate, defined as the ratio of the population aged 65 or older to the population aged 15–64

(6) DEP = the total dependency rate, defined as the ratio of the population aged 0–14 or 65 or older to the population aged 15–64

(7) INFL = the rate of change of the consumer price index

(8) A constant term

The lagged saving rate is included to test for the presence of inertia, persistence, or habit formation. The income growth rate is included to test the validity of the life-cycle hypothesis, and the coefficient of this variable will be positive if habit persistence is present and/or if growth is cohort-specific, as the life-cycle model assumes. The real interest rate is included to test for the impact of financial variables, and we would expect its coefficient to be positive if the substitution effect more than offsets the income effect. The predicted impact of the demographic variables is discussed in Section 14.3, and the inflation rate is included as a proxy for price uncertainty and/or macroeconomic stability more generally (as done by Loayza, Schmidt-Hebbel, and Serven (2000) and Schrooten and Stephan (2005)), and a constant term, which corresponds to the coefficient of a time trend because first differences are taken (see Section 14.6 below), is included in some variants.

Finally, the real growth rate of per capita gross provincial product is used as an instrument in the level equation, as discussed below.

The data we use in our analysis are panel data for 1995–2004 on Chinese provinces. All variables are available for urban, rural, and all households with the exception of the nominal interest rate, which is available only for the country as a whole, and thus we are able to obtain separate results for urban, rural, and all households and for a pooled sample of urban and rural households.

All data from China's household survey and national accounts data are taken from the *China Statistics Yearbook*, all demographic data are taken from the *China Population Statistics Yearbook*, and data on nominal interest rates are taken from the International Monetary Fund's *International Financial Statistics*.

Data were available for all thirty-one provinces for the ten-year period from 1995 to 2004 with the following exceptions: data were not available for Chongqing Province during the 1995–6 period because this province did not become independent of Sichuan Province until 1997, and data on the CPI and/or on household income and consumption were not available for Tibet Province during the 1995–8 period. These missing values caused the number of observations to decline from 310 to 304. Moreover, one year's worth of data were lost because the income growth rate was used as an explanatory variable. This reduced the number of observations further from 304 to 273 and means that the sample period for most provinces was nine years (1996–2004). Finally, because the lagged real growth rate of per capita

Table 14.3: Descriptive statistics

Variable	Obs	Mean	Std. Dev.	Min	Max
SR (all)	272	0.230	0.057	0.087	0.390
SR (urban)	272	0.207	0.041	0.077	0.313
SR (rural)	272	0.255	0.097	−0.044	0.494
YOUNG (all)	272	0.312	0.086	0.116	0.527
YOUNG (urban)	272	0.257	0.053	0.110	0.420
YOUNG (rural)	272	0.376	0.093	0.136	0.596
OLD (all)	272	0.102	0.027	0.043	0.219
OLD (urban)	272	0.106	0.028	0.027	0.225
OLD (rural)	272	0.108	0.029	0.063	0.314
DEP (all)	272	0.414	0.084	0.220	0.655
DEP (urban)	272	0.363	0.048	0.245	0.539
DEP (rural)	272	0.483	0.088	0.262	0.771
NINT (all)	272	0.033	0.018	0.020	0.075
INFL (all)	272	0.017	0.031	−0.033	0.116
INFL (urban)	272	0.016	0.032	−0.034	0.116
INFL (rural)	272	0.017	0.031	−0.037	0.116
RINT (all)	272	0.016	0.022	−0.041	0.068
RINT (urban)	272	0.016	0.022	−0.041	0.067
RINT (rural)	272	0.015	0.024	−0.041	0.072
CHGDP (all)	272	0.094	0.050	−0.272	0.228
POP	272	4126.225	2601.504	262.000	11430.000
CHPOP	272	8.613	18.023	−49.865	188.721
INCOME (all)	272	3844.672	2097.599	1511.344	14573.670
INCOME (urban)	272	6643.530	2341.563	3353.940	16682.820
INCOME (rural)	272	2521.854	1126.045	1100.590	7066.330
CONS (all)	272	2938.318	1591.129	1323.966	11248.800
CONS (urban)	272	5239.805	1771.079	2767.840	12631.030
CONS (rural)	272	1848.667	839.803	880.650	6328.849
RURAL_RATIO	272	0.692	0.151	0.219	0.864
CPI (all)	272	101.663	3.081	96.700	111.600
CPI (urban)	272	101.645	3.168	96.600	111.600
CPI (rural)	272	101.736	3.078	96.300	111.600
CHY (all)	272	0.073	0.034	−0.037	0.191
CHY (urban)	272	0.073	0.042	−0.039	0.231
CHY (rural)	272	0.060	0.052	−0.101	0.331

Source: Authors' calculations based on China Statistics Yearbook, 1996–2005, China Population Statistics Yearbook, 1996–2005, and International Financial Statistics, 1995–2005.

gross provincial product was used as an instrument, yet another observation for Chongqing Province (that for 1998) had to be dropped, causing the final number of observations to be 272.

Descriptive statistics on the variables used in our analysis for the final sample of 272 observations are shown in Table 14.3.

14.6 Estimation Method

In this section, we briefly describe our estimation method. Following Loayza, Schmidt-Hebbel, and Serven (2000) and Schrooten and Stephan (2005), we use a generalized-method-of-moments (GMM) estimator applied to dynamic models using panel data. We use this estimator for at least three reasons: (1) Inertia is likely to be present in annual data, and it seemed desirable to use a dynamic specification to allow for it. (2) Some of the explanatory variables (such as RINT and CHY) are likely to be jointly determined with the saving rate, and it seemed desirable to control for the potential joint endogeneity of the explanatory variables. (3) There is the possibility of unobserved province-specific effects correlated with the regressors, and it seemed desirable to control for such effects.

Following Loayza, Schmidt-Hebbel, and Serven (2000) and Schrooten and Stephan (2005), we use the alternative 'system GMM estimator' proposed by Arellano and Bover (1995) and Blundell and Bond (1998), which reduces the potential biases and imprecision associated with the usual difference estimator by combining, in a system, the regression in differences with the regression in levels.

14.7 Estimation Results

In this section, we present our estimation results (see Horioka and Wan (2007) for more details).

Looking first at the coefficient of SR(-1) (the lagged saving rate), this coefficient is always positive and highly significant, indicating strong inertia, persistence, or habit formation. This coefficient ranges from 0.476 to 0.844, implying a long-run effect that is 1.91 to 6.14 times the short-run effect.

Looking next at the coefficient of CHY (the income growth rate), it is always positive and highly significant, ranging from 0.192 to 0.536. These figures imply that a one percentage point increase in the income growth rate causes a 0.19 to 0.54 percentage point increase in the household saving rate. Moreover, the long-run impact of the income growth rate is 1.9 to 6.4 times these figures.

Looking next at the coefficient of RINT (the real interest rate), it is positive and significant in most cases, which suggests that the interest elasticity of saving is positive.

Looking next at the impact of the demographic variables (YOUNG, OLD, and DEP), the coefficient of OLD is never significant and the coefficients of YOUNG and DEP are negative and significant, as expected, only in one of the four samples (the pooled sample of urban and rural households).

Looking next at the coefficient of INFL (the inflation rate), it is sometimes negative and significant, which suggests that inflation may have a negative impact on the household saving rate in China.

Looking finally at the constant term, which represents the coefficient of a time trend, it is positive and often significant, suggesting that there is an upward trend in China's household saving rate.

We also tried adding year dummies and the level of per capita household disposable income as additional explanatory variables, but we dropped them from the final specification because their coefficients were not statistically significant.

14.8 Conclusion

In this study, we presented data on saving rates and related variables in China and conducted an econometric analysis of the determinants of the household saving rate using a life cycle model and panel data on Chinese provinces for the 1995–2004 period from the household survey conducted by the Chinese government. To summarize our main findings, we found that China's saving rate has been high and that it has generally shown an upward trend over time and that the main determinants of variations over time and over space in China's household saving rate are the lagged saving rate, the income growth rate, (in many cases) the real interest rate, and (in some cases) the inflation rate. However, we found that the variables relating to the age structure of the population have the expected impact on the household saving rate in only one of the four samples. These results provide mixed support for the life-cycle hypothesis and are also consistent with the existence of inertia or persistence.

Turning to the implications of our findings, our finding that inertia or persistence are strong implies that there will not be a dramatic decline in China's household saving rate, and our finding that the income growth rate has a positive impact on the household saving rate implies that China's household saving rate will remain high as long as the growth rate remains high. However, if the growth rate tapers off, we can explain a gradual decline in the household saving rate.

Thus, it seems likely that China's household saving rate will remain high in the short to medium run, and to the extent that this causes China's current account surplus to remain high, this may cause continued frictions with the United States and China's other trading partners.

To alleviate such frictions, it may be desirable to implement the following five-point plan: (1) improve the infrastructure of the economy, (2) increase the availability of consumer credit, (3) improve social security, (4) relax the one-child policy and other population control measures, and (5) further strengthen the Chinese yuan.

Since investments in infrastructure count as investment and since such investments will stimulate private investment in plant and equipment, our first recommendation will raise the level of investment spending in China, thereby causing her current account surplus to narrow, and will, at the same time, improve the well-being of the Chinese people. In China, the level of infrastructure in rural areas lags behind that in urban areas, and thus China

Appendix for Figures 14.1, 14.2, 14.3.

Year	National gross investment as a ratio of GNP (percent)	National gross investment as a ratio of GDP (percent)	Per capita GDP (in yuan at 1952 prices)	Total population (in millions)	Life expectancy at birth (in years)	Ratio of the population aged 0–14 to the population aged 15–59	Ratio of the population aged 60 or older to the population aged 15–59	Ratio of the population aged 0–14 or 60 or older to the population aged 15–59
1949				541.67				
1950				551.96	40.8	0.57	0.13	0.70
1951				563				
1952	21.7		119.0	574.82				
1953	23.1		137.3	587.96	40.3	0.64	0.13	0.77
1954	25.5		136.1	602.66	42.4			
1955	22.9		140.4	614.65	44.6	0.67	0.14	0.81
1956	24.4		154.4	628.28	47			
1957	24.9		154.9	646.53	49.5			
1958	33.9		184.1	659.94	45.8			
1959	43.8		197.0	672.07	42.5			
1960	39.6		192.9	662.07	24.6	0.72	0.13	0.86
1961	19.2		140.9	658.59	38.4			
1962	10.4		126.9	672.95	53			
1963	17.5		141.1	691.72	54.9			
1964	22.2		168.4	704.99	57.1	0.77	0.13	0.89
1965	27.1		199.7	725.38	57.8	0.76	0.13	0.89
1966	30.6		211.9	745.42	58.6			
1967	21.3		197.5	763.68	59.4			
1968	21.1		186.4	785.34	60.3			
1969	23.2		206.3	806.71	60.8			
1970	32.9		233.9	829.92	61.4	0.74	0.13	0.87
1971	34.1		246.7	852.29	62			
1972	31.6		251.9	871.77	62.3			
1973	32.9		267.0	892.11	63			
1974	32.3		266.3	908.59	63.4			
1975	33.9		279.5	924.2	63.8	0.74	0.13	0.87
1976	30.9		269.6	937.17	64.2			
1977	32.3		288.3	949.74	64.6			

Year						Young Dep.	Old Dep.	Total Dep.
1978	36.5	38.2	320.1	962.59	65.1			
1979	34.6	36.2	345.3	975.42	65			
1980	31.5	34.9	359.4	987.05	64.9	0.62	0.13	0.75
1981	28.3	32.3	373.1	1000.72	64.8			
1982	28.8	32.1	393.1	1016.54	64.7	0.57	0.13	0.70
1983	29.7	33	427.8	1030.08	64.63			
1984	31.5	34.5	496.5	1043.57	64.55			
1985	35	38.5	547.0	1058.51	66.6	0.49	0.13	0.62
1986	34.7	38	578.3	1075.07		0.47	0.13	0.61
1987	34.1	36.7	622.4	1093		0.46	0.14	0.59
1988	34.5	37.4	644.6	1110.26				
1989	33.8	37	618.5	1127.04		0.42	0.14	0.56
1990	32.8	35.2	659.8	1143.33	68.55	0.43	0.13	0.57
1991	32.8	35.3	722.0	1158.23		0.44	0.15	0.59
1992	34.3	37.3	809.1	1171.71		0.44	0.15	0.59
1993	38.7	43.5	895.6	1185.17		0.43	0.15	0.58
1994		41.3	956.4	1198.5		0.43	0.15	0.58
1995		40.8	1013.1	1211.21	69.7	0.42	0.16	0.58
1996		39.3	1069.7	1223.89		0.41	0.17	0.57
1997		38	1126.3	1236.26		0.39	0.17	0.56
1998		37.4	1196.6	1247.61		0.38	0.17	0.55
1999		37.1	1242.5	1257.86		0.37	0.17	0.54
2000		36.4	1333.2	1267.43	71.38	0.34	0.16	0.50
2001		38	1429.7	1276.27	71.62	0.34	0.17	0.51
2002		39.2	1550.3	1284.53	71.86	0.32	0.18	0.49
2003		42.4	1704.2	1292.27	72.22	0.30	0.18	0.48
2004		44.2	1912.3	1299.88	71.96	0.28	0.18	0.46

Note: Young Dependency Ratio is defined as the ratio of the population aged 0–14 to the population aged 15–59. Old Dependency Ratio is defined as the ratio of the population aged 60 or older to the population aged 15–59. Total Dependency Ratio is defined as the ratio of the population aged 0–14 or 60 or older to the population aged 15–59.

should give priority to improving the infrastructure (the provision of water and electricity, the road system, etc.) in rural areas, as proposed by Professor Justin Yifu Lin of Peking University.

Our second and third recommendations will lower China's household saving rate, thereby causing her current account surplus to narrow, and will, at the same time, raise the well-being of the Chinese people.

Our fourth recommendation will raise China's youth dependency ratio and lower her household saving rate, thereby causing her current account surplus to narrow, and will, at the same time, improve the well-being of the Chinese people by enabling them to have more children.

Finally, our fifth recommendation will cause a decline in China's exports and an increase in her imports, thereby causing her current account surplus to narrow, and will, at the same time, improve the well-being of the Chinese people by enabling them to buy imported goods more cheaply.

Thus, our recommendations will enable China to reduce her saving-investment imbalance and current account surpluses, thereby alleviating strains with other countries, and will, at the same time, enable her to improve the well-being of her people. They would thus enable her to kill two birds with one stone.

In the long run, however, China's household saving rate can be expected to taper off assuming the growth rate tapers off, and thus, in the long term, China may well suffer from current account deficits rather than current account surpluses.

References

Arellano, Manuel, and Bond, Stephen (1991), 'Some Tests of Specification for Panel Data: Monte Carlo Evidence and an Application to Employment Equations,' *Review of Economic Studies*, 58(2) (April): 277–97.

Arellano, Manuel, and Bover, Olympia (1995), 'Another Look at the Instrumental Variable Estimation of Error-Components Models,' *Journal of Econometrics*, 68(1) (July): 29–51.

Banister, Judith (1984), 'An Analysis of Recent Data on the Population of China,' *Population and Development Review*, 10(2) (June): 241–71.

—— (1987), *China's Changing Population* (Stanford, CA: Stanford University Press).

Blundell, Richard, and Bond, Stephen (1998), 'Initial Conditions and Moment Restrictions in Dynamic Panel Data Models,' *Journal of Econometrics*, 87(1) (August): 115–43.

Bond, Stephen (2002), 'Dynamic Panel Data Models: A Guide to Micro Data Methods and Practice,' CEMMAP Working Paper CWP09/02, Department of Economics, Institute for Fiscal Studies, London.

The Economist, 'The Frugal Giant,' September 24–30, 2005, pp. 12–14 of 'A Survey of the World Economy.'

Horioka, Charles Yuji, and Wan, Junmin (2006), 'The Determinants of Household Saving in China: A Dynamic Panel Analysis of Provincial Data,' National Bureau of Economic Research Working Paper No. 12723 (December).

―― and ―― (2007), 'The Determinants of Household Saving in China: A Dynamic Panel Analysis of Provincial Data,' *Journal of Money, Credit and Banking*, 39 (8) (December).

Kraay, Aart (2000), 'Household Saving in China,' *World Bank Economic Review*, 14(3) (September): 545–70.

Lin, Justin Yifu (1992), 'Rural Reforms and Agricultural Growth in China,' *The American Economic Review*, 82(1) (March): 34–51.

Loayza, Norman, Schmidt-Hebbel, Klaus, and Serven, Luis (2000), 'What Drives Private Saving across the World?' *Review of Economics and Statistics*, 82(2) (May): 165–81.

Modigliani, Franco, and Cao, Shi Larry (2004), 'The Chinese Saving Puzzle and the Life-Cycle Hypothesis,' *Journal of Economic Literature*, 42(1) (March): 145–70.

Roodman, D. (2005), 'xtabond2: Stata module to extend xtabond dynamic panel data estimator,' Center for Global Development, Washington, DC; <http://econpapers.repec.org/software/bocbocode/s435901.htm>.

Schrooten, Mechthild, and Stephan, Sabine (2005), 'Private Savings and Transition: Dynamic Panel Data Evidence from Accession Countries,' *Economics of Transition*, 13(2): 287–309.

Windmeijer, Frank (2005), 'A Finite Sample Correction for the Variance of Linear Efficient Two-Step GMM Estimators,' *Journal of Econometrics*, 126(1) (May): 25–51.

Data Sources

Central Intelligence Agency, *CIA World Factbook* <http://www.indexmundi.com/g/g.aspx?c=ch&v=30>.

Department of Population, Social, Science and Technology Statistics, National Bureau of Statistics of China (ed.), *China Population Statistics Yearbook*, 1991–2005 editions. Beijing: China Statistics Press.

International Monetary Fund, *International Financial Statistics*, 1995–2005. Washington, DC.

National Bureau of Statistics of China (ed.), *China Statistical Yearbook*, 1988–2005 editions (Beijing: China Statistics Press).

United Nations (2002), *World Population Prospects: The 2002 Revision* (New York: United Nations).

Index

acid rain 31, 43
  and fossil-fuel burning 22
AFTA (ASEAN Free Trade Area) 87
  and establishment of 89
  and rules of origin 98
agriculture:
  and Doha Round 151
  and impact of black carbon 33 n19
air freight, and projected demand for 15–16
air pollution, and China 29–34
  and acid rain 31
  and black carbon emissions 32–4, 43–4
  and costs of 29
  and emissions trading systems 32
  and fossil-fuel burning 22
  and improvements in 29–30, 43
  and particulate emissions 30
  and price-based charging 32
  and sulfur dioxide emissions 31–2, 43
Alessie, R 381
APEC (Asia Pacific Economic Cooperation) 6
  and assessment of 114, 120–1, 132–7
    analysis of leaders' declarations 121–5, 130
    analysis of projects 126–31
  and consistency and coherence of 114, 132, 137
  and disappointment with 114, 119
  and expanded goals of 113–14
  and institutional framework 118–19
  and objectives of 113, 118
  and potential influence 119–20
  and preferential trade arrangements 115–16
    best practice recommendations 117–18
    recommendations for 114
    role in controlling 119, 132
  and trade liberalization 87
ASEAN (Association of South East Asian Nations):
  and China 89–91
  and East Asian Vision Group 91
  and free trade agreements 51, 88
    ASEAN-China FTA 104, 154–5
    ASEAN-Korea FTA 160
    constraints on regional integration 104–5

emergence as hub 106–7
recent developments in 89–91
rules of origin 98
and hub-and-spoke bilateralism 68–9
see also AFTA
Asia Pacific Economic Cooperation, *see* APEC
Asia Pacific Partnership for Clean Development
  and Climate (APPCDC) 44
Asian Bond Market Initiative (ABMI) 104, 245, 246
Asian Currency Unit (ACU) 246
Asian Development Bank (ADB) 51, 180, 197, 371
  and Asian Currency Unit 246
Association of South East Asian Nations, *see*
  ASEAN
Australia, and free trade agreement with
  China 157–8

Bae, K-H 169
Baldwin, R E 53, 95, 103
Bank for International Settlements (BIS) 172
  and Committee on the Global Financial
  System 206
bank lending, and geographical distribution
  of 175–8
Bank of Thailand 204
  and bond holding 227
  and removal of governor 210
banking crises, and financial services
  liberalization 342, 357
banks, *see* foreign banks, and China
Berg, A 234
Bhagwati, Jagdish 53
bilateral free trade agreements, *see* free trade
  agreements
black carbon emissions 32–4, 43–4
Blanchard, O 196
Bleakley, H 248
Bogo Declaration 87
bond market liquidity (Thailand) 201–2
  and definition of liquidity 206
  and determinants of 206–7
  and dimensions of 206

bond market liquidity (Thailand) (*cont.*)
  and empirical results of study:
    aggregate level regression 220–2
    final equation 219–20
    modelling volatility 218–19
    using EGARCH estimation 216–18
    using least squares estimation 216
  and measurement of 207–8
    bid-ask spread 207–8
    trade frequency 207
    trading volume 207
  as obstacle to market development 201
  and policy implications of study 230
    announcements by authorities 222
    auctions 228–9
    bond holding 227–8
    increasing market participants 223
    issuing practice 224–6
    private repo market 223
    reducing excessive volatility 222–3
    short selling 223
    trading volume 224
  and role of 201, 205–6
  and Securities Position Adjustment
      Facility 227
  and structure of market:
    development of 229–30
    post-1997 growth 203
    pre-1997 202–3
    profile of 204–5
    Thai Bond Dealing Centre 205
    underdevelopment of 203–4
  and Thai Bond Dealing Centre 205, 211
  and theory and methodology of study:
    adverse selection 209–10
    basic model and rationale 208–10
    data in the estimation 212
    data source 210–11
    inventory control 209
    order processing costs 209
    trading volume 208–9, 210, 212
    volatility 208, 210, 212
Borio, C 205, 207
BP 11
Brazil, as trade hub 65–6

Cao, S H 373
capital account liberalization, and China:
  and capital controls 329–30
  and effects of 312
  and foreign banks 342
  and outward direct investment 330–1
  and qualified institutional investor
      schemes 331
    domestic institutional investors 332–3
    foreign institutional investors 331–2
  and resident deposit conversion 333–6

capital controls, and effectiveness of China's
      312–13
  and assessment of 313, 325, 329, 336–7, 355
  and capital account liberalization 329–30
    effects of 312
    outward direct investment 330–1
    qualified domestic institutional investor
        scheme 332–3
    qualified foreign institutional investors
        scheme 331–2
    qualified institutional investor
        schemes 331
    resident deposit conversion 333–6
  and cross-border flows 313–14
  and flow evidence on 325
    cross-border flows 326–7
    discriminating regime 325–6
    dividend/interest payments 327
    foreign currency bank deposit flows 327–8,
        333–6
    net flows of errors and omissions 328–9
    remittance inflows 326
  and foreign banks 342, 355, 357
  and monetary independence 321–2, 324–5
    China-America interest rate
        differentials 322–4
  and onshore/offshore renminbi yield
      differentials:
    measurement of 315–17
    People's Bank of China bills 319–21
    three-month China interbank-offered rate
        (Chibor) 317–19
  and regime features 329–30
capital inflows, and China 276–7
  and Asian crisis 277, 303–4
  and cross-country comparison 277–8
  and evolution of 277–8
  and explaining composition of 303–4
    domestic financial institutions 307–8
    governance effects 308
    impact of Asian crisis 303–4
    incentives affecting FDI 304–6
    mercantilist explanation of 306–7
    pragmatic strategy 303
    restrictions on FDI 305–6
  and external debt 286–9
    maturity structure 286
    trade credits 286–9
  and foreign banks 354–7, 362–3
    borrowing from head offices 355–7
    short term bank loans 355
  and foreign direct investment 142, 275,
      278–86, 302–3
    domestic financial institutions 307–8
    FDI outflows 285–6, 330–1
    geographical distribution of 284–5
    governance effects 308

growth of 276, 277
incentives for 304–6
mercantilist explanation of 306–7
restrictions on 305–6
'round-tripping' from Hong Kong 283
sectors invested in 284
as share of emerging market FDI 278–81
sources of 282–4
and foreign exchange reserves 259, 261,
   289–99
accumulation of 289–92
cushion for financial sector 298
decomposition of 292–3
'hot money' 292, 293
implications of build-up of 296–9
import coverage 296–7
monetary base coverage 298
risks of high level of 298–9
short-term debt coverage 297
valuation effects 293–5
and growth of 276
and right composition of 302–3
capital markets, and underdevelopment in East
   Asia 195
carbon dioxide emissions 18–19
and climate change policy 35
and developing countries 35–7
and environmental policy 20–1, 44–5
and global policy 37
and growth in 8–9
and Kyoto Protocol 35–6
and market-incentives for reduction 37–8
carbon tax 37–9
permit trading 39
and McKibbin Wilcoxen Blueprint 40–3,
   44–5
and projected emissions 19, 24, 26
and requirements for effective policy 39–40
and share of global emissions 21–2
CGE models 93 n3
Chelley-Steeley, P L 195
Cheung, Y-W 322–3
ChevronTexaco 12
Chiang Mai Initiative (CMI) 104, 170, 197, 245
Chile, and free trade agreement with
   China 156–7
China:
air pollution 29–34
acid rain 31
black carbon emissions 32–4, 43–4
costs of 29
emissions trading systems 32
fossil-fuel burning 22
improvements in 29–30, 43
particulate emissions 30
price-based charging 32
sulfur dioxide emissions 31–2, 43

and competitiveness 163–4
hyper-competitiveness 164
and economic reform 371
impact of WTO membership 149
and exchange rate policy 164
and exports 87–8
growth of 145, 268, 269–70, 272, 273
and fiscal policy 266–7, 271, 273
debt balance/GDP ratio 266–7
inflation control 254–5
and foreign banks 345–6
arbitrage opportunities 355, 357
asset size 348
borrowing from head offices 355–7
cross-border capital flows 354–7, 362–3
customers 348–51
forms of entry 348
funding sources 351–3
impact of 341–2, 362–3
location of 348
motives for entry 348
short term bank loans 355
and foreign direct investment 145, 275,
   278–86, 302–3
domestic financial institutions 307–8
FDI outflows 285–6, 330–1
foreign bank entry 348–51
geographical distribution in 284–5
governance effects 308
growth of 276, 277
incentives for 304–6
mercantilist strategy 306–7
restrictions on 305–6
'round-tripping' from Hong Kong 283
sectors invested in 284
share of FDI to emerging markets 278–81
sources of FDI 282–4
and foreign exchange reserves 259, 261,
   289–99
accumulation of 289–92
cushion for financial sector 298
decomposition of 292–3
'hot money' 292, 293
implications of build-up of 296–9
import coverage 296–7
monetary base coverage 298
risks of high level of 298–9
short-term debt coverage 297
valuation effects 293–5
and free trade agreements 89–91, 146, 154,
   158
ASEAN-China FTA 104, 154–5
Australia 157–8
Chile 156–7
competitiveness 163–4
as force for global liberalization 159–61
fortress Asia fear 161

China: (*cont.*)
  and free trade agreements (*cont.*)
    Hong Kong 154–5
    hyper-competitiveness 164
    implementation of 163
    India 158
    Macao 155
    motives for 109, 158–9, 162–3
    New Zealand 157
    Pakistan 158
    pragmatic approach to 159
    regional policy 93
    rules of origin 98
    scope of 159
  and global integration 275
    cross-border flows 314
  and governance:
    impact of WTO membership 149
    institutional capacity 163
  and hub-and-spoke bilateralism:
    Japan-China two-hub system 70–1, 88, 109
    as trade hub 67–9, 70, 107–8, 161
  and imports 88
    energy 7, 9, 11, 12–13, 22
    growth of 145
    intra-regional trade 87
    projected value of 6
    raw materials 14–16
    reliance on 7–8, 11, 16, 88
  and inflation 254, 272
    control of 254–5, 256
    economic growth 273
    monetary policy 257
  and Japan, rivalry between 93
  and multilateral trading system:
    impact on 145–7
    World Trade Organization 148–54
  and regional economic integration 105
  and state-owned enterprises, losses of 270–1
  and Taiwan 152–3
  and tariff regime 149–50
  and World Trade Organization:
    accession commitments 148–51
    accession to 145, 146
    annual Transitional Review
      Mechanism 153
    compliance with 6, 146, 163
    concerns over membership 146
    participation in 151–4
    Taiwan 152–3
  see also capital account liberalization; capital
    controls; economic growth; energy;
    monetary policy; savings rate
China National Offshore Oil Corporation
  (CNOOC) 11, 12
China National Petroleum Corporation
  (CNPC) 11, 12

China Petrochemical Corporation
  (Sinopec) 11, 12
Chinese Communist Party (CCP), and
  legitimacy of 7
Chinn, M D 322–3
climate change:
  and fossil-fuel burning 22
  and global policy 37
  and greenhouse gases 35
  and Kyoto Protocol 35
  see also carbon dioxide emissions;
    environmental policy
Closer Economic Partnership Arrangement
  (CEPA) (Hong Kong and Mainland
  China) 154–5
coal, and China:
  and air pollution 9, 30
  and environmental impact 22
  and fragmented nature of market 10
  and growth in electricity-generating
    capacity 9
  and inefficiency of electricity-generating
    plants 10–11
  and projected consumption of 8, 19, 43
  and projected demand for 4
Committee on the Global Financial System
  (CGFS) (BIS) 206
ConocoPhillips 12
Cooper, Richard 37
Coordinated Portfolio Investment Survey
  (CPIS) (IMF) 172
Cowan, K 248
crises, *see* banking crises; financial crises
cumulation problem, and free trade
  agreements 77
currency conversion, and liberalization
  333–6
currency speculation, and foreign exchange
  reserves 243–5, 250
customs unions, and anti-spoke strategies
  72–4

Danthine, J-P 196
Darfur 12
De Gregorio, J 236
Deng Xiaoping 371
Denmark 72
Devakula, Pridiyathorn 210
developing countries:
  and carbon dioxide emissions 35–7
  and financial globalization:
    composition of capital inflows 301–2
    economic growth 299–300
    volatility 300–1
  and Kyoto Protocol 35–6
  see also emerging markets
Direction of Trade data set 179

Doha Round 6, 92
  and Chinese participation 151–2
  and financial services liberalization 343
  see also World Trade Organization
D'Souza, C 207, 208

East Asia:
  and hub-and-spoke bilateralism:
    anti-spoke strategy proposal 80–2
    implications of 69–70
    Japan-China two-hub system 70–1, 88, 109
  and market-driven regionalism 52
  and trade hubs 67–8
    regional agreements 68–9
  see also APEC; ASEAN; financial crises;
    financial integration; free trade
    agreements; hub-and-spoke bilateralism;
    regionalism
East Asian Vision Group (EAVG) 91
economic growth, and China 254, 371
  and economic bottlenecks 269
  and energy demand 4–6
  and enterprise profitability 269, 270–1
  and environmental impact of 18–19
  and global economic engagement 145
  and household consumption 271
  and impact of 18
  and inflation 256, 273
  and investment 270, 272
  and monetary policy 256, 257
  and net export growth 268, 269–70, 272, 273
  and peace 7
  and price indices 268–9
  and productivity 24–6
  and projected growth rates 1–4, 24–6, 371
    adverse scenarios 7
    and prospects in 2006 268–71
    actual performance 272
  and sources of 24
  and stop-go pattern 254–5
  and uncertainties over 268
economic growth, and financial
    integration 299–300
Eichengreen, B 169, 192, 195, 322, 323
electricity, and China:
  and fragmented nature of market 10
  and growth in generating capacity 9–10, 22
  and inefficiency of generating plants 10–11
  and state-owned enterprises 10
EMEAP (Executives' Meeting of East Asia-Pacific
    Central Banks) 204 n2
emerging markets:
  and banking crises 342, 357
  and financial globalization:
    composition of capital inflows 301–2
    economic growth 299–300
    volatility 300–1

and foreign banks, impact of 341–2
and impact of financial services liberalization
    on bank loans to 357–9, 362–3
  capital controls 362
  country risk indicators 361
  economic linkages 361
  empirical results 359–62
  GATS commitments 361–2
  gravity model 358–9
  gravity variables 359–61
  institutional quality 361
energy, and China:
  and air pollution 29–34
  and determinants of use of 24
  and energy intensity 22
  and environmental impact of use of 29–34
    responses to 35–43
  and fragmented nature of market 10
  and G-Cubed model for projecting use
    of 45–7
  and growing demand for 18
  and growth in electricity-generating
    capacity 9–10
  and imports of 7, 9, 11, 12–13, 22
  and inefficiency in use of 10–11
  and projected consumption of 8, 11, 13–14,
    19, 20, 24–9
  and projected demand for 4–6
  and share of world energy use 21
  and sources of demand for 23
  and sources of supply 23
  and state-owned enterprises 10
  and strategy 11
Enterprise for the Americas Initiative (EAI)
    61
environmental policy:
  and acid rain 31
  and black carbon emissions 32–4, 43–4
  and carbon dioxide emissions 20–1, 44–5
    carbon tax 37–9
    Kyoto Protocol 35–6
    McKibbin Wilcoxen Blueprint 40–3,
      44–5
    market-incentives for reduction 37–8
    permit trading 39
    requirements for effective policy 39–40
  and climate change policy
    developing countries 35–7
    global state of 37
    Kyoto Protocol 35–6
  and emergence of 19–20
  and emissions trading systems 32
  and impact of economic growth 18–19
  and impact of energy use 29–34
  and Kyoto Protocol 35
  and price-based charging 32
  and progress in 21

environmental policy: (*cont.*)
    and responding to energy-related
        issues 35–43
    and sulfur dioxide emissions 31–2, 43
Essevadeordal, A 99
European Economic Community (EEC) 103
European economic integration 103
European Free Trade Association (EFTA) 103
    and anti-spoke strategy 74–7
European Union:
    and climate change policy 37
    as customs union 72
        Turkey 73–4
    and free trade agreements 61
        European Free Trade Area 74–7
        rules of origin 99
    and investment in China 283–4
    and monetary integration 196
exchange rate crisis, *see* financial crises
exchange rate regime:
    and crisis prevention 237–40, 249
    and financial integration 196–7
exports, and China 87–8
    and growth of 145, 268, 269–70, 272, 273
external debt:
    and China 286–9
        maturity structure 286
        trade credits 286–9
    and volatility 301
ExxonMobile 11

financial crises, and East Asia:
    and 1997-98 crisis:
        impact of 233
        lessons of 236
        reactions to 233
        unpredictability of 234–5
    and crisis prevention 236
        accumulation of foreign exchange
            reserves 240–5, 250
        corner exchange rate strategy 249–50
        exchange rate regimes 237–40, 249
        monetary cooperation 245–6, 250
        structural reform 237
    and economic resilience 250
    and financial liberalization 250, 341–2,
        357
    and incidence of 233–4
    and likelihood of 249
    and vulnerability to 246, 249
        financial vulnerabilities 247–9
        macroeconomic vulnerabilities 246–7
        non-financial vulnerabilities 247
financial globalization:
    and composition of capital inflows
        301–2
    and economic growth 299–300

    and macroeconomic policy 300
    and volatility 300–1
    and vulnerability to risks of 301–2
financial integration, and East Asia 168–71,
        197–8
    and assessing degree of 170–1
    and benefits of 169
    and geographical distribution of assets 171
        bank lending 175–8
        data 171–2
        portfolio investment 172–5
    and global integration 168
        comparison with Europe 184–5, 186–7
        risk-sharing 191–2
        strength of 169
    and gravity-model test of 179–87
    and regional integration 168
        comparison with Europe 184, 185–6
        exchange rate regime 196–7
        financial intermediation 170
        home bias 194
        impact on regional cooperation 170
        institutional/structural constraints
            194–5
        justification for 169–70
        lack of encouragement of 169
        monetary integration 169–70, 196
        portfolio diversification 192–4
        risk-sharing 191–2
        strength of 168–9
    and risk-sharing 169
        comparison with Europe 191–2
        empirical results 190–2
        regional versus global 187–90
financial markets, and underdevelopment in
        East Asia 195
    see also bond market liquidity (Thailand)
financial sector, and financial crises 247–9
financial services liberalization 341
    and financial crises 341–2, 357
    and foreign banks in China 345–6
        arbitrage opportunities 355, 357
        asset size 348
        borrowing from head offices 355–7
        cross-border capital flows 354–7
        customers 348–51
        forms of entry 348
        funding sources 351–3
        impact of 341–2
        location of 348
        motives for entry 348
        short term bank loans 355
    and General Agreement on Trade and
        Services 341
        financial services trade liberalization
            negotiations 342–5
        modes of supply 344–5

and impact on bank loans to emerging
   markets 357–9, 362–3
   capital controls 362
   country risk indicators 361
   economic linkages 361
   empirical results 359–62
   GATS commitments 361–2
   gravity model 358–9
   gravity variables 359–61
   institutional quality 361
fiscal policy, and China 266–7, 271, 273
   and debt balance/GDP ratio 266–7
   inflation control 254–5
Fleming, M 208
Flood, R 246
Folkerts-Landau, D 226
foreign banks, and China 345–6
   and arbitrage opportunities 355, 357
   and asset size 348
   and borrowing from head offices 355–7
   and cross-border capital flows 354–7, 362–3
   and customers 348–51
   and forms of entry 348
   and funding sources 351–3
   and impact of 341–2, 362–3
   and location of 348
   and motives for entry 348
   and short term bank loans 355
foreign currency deposits, and
   liberalization 333–6
foreign direct investment (FDI):
   and China 145, 275, 278–86, 302–3
      domestic financial institutions 307–8
      FDI outflows 285–6, 330–1
      foreign bank entry 348–51
      geographical distribution in 284–5
      governance effects 308
      growth of 276, 277
      incentives for 304–6
      mercantilist strategy 306–7
      restrictions on 305–6
      'round-tripping' from Hong Kong 283
      sectors invested in 284
      share of FDI to emerging markets 278–81
      sources of FDI 282–4
   and hub-and-spoke bilateralism 51–2
      competition for investment 58–9
      'noodle bowl' problem 52, 109
   and volatility 301
foreign exchange reserves:
   and China 259, 261, 289–99
      accumulation by 289–92
      cushion for financial sector 298
      decomposition of 292–3
      'hot money' 292, 293
      implications of build-up by 296–9
      import coverage 296–7

monetary base coverage 298
      risks of high level of 298–9
      short-term debt coverage 297
      valuation effects 293–5
   and crisis prevention 240–5, 250
   and optimum levels 296
Francois, J F 97
Frankel, J 358 n10
Fratzscher, M 196
free trade agreements (FTAs), and East
   Asia 87–9, 108–9
   and APEC best practice
      recommendations 117–18
   and assessment of quality of 101–2
      market access 102–3
      rules of origin 101–2
      tariff elimination 101
   and China 89–91, 146, 154, 158
      ASEAN-China FTA 104, 154–5
      Australia 157–8
      Chile 156–7
      competitiveness 163–4
      as force for global liberalization 159–61
      fortress Asia fear 161
      Hong Kong 154–5
      hyper-competitiveness 164
      implementation of 163
      India 158
      Macao 155
      motives for 109, 158–9, 162–3
      New Zealand 157
      Pakistan 158
      pragmatic approach to 159
      regional policy 93
      rules of origin 98
      scope of 159
   and competitive regionalism 104
   and costs of 108, 116
   and domino effect 59–61, 103–6
   and economic effects of 93–8
      capital accumulation 95–6, 97–8
      dynamic gains 93–4
      gross domestic product 94–6
      impact of coverage area 96–7
      investment incentives 95
      trade creation/diversion 93, 94
      variation in magnitude of 98
   and economic reform 92–3
   and emergence of regional hub:
      ASEAN 106–7
      China 67–9, 70, 107–8
      Japan 67–9, 70, 107
   as force for global liberalization 159–61
   and motives for 162
   and 'noodle bowl problem' 52, 53–4, 109,
      161–2
   and political/strategic motives 109

free trade agreements (FTAs)... (*cont.*)
  and proliferation of 51, 88
    consequences of 103–8
    dangers of 109
    factors behind 91–3
  and protectionism 109
  and recent developments in 89–91
  and regional integration 103–4, 108–9,
    110
    constraints on 104–5
  and rules of origin 98, 99–101, 109–10
    compared with European Union 99
    compared with United States 98–9
  and types of 91
  see also hub-and-spoke bilateralism
Fujii, E 322–3
Fung, S-S 169

Gaa, C 207, 208
Gadanecz, B 169
Garbaccio, R F:
  and air pollution 29
  and carbon dioxide emissions 37
Garber, P 246
gas, and China:
  and domestic production 13
  and electricity-generating capacity 10, 13
  and imports of 9, 13
  and projected consumption of 8, 11, 13–14
G-Cubed model 45–7
General Agreement on Tariffs and Trade
  (GATT), and regional trade
  agreements 89 n2
General Agreement on Trade and Services
  (GATS) 341
  and financial services trade liberalization
    negotiations (FSTLN) 342–5
    modes of supply 344–5
  and impact on bank loans to emerging
    markets 357–9, 362–3
    capital controls 362
    country risk indicators 361
    economic linkages 361
    empirical results 359–62
    GATS commitments 361–2
    gravity model 358–9
    gravity variables 359–61
    institutional quality 361
Giavazzi, F 196
Gilbert, J P 94
globalization, *see* financial globalization
Goldstein, M 226, 248, 334
gravity model:
  and financial integration 179–87
  and loans to developing economies
    358–9
    empirical results 359–62

greenhouse gases:
  and climate change 35
  and G-Cubed model for projecting
    emissions 45–7
Guangdong Province 285 n4
  and foreign direct investment 284

Ho, C 315
Ho, M S:
  and air pollution 29, 30
  and carbon dioxide emissions 37
home bias, and portfolio investment 194
Hong Kong, and Mainland China:
  Closer Economic Partnership
    Arrangement 154–5
  foreign direct investment 283
household saving, *see* savings rate
Huang, Yasheng 307
hub-and-spoke bilateralism:
  and allocation effects:
    'noodle bowl effect' 53–4, 109
    restricted pro-competitive effect 54
  and anti-spoke strategies:
    customs union 72–4
    East Asian Free-Trade Union 80–1
    European Free Trade Area 74–7
    Japan-Korea Free Trade Agreement
      Union 81–2
    Mexico 77–9
    Singapore 77
  and domino effect 59–61
  and East Asian regionalism 61
    ASEAN as hub 106–7
    China as hub 67–9, 70, 107–8, 161
    implications for 69–70
    Japan as hub 67–9, 70, 107
    Japan-China two-hub system 70–1,
      88, 109
  and foreign investment 57–8
    competition for 58–9
  and 'hub-ness' measurement 62–4
    Brazil 65–6
    East Asian regional agreements
      68–9
    Japan, China and Korea 67–8
    United Sates 65
  and location effects 54–6
    industrial hysteresis 56
  and marginalizing tendencies of 54
  and mercantilist view of trade
    negotiations 56–7
  and 'noodle bowl problem' 52, 53–4,
    109, 161–2
  and political economy of 57–9
  and political effects of 52
  and problematic nature of 51–2
  and protectionism 57–8

and trade diversion 53
see also free trade agreements; preferential
    trade arrangements
Husky Oil 12
hydroelectric power, and China 9
    and electricity-generating capacity 9, 22
    and projected consumption of 8

imports, and China:
    and energy 7, 9, 11, 12–13, 22
    and growth of 145
    and intra-regional trade 87
    and projected value of 6
    and raw materials 14–16
    and reliance on 7–8, 11, 16, 88
India:
    and free trade agreement with China 158
    and population growth 2, 3
    and projected growth rates 2
inflation, and China 254, 272
    and control of 254–5, 256
    and economic growth 256, 273
    and monetary policy 257
Inoue, H 225
interest rates:
    and arbitrage opportunities 355
    and China-America interest rate
        differentials 322–4
    and Chinese monetary policy 263–5, 271
    and onshore/offshore renminbi yield
        differentials:
    measurement of 315–17
    People's Bank of China bills 319–21
    three-month China interbank-offered
        rate 317–19
international economic organizations, and
    China's role in 6
International Energy Agency (IEA) 9, 10
International Financial Statistics (IFS) 179
International Monetary Fund (IMF):
    and Coordinated Portfolio Investment
        Survey 172
    and East Asian financial crisis (1997–98) 240
    structural reforms 237
international relations, and Chinese economic
    policy 16–17

Japan:
    and China:
        investment in 283
        rivalry between 93
    and climate change policy 37
    and free trade agreements 89, 107, 161
        economic reform 92–3
        motives for 109
        regional policy 93
        rules of origin 100

and hub-and-spoke bilateralism:
    anti-spoke strategy proposal 80–2
    Japan-China two-hub system 70–1, 88, 109
    as trade hub 67–9, 70, 107
    and population decline 2, 3
    and projected growth rates 2
    and regional economic integration 105
Jeanne, O 243
Jeon, J 169
Jiange Li 11
Jiangsu Province, and foreign direct
    investment 284–5
Jorgenson, D W
    and air pollution 29, 30
    and carbon dioxide emissions 37

Kaminsky, G 234, 250 n10
Kawai, M 358 n10
Kawasaki, K 94
Kazakh oil pipeline 12
Keil, M W 169
Kerr-McGee 12
Kim, S 169, 171, 196
Kim, S H 169, 171, 196
Kireyev, A 357
Kiyota, K 94
Kono, M 357
Korea:
    and free trade agreements:
        Korea-ASEAN 160
        rules of origin 100
    and hub-and-spoke bilateralism:
        anti-spoke strategy proposal 80–2
        emulation of Mexican strategy 79
        free trade agreements 79–80
        as trade hub 67–9
    and investment in China 283
Korea International Trade Association
    (KITA) 160 n22
Kraay, A 373
Krugman, P 54, 246
Kyoto Protocol 21, 35
    and developing countries 35–6
    and limitations of 35–6
    and property rights 43

Lane, P 313 n2
Lee, J-W 196
Lewis, K K 194
liberalization, *see* capital account liberalization;
    financial services liberalization; trade
    liberalization
'Like-minded Group' 152 n10
Lin, Justin Yifu 392
Linnan, D K 119
liquidity, *see* bond market liquidity (Thailand)
Liu, L 358 n10

Lizondo, S 234
Loayza, N 385, 387, 388
Lusardi, A 381

Ma, G 315
Macao, and free trade agreement with
China 155
McCauley, R 169, 207, 224, 225, 315
McDonald, B J 97
McKibbin, W 37, 39
McKibbin Wilcoxen Blueprint, and climate
change policy 40–3, 44–5
McKinnon, R 323 n8
macroeconomic factors, and financial
crises 246–7
Maddison, Angus 2
Manning, R A 119
Mares, A 206, 222–3
market access, and free trade agreements 101,
102–3
market exchange rates, and comparing
economies 3–4
market-driven regionalism 52
Martinez, L 250 n10
Menon, S 33
Mercosur (Southern Common Market) 65–6
Mexico:
and anti-spoke strategy 77–9
and NAFTA 61, 78
and pursuit of hub status 77–9
Milesi-Ferretti, G M 313 n2
Modigliani, F 373
Mohanty, M S 207, 223, 225
monetarism, and Chinese monetary policy 257
monetary cooperation, and crisis
prevention 245–6, 250
monetary integration, and regional financial
integration 169–70, 196–7
monetary policy, and China 256–66, 271, 273
and central bank bills 261
and economic growth/inflation balance 257
and effectiveness of 258, 265–6
and implementation of 258
inflation control 254–5
and interest rates 263–5, 271
and monetarism 257
and monetary base 258, 259, 261
and monetary multiplier 258, 262–3
and money supply 257, 271
growth rate 258
influence of 258
and objectives of 256
conflicts between 265–6
economic growth 256
exchange rate stability 257
inflation control 256
and open market operations 258, 259–60

and problems with:
conflicting objectives 265–6
lack of benchmark interest rate 266
multiple targets 266
and reserve money 258–60
and reserve requirements 262, 263
and sterilization policy 259–61
Mundell, R 323 n8

NAFTA (North American Free Trade
Agreement):
and domino effect 61
and origins of 78
and rules of origin 98–9
Nakada, M 43
National Development and Reform
Commission (NDRC) 22, 269
natural gas, see gas
Network of East Asian Think-Tanks (NEAT) 91
New Zealand, and free trade agreement with
China 157
Nordström, H 97, 152
North American Free Trade Agreement, see
NAFTA
nuclear power, and China 9
and electricity-generating capacity 9–10
and expansion of 22, 43
and projected consumption of 8

Obstfeld, M 247
OECD (Organisation for Economic
Co-operation and Development) 120
Oh, Y 169
oil, and China:
and development abroad 12
and domestic production 11
and equity oil investments 12
and exploration for 9, 11–12
and imports of 7, 9, 11, 12–13
and projected consumption of 8, 11, 19
and projected demand for 4, 6
and projected prices of 5
and reorganization of industry 11
and state-owned enterprises 10
'one-child policy' 372
OPEC (Organization of the Petroleum
Exporting Countries) 5
Organisation for Economic Co-operation and
Development (OECD) 120
Osaka Action Agenda (OAA) 118 n5

Pakistan, and free trade agreement with
China 158
Park, Yung Chul 169, 192, 195
Patillo, C 234
PBOC, see People's Bank of China
peace, and economic growth 7

People's Bank of China (PBOC) 271
  and interest rates 263–5
  and monetary multiplier 263
  and open market operations 258, 259–60
  and reserve requirements 262, 263
Phalapleewan, A 169
population, and projected trends in 2, 3
population policy, and China 372
Portes, R 181, 358 n10
portfolio investment, and financial
      integration:
  geographical distribution of 172–5
  home bias 194
  portfolio diversification 192–4
Prasad, E 328
preferential trade arrangements (PTAs):
  and APEC:
    best practice recommendations 117–18
    role in controlling 119
  in Asia and the Pacific 115–18, 132
    APEC members 115–16
    concern over 116, 132
    costs of 116
    as obstacle to trade 116–17
  and growth of 114
  see also free trade agreements; hub-and-spoke
      bilateralism
price controls, and energy 10
PricewaterhouseCoopers (PwC) 304–5
productivity, and economic growth 24–6
property rights, and Kyoto Protocol 43
protectionism:
  and free trade agreements 109
  and hub-and-spoke bilateralism 57–8
purchasing-power parity (PPP), and comparing
     economies 3–4
Putin, Vladimir 13

Qingtai Chen 11
qualified institutional investor schemes, and
    China 331
  and domestic institutional investors
    332–3
  and foreign institutional investors 331–2

Rajan, R S 169
Ravenhill, J 119, 126
raw materials, and China:
  and imports of 14–16
  and reliance on imports 7, 11
regional trade agreements 89 n2
regionalism, East Asian 52
  and hub-and-spoke bilateralism:
    anti-spoke strategy proposal 80–2
    implications of 69–70
    Japan-China two-hub system 70–1,
      88, 109

and trade hubs 67–8
  regional agreements 68–9
  see also free trade agreements; hub-and-spoke
      bilateralism
Reinhart, C M 234, 250 n10
Remolona, E 207, 224, 225
renewable energy 22, 43
Rey, H 181, 358 n10
risk-sharing 169
  and null hypothesis 187, 188
  and regional versus global 187–90
  empirical results 190–2
Rose, A K 358 n10
Royal Dutch/Shell Company 1
rules of origin:
  and customs unions 73
  and East Asian free trade agreements 99–101,
    109–10
    quality of agreements 101–2
  and European Union 99
  and free trade agreements 98
  and NAFTA 98–9
  and trade agreements 53–4, 77
  and United States 98–9
Russia, and energy supplies to China 12–13

Saudi Arabia 5, 12
savings rate, and China 307
  and age structure of population 372, 374,
    380, 388–9
  and data on:
    age structure of population 375–7, 381
    life expectancy 375
    national gross investment rate 374–5
    rural and urban households 378–80
  and dependency ratio 374, 377
  and determinants of 389
    data sources 386–7
    estimation method 387–8
    estimation model 385–6
    estimation results 388–9
  and economic frictions caused by 372, 389
    alleviation of 392
  and future trends 389, 392
  and habit formation 389
  and high level of 372, 389
  and life-cycle model 374, 377, 389
  and literature survey 373–4
  and theoretical model 381–5
Schiff, M 93
Schmidt-Hebbel, K 385, 387, 388
Schmukler, S 250 n10
Schrooten, M 385, 387, 388
Schreifels, J 29
Schuknecht, L 357
Scollay, R 94
Serven, L 385, 387, 388

Shell 11
Shih, Y C 223
Shin, K 196
Simmons, Mathew R 5
Singapore:
  and free trade agreements 68, 77, 88, 89
    rules of origin 99–100
  and investment in China 283
Sonakul, Chatu Mongkol 210
South African Customs Union (SACU) 72
Spiegel, M M 196, 358 n10
State Administration of Foreign Exchange
    (SAFE) 353 n7, 355
State Environmental Protection Agency (SEPA)
  and air quality 29
  and monitoring/enforcing activities 30
state-owned enterprises (SOEs):
  and energy industry 10
  and losses of 270–1
Steeley, J M 195
Stephan, S 385, 387, 388
Stern, S 119
stock markets, and size of 237, 238
Streets, D G:
  and acid rain 31
  and black carbon emissions 32, 33
structural reform, and crisis prevention 237
Sudan, and Chinese financial support of 12
sulfur dioxide emissions 31–2
  and emissions trading systems 32
  and reduction of 43

Taiwan:
  and China 152–3
    investment in 283
  and foreign exchange controls 334, 335
tariffs, and China 149–50
tax revenues 3
technology, and Chinese reliance on external
    sources 7–8
Thai Bond Dealing Centre (Thai BDC) 205,
    211
Thailand:
  and financial and economic crisis
    (1997) 202–3
  and foreign exchange reserves 240–3
  and role of banks 202
  see also bond market liquidity (Thailand)
Three Gorges Dam, and electricity-generating
    capacity 9, 22
Tornell, A 250 n10
trade, and intra-regional trade 87
trade agreements, see free trade agreements;
    hub-and-spoke bilateralism
trade deflection 74
trade liberalization 87
  and slow progress of 92

see also free trade agreements; hub-and-spoke
    bilateralism; preferential trade
    arrangements
Tseng, W 304 n26
Turkey, and European Union 73–4
Turner, P 248

Ueta, K 43
United Nations Earth Summit (Rio de Janeiro,
    1992) 35
United Sates:
  and China:
    investment by 286
    investment in 283–4
  and climate change policy 37
  and free trade agreements 61
    rules of origin 98–9
  and NAFTA 61, 78
    rules of origin 98–9
  and population growth 2, 3
  and projected growth rates 2
  as trade hub 65
Unocal 12
Urata, S 94, 358 n10

Valckx, N 357
Venables, A 53, 95
Venezuela 5
volatility:
  and financial integration 300–1
  and Thai bond market 208, 210, 212
    modelling 218–19
    reducing 222–3
von Thadden, E-L 196

Wang, Y 169, 171, 196
Wei, S-J 303, 304, 306, 328
Weitzman, M L 39
Wen Jiabao 30
Westermann, F 250 n10
Whalley, J 78
Wilcoxen, P 37, 39
Willett, T 169
Williamson, J 240
Winters, L A 93
World Bank:
  and air pollution 29
  and Chinese external debt 289 n8
World Health Organization (WHO) 31
World Trade Organization (WTO):
  and accession requirements 147–8
  and China:
    accession commitments 148–51, 341
    accession to 145, 146
    annual Transitional Review
      Mechanism 153
    compliance with 6, 146, 163

concerns over membership 146
participation of 151–4
Taiwan 152–3
and General Agreement on Trade and
Services 341, 342–5
and regional trade agreements 89 n2
and slow progress of trade liberalization
92

Wyplosz, C 243, 250 n10

Yamazawa, I 113
Yang, D Y 169
Yang, J 29, 208
Yangtze River Delta region 285 n4

Zebregs, H 304 n26